The Spirit's Tether

THE SPIRIT'S TETHER

Family, Work, and Religion among American Catholics

MARY ELLEN KONIECZNY

OXFORD
UNIVERSITY PRESS

OXFORD
UNIVERSITY PRESS

Oxford University Press is a department of the University of Oxford.
It furthers the University's objective of excellence in research, scholarship,
and education by publishing worldwide.

Oxford   New York
Auckland   Cape Town   Dar es Salaam   Hong Kong   Karachi
Kuala Lumpur   Madrid   Melbourne   Mexico City   Nairobi
New Delhi   Shanghai   Taipei   Toronto

With offices in
Argentina   Austria   Brazil   Chile   Czech Republic   France   Greece
Guatemala   Hungary   Italy   Japan   Poland   Portugal   Singapore
South Korea   Switzerland   Thailand   Turkey   Ukraine   Vietnam

Oxford is a registered trademark of Oxford University Press
in the UK and certain other countries.

Published in the United States of America by
Oxford University Press
198 Madison Avenue, New York, NY 10016

© Oxford University Press 2013

Library of Congress Cataloging-in-Publication Data

Konieczny, Mary Ellen.
The spirit's tether : family, work, and religion among American Catholics /
Mary Ellen Konieczny.
pages cm
Includes bibliographical references and index.
ISBN 978–0–19–996579–3 (pbk. : alk. paper)—ISBN 978–0–19–996577–9 (cloth : alk. paper)
1. Families–Religious aspects–Catholic Church.   2. Catholic Church–United States.
3. Families–United States.   4. Catholic Church–Doctrines.   I. Title.
BX2351.K66 2013
282'.7309051—dc23
2012050009

In memory of
Joseph Cardinal Bernardin
1928–1996

"Draw us in the Spirit's tether,
For when humbly in your name,
Two or three are met together,
You are in the midst of them.
Alleluia! Alleluia!
Touch we now your garment's hem.
"As disciples used to gather
In the name of Christ to sup,
Then with thanks to God the Father
Break the bread and bless the cup.
Alleluia! Alleluia!
So now bind our friendship up.
"All our meals and all our living
Make as sacraments of you,
That by caring, helping, giving,
May we be disciples true.
Alleluia! Alleluia!
We will serve with faith anew."

Contents

Preface

IT IS CUSTOMARY to dedicate a first book to those family members who have most supported one along the way, and in my case, that person is undoubtedly Chris Chwedyk, my husband. But as this book drew near its completion, Chris and I found ourselves discussing how and why this book has taken the shape that it did—and then, the possibility of departing from this custom. The result of our conversation is a book dedicated to the person who, more than any other, inspired in me a passion to understand how the family, and the everyday lives and routines of families, are intertwined with the growing moral polarization I have witnessed among Catholics throughout my adulthood.

Prior to my graduate training in sociology, I worked for the Catholic Archdiocese of Chicago. I moved to Chicago in 1985 and began working for the Archdiocese after having earned a graduate degree in Theology, spending two years working in college campus ministry, and then working for seven years in Archdiocesan administration: four as an Associate Director in the Vocation Office and three as the Director of Ministry in Higher Education.

During those years, Joseph Cardinal Bernardin was the archbishop of Chicago. Many will remember him, of course, as a prominent and powerful figure within the American Catholic Church. He was a strong leader, known for his intelligence and political acumen. He was also a caring pastor and a gifted and earnest teacher.

The strength of Bernardin's leadership within the Chicago Archdiocese has been evident since his death in many ways, including in his lasting influence upon those who knew him and worked for him. His influence on the way I think about the Catholic Church is encapsulated in two of his initiatives: his development of a "consistent ethic of life" approach to public moral issues and his Common Ground Initiative, meant to encourage Catholics to engage one another civilly despite differences and work for society's betterment. Both efforts were grounded in his belief and assent to the authenticity of Catholic moral teachings and its teachings about the church. Both efforts acknowledged the contemporary controversies that continue to divide Catholics, and both were meant to promote unity among Catholics while acknowledging differences among them. Bernardin's vision was one in which Catholics should be challenged to live out a faith that does not fit neatly into political categories of right and left—one in which Catholics are encouraged to embrace the totality of Catholicism while compassionately recognizing and challenging weakness and human imperfection in individuals and social institutions.

But in the years since Bernardin's death, American Catholics as a whole appear to have grown more polarized and more contentious, and the divisions among them more publicly political. It has saddened me to see some on either side of this division try to use or remake Bernardin's legacy for their own ends, and even to situate him on one side of the divide. I find this ironic since it was this very kind of division that he determinedly worked against.

In the spirit of Cardinal Bernardin, I think that moral polarization in the United States generally, and in the Catholic Church, is largely counterproductive for democracy and impedes human flourishing. Acknowledging this stance, however, I have been scrupulous in pursuing this study with as much objectivity as possible and with a commitment to allowing the voices of my interlocutors to speak for themselves. This approach, it seems to me, is also in Bernardin's spirit, since his efforts were grounded in dialogue and respect for others.

My husband and I have had many conversations about these things over the last few years. And when I asked him, "What do you think of me dedicating the book to Cardinal Bernardin?" he answered immediately, "Of course. Who would be more appropriate?" So it is for this reason that the book is dedicated to Cardinal Bernardin. This dedication comes not just from me, but with Chris's understanding and generosity. I am grateful to them both.

Acknowledgments

IT IS HUMBLING task to write a book, especially for the first time. It would not have been possible for me to complete this project without the support and guidance of many people.

I am especially grateful to Martin Riesebrodt, who served as the chair for the dissertation that forms the basis for this book. Martin piqued my curiosity about theoretically informed research and taught me how to use social theory and good empirical studies in striving to think creatively about the social world. He exemplifies creativity and intellectual honesty—qualities I very much admire and strive to emulate in some small way. I am most grateful for his rather remarkable patience with me and for the wisdom with which he mentored me.

I am also grateful to Mark Chaves, Omar McRoberts, and Leslie Salzinger, who with Martin formed my dissertation committee. These accomplished scholars provided me with much support and helpful feedback throughout my research and dissertation writing. Andrew Abbott, Andreas Glaeser, Gary Herrigel and Genevieve Zubrzycki also provided me with support, advice, and thoughtful feedback during the period of this project's design and early execution. Emily Barman, Kelly Chong, Bryan Froehle, Deborah Kapp, Loren Lybarger, David Sikkink, Brian Starks, Steve Warner, Melissa Wilde, David Yamane, Michele Dillon, Brad Wilcox, M.J. Murray-Vachon, Mary Hallan Fiorito, the 2001–2002 Fellows at the Center for the Advanced Study of Religion at Yale, and members of the Chicago Group for the Study of Religious Congregations all generously read and perceptively commented on chapters of this manuscript.

Thank you, to Oxford editor Theo Calderara, and, to my colleagues at Notre Dame, who have generously provided support as this book took shape. Thanks are due especially to Christian Smith, who read an earlier version of this manuscript and gave me useful and encouraging comments, and to Meredith Whitnah, my graduate assistant, who has helped me enormously, providing research assistance, reading and commenting on chapters, tracking down citations, and copyediting. Thank you also to Karen Hooge, Aaron Sant-Miller, and Daniel Escher, who provided research assistance. I am grateful to Jane Pitz for creating the concept that directed my choice of the book's cover photo. And thank you to the Cushwa Center for the Study of American Catholicism at Notre Dame, especially to Tim Matovina and Kathleen Sprows Cummings, for graciously inviting me to be a Fellow there during the completion of this manuscript. They provided me with advice, mentoring, and many intellectually stimulating conversations.

Thank you to the Center for the Advanced Study of Religion at Yale for providing me with a dissertation fellowship and also to the Woodrow Wilson Foundation, which awarded me a Charlotte W. Newcombe Dissertation Fellowship. The financial support I received from these two organizations was crucial in accomplishing a draft manuscript. Thank you also to the Institute for Scholarship in the Liberal Arts at Notre Dame, who provided support for the development of the book's index. Thanks are also due to the University of Chicago Social and Behavioral Science Institutional Review Board for assisting me in the process of appropriately designing my field research and interviews; the research was conducted under protocol #00-199.

My family deserves much more than thanks for their abundant tolerance, ready companionship, and persistent humor (often at my expense). Florence Konieczny, my mother, has provided support of many kinds throughout these years. Renata and Joseph Chwedyk, my in-laws, spent many days with my sons throughout my graduate training at the University of Chicago. Chris Chwedyk, my husband, has provided love and support through the many years it has taken to bring this project to completion. John and Peter, our sons, have given me enormous joy through the years of this project—cheering me (usually unknowingly) in periods of difficulty, diverting me with the thrills of innumerable baseball and basketball games and soccer matches, teaching me about their passions for film and music, and allowing me to companion them as they move into adulthood.

Finally, it is with profound admiration that I thank the pastoral staffs and people of Our Lady of the Assumption and St. Brigitta parishes. Members of both congregations drew me into the Spirit's tether, in welcoming me to worship with them, learn with them, and share small parts of daily life with them. Although these two congregations worship and live in very different ways, I repeatedly witnessed sincerity, integrity, and virtue in their different forms of practice and ways of living. In my interviews with parishioners, I was humbled by their honesty, comforted by gracious responses to my awkwardness, and edified by individuals' willingness to talk about the intimacies of their everyday lives. I ask patience with any mistakes I have made along the way, and it is my hope that they and their peers might find this study interesting and useful.

The Spirit's Tether

Introduction

*Is it possible for us to join hands in common effort? As citizens
of a vibrant and varied democracy, how do we engage in vigorous
debate? How does each of us remain firm in our principles, and
fight for what we consider right, without demonizing those with
just as strongly held convictions on the other side?*

PRESIDENT BARACK OBAMA *May 17, 2009*

THIS WAS ONE small portion of the commencement address given by President
Barack Obama at the University of Notre Dame in May of 2009—an event that
had been the subject of public controversy for months. Upon the news that Notre
Dame had invited Obama to deliver the commencement address and to receive
an honorary doctor of laws degree, groups of Catholics and others argued that
Obama's pro-choice positions made him an inappropriate choice to be honored
by a Catholic university, especially with an honorary degree, since the Catholic
Church condemns abortion. But other Catholics, including former president
Theodore Hesburgh, defended the invitation, pointing to the many issues on
which Obama's positions are consistent with Catholicism's moral beliefs and
appealing to the role that universities play—Catholic universities among them—
as arenas for thoughtful dialogue about contentious issues.

President Obama's questions to the 2009 commencement assembly at Notre
Dame are significant not only because they are a response to the controversy itself
but also because they reflect a broader societal environment in which civil discourse about controversial issues, like abortion, is increasingly rare and is often
replaced by incivility or a refusal to engage at all. Because Catholicism has historically valued and maintained unity among diverse peoples with a plurality of
perspectives, traditions, and ways of living, these questions are particularly critical for Catholics. Catholicism therefore also offers a unique opportunity to better
understand why, in the contemporary United States, disagreement about deeply
felt moral issues has devolved into a polarization that rejects both authentic argumentation and the search for common values and objectives—a situation that has
too often obstructed efforts to find constructive solutions to pressing societal and
ecclesial problems.

In fact, the debate surrounding President Obama's visit to Notre Dame clearly
brings into view the fault lines of contemporary American Catholicism. In the

political sphere, Catholics are divided on family-related issues, with abortion the most contentious among them. They are likewise polarized on ecclesial issues, including the role and constitution of hierarchical authority in the church and women's roles in church and society. Significantly, the debate around Obama's visit did not center primarily on the morality of abortion. Instead, it revolved around how Catholic beliefs about the immorality of abortion should figure in whether the president should be honored by a Catholic university. Catholics with pro-life views took positions on *both* sides of this debate. An April 2009 Pew poll found that 50 percent of U.S. Roman Catholics supported Notre Dame's invitation to President Obama and 28 percent opposed it.[2] The numbers also showed that the opposition was concentrated among white Catholics who attend church regularly, with 37 percent supporting the visit and 45 percent opposing it.[3] A petition calling upon Notre Dame to rescind the invitation garnered more than 360,000 signatures.[4] A significant portion of the U.S. Catholic bishops, 83 of 429[5] (19.3 percent), signed a letter criticizing the visit on the grounds that it violated a 2005 pronouncement of the U.S. Catholic Conference of Bishops, which asserted that Catholic institutions should not honor public figures who act against Catholic teachings.[6] This reasoning figured prominently in Harvard professor Mary Ann Glendon's decision to decline the Laetare Medal, Notre Dame's highest honor, at the ceremony. In a public letter, she explained that she "could not help but be dismayed by the news that Notre Dame also planned to award the president an honorary degree... to honor a prominent and uncompromising opponent of the Church's position on issues involving fundamental positions of justice" and that Notre Dame's act disregarded the U.S. bishops' request that Catholic institutions should not give "awards, honors or platforms which would suggest support for [such] actions."[7] Glendon's objections reflected those of many Catholics who opposed Notre Dame's invitation to Obama.

As the larger public debate unfolded, the controversy also played out on and around the Notre Dame campus. A cadre of pro-life activists of various denominations demonstrated regularly at the university's gates and flew a small banner on an airplane over the campus daily. A student debate was held at the university, and Notre Dame's student newspaper, *The Observer*, received a flood of letters regarding Obama's visit. Of 612 letters received, 313 were from alumni, with 30 percent supportive of the invitation and 70 percent against it.[8] But among the 282 letters from students, the totals were reversed: 73 percent in favor and 27 percent against. Ninety-seven percent of Notre Dame's seniors approved of Obama's selection as a graduation speaker, while 26 of the 2,900 graduates chose to protest Obama's appearance by attending a service at Notre Dame's Grotto instead of the graduation, and several more attended their graduation but marked their mortar boards in protest.[9]

Broader political motives no doubt contributed to the controversy, but recent developments in U.S. Catholicism also played an important role—perhaps especially church leaders' "deprivatization" of religion and the increasing outspokenness on issues of moral concern[10] of bishops elevated during the papacy of John Paul II, who have tended to focus their public statements especially on issues like abortion.[11] At the same time, the linking of Catholic identity, and the debate over what should constitute Catholic identity generally, with issues related to the family is not only a historically specific result of changes in ecclesial and secular politics but also, and perhaps even more important, a consequence of the cultural and socioeconomic pressures faced by American families in the last few decades. Thus the polarization we witness in the Catholic Church today is not merely a product of conflict among elites, but one constituted among ordinary Catholics.

By studying the relation of religion and family among American Catholics in local parish settings, we can better understand how polarizing tendencies among them are supported, shaped, and intensified, since it is in these local cultures where religion and family life are intimately and emotionally related. I contend that moral polarization within Catholicism, while perhaps most obviously manifested in political conflicts surrounding the family, is not only shaped by elites and public figures but also constituted in the institutions and local cultures of everyday life in which Catholics interact with one another. Therefore, this book asks: How do religious institutions exert influence upon family life? And how do local religious cultures and their production, as well as religious perspectives on the family generally, contribute to the moral polarization observed in cultural conflicts about the family? Answers to these questions are undoubtedly complex, but my aim in this book is to provide one discrete and important piece of the explanation: to show how and why issues of cultural conflict over the family come to matter to ordinary Catholics involved in their parishes.

Problem and Thesis: Cultural Conflicts about the Family among American Catholics

Cultural conflicts about the family—including those surrounding women's social roles, the debate over abortion, and in more recent years, debates about stem cell research, same-sex marriage, and contraception—have intensified over the last half century, roughly in parallel with significant changes in the structure of the American family and a growing plurality of family forms. Social scientists and public intellectuals have investigated religion's role in these cultural conflicts primarily through the lens of the so-called culture wars, but the bulk of current scholarship has contributed to understanding the resonance of these conflicts among ordinary Americans in only a limited way.

This debate was catalyzed by James Davison Hunter,[12] whose culture wars thesis contends that the structure of public cultural conflicts in the United States—including those concerning the family, education, law, art, and politics—has become one of increasing polarization in recent decades. Hunter argues that religion plays a constitutive role in these conflicts: the groups pitted against one another hold competing moral visions that are fundamentally religious, with traditionalists pitted against progressives.[13] Critics, including Alan Wolfe and Paul DiMaggio, have hotly disputed Hunter's thesis by claiming that any culture war is being waged by elites, not ordinary Americans, and, defending this claim primarily with opinion data showing that Americans are not polarized on most issues, that public opinion consists in a plurality of perspectives and that the majority holds moderate views.[14] Recent studies, however, suggest that this moderate majority is shrinking.[15] Moreover, Robert Putnam and David Campbell have recently contended that the relevant fault line regarding moral polarization—and they do agree with Hunter about the empirical reality of polarization—is between those who are religious and those who are secular, with the most religious Americans tending to take conservative positions on politically contentious issues, especially those surrounding sexuality, and secular Americans prone to take liberal positions.[16] Although Putnam and Campbell's work helpfully demonstrates growth in secularism in the United States, by framing the conflict in this way, they appear to equate more liberal religious orientations with secularism. They thereby shift attention away from some of the very real differences that exist among *religious* Americans, which we see played out both in research on their attitudes and practices and in the public sphere.

In general, survey research indicates that between 10 and 20 percent of the American public is intensely polarized around culture wars issues but that larger minorities, about half the population, actually hold the same worldviews, even though their views on particular issues are less extreme.[17] At the same time, the studies that critics have used to counter Hunter's thesis *do* reveal attitudinal polarization around family-related issues such as abortion and same-sex marriage.[18] Some critics see these latter findings as significant because they are the *only* arenas where polarization is evident in survey research—thus giving evidence that there is no broad culture war.[19] But these findings also represent a missed opportunity, because they document the emergence of a significant cleavage in how Americans regard the family—one that has received little scholarly attention. In fact, social scientific tests of the culture wars hypothesis generally reflect a rather narrow definition of polarization, in which scholars look for large proportions of attitudes at either extreme of a political or cultural question. However, moral polarization is constituted not only by attitudes but also, more important, by how groups experience and respond to antagonism over such conflicting attitudes and perhaps particularly by the emotional responses that sustain antagonism. Antagonism and

emotion in conflict are fed by social processes within groups,[20] but survey measures neither capture nor reflect this reality. Moreover, while existing measures
have given some insight into those at the poles, we know relatively little about how
those in the middle—that is, those with more moderate attitudes—make choices.

Hunter's thesis, though perhaps too broad, helpfully highlights religion's role
in moral polarization. Its critique has somewhat clarified the scope of ordinary
Americans' attitudes toward cultural conflicts in the public sphere. However, arguments about whether there is a culture war have diverted scholars' attention away
from important questions about the institutional and cultural local-level processes
constituting moral polarization when and where it does exist and how polarization
might emerge from Americans' plurality of perspectives. And while some other
studies, especially those documenting how conservative religion is intertwined
with particular family patterns, have usefully illuminated the conservative pole in
the cleavage over family-related issues,[21] scholars have rarely compared religion
and family in theologically diverse congregations of a particular tradition or investigated the social processes by which religion and family intertwine, much less
attempted to explain moral polarization.

Thus, to better understand religion's role in how ordinary Americans have
become divided around contemporary cultural conflicts about the family, we
must grasp more fully local congregations' roles in how their families engage the
challenges of everyday life, how congregational cultures support them, and what
cultural processes sustain polarizing tendencies within them. The prevalence of
mundane congregational conflicts over the family—for example, conflicts between
working and stay-at-home mothers, over how to address issues of sexuality with
children, or over how to respond to same-sex couples or single parents—demonstrates that religious people's involvement in conflicts over the family are neither
merely rhetorical nor political, but are part of the concrete substance of daily life.
The quotidian qualities of these local conflicts are another reality that often has
been overlooked in analyses of public cultural conflicts.[22] We already know that
churches can be important sites for filtering public discourse about the family
and, more generally, for providing institutional support for particular worldviews
and ethics. Thus it is in congregations where the local-level polarization processes
connecting religion and the family are most likely to be found.

To more fully understand individuals' involvements in public conflicts over the
family, we must work to better understand how men and women actually forge
marriages, rear children, and make choices surrounding work-family balance
within their particular economic and cultural contexts, simultaneously exploring
when and how religion matters in these efforts. In other words, explaining how
public politics surrounding the family have become divisive at local levels involves
not only individuals' beliefs about family-related issues but also their experiences
and acts of domestic politics. Therefore, the central project of this book is to

present a close and detailed analysis of local religious cultures of family life. In so doing, I aim to identify when and how these cultures produce and support polarizing tendencies that emerge in cultural conflicts about the family.

Catholicism is a promising case study for this analysis not only because of its prominence on the American religious landscape—it is the largest American denomination, approximately 29 percent of U.S. religious practitioners[23]—but also because it is a church that, by contrast with Protestant denominations, is characterized historically by pluralism. At the same time, in the last several decades, it has participated in a general restructuring of U.S. religion that, as Robert Wuthnow claims, has made denominational boundaries less salient than intradenominational liberal-conservative differences.[24] Of course, some characteristics of the religion-family nexus in this study will be particular to Catholics—perhaps especially those resulting from the Catholic Church's reforms in the Second Vatican Council (1962–1965) and their implementation.[25] Nevertheless, Catholicism allows us to examine how plural perspectives on religion and family have aligned into polar positions within a single denomination and also affords us an opportunity to observe how this happens *despite* continued intragroup and intergroup pluralism, thus promising to inform our conception of moral polarization and the religious politics of the family generally.

This study also aims to contribute to knowledge of contemporary Catholicism's impact on members' families. Despite rich scholarship on the history of religion and family within Catholicism[26] and a tradition of survey research that has deeply explored Catholics' attitudes on issues of gender and sexuality, especially as they cohere with or depart from church teachings and attitudes predominant among Americans generally,[27] we still know relatively little about how religion figures sociologically in American Catholics' efforts to cope with family change over the last half century. Thus, in exploring how and to what extent Catholic families' goals, problems, and everyday choices inform their perceptions of contemporary issues surrounding family life, and how Catholicism is intertwined in their perceptions and responses, we can gain a better understanding of Catholicism's distinctive effects on family life. How do Catholics' domestic politics reflect their dilemmas, constraints, and hopes, and how does religion matter as they respond to life challenges? What is at stake for ordinary Catholics in broader public debates about the family, and how do these debates play out locally? Why do couples choose to bring their families to church at all, when even in today's religious culture of choice, belonging involves at least some measure of submission to religious authority and therefore introduces constraints on their choices? And how does the parish matter when Catholics are making points of connection between faith and family life?

Answering questions like these involves delving into the everyday lives and faith journeys of families. Throughout the course of this study, in conducting

20 months of ethnographic research in two Midwestern Catholic churches, I have paid particular attention to the individual stories, collective rituals, and other activities of parish members.[28] Located in two roughly similar middle-class urban neighborhoods of the same city, Our Lady of the Assumption is a religiously conservative church,[29] and Saint Brigitta is theologically progressive. Utilizing comparative methods, this study brings to light the ways in which Catholics who embrace different styles of religious identity form marriages, craft family routines, and cope with the strains and pressures of balancing work and family life. As I explore how parishioners' responses to family-related issues vary by factors including generation, family background, and career trajectories, even among groups with similar class backgrounds, I will demonstrate that parish life and the religious identities nurtured therein provide particular perspectives on families' life problems that support and shape responses to them. And in the process of working out their domestic politics, I show how the emotional and symbolic content of the religious resources that help families meet these challenges resonates with particular streams of public politics.

It is important to acknowledge that Catholic families can, and no doubt sometimes do, find religious support for family life in arenas beyond the parish. But this study focuses on parish contexts because, although the church is also encountered through voluntary organizations, media, and public figures like bishops, theologians, and the pope, parishes are ordinarily the primary way in which most Catholics experience their church. As in other U.S. denominations, cultural pluralism and religious subcultural expressions flourish in Catholic congregations.[30] Historically, this pluralism has been constituted by groups of people who were born into particular social classes, ethnicities, and regions—in other words, Catholic pluralism was based on ascribed differences. But as other studies have shown and this study illustrates,[31] in today's religious landscape, pluralism also comprises identities based in distinctive sets of chosen values, desires, and perceptions of the world[32]—that is, achieved identities—even among cradle Catholics whose religious observance has often been conceptualized in primarily ascriptive terms.

Parishioners at Assumption and Saint Brigitta represent two somewhat broadly different types of chosen, or achieved, Catholic identities, even though members are also at least partly characterized by the ascriptive identities of social class. Each church, moreover, represents a particular local expression of Catholicism closer to the poles of U.S. Catholic practice than to the middle, but one whose individual elements are typical enough to make each one useful for understanding similar expressions in other settings. Thus, although each setting is unique and therefore reveals interconnections between faith and family that may be in some ways particular to them, they are also embedded in and reflect much of the larger shared cultural repertoires of American Catholics. Their distinctive similarities, together with their differences, provide an unusually clear view into a particular and important swath of contemporary American Catholicism. Both churches, while somewhat racially diverse, have primarily white middle-class memberships descended from upwardly mobile Catholics of an older immigrant church, and, therefore, they are members of a group that is today socially influential within U.S. Catholicism and in society at large. At the same time, Assumption and Saint Brigitta also differ in significant ways that bear on particular manifestations of Catholicism. Saint Brigitta expresses a post–Vatican II religiously progressive spirit in its contemporary and participatory worship style and in preaching and parish groups that emphasize the religious demands of social justice. By contrast, Our Lady of the Assumption reflects a retraditionalization in worship, devotional practices, and religious teachings, in which older Catholic traditions are recovered, employed in circumstances other than those in which they were originally practiced, and attributed meanings that respond to new social conditions. In addition, Assumption especially emphasizes explicit adherence to Catholic teachings on human sexuality. Together, these parishes allow us to observe how two groups whose Catholic practice and doctrinal emphases are quite different, but whose beliefs and practices are each recognizable in many Catholic settings, perceive and respond to the challenges of sustaining marriages, raising children, and balancing work and family life.

The central claim of this book is that, while public political attitudes are indicative of moral polarization and elites play important roles in shaping and constraining debates about the family, polarization is also constituted among Catholics through local-level social processes. Two parish-level processes—one involving the expression of congregational metaphors and the other involving religious identity construction—have contributed to the constitution of different cultures and structures of family life among Catholics in ways that foster moral polarization.[33] Central church metaphors, expressed paradigmatically in parish worship, present models for social relations that have affinities with, and are transposable to, family life. Different metaphors support different models of the family, which are contested symbolically in conflicts over family-related issues. And the construction of Catholic identities in parishes both creates in-group solidarity and distinguishes them from others, including other Catholics. Opposed identities are established in the different discourses through which parishioners articulate the beliefs and practices they understand to be authentically Catholic. In part I of this book, I demonstrate how these two processes actually work locally, focusing on congregational metaphors in chapter 1 and identity construction in chapter 2. I explore the ramifications of these processes for family life and its relation to public politics in the chapters analyzing particular aspects of domestic politics in chapters on marriage (chapter 3), childrearing (chapter 4), and mothers' work-family balance (chapter 5) in part II.

Processes involving congregational metaphors and religious identity construction foster polarizing tendencies at Assumption and Saint Brigitta because they both support families' domestic politics and construct identity boundaries against other Catholics in ways that are strongly emotional. Antipathy is more intense between those that belong to the same group—in this case, among Catholics—than those who do not, for as Georg Simmel observes, "antagonism on the basis of a common kinship tie is stronger than among strangers."[34] In fact, he remarks that this is particularly true in churches where even small differences can become significant sources of conflict. This is the case because although churches espouse causes, which Simmel understands to be fundamentally objective and impersonal, they are held together as groups by members' similarity and interpersonal intimacy. In addition to these emotional factors, the intensity of religious conflict is also exacerbated, according to Simmel, by the logical irreconcilability of dogmatic differences, even when they are relatively small. This study will show that although the markers of family-related conflict between conservative and progressive Catholics are often related to doctrine, these conflicts are not just about beliefs, but also have experiential and emotional dimensions in their concrete implications for people's lives. They are thus at once rational, emotional, and personal. Even in a church that has historically tolerated pluralism and where the impulse is to remain unified rather than to separate, such overdetermined boundary drawing increases the likelihood of polarization.

Methodological Notes and Description of Cases

Two prefatory notes conclude this introduction: a discussion of the social scientific details of the study and a brief introduction to Assumption and Saint Brigitta parishes and how they fit into the broad swath of American Catholicism.

Data and Methods

Because this book seeks to understand social processes underlying the relation between religion and family and their role in moral polarization, Assumption and Saint Brigitta were selected for study based on a combination of demographic and socioeconomic similarities and differences in religious orientation and practice. Because of the similarities of the congregations, I am better able to isolate the reasons for their differences.

The study comprises 20 months of ethnographic field research and 38 open-ended interviews conducted at Assumption and Saint Brigitta during the years 2000 through 2002, together with subsequent occasional visits to each church and follow-up conversations with parishioners. Fieldwork included regular attendance at Sunday masses and other worship services; participation and observation at parish events including lectures, discussions, and celebrations; and numerous informal conversations. Quantities of written material, including parish bulletins, flyers, and letters, were gathered, as were books and periodicals on religion and family recommended by parishioners.

I attended each of the regular Sunday masses offered at each parish at least twice and attended one Sunday mass at each parish on a regular basis: the 10:00 A.M. Sunday mass at Assumption and the Saint Brigitta Sunday morning gym mass. These masses were chosen for substantial periods of participant observation because parishioners and pastors in each setting described them as ones that families with children disproportionately attended and/or ones that particularly catered to or tried to attract families.

Interviews with parishioners, lay leaders, and staff totaled 19 in each setting: 21 women and 17 men in all and a roughly equal number of men and women at each parish. I identified interview candidates through staff recommendations and parish and diocesan networks and made final selections based on their fit with the theoretical questions of the study. Most of those interviewed attended the focal Sunday services, and parents with children at home were oversampled. Interviews were conducted in several different locations, including restaurants, participants' work locations, and my home, but the majority of interviews took place in congregants' homes. Interviews usually ran about two hours, during which respondents were asked about their upbringings, educational experiences, aspirations, work and family life, the roles religion has played in their lives, and current family religious practices. I allowed discussions of public conflicts over family-related issues, including hot-button issues like homosexuality and abortion, to emerge from these narratives, generally permitting their narrators to determine their importance rather than prompting them (which I did only occasionally). I tape-recorded interviews and prepared verbatim transcripts for all respondents except four individuals who requested that they not be recorded and whose responses I reconstructed as interview notes immediately afterward.

Among those interviewed in each congregation were groups of young parents with small children in the home who were friends with one another. These parents were members of groups that I spent significant time with at parish events and in more private settings. The friendship group I spent the most time with at Assumption was the result of a larger friendship network encouraged by the pastor and sustained by the connectedness of the women in the circle, many of whom gathered their children for play dates, occasionally traded child care, and met for a book group. Many of those in the friendship group I worked with at Saint Brigitta were college friends. They met regularly as a faith-sharing group, and their lives were also intertwined in the activities of their children. Members of these groups figure significantly in the accounts presented in the following chapters.

Our Lady of the Assumption and Saint Brigitta in the Context of American Catholicism

Assumption and Saint Brigitta are similar to one another—and to a segment of urban Catholic churches generally—in size and family composition, and they are similar to one another socioeconomically and in some other respects. They differ primarily in their religious orientation and practice.

DEMOGRAPHIC AND SOCIOECONOMIC CHARACTERISTICS.
Both Our Lady of the Assumption and Saint Brigitta parishes are comprised largely of middle- to upper-middle-class congregants, both display a generational balance, and both have large numbers of young adults and families with young children (see table I.1 for related descriptive statistics of the parishes and the interview sample). Set in diverse and gentrifying neighborhoods, both congregations are class-heterogeneous. But each draws large numbers of highly educated professionals, including attorneys, entrepreneurial and managerial businessmen and women, and doctors; these congregants are situated squarely within the Catholic middle classes, which are the majority of U.S. Catholics. Although the median household income in the neighborhood surrounding Assumption ($53,836) is higher than that at Saint Brigitta ($38,068), this income difference is not necessarily mirrored in these parishes. The higher median income at Assumption is in part the result of recent rapid gentrification, prompting an influx of higher earning professionals into the neighborhood, but several of those interviewed had moved from within the parish boundaries and commuted from less expensive areas to attend church on Sunday—suggesting that the actual median income of active parishioners is somewhat lower than the total of those living within the parish boundaries and therefore closer to that of worshippers at Saint Brigitta.

Both parishes are large compared with U.S. congregations generally (their median size is 400) but medium-size for urban U.S. Catholic churches, with total Sunday attendance averaging 1,012 at Saint Brigitta and 1,651 at Assumption from 2000 to 2002.[35] This study focuses on the worship environments and practices of the 10:00 A.M. Sunday mass at Assumption and the Saint Brigitta Sunday morning gym mass. The 10:00 A.M. Assumption mass averages 400 to 550 individuals and draws families from the city and suburbs who are attracted by Assumption's conservative theology and practice, friendship connections, and its well-known network of like-minded people. By contrast, the Saint Brigitta gym mass averages 100 to 125 individuals and draws families who tend to live in or near the church neighborhood. Father Theo, the pastor of Saint Brigitta parish, describes the gym mass as drawing "returning Catholics who might be skittish about actually reentering a church building," and indeed, many regulars there previously had been

Table 1.1 Organizational and Demographic Characteristics

Parishes	Assumption	St. Brigitta
Mean Sunday mass attendance[1]	1,651	1,012
Focal mass attendance (range)	400–550	100–125
Median household income[2]	$53,836	$38,068
Interview sample		
Occupation/background[3]		
For-profit/business[4]	10	6
Nonprofit/helping[5]	9	13
Distance from church		
Within/near parish boundaries	8	17
5 or more miles from church	11	2
Number of children		
Mean	3.5	2.25
Median (range)	3 (1–12)	2 (1–7)
Age cohort[6]		
Pre–Vatican II	2	3
Vatican II	7	9
Post–Vatican II	10	7

1 Based on average of diocesan October counts 2000–2002:

2000   2001   2002
Our Lady of the Assumption: 1,538   1,679   1,735*
St. Brigitta: 1,074   1,003   960

* Note: During October 2002, OLA performed a mass celebration the canonization of Josemaria Escriva, so this figure reflects an exceptionally high mass attendance that Sunday.

2 Thanks to diocesan officials for providing these figures, which are weighted averages computed with census data (2004).

3 Figures include current occupation, profession, or occupational background for participants who have temporarily left the workforce (5 at Assumption and 3 at St. Brigitta).

4 Includes attorney, administrator/secretary, business/sales, economic analyst, information technician, writer.

5 Includes childcare provider, church worker, nonprofit religious worker, nurse, psychologist, social worker, teacher.

6 I use Davidson and colleagues' (1997) classification of these generations: Pre-Vatican II Catholics were born in the 1930s or before, Vatican II Catholics from 1941 to 1960, and Post–Vatican II Catholics in 1961 or later.

inactive out of anger, frustration, or apathy. Participants often were publicly critical of the institutional church. At the same time, several said they attended the gym mass because it was an "intentional community," that is, a mutual support group committed to a common life of faith.

Both parishes are situated in city neighborhoods that are ethnically diverse and gentrifying, and each exhibits some racial diversity among its membership. Saint Brigitta is situated in a neighborhood far more diverse than its Sunday parishioners. While I encountered Latinos, Asians, and African Americans at Sunday mass, they were a relatively small portion of the congregation. By contrast, Sunday attendance at Our Lady of the Assumption reflects more ethnic diversity, and the parish draws Latino and Polish members—often from outside its parish boundaries. Since Sunday masses are offered in Spanish and Polish as well as English, these worshippers mostly attend services in the languages and traditions of their countries of origin, which I attended occasionally. And while I included individuals with varied racial and ethnic backgrounds when it made sense to do so, the analysis of specific racial groups or ethnic immigrants—an important line of research that is being pursued by others[36]—is beyond the scope of this study.

Religious orientation and practice

The similarities just noted allow the comparison of two groups who are similar in many respects and vary mainly in religious orientation and practice. Assumption and Saint Brigitta differ significantly here (see table I.2).

Saint Brigitta magnifies progressive tendencies within the Conciliar (Vatican II) generation of U.S. Catholics, distinguishing itself from mainstream Catholic

Table I.2 Religious Characteristics

	Assumption	St. Brigitta
Theological orientation	Neotraditional; "Orthodox"	Progressive
Teaching emphasis	Church doctrine on sexual morality	Social justice
Dominant image of congregation	Church as holy family	Church as community of equals
Worship and devotional practice	High style of worship: novenas, rosary, confession	Low style of worship: lay preaching, faith sharing, general absolution
Concept of God	Transcendent	Immanent; incarnational

parishes not so much in its religious orientation as in its relative intensity. Parish staff and leaders tend to espouse a theology that emphasizes God's immanence, that is, one that understands the presence of God to be found primarily in the environments and activities of everyday life. The ritual practice at Saint Brigitta reflects the *aggiornamento* of the Second Vatican Council—that is, the church's modernization or "bringing up to date" accomplished by the council[37]—and the parish has retained the spirit of experimentation in its worship that characterized the period of postconciliar reform. Worship practices are meant to elicit the active participation of the assembly and individuals within it, often by multiplying ritual roles to involve as many church members as possible. Several ritual practices stretch the boundaries of Catholic practice in their involvement of laity: lay homilists routinely serve as preachers at Sunday masses, a dialogue homily elicits congregational participation at a casual community-focused mass in the school gymnasium, the parish offers general absolution at seasonal reconciliation services, and a cadre of liturgical dancers performs monthly at Sunday services at the gym mass and in the church.

One of the most striking things about Saint Brigitta is the profusion of parish groups and organizations; new registrants receive a parish directory listing more than 60 different groups with information on whom to contact to learn more about each of them. Although these groups are quite diverse, activities concerned with religiously defined issues of social justice are particularly numerous. Moreover, parishioners often use liberal religious and secular political concepts to address their disagreements with church rules (such as the all-male celibate priesthood), linking them with secular issues of social justice. Saint Brigitta stresses a self-revelatory religious sensibility in both its worship and program offerings, which include 15 to 20 ongoing small faith-sharing groups.

By contrast, Assumption practices a retraditionalized Catholicism that emphasizes transcendent images of God, especially in its high style of worship, and traditional devotional practices like the rosary. The parish integrates Vatican II reforms, upholds older traditions, and emphasizes church doctrines on sexuality. Priests and most parishioners preferred the term *orthodox*—rather than *conservative* or *traditionalist*—to describe their Catholicism, emphasizing a sense of fidelity to the church's doctrines, morals, and Magisterium.[38] Assumption's emphasis on the church prohibition of artificial birth control is, in parishioners' words, a litmus test for orthodoxy; they talked of "choosing to welcome children" rather than following materialistic pursuits that might delay childbearing or preclude a large family. And indeed Assumption has larger families (see mean number of children in table I.1) than Saint Brigitta.[39]

Our Lady of the Assumption Church has many members who are affiliated with Opus Dei.[40] By contrast with other expressions of doctrinally conservative Catholicism and churches characterized as conservative dissenters where masses of the Tridentine Rite are said in Latin,[41] masses at Our Lady of the Assumption are said in the vernacular and according to the *Novus Ordo* (the new order of the mass instituted after Vatican II).[42] Devotional practices such as novenas, communal recitation of the rosary, and adoration of the Blessed Sacrament are frequently offered, as is the sacrament of confession.

Although many of these values and attitudes are shared by the Catholic right generally, the portrait of the typical conservative Catholic found in scholarly literature—an educated, middle-class religious traditionalist who experienced the Catholic Church prior to Vatican II and grieves its loss[43]—is not the most common churchgoer at Assumption. Instead, the average Assumption parishioner is much younger, and many are not old enough to remember the council, much less the church that existed before it. Younger members often said they were attracted to conservative Catholicism because of its teachings on issues of sexuality and family life, a broader phenomenon in American religion charted especially in ethnographic studies focusing on gender and religion.[44]

The similarity in the intensity and singularity of religious orientations at these two parishes is at least partly a result of history. As Jerome Baggett explains in his study of a diverse set of six Catholic Bay Area churches, Catholic churches can grow to be characterized by a singular religious orientation through a process of "de facto congregationalism,"[45] whereby like-minded people gravitate to churches with particular sensibilities, and these churches over time come to more strongly emphasize the traditions and practices most valued by parishioners.[46] Our Lady of the Assumption grew through such a process over the decade prior to this study as a result of the congregation's staunch doctrinal orthodoxy. And the long tenure of the pastor at Saint Brigitta similarly solidified a milieu where theological liberalism is dominant. In this sense, Assumption and Saint Brigitta are perhaps different from most U.S. Catholic parishes, which might be described as middle of the road and often exhibit a greater range of religious orientations and viewpoints among parishioners than do these two particular settings.

Thus these churches fundamentally differ according to their religious orientations in ways analogous to the religious categories described by Robert Wuthnow and James D. Hunter, a religious landscape where the salient religious differences are religiopolitical and occur primarily within religious denominations rather than among them.[47] And yet, each of these parishes does not fall unproblematically into these categories. As described in the chapters that follow, parishioners at both churches often disagree internally about public politics, and involved parishioners at these two churches sometimes agree more than disagree on the moral status, if not the rationales, of issues as profoundly polarizing as abortion and economic strategies for the alleviation of poverty. Thus these congregations reveal the ambiguities of lived experience in Catholics' domestic politics and, at the same time, help us to understand how they approach cultural conflicts about the American family at the turn of the 21st century.

PART ONE

The Churches

I

Worship

Our Lady of the Assumption Church
Sunday, ten o'clock in the morning.
The massive white dome of the church rises above the red-brick
Roman Renaissance-style structure.[1] The church was built in
the early decades of the 20th century to serve as the heart of the
surrounding immigrant neighborhood. Nearly a hundred years
later, the sight of rehabilitated old brownstones, the new construction of single-family homes built on 25-foot lots purchased
as teardowns, and the luxury autos parked along either side of
crowded neighborhood streets provide ubiquitous evidence of gentrification. In the midst of this urban revitalization, the church
still stands tall above the neighborhood. This morning, its dome
and spires glisten in the sunlight.
The streets are busy and congested, and people clog the sidewalk
in front of the church steps. Some are on foot, but most arrive
at the church in small sedans, vans, or sport utility vehicles.
Many are suburban residents who live nearer to other Catholic
churches.
As singles and families, young and old, enter the church, they
encounter the familiar sign at the door to the nave. It begs those
who would enter, out of respect for the Lord, to be modest and
appropriate in their dress—and specifies immodesties to be
avoided, including shorts, backless dresses, and bare midriffs.
Most walk past the sign with nary a glance.
They enter the church. It is a large church by almost any standard: three-fourths the length of a football field, well over a hundred feet wide, and eight stories high at the top of its main dome.
Inside the church, four banks of pews run across its width in the
nave,[2] with enough seating to accommodate 2,000. Four heavily
decorated arches frame each side of the barrel-vaulted nave and
mark the stained-glass windows that line its exterior walls. A gold
baldacchino enshrines the tabernacle behind the marbled main

altar;³ *statues of the Blessed Mother, Saint Joseph, and Saint Thérèse of Lisieux form the heart of devotional shrines throughout the nave. Above the main altar, the half-domed ceiling is painted with a mural of the Virgin Mary, for whom the church is named. Sixty-eight stained-glass windows allow natural light to stream into the church. A dozen brass chandeliers make it luminous even when it is cloudy. In the evenings, the chandeliers and banks of vigil lights create a soft glow in the church.*

The newly arrived walk up the side aisle and pass a line of people waiting near the doors of the confessional. The confessional line remains intact through most of mass each Sunday; as the faithful in line receive the sacrament and return to their pews, new penitents join the line to wait for their turn. Father James, one of two priests assigned to the parish, has said that although hearing confessions during Sunday mass is technically not allowed by the Catholic Church, the bishop has witnessed this practice during visits to Assumption and does not object.

In twos and threes, people genuflect,⁴ cross themselves, and move into pews, where they kneel. As the bells sound the hour, people are still arriving. A diminutive middle-aged woman, well-groomed and wearing a tailored suit, walks up to the lectern in the sanctuary and formally greets the congregation. "Today is the second Sunday of Lent," she announces. She is Christina McKenna, the principal of the grade school, and one of a small group of lay lectors who read the scriptures each Sunday.

The mass begins. All rise, and the choir begins to sing a familiar old hymn, "The King of Love My Shepherd Is," as the procession, led by altar boys in red cassocks and white surplices,⁵ begins from the door to the right of the sanctuary. The boys' faces are scrubbed and their hands are folded, with fingers pressed together and wedged into their chins. Gym shoes peak out from below their cassocks. One boy leads with a cross, two with tall candles on processional stands follow him, and four more altar boys march behind them in pairs.

Father Aidan MacInerny, Assumption's pastor, walks behind them in procession, wearing a purple chasuble over a thin white alb that only partially hides the black cassock that is his daily uniform.⁶ He is tall and thin, with a long face and rimless spectacles. His balding head and graying hair reveal his sixty years, but his energetic demeanor belies them. He walks briskly behind the altar boys, hands folded in front of him, with long fingers pointing heavenward, his ascetic face tense with concentration.

There are at least 500 in the congregation this morning. Drawn from nearby urban neighborhoods and some far-flung upper-middle-class suburbs, the congregation reflects the several different groups that invest themselves in the life of Assumption parish. The front banks of pews are occupied primarily by young families. One sees many families with three or four or five small children, dressed in their Sunday best. A few mothers and their daughters cover their heads with lace mantillas or chapel veils in a traditional sign of obedience to norms of modesty for women. Interspersed among the families, single young adults sit in small groups. The women among them are dressed formally and smartly, as they might for business meetings during the week. Older couples noticeably dot the mostly young, mostly white congregation in the front half of the church, as do several African American and Latino men and women. As one travels toward the back of the church, one sees more singles and couples, the dress code becomes casual and the clothes worn less expensive, and racial diversity within the congregation becomes more apparent.

Father Aidan processes up the main aisle and past the altar rail to the altar, where he genuflects deeply, kisses the altar, and takes his place in front of an ornate chair on one side of the sanctuary. He formally addresses the congregation with the words, "The Lord be with you." Father Aidan's voice resounds throughout the church. He pronounces the customary greeting with elongated vowels, betraying his Northeastern U.S. origins. His manner is at once warm, avuncular, and formally reverent. Parishioners frequently describe him as holy or saintly.

As the mass continues, the choir leads musical responses interspersed with congregational and priestly prayers. The congregation's worship is formal and comfortably routinized; they stand, sit, and kneel on cue, and alternately sing, speak, listen, and pray silently. The numerous children in the congregation can hardly be heard. Parents muffle children's protests with loving instruction, and the great domed ceiling of the church absorbs the occasional cries for attention and activity.

The ritual approaches its climax in the Eucharistic Prayer. The conclusion of a plainchant Hosanna is the signal for the congregation to kneel, and Fr. Aidan reverently prays the Roman Canon. Some heads are bowed, and some look forward, staring. Others look around, distracted. At the consecration, Fr. Aidan raises the large white host with both hands high above his head,

his gaze following the host. Bells ring, three long peals to mark
the moment. The rite is repeated with the chalice. Most of the
congregation gaze; many cross themselves, and then they bow
their heads. A mother in the front bank of pews quietly whispers
to her young son, "It's Jesus now." A moment of silent prayer
follows—even the children are still—and then the choir chants a
response to the grace of that sacramental moment.

Saint Brigitta Church
Sunday, ten thirty in the morning.
In a neighborhood six or seven miles to the north of Our Lady
of the Assumption Church, in another gentrifying city neighbor-
hood, the streets encircling Saint Brigitta Catholic parish are full
of people in transit. Music and sonorous prayer can be heard
emanating from the gray stone Gothic church, as worshippers
cross the street in front of it and enter the multipurpose parish
building, where another mass is about to begin. A banner hung
on the stair railing in front of this building announces and wel-
comes any who would come to "The Saint Brigitta Mass in the
Gym."
People file slowly up the stairs and into the gymnasium. The
interior of the gym is drab and old, worn with decades of school-
children's play and the activities of numerous parish events. Its
large arched windows match the Gothic style of the church, but
the remaining architectural features of the space are all more
functional than decorative. The bottom half of the gym walls are
robin's-egg blue, with plain concrete block above, and a clock and
a couple of old advertisements from local businesses hang high
above the gym floor on one long wall. A stage concealed by a cur-
tain occupies the far south end of the gym. In the middle of the
gym, three rows of steel folding chairs are set up in a semicircle,
with a makeshift aisle down the center; racks of bleachers have
been placed behind the chairs. A wooden ambo is positioned at
the head of the semicircle. At the far end of the gym stands a
wooden altar, flanked by a large wooden cross draped in bur-
lap. Behind the altar is a white backdrop with a multicolored
patchwork cross hand-quilted upon it. A basketball hoop hangs
incongruously above the backdrop; organizers have chosen not to
disguise or hide it.
At ten thirty, when the mass is advertised to start, the gym is only
about a third full, and seven or eight musicians are practicing.
As worshippers enter the gym, greeters hand them music sheets

and bulletins. By ten forty-five, the congregation is small but swelling, with about a hundred people sitting in folding chairs and on bleachers. The mass is ready to begin. The congregation is overwhelmingly white, middle-class professionals, belying the racial and economic diversity of the surrounding neighborhood. There are between 75 and 125 people in attendance at the gym mass each Sunday. Masses held in the church building draw larger numbers, where today at ten o'clock, Sunday worshippers number upward of 700 or 800.

There are several families with children in the congregation. Parents range from young adults in their 30s to more mature parents in their 40s and early 50s. Many have one or two or three small children. There are also many active seniors, and some older singles and couples accompanied by one or two teenagers. Many dress in jeans or in other casual attire.

The casual sensibility of the group extends to the character of the service. The music is a blend of folk, contemporary country, and gospel styles, and as mass begins, piano, guitars, and mandolin accompany voices raised in song. The song is "Earthen Vessels"; written in the 1970s, it has a contemporary sound. Father Pierre, a young Caribbean priest from a religious order who often celebrates mass in the gym, arrived just a few minutes earlier and stood adjusting his vestments in the gathering space at the back of the assembly as the music began. Now he walks perfunctorily up the makeshift main aisle, stands beside the altar, and welcomes the congregation. Father Pierre has close-cut curly black hair, a dark complexion, and bright brown eyes. Speaking in heavily accented English, he tells the congregation, "You are all loved, you are treasures. Now greet each other, and tell each other 'You are a treasure.'" The large gymnasium with its two-story ceiling explodes with noise, its lively acoustics magnifying the din. Steel chairs scratch and clang as friends and family reach across chairs to embrace one another. Children stomp on the bleacher seats, reaching over to shake hands with the friend above, below, or to one side of them. After a moment, Father Pierre quells the noisy camaraderie, speaking above it until all retire back to their seats. "Now that we have greeted one another, let us pray." Together the congregation utters the prayers of the opening rite.

Then a 30ish woman, Kate Burton, who together with her husband is coordinating the gym mass this year, approaches the lectern. She proclaims the day's scriptures, first reading from the

Hebrew Scriptures, then from the New Testament, pausing and singing with the congregation as the musicians lead the psalm response between the readings.

At the Gospel, Joe Moran, a slight, graying man with a well-groomed mustache and full beard, comes from the congregation and stands in front of Father Pierre. The priest places his hands on Joe's head in blessing as the congregation prays. Joe is a resigned Catholic priest who now directs a foundation for the education of disadvantaged youth. He crosses himself, approaches the ambo, and dramatically proclaims a reading from the Gospel of Luke. It is the story of the Pharisee and the tax collector praying in the temple.[7]

Then he drags a large flip chart from behind the musicians and begins to preach. "People are prone to see prayer," he says, "as petition or as bargaining," and he writes these words in the first of two columns he has drawn on the flip chart. "But Jesus wants us to understand prayer differently—as something which will produce a radical change in us, not God," and he writes the word change *in large letters in the second column. He goes on to explain what he means by telling stories of people he knows from his work and from Saint Brigitta. Then he asks the congregation, "How is it that you understand prayer? What moments of prayer have changed you?"*

One at a time, men and women rise from their seats and talk about their experience of prayer. An older man tells a story of how, in praying for his dying father, he found himself struggling but eventually was comforted and changed. A middle-aged woman stands to say she doesn't like to pray in a disciplined way but just lets prayer happen in her life. Joe calls on one person after another, responding to several of the comments with brief remarks of encouragement and support, alternately displaying the skills of an organizational psychologist and a motivational speaker. When five or ten minutes have passed, he deftly wraps up the dialogue and begins the Prayer of the Faithful.

After petitionary prayer and the congregational singing that follows it, Father Pierre invites the congregation to join him at the altar. He leads the Liturgy of the Eucharist. Some of the congregation seem to concentrate at prayer; others scan the group or watch what is going on around them. Small children play with one another at the edges of the congregation. A couple of teens look bored and distracted.

*The congregation is orderly until the Sign of Peace. It is a boister-
ous ritual, with most people exchanging hugs, kisses, and enthusiastic greetings. Many greet one another with affection rooted in
years of familiarity and shared experience. After a few minutes,
the musicians intone the Lamb of God to gather people back
to the altar. The Eucharistic bread is broken, cups of wine are
poured, and communion is distributed.*

*Announcements after communion are an informal affair. Ken
Burton, Kate's husband, reads a few brief items, and others in
the congregation add a couple more. Ken then asks if anyone
is here for the first time. The congregants with whom they have
come introduce each of the new worshippers in turn, and each is
greeted with a round of applause.*

*The presider leads the closing rite, and the music group leads the
congregation in song to close. When the song is over, the congregation applauds. The chairs and bleachers are gathered up, and
the gym is transformed from prayer to social space. Coffee and
juice are poured. Children and teens pull basketballs out of an
equipment closet and start an impromptu game. The congregation begins an ebullient social hour.*

Worship and Congregational Metaphors: Imagining and Practicing Social Relations

As these descriptions illustrate, two distinctly different worship styles are evident
in the Sunday masses celebrated at Assumption and Saint Brigitta.[8] Their contrasting styles are significant not only because they reflect the different aesthetic
sensibilities present in these two parishes but also, more important, because these
two ways of worshipping enact different central metaphors for the church that
express and support each parish's social life. In this chapter, I show that these central metaphors—of the church as a family at Our Lady of the Assumption and the
church as a community at Saint Brigitta—express and support different normative
patterns of social relations. In so doing, they present models for social relations
that have affinities with, and are transposable to, other life arenas having consequences for families. Because these metaphors entail particular understandings
of how church and family should be organized, they support polarizing tendencies
among Catholics surrounding family-related issues.

   This chapter therefore explores the two distinct and diverging ecclesial milieus
at Assumption and Saint Brigitta through a close analysis of these worship styles.
The worship style at Our Lady of the Assumption draws heavily on the practices
of mid-twentieth-century devotional Catholicism, which are woven into the New

Order of the Mass instituted by the Second Vatican Council. The aesthetics, discourses, and practices of worship and devotions at Assumption help to constitute the central image of the church as a sacred family, one that is closely linked to the hierarchical Catholic Church. Their aesthetic and ritual practices evoke the transcendent holy, thereby providing a familiar setting in which parishioners cultivate dispositions of humility and reverence and affirm retraditionalized relations of authority. By contrast, the style of Sunday worship and faith-sharing practices at Saint Brigitta embraces and extends the spirit of church reform practiced with particular intensity in the two decades following Vatican II. The gym mass embodies this spirit by emphasizing lay participation, expressive worship, welcoming and casual dispositions, and a sense of the sacred perceived first and foremost in the ordinary experiences and objects of everyday life. Worshippers in the gym consider themselves a community. The image of the church as a community of unique but equal members, whose authority relations involve significant autonomy, pervades the sensibility of parish worship and social interaction.

The contrast of these central metaphors emerges with particular clarity through the following analysis of each parish's worship practices, which both reflect and help to structure the distinctive aspects of their social relations and the behaviors they consider to be normative. In fact, because of the centrality of the sacraments for Catholics and their highly embodied rituals, worship has the capacity to express core religious metaphors and dispositions of sacredness richly: not only through singing and speech but also through gesture, touch, sight, and the emotions produced in believers through embodied ritual prayer.[9] I maintain that, in the expression of these ecclesial metaphors, Catholic worship has the capacity to reveal how post–Vatican II divisions in the Catholic Church are rooted in different understandings of the ways in which church and family are to be organized, which form a basis for moral polarization surrounding family life. Before moving on to demonstrate this claim, I first explain how social processes involving the extension of these metaphors into the arenas of everyday life have the capacity to constitute family life, as well as families' perceptions of the cultural conflicts about the family which concern them.

Imagining the Church and Central Metaphors of the Social

Closely examining the central church metaphors enacted in worship at Our Lady of the Assumption and Saint Brigitta will allow us to understand how and why the expression of these metaphors in church life have affinities with the organization of family life in each congregation. To explain why this is so, I draw on a set of theoretical ideas about how symbols and cultural patterns can both reflect and shape social relations and social action.

Scholars from diverse traditions, including anthropologist Clifford Geertz and social historian William Sewell Jr., have employed Durkheimian ideas to show how metaphors, symbols, models, or other cultural patterns—which Sewell terms *cultural schemata*—can summarize the central aspects of a group's beliefs, social relations, structures, norms, and other aspects of social life.[10] For example, in his well-known essay on the Balinese cockfight, Geertz shows how the ritual of the cockfight reveals the social relations and beliefs of the Balinese.[11] Similarly, in "Religion as a Cultural System," he theorizes that religion is both a "model of and model for reality."[12] This theoretical perspective has been employed by others to show how religious images have the capacity both to synthesize perceptions of the world and to suggest responses to that world. For instance, Karen McCarthy Brown shows how the possession performances of *vodou* spirits provide both models of the capriciousness of Haitians' lives and models for surmounting difficulties in the various arenas of life with which these spirits are associated.[13] Working out of different traditions of scholarship but similarly theorizing a connection between congregational or church models and social life, sociologist Penny Edgell Becker and theologian Avery Dulles each discuss the social effectiveness of church models in how they reflect and shape social relations and normative behaviors in the churches that claim them.[14] For example, Dulles speaks of Catholic Church models present in Vatican II documents—including the church as institution, communion, sacrament, herald, and servant—as suggesting "attitudes and courses of action; they intensify confidence and devotion. To some extent they are self-fulfilling: they make the Church become what they suggest the Church is."[15] At the same time, he acknowledges: "To be fully effective, images must be deeply rooted in the corporate experience of the faithful."[16]

Similarly, Sewell explores the relation between cultural patterns, individual agency, and social life in the wider world but extends his theory even more broadly.[17] In so doing, he explicitly explores how particular cultural schemes—metaphors, routines, and assumptions that comprise the rules of social life—come to be reproduced or transposed in arenas of social life beyond the ones in which they originated. Sewell thinks of these cultural schemes, together with resources, as comprising social structures. In ways similar to religious images that are "models of and models for reality," Sewell understands cultural schemes as one kind of "dual" social pattern, in that cultural images both influence people's choices and are sustained by their actions; that is, "Structures shape people's practices, but it is also people's practices that constitute (and reproduce) structures."[18] By contrast with Geertz, Sewell's primary emphasis is not on the beliefs that underlie these schemes, but on their practice. Most important, he observes that these schemes are transposable and "can be applied across a wide range of circumstances," including contexts outside those where they were first learned.[19] In a similar way, Pierre Bourdieu observes that people's ability to transfer cultural patterns or schemes from one setting to another through analogy "makes possible the achievement of infinitely diversified tasks ... permitting the solution of similarly shaped problems."[20]

In explaining the affinities between the central ecclesial metaphors at Assumption and Saint Brigitta and families' marriage, parenting, and work-family balance routines throughout the chapters of this book, I claim that the enactments of these metaphors help to produce, support, and reproduce particular sets of group relationships, dispositions of the self, and ultimately, different ways of engaging the wider world. In the analysis that follows, I demonstrate how the conduct of worship enacts particular authority relations. Congregants draw on these relations as they speak about and engage in devotional practices, in which their religious practices intersect with the concerns of everyday life. I also show how the dispositions of worship are not just normative enactments, but can be practiced with the aim of cultivating attitudes and behaviors desired by congregants (a point I explain at more length in the next section).

These metaphors are recognizable in both in church practices and social organization and in the beliefs people hold about what church means; therefore, both religious authority and morality are interwoven in them. These models are local, but they also imply particular patterns of relationship with the larger church and the wider world. Their connections between religion and family are sometimes explicitly articulated, and at other times are a part of the common sense of these congregations. However, it is important to note that whether particular religious schemes or models are transposed onto the family, or vice versa, is an empirical question. Throughout part 2 of the book, I demonstrate not only how these religious metaphors have affinities with family life but also how their characteristics are useful for congregants, as I show when and how these schemas are transposed.

Sacredness, Shaping Selves, and Social Relations

The analyses of this chapter show not only how these images are present and enacted at Sunday masses and in group spiritual practices but also how they are intertwined with particular religious dispositions and with the expressions of the bonds of authority, solidarity, and caring they cultivate. As the worshipping congregations at Assumption and Saint Brigitta express dominant models of the church through worship, they are also producing, expressing, and presenting particular senses of sacredness. These congregations' different perceptions of the sacred in turn support the particular forms of social relations enacted in their central metaphors—especially congregational authority relations, which involve the practice of morally significant dispositions. In other words, as Geertz observes, religion is not only effective in its presentation of models of and for reality but also evokes "moods and motivations" in practitioners.[21] In Geertz's view, these sentiments' primary role is in producing the plausibility of belief. However, in my view, they also comprise dispositions having profoundly moral and relational dimensions.

As we see in the descriptions at the beginning of this chapter, Sunday worship at Assumption strongly evokes the sacred as transcendent, especially through its setting, music, and the formal manner in which the mass is celebrated. By contrast, the congregation worshipping in the Saint Brigitta gym creates an immanent sense of sacredness in the ordinary through its mundane setting, the ritual objects used, the informality of its worship, and its emphasis on making congregants' life events explicit in public prayer. As they practice these different senses of the sacred, congregants also cultivate dispositions and habits they deem useful for moral living, both actively and passively. In fact, many at Assumption and Saint Brigitta engage in worship and religious devotions not just out of obligation or to express or build social solidarity, but to cultivate strengths and habituate themselves to respond to life situations in ways they consider virtuous or moral. In Aristotelian and Thomistic thought, the result is the formation of a *habitus*, that is, an inner ethical character that shapes one's moral actions.[22]

In understanding how this takes place, I draw on the work of Saba Mahmood,[23] who has reclaimed these ancient and medieval philosophical meanings of *habitus* to explain how individuals intentionally cultivate particular dispositions through religious practice.[24] The Aristotelian and Thomistic understandings of *habitus* she employs causally relate bodily and mental practice to the development of virtue.

Mahmood argues that the different ways in which groups perceive the self and construct social ties—especially authority relations—lead to different interrelationships among ritual, emotions, and practical activity, depending on the context. In other words, ritual doesn't just constrain people through imposing a worldview, but rather, people can creatively use ritual for their own ends. They can assert themselves with a relative amount of freedom (that is, agency) within the constraints of the ritual. Mahmood argues that ritual allows such agency because, although ritual has often been conceived by scholars as socially prescribed, conventional, and fundamentally different from the informal pragmatic actions that orient daily living, religion as it is actually lived does not strictly separate its rituals from everyday life.[25] Thus the images created in worship, the sentiments evoked, and the habits cultivated have implications for people's everyday lives. Even in contexts that involve significant constraints, individuals can and do exercise agency by creatively making use of religious practices and authority relations as they attempt to shape their internal dispositions and reactions to the life situations they come upon.[26]

These observations have important implications for how we understand the practice of worship at Assumption and Saint Brigitta. In looking at the dispositions people cultivate and the authority relations expressed at Sunday worship, together with ways in which congregants use these relations and perform these dispositions in living everyday life, we can observe how perceptions of moral living are enacted in practice, as well as how worship and religious authority concretely become resources for perceiving and acting in the world outside the church. The social processes involved in the production of churches' central ecclesial metaphors, together with the cultivation of their attendant dispositions, are a first step in understanding how and why parish religious practice contributes to supporting and shaping particular perceptions of and solutions to the problems of families, as well as the family-related issues that have the capacity to symbolize them.

Our Lady of the Assumption: the Church as a Holy Family

At Our Lady of the Assumption, the central metaphor for the church enacted during worship is that of a family striving for holiness, one that is closely linked with the institutional and hierarchical traditions of the Catholic Church. This metaphor is especially evident in preaching and other public discourse at Assumption and is intensified in its analogical relationship with the many families in the pews who portray the domestic church. At the same time, the aesthetics of the setting, the conduct of ritual practices, and talk of the holy together evoke the *mysterium tremendum et fascinans*,[27] providing a familiar setting for the cultivation of humble and reverent dispositions and retraditionalized relations of church authority that are implicated in the sacred family.

The Church as a Family Striving for Holiness

Amid the sense of the transcendent sacred evoked in Sunday celebrations of the mass and the multiple images of the church communicated through word and sacrament, the congregation comes to know and express itself fundamentally as a faithful religious family, one whose members strive to become holy. Although concern for families is ubiquitous in churches more generally,[28] at Assumption the family is a particularly central religious image whose contours are supplied by the religious symbols, devotions, and moral teachings of the Catholic tradition and further supported by the presence of and ministry to its participating families. During Sunday mass and in other parish rituals and settings, this image imbues both familial and congregational roles and relationships with expectations of nurture, protection, and trustworthiness.

The analogical relationship between church and family

At Assumption, the relationship between the church as a family and individual families, especially nuclear families and traditional roles, is interdependent and analogical. In other words, in imagining the church as a family, the congregation and its leaders—especially the priests of the parish—draw on people's experiences of family to draw out the ways in which the church is a family. This image of the sacred family is constructed discursively through the interplay of perceptions of family drawn both from stories and writings about sacred figures in Catholicism and from everyday family experiences. The focus on ministry to families at Assumption further emphasizes and brings the image of the church as family into relief. This image of the church as a family, then, also affirms and teaches parishioners about the constitution and moral conduct of the "good family."

Assumption's pastoral family focus is well-known among involved Catholics throughout the diocese. Father Aidan strives to make families feel at home by introducing parents to each other so that they will have a network of friends at the parish. Once married couples are established at Assumption, worship provides both a sense of belonging and a strong affirmation of a particular religiously centered style of family life for nuclear families. For June Schweickert, 35, a mother of an infant, a toddler, and three school-aged children, Assumption is a good fit because "You feel comfortable bringing your whole family. You can go to the back [of the church] with your crying baby and there are other crying babies." Many large nuclear families attend Sunday mass all together, and the children of these families are enfolded patiently into the congregation and encouraged to participate quietly and let themselves be drawn into the ritual by its power and their parents' catechesis. If they become noisy or distracting, parents take them to the back of the church, where they will be less disruptive until they are quieted. When mass is over, parents take their children from statue to icon to mural, telling the stories they depict. And at times when the church is nearly empty, one occasionally sees a mother seated in a pew nursing her infant. These nurturing practices help to construct the church itself, even amid its artistic grandeur, as a setting for the domestic practices of families who belong to the family of the church.

The images of saintly figures that adorn the church's walls, shrines, and alcoves also often represent images of family, presenting visual expressions, stories, and traditions that contribute to the construction of the image of the church as a family. Older worshippers will especially recognize the extended family of the communion of saints in the statues and murals throughout the church, but even younger Catholics less schooled in the church's history and traditions recognize the significance of the Holy Family—the nuclear family of the historical Jesus, his mother Mary, and his earthly father Joseph. Mary, the church's patroness, is represented visually in several places in the church and prominently depicted alongside Joseph in the baldacchinos flanking either side of the sanctuary. The baldacchino to the left surrounds a statue of Joseph holding the child Jesus, and the one to the right surrounds a statue of Mary cradling the infant Jesus, with the image's title, "Mother of the Fairest Love," inscribed on the statue's base. In this setting, the congregation often hears family stories of saints during Sunday homilies. These stories reinforce the image of the modern nuclear family and the very particular roles of the mothers, fathers, and children who inhabit this family structure.[29]

During Sunday homilies, the most frequently discussed family relationships drawn from the Catholic tradition are those of the Holy Family and those of God the Father, Jesus the Son of God, Mary the Blessed Mother—and the church and its members. The Holy Family is often talked about by drawing comparisons with parishioners' own experiences of family, constructing an analogical relationship between the Holy Family of scripture and tradition and the nuclear families in the congregation. Although Assumption's members' family patterns are pluralistic— the parish has single parents and blended families as well as nuclear families— the nuclear family is well represented at Assumption, and its form is a privileged ideal mirrored and sacralized in the Holy Family. Priests emphasize Mary as the mother who bears children and cares for and nurtures her family. Joseph, her husband, is presented as the father who protects the family and teaches their children. In this context, Jesus is often spoken of as the loving, wise, and faithful child. Priests encourage parishioners to reflect on the Holy Family in shaping their family routines, and at the same time, experiences of ordinary families are resources that priests and church leaders employ in imagining the church as a family. For example, Father James explains the devotional practice of saying the rosary in a Sunday bulletin letter by writing:

> I have often compared the rosary to a "family album." Some of us, when we were small, would look at the photo album that recorded our family history. Then maybe we would climb into our mother's lap and ask her to explain the pictures: Who was the lady in the funny hat that came to your and Dad's wedding? Is this what my big brother looked like when he was a baby?
>
> When we say the rosary, we turn to our Mother, the Blessed Virgin, and try to see, through her eyes, the events through which God's mercy have been manifested in the world.

Father James explains and encourages this devotional prayer by linking it to images of everyday family life. In praying the rosary, practitioners repeatedly pray the Our Father, Hail Mary, and Glory Be while meditating on the rosary's mysteries—which are events from the life of Jesus and the Holy Family as seen through the eyes of the Blessed Mother. Father James's message is that salvation history is understandable through analogy to one's family history, and that the church's history, as seen through the Blessed Mother's eyes, is a family history that is also theirs. In this way, he draws a connection between the family roles people experience in everyday life, the central doctrines of Christianity, and parishioners' belonging to the family of the church.

Similarly, other kinds of formal and personal prayer at Assumption cement the analogical relationship between ordinary families and the family of the church. For example, in a homily one Sunday evening, Father Stephen, a priest in residence at Assumption who frequently says Sunday masses, discussed the practice of prayer concretely for the congregation by saying:

> Meditation is imagining, like we do with the mysteries of the rosary, or just being in the presence of God. And continual prayer is offering everything up to God during the day, and can be punctuated with ejaculations from litanies, such as "Jesus, I love you," or "Mary, Queen of Families, pray for us." One can offer one's work, one's leisure, and even one's sleep.

Father Stephen talks about meditation, and especially about continual prayer, in concrete terms that encourage parishioners to think of how they can make prayer a part of daily life. He embeds this discussion in the ordinary rhythms of the day, offering short examples of simple prayers that would be appropriate for his audience. With the particular example of "Mary, Queen of Families," Fr. Stephen both connects with the parish's many families and reminds them of their common identity in the church as a family.

Motherhood and the Blessed Virgin Mary

These examples not only show the contours of the analogical relationship between family life and the church as a family at Assumption but also reveal the prominence of the Blessed Mother in the devotional life of the parish. In fact, Mary is a particularly central and enduring presence in worship and devotions at Assumption. Historically and in the present, Mary is an important figure among Catholics, even though Marian devotions such as novenas and public recitation of the rosary fell out of public practice in many U.S. parishes after Vatican II.[30] By contrast with many of the parishes in the diocese in which it is situated, Mary remains a presence in the traditional devotions practiced there. Mary is preached about, invoked in litanies, and remembered privately and publicly as congregants finger their rosaries. She is prayed to at the 10 A.M. mass each Sunday after communion when the congregation pauses to recite the Angelus.[31] During Evenings of Reflection, when speakers lead women in reflections upon God, their everyday work, and their household and family duties, they do so also with prayer—for instance, leading retreatants in the Hail Mary along with their lessons, thereby reminding them of the Blessed Mother's modeling and patronage of motherhood. Mary is especially present during Marian feasts, in her months of May and October, and in the frequent practice of the congregation's devotional prayer. At Assumption, Mary is not simply the subject of sacred art and statuary, nor is she merely a private devotional figure for a few; rather, she is a constant presence at worship, a central moral figure, and a comforting and guiding presence in many of its members' everyday lives. Mary is addressed by many titles during worship, and several of those titles explicitly concern her role as mother of the church.

Marian devotion is important at Assumption not only because Mary is a model for mothers but also because Mary is central to both church doctrine and popular piety historically; thus, the practice of Marian traditions at Assumption facilitates practitioners' connection to the institutional church. We can see this in a December event during my field research, when the parish celebrated the Novena to the Immaculate Conception. During the ten days of the novena, a tall statue of Mary remained in front of the altar of the church, with several dozen red roses blooming in brass vases on her left and her right. Each evening, about 300 people—most of them young mothers, many with babies and toddlers accompanying them—gathered in the church to honor and petition her.

During one of these evenings, the novena was led by a priest wearing a black cassock and white surplice and a young man dressed a navy blue suit and tie. With the young man kneeling on the sanctuary steps in front of the statue of Mary and the priest standing at the lectern nearby, they led the joyful mysteries of the rosary. Together with the congregation, they continued the prayer until it was finished, ending with the short traditional prayer, Hail Holy Queen, which the congregation recited from memory.

The mass followed. During the homily, Father Aidan spoke of Mary, saying,

> Christ is the founder of the church, and Mary is his mother. For this reason, Mary is the Mother of the Church. Mary is concerned for the church; in good times and in bad times, she is always concerned.
>
> One of the Church Fathers compares the church to a boat—like the boats Jesus traveled on in the gospels, which would sometimes be tossed around and take on water, but never sank. And the wind and the sea obey, they obey Jesus.
>
> The church is like this. There are some storms in the church. After many years, hopefully we are coming out of a storm now. But Mary is always concerned for the church, and wants us to be concerned for the church. Let us pray to Mary, and bring our concerns to Mary, Mother of the Church.

In his homily, Fr. Aidan emphasizes that Mary is not only the mother of Jesus or "our mother" in some general sense but also, in a central way, the mother of the church. This is a long-standing Catholic teaching, of course, but what is important here is that Father Aidan underscores this role for the congregation, evoking the image of the church as family through his discussion of Mary's motherhood of the church. He thereby ties Assumption to the larger church and underscores Mary's concern for the Assumption family gathered in prayer and for the church as a whole.

The perceptions of the church that underlie Father Aidan's words reflect a particular model of congregational social relations vis-à-vis the broader church. When he talks about Mary as mother of a church that is "coming out of a storm," he is speaking from the common perception at Assumption that, since Vatican II, the church has been weathering a period of confusion and conflict over doctrine, morality, and authentic church practice. Father Aidan's homily affirms the church's enduring hierarchical authority and enunciates a fervent statement of hope for the future of a newly traditional church—one that is both reformed and grounded in church traditions perceived by parishioners to be authentic. When I spoke with him briefly after the novena that evening and mentioned that it had been years since I had attended one, he said, "Yes, I think they're coming back, thank God." In our conversation, he expressed the hope that the future of the church will be sustained by the renewal and recovery of traditions of prayer like the novena. Such practices have an appeal in Assumption's milieu, both because they represent tradition and because they are experienced and interpreted in ways that affirm the nuclear family ideal in a societal context of plural family forms, where that ideal is perceived to be threatened.

At the same time, the presence of so many women with small children at the novena demonstrates the contemporary salience of Mary as a devotional figure for mothers at Assumption. Mary's presence at Assumption, especially her exemplary caring, nurturing, and modeling of women's experience, is so much a part of the taken-for-granted common sensibility of the parish that the symbolic dimensions of her presence at prayer are expressed primarily in subtle ways. Some women spoke explicitly of their connections to Mary in their everyday lives, and others represented their devotion in simple displays of Marian images, such as Lladró statuettes or *l'art Saint-Sulpice* prints of Mary, in their homes.[32] In this retraditionalized style of Catholicism, Mary's maternal roles are intensified since, for Catholics at Assumption, Mary's maternity and nurturance are central virtues that speak to routine practices and everyday lives, especially the lives of the parish's women, in ways that are both distinct from and dependent upon tradition.

Fatherhood and paternal images

Although the Blessed Mother is an extremely important figure at Assumption, family imagery is not concentrated only in Mary; paternal images also enter into the metaphor of the church as a family. As in most Christian churches, God is routinely spoken of as a father, and this no doubt strengthens the corporate identity of the church as a family. But the attention given to Saint Joseph, and the ways in which priests are fathers to their congregation, are particularly illustrative of how Assumption's central ecclesial metaphor incorporates, symbolizes, and sacralizes the roles and social relations of fatherhood. For example, in another of his bulletin letters, one on the Sunday anticipating Saint Joseph's feast day, Father James writes:

> March 19, the Solemnity of St. Joseph, is a good opportunity for us to look at the life of this holy Patriarch. He is invoked under many titles: Spouse of Mary, Patron of the Church, Guardian of the Redeemer, patron of a holy death, patron of the interior life (our life of union with God) and patron of workers.
>
> St. Joseph is a great example for us: he was a man who fulfilled God's will, adapting his life to God's plan. That life was not easy: for instance, he had to flee Egypt with Mary and Jesus at a moment's notice; there, he had to start work as a carpenter wherever he could. After a few years, following God's command, he had to go back to Nazareth once more. With his hard work, he provided for Jesus and Mary. Joseph's life teaches us the value of ordinary work, done for the love of God.
>
> St. Joseph is the patron of the spiritual life. After the Blessed Virgin Mary, he is the one who was closest to Jesus.

Here, Father James writes about Joseph's multiple roles, which go beyond his role as a father to his significance as a role model of the spiritual life. But Saint Joseph's other roles are all grounded in his role as a "holy Patriarch." Father James evokes the image of the father as a protector in the flight to Egypt and the father as a breadwinner in his work as a carpenter—even using the common parlance, "provider." In his discussion of the life of Saint Joseph, Father James evokes a contemporary image of a virtuous father at Assumption, even though Joseph's life narrative is one that occurred in a distant past, in circumstances far different than the present.

In the image of the church as a family, priests also play a paternal role; parishioners at Assumption have an everyday experience of their priests relating to them as spiritual fathers. The analogy of priesthood and spiritual fatherhood occurs often in discourse; one good example is a Sunday homily that Father Anthony, a visiting priest, gave about encouraging vocations to the priesthood and religious life. He compared the church to the "good Catholic family," saying,

> Priests learn to be good priests through the example of their own fathers. For just as a father cares for and directs his family—his wife and children— so, in a similar way, the Magisterium "fathers" Catholics in its teachings,

and priests are spiritual fathers for their parish family—and God is the father of all his people.

Just as fathers protect their families and teach their children about how to be good people, so priests do the same for their parishioners. Therefore, from the time they are children, fathers show their boys, through example, how to be good fathers themselves—and for some of them, this is how they will first learn to be good priests.

Sentimental discourses like this one both sacralize roles within individual families and express congregational social relations as familial. Father Anthony's words identify the paternal leadership of fathers with the religious leadership of priests, revealing how the roles and relationships in the nuclear family are experiences that can be used to understand the Holy Family and also can be transferred into images reflecting congregational social relations and the wider church. Priests are to care for their people spiritually as ordinary fathers care for their families—with spiritual wisdom, leadership, and a spirit of protection. And Father Anthony extends this familial imagery by speaking of how they are also married to the church, saying,

Further, priests are the fathers for their people, and spouses of the church—that is, the church is their bride. It is their bride that tells them how to be priests....At the same time, he learns from his people that life begins at conception, and that homosexuality is wrong.

Here, Father Anthony plumbs the connection between spiritual and physical fatherhood in ways that allow him to speak from "experience" about sexual morality, learned from his parishioners who are biological fathers. For Father Anthony, the parish's nuclear families and their ways of life produce important experiential knowledge that confirms the church's teachings on human sexuality. This is something that he cannot do on his own, but must learn from those he fathers, since he lives a life of celibate chastity. Significantly, he explicitly mentions church teachings about the immorality of abortion and homosexual sex—fault lines in public debates over the family—asserting that he learns of their moral status from the families in the pews as they live out their sexuality according to church norms. But more than this, he symbolically ties the church's stands on abortion and homosexual sex to families and to the church as a family—showing the authoritative connection in this milieu between a particular familial social organization and moral conduct. In this brief mention, then, Father Anthony reinforces the link between families' everyday lives, a particular familial and church social organization, and public cultural conflicts about the family.

The fatherly image of the priest that Father Anthony articulates in this homily, then, is a retraditionalized one, anchored in particular practices that evoke older Catholic images of priests as spiritual fathers and express a sense of authority that goes beyond mere metaphorical fatherhood. Like Father Aidan's homily about Mary as the mother of the church, Father Anthony evokes an image of fatherhood directly tied to the church's hierarchically organized authority to teach and govern. Significantly, what Father Anthony says about learning sexual morality from his people provides experiential authority for his own and, ultimately, the church's authority and its paternally oriented structure.

In fact, parishioners at Assumption routinely call priests "Father" not merely as a convention, but because the paternal dimension of priests' relationships with their parishioners is integral to their role. As in Catholic parishes generally, priests meet the spiritual needs of their congregants in multiple ways: this takes place not only through the sacraments, through blessing objects and people, in praying for those who ask, and in comforting the distressed but also and especially in providing moral guidance and admonishment to congregants. At Assumption, this relationship takes the form of a paternal authority dependent upon images of traditional and personal social relations—but at the same time, ones that are imbued with authority because of priests' acknowledgment of their parishioners' vocations, their active demonstration of care for their people, and the holiness parishioners perceive in them.

Disposing Oneself in Response to the Mysterium Tremendum: *Strength in Humility*

Dispositions of the worshipping body are produced through the same ritual by which the church is imagined as a family, created especially in the sights and sounds of its aesthetic environment, congregational participation in gesture and song, the routines of vocal and silent prayer and devotional practice, and public preaching. While not everyone participates or responds in the same way, these practices embody particular dispositions that constitute elements of the *habitus* of worshippers—especially humility and reverence—in tandem with a numinous sense of the sacred.

Sacredness and virtuous dispositions

Humility and reverence are perceived and experienced as appropriate responses to the transcendent sacred experienced in worship, ones that direct the congregation's attention to God and de-emphasize the actions of individuals during worship. This de-emphasis of the self goes along with other congregational dispositions valued here: prayerfulness, respect and awe of the transcendent, and charity. These dispositions are understood as virtues for moral living generally and are perceived as comprising the strength of character desired by those who practice this style of Catholicism. These occur within a set of social relations that affirm the authority of those who practice these virtues, especially those who lead the congregation.

The numinous style of the sacred encountered at Assumption begins with the church building itself; the aesthetic and appointments of the Roman Renaissance-style church create a fitting setting for the evocation of a transcendent God. The material culture in Assumption's church is aesthetically rich, especially in artistic objects in the realistic style of *l'art Saint-Sulpice*. These objects, together with Assumption's architecture, ritual objects, and practices, represent a strong theology of transcendence and the reinvigoration of a Catholic traditionalism often identified with the church before Vatican II. The normative response of worshippers to the environment and the ritual is one of reverent humility.

Humility is expressed in the dispositions of those who perform focal roles or ministries during the mass. For example, the choir, accompanied by an organist, performs from the loft that runs along the back of the church's nave. Therefore, their performance is virtually unseen and blends into the mass, rather than being a focal point of worship. And although choir members demand of themselves a professional musical quality, they resist common secular idioms of performance and instead de-emphasize themselves as individuals and as a group. Other ritual actors display similar dispositions. While lay readers, altar servers, singers, and priests appear to take pride in doing their jobs well, they practice their roles without drawing attention to themselves or the creativity of an individual performance.

The importance of humility in Assumption's religious style becomes obvious when this norm is breached. Unintentionally, I breached this norm one Sunday when I met Gerry Godfrey while browsing in the parish bookstore. Gerry is a tall, lumbering man of indeterminate middle age, with dark curled hair cut close to his long face, dark horn-rimmed glasses, and a cheerful demeanor. He is an involved and trusted lay leader in the parish and had been the lay lector that morning, reading the Old and New Testament readings for that day prior to the Gospel. Exchanging pleasantries with him, I said, "I really appreciated the way you read the scriptures today. You read so clearly and so prayerfully." Gerry looked startled and embarrassed. He blushed. Then he smiled warmly, gathered his composure, and said, "Well, that will just motivate me to do even better, then!" with a bit of a nervous laugh. Gerry appeared pleased but baffled. He changed the subject.

Gerry was startled because, by emphasizing his individual contribution at worship, I had inadvertently breached the congregational norm that links the cultivation of humility with the de-emphasis of the self. It is unusual for people to comment on the ritual performances of laity at Assumption; except for an occasional comment about the quality of the music, I never heard anyone compliment, criticize, or otherwise talk about how laity exercised their worship roles.

This contrasts with the practice at other Catholic churches, including Saint Brigitta, where lay leadership in worship often entails just these sorts of evaluations and emphasizes parishioners' individual contributions to the parish. Karen Keeley, who attended Assumption throughout her twenties, drew attention to these different sensibilities when discussing Assumption's attraction for her young adult friends. Picking up a diocesan Young Adult Ministry brochure, she read the titles of a few educational offerings that, she observed, presented Catholicism as a vehicle for individual self-affirmation and meeting one's social needs. Young adults at Assumption don't think about their Catholic faith this way at all, she explained, saying emphatically, "They know that it's not about *them*." Karen's comment reveals that the humility practiced at Assumption's worship is not only a response to a transcendent sense of the sacred but also a valued moral attitude to be practiced in everyday life.

Like humility, reverence is a response to the transcendent sacred, a virtue cultivated at worship, and one to be practiced in daily life. This disposition is reflected and cultivated in the actions of priests and congregants. In priests' words and actions—genuflection, bowed heads, and arms precisely extended to the shoulders in a traditional gesture for Christian prayer—they express reverence for God and emphasize that the church is a holy place. Father Aidan always reads the Gospel with his hands pressed together against his breast, fingers extended up to his chin, expressing prayerful supplication. This ritual disposition also serves as a signal through which parishioners draw boundaries with other Catholics; some parishioners criticized priests at other parishes who do not enact reverence in this fashion but, as worshipper Philip Fitch explained, celebrate the mass like "cape twirlers" who draw attention to themselves.

As with humility, reverence is a normative disposition at Assumption—and the importance of reverence also becomes evident when this norm is breached. This happened after mass one Sunday. While I was talking with the Williamses at the entrance to the nave of the church, Pam Williams saw the McMichaels, another parish family, and urged us to hurry up the main aisle to speak with them. The families greeted one another warmly at the front of the church, but in the midst of these greetings, Father Stephen emerged from a nearby confessional and frowned, scolding us for talking in the church. "I'm hearing confessions here, and I can hear you quite clearly! You shouldn't be talking in church! If you wish to socialize, please go outside," he said. Chastised and embarrassed, we guiltily left the church and walked out onto the front steps to continue talking, the joyous mood of our socializing temporarily broken. Pam said later that she and her friends know that the priests prefer that they not socialize in church, and they try to be respectful. And the priests generally try to balance the maintenance of a strong sense of the sacred with the recognition that young adults often remain parishioners because of the social networks they establish at church. But when these younger worshippers socialize in the church, they reveal the habits of a generation more familiar with a casual church etiquette than the norm of reverence.

Thus although humility and reverence are important elements of Assumption's religious style, they are not practiced uniformly among all worshippers. Individuals participate in the mass in diverse ways, ranging from those who appear full of attention, to those disposed with a taken-for-granted familiarity, to others who are evidently distracted or bored or somnolent. A good example of this diversity is found in parishioners' reactions after a special Friday evening celebration of the *Novus Ordo* mass in Latin. The bishop presided, a visiting choir performed Latin hymns, there were a large number of celebrants and servers in the procession, and the church was redolent with incense. I sat in a pew filled with young adults beside a young man, about 25 years of age, who sang and responded in perfect Latin. Others in the pew sometimes stumbled over the responses; some stared at their missals in silence as music and vocal prayer resounded. When the mass ended, these young people gathered in an aisle and whispered to one another in animated tones, "That was awesome!" A group of older women passed by, and one stooped with age said to her companion, "I did this half my life, but I'd forgotten it all." Julia Flaherty, who came with her husband and three preschool children, commented, "It was so long!" These responses to the Latin mass show the ways in which dispositions like reverence are more or less constantly being formed at Assumption, even as they are sometimes breached and sometimes accommodated to other parish sensibilities and needs. They also suggest that cohort and generational differences in life situations and memories figure in congregants' response to worship, with Vatican II and older cohorts accustomed to the practice of these dispositions, and those in post–Vatican II generations striving to cultivate them. At the same time, Catholics at Assumption regularly act as to draw attention to the practices of humility and reverence as an expression of boundaries that define this milieu over against others.

Virtue and authority

A brief example of ritual practice outside Sunday mass—the sacramental practice of confession—serves to bring together how this cultivation of dispositions, the church's central metaphor as a family, and relations of authority are intertwined. Whereas most Catholic churches offer confession for an hour or two each Saturday afternoon, Assumption offers 17 hours of confession time weekly. Parishioners appreciate the availability of confession and practice confession frequently. They speak of the priests at Assumption as helpful confessors and of having experienced "beautiful confessions." Parishioners, moreover, do not just confess sin during their practice of the sacrament but also seek counsel from priests. This was illustrated during a picnic conversation I had with a few parish women one afternoon, when one of them, Donna, and I discovered that we had both attended the same communal penance service at a parish in a nearby suburb, and we compared notes.

The communal penance service conducted at Saint John of the Cross church earlier that month had included singing and readings, a brief homily and an examination of conscience, and individual confessions. For confessions, the congregation was instructed to form lines in front of each of the priests, who stood at the head of each of the aisles near the church's sanctuary, and to mention to the priest just one or two faults each considered most urgent. Each penitent took just a minute to speak to the priest, who then laid hands on the penitent's head, performed the sign of the cross, and gave him or her absolution. Donna evaluated the service by saying,

> I suppose it is a good thing for Catholics who wouldn't go [to confession] otherwise, but it's awkward not to be able to have your confession in the privacy of the confessional. The next person in line was standing only ten feet away! If you really had something important to discuss, you couldn't do it. And I had the feeling that the priest wasn't really listening to me when I was making my confession.

For Donna, the importance of confession is not only as a place to seek God's sacramental forgiveness for their faults but also as a place where one can discuss things important to her daily life. It is an interaction that is somehow intimate, a relationship of connection where the priest is expected to listen. The priest's listening, his responses, and his advice matter. Confession is not only one of several sites where the priest's sacramental role is exercised; it is also a setting where the priest acts as a paternal guide.

In response to Donna's observations, her friend Andrea, an energetic, red-headed mom, mused, "Why do you think so many Catholics are willing to spend money on therapy, and so few will go to confession? What's up with that? It seems like a big waste of money to me." Andrea's drawing of a connection between confession and psychotherapy further illuminates how this relationship between the priest confessor and the penitent is not merely traditional but has been reshaped to fit contemporary social circumstances. On the one hand, Andrea's comment is a curious one, since members of this milieu often criticize, as Andrea did indirectly, the therapeutic orientation of other mainstream middle-class cultures. But her drawing of a connection between the value of confession and that of therapy also suggests that receiving counsel in confession is an important way in which parishioners can receive moral guidance and insight into behavior in themselves that they perceive to be sinful. Moreover, Andrea's criticism of the service reveals how authority relations between priest and people are interwoven with parishioners' expectations of priests in confession and their critical evaluation of them, as well as with habitual independent examinations of one's own actions and motivations. At Assumption, then, authority relations between priest and people rooted in the church's patriarchally organized priesthood are not unreflective. Instead, they constitutively involve deliberation, agency, and choice within the social and perceptual frameworks of their culture.

We see, then, that the images, ritual actions, discourses, and informal conventions practiced at Sunday mass at Assumption create a particular style of Catholic identity that simultaneously communicates reverence for the sacred and a welcome to families by blurring the boundaries between ritual and everyday concerns. At Assumption, the image of the family striving for holiness provides a model for parish social relations and at the same time affirms the modern nuclear family and its ideal social relations. In stories of the nurturing maternity of Mary and her care for her people; in the paternal relations between priest and people and priests' solicitous teaching, admonition, and compassion; and in the visible presence of mothers, fathers, and children in the religious imagery of the church and in the pews, the central symbol of the church as family is evoked. This sacred image of family draws on the social organization of the modern nuclear family as an ideal, is connected to the Catholic past through retraditionalized symbols and practices, vivifies hierarchical models of church authority, and is imbricated into a numinous sense of the sacred that expresses and cultivates dispositions that resonate with this social organization. This image of the family occupies a central place in imagination and practice at Assumption, constituting and supporting a particular style of Catholic identity in the practice of religious devotions, in parish social relationships, and in moral teachings—including those at one pole in cultural conflicts about the family. In the abundant religious imagery surrounding the family and the multiple meanings its symbols evoke, this particular normative image of the family is sacralized.

Saint Brigitta: The Church as a Community of Equals

At Saint Brigitta, the style of Sunday worship reflects and seeks to extend the church reforms initiated and practiced following the Second Vatican Council. Those who worship in the Saint Brigitta gym each Sunday, including its many families, think of themselves as a part of a community and ritually practice community in warm interactions and self-disclosing public dialogue with one another. The gym mass, which paradigmatically expresses the metaphor of the church as community valued in the parish broadly, enacts the image of community as it emphasizes lay participation and empowerment, expressive elements of worship, a casual style, and an immanent sense of the sacred. This eccesial metaphor constitutes a local culture enacting different dispositions of the *habitus*, different social relations, and supporting a different basis for moral decision making than at Assumption—one that tends to view public cultural conflicts about the family from a second pole.

The Church as a Community of Equal Members

Saint Brigitta parish members understand themselves first and foremost as a participatory community with ideals of human dignity and equality underlying its leadership, decision making, and authority relations. The experience of a felt sense of community is highly valued among parish leadership and involved parishioners, and the church as community is the central metaphor for congregational belonging, a significant aspect of religious identity, and a symbol for moral action. During worship, meetings, and parish events—and in a particularly intense way at the mass in the gym—this image of the church reflects and structures democratically oriented social relations among parish members, reclaims traditions and scriptures that inspire this model, and expresses relations of authority locally and with the larger church.

Community and worship, local and universal

Most regular participants said they attend the gym mass because it is an "intentional community." By this term, they denote an understanding of the church that stands in contrast to institutional and hierarchical models of Catholicism. It is a more locally oriented model than Dulles's model of the church as a mystical communion but mirrors the sociological concepts of *Gemeinshaft* (community) and primary group Dulles uses in describing communion.[33] At Saint Brigitta, local expressions of the unity of community tend to receive the most emphasis, especially those deriving from and practiced in face-to-face interactions with individuals who are mostly known to one another. When people describe the sense of community at the gym mass, they speak of friendship, warmth, welcome, and the practice of a common life of faith at a local level. For many in the gym, this experience of the local church is experientially linked with the larger church, much as in Dulles's model. For example, Rick McNeill describes his experience of the church as community by saying, "I've come to realize the value of community. Not only the community in the local church, but in the worldwide church, has come to have some sort of meaning to me that I lean on." But others emphasize the importance of their local experience of church. Bryan O'Lear expresses this view, saying,

> I experience myself as a marginal Roman Catholic now. I'm a member of this local church community, part of a group of people that I feel very

connected with. But I have serious doubts that I would feel any need to go to mass or participate in the Catholic Church if I wasn't connected to a meaningful local community.

And in fact, many of the regulars at the gym mass are involved in networks of friendship in daily life. Although friendship networks are also present at Assumption, the greater concentration of Sunday worshippers within or near the parish's boundaries facilitates a greater density of these networks at Saint Brigitta. The image of the church as community expresses and supports these networks.

Even though the primary image of the church celebrated in the Saint Brigitta gym is one of community, not family, many families worship there regularly, and being a family member is a part of one's identity in community. In fact, Maggie McNeill characterized her sense of belonging to the gym mass community as in part related to her role as a parent of an infant and toddler son, saying, "I felt a little less connected to the community before we had Robbie and Rachel....I remember when I was pregnant with Robbie, feeling like it was a badge of inclusion into the club." Moreover, among the families with children who frequent the gym mass, parents share and trade child care, arrange play dates for their children, and belong to small faith-sharing groups that pray and dine together in one another's homes. Newer parents rely on those with older children to be mentors and role models. Of course, the dense and long-standing connections that many members of the gym mass have with one another also encompass those who are single or whose children are grown and are not limited to those among families with children. The metaphor of the church as a community at Saint Brigitta is made explicit in worship, with parish leaders fashioning rituals to produce and support a felt sense of community within the worshipping congregation.

How organizers produce the church as a community in the Saint Brigitta gym begins with the very choice of the space in which the Sunday congregation worships; the plainness and mutability of the environment allows parishioners to enact this image of the church in specific ways. This space is diametrically distinct from Assumption's church. It is aesthetically unremarkable, with a gray stone exterior, high ceilings, and a spare and institutional interior space; it was originally designed to accommodate parish assemblies and sporting events. It is an ordinary space that does not easily dampen sound or contain silence. But its very ordinariness makes it an appropriate space for the experience of community because it is versatile, and its acoustics foster a convivial ambiance by magnifying the enthusiastic expression of a communal sensibility that places sociability at the center of its self-expression.

Organizers modify the gym for Sunday mass with the addition of seasonal decorations, ambo (i.e., lectern), altar, musical instruments, and steel folding chairs and bleachers. They recraft the space so that, on Sunday mornings, the altar is more or less at the center of worship, with the altar, ambo, and musicians forming one half of a circle, and the congregation comprising the other half. This seating pattern creates no singular focal point for the mass, thereby drawing attention to the actions of ordinary congregants and the congregation as a whole.

The practice of church as a community begins from the moment one steps into the gym, where one is greeted by parishioners assigned to welcome worshippers, and continues through the congregational welcome given newcomers before the dismissal and into the social hour after mass. Community is practiced in multiple ways, from the distribution of liturgical ministries to as many congregants as possible to the incorporation of the group's youngest members as they play at the margins of the semicircle. Three moments during the gym mass stand out as paradigmatic expressions of Saint Brigitta's self-understanding as community: the dialogue homily, the Sign of Peace, and the social hour at the end of mass. The single most important and illustrative of these is the dialogue homily.

Joe Moran's preaching and the dialogue that followed, chronicled at the beginning of this chapter, is a good example of how the dialogue homily proceeds. After the Gospel has been proclaimed, the preacher speaks for five to seven minutes. Preachers close their homilies by asking a question that is meant to elicit the congregation's response in the dialogue portion of the homily. The homilist directs the dialogue, calling on people one after another, and closing it when comments have gone on for about ten minutes. During the dialogue, people stand in turn and speak from their places in the congregation. Speakers generally try to model their comments on the homilist's style, relating a problem or situation or telling a story and then evaluating the narrative they present with their interpretation of a Christian or moral response.

Although the dialogue is conventional, it is unscripted, and therefore it sometimes produces difficult moments when speakers breach its norms. Sometimes people hold the floor and speak for longer than is customary, and preachers then often try to interrupt them or use subtler bodily cues to encourage them to end their comments. At other times, especially around issues of public politics, disagreement bubbles beneath the surface of parishioners' comments and threatens to erupt into open conflict. Conflict is usually diffused before it becomes overt, but occasionally conflict emerges before it can be contained. This happened at one Sunday gym mass in the previous year, when a group of parishioners gave a presentation about a protest trip they had made to the School of the Americas during the homily time.[34] Congregational dialogue responses following the presentation evolved into a debate of conflicting political views, and parishioner accounts of the debate suggest that it was heated and uncomfortable. It was an important enough event at Saint Brigitta that several people spoke of it unprompted a year later; even some of those who affirmed the politics of the protest did not think the presentation to be appropriate during the dialogue homily. In discussing this event, Louis Beltrami, the pastoral associate, explained that political debate and conflict during the dialogue defeats its purpose, since the dialogue is meant to be a free airing of worshippers' sentiments and spiritual insights. In other words, the dialogue homily is imagined as an opportunity for self-expression, enrichment, and group sharing and not a forum for critique and intellectual or political interchange. But this can be a delicate line to walk in a community setting where a significant number of regular members perceive action on behalf of issues of social and political justice to be foundational to religious faith.

The dialogue homily ritualizes and helps to makes normative Saint Brigitta's self-understanding of the church as a community grounded in the importance of individual contribution, sociability, welcome for newcomers, tolerance and respect, and lay leadership. Underlying all these characteristics is the assumption of a fundamental equality among all who participate in worship and in the life of the church.

Community and equality, autonomy and authority

Discourse about community at Saint Brigitta reflects the fundamental importance of the value of equality and sometimes serves to further emphasize and flatten relations involving church authority in ways that reflect the valuing of human equality among members prior to any distinctions between them. This value is considered to be a moral imperative. Involved parishioners actively work to create this sensibility in their local setting, but many, and especially those who attend the gym mass, believe that the larger Catholic Church should better and more fundamentally embody this model of church as community and privilege it over more hierarchical models of the church.

This sensibility is illustrated not only at the gym mass but also in the practices of the parish's many faith-sharing groups. These groups, consciously modeled upon *communidades de bases*,[35] are at once a form of lay mobilization and a vehicle for participants to shape themselves through spiritual exercises and group conventions. Like Sunday worship, faith-sharing groups combine sociability with serious discussion; they provide a setting for reflection on experience and a method in which participants work out and articulate the relation between religious practice and the problems, choices, and experiences of daily living. They are an important context for comprehending the self-understanding of church as community at Saint Brigitta because they are understood within the parish as a primary tool for building and sustaining it.[36]

During the period of my field research, 17 permanent faith-sharing groups met regularly, some even weekly, throughout the year. Members of these groups develop close relationships that foster not only the prayer and discussion for which the groups are formed but also friendship, the sharing of meals, social time, and even child care. About 20 additional groups were organized during the Lenten season when I regularly attended Saint Brigitta.

Faith-sharing groups consist ideally of about ten people, and they generally meet in homes or in parish meeting rooms. Lenten faith-sharing groups met weekly, preparing for their meetings by reading the Sunday scriptures and chapters from a book of theological reflections written for laity. Groups convened for an hour every week at a prearranged time; my group of seven women and two men met on a weekday morning. The group was diverse in generation and lifestyle and included a young mother in her mid-30s, a couple of fathers of a similar age with small children, a couple of grandmothers in their 60s, and some never-married women who were middle-aged and older.

Each week, our group leader began the faith sharing by having us read the assigned book chapter aloud, with each person in the group taking a paragraph in turn until we had finished. Participants took some quiet time to think about what had been read, and the leader then encouraged discussion by probing the questions at the end of the chapter. One after another, group members took turns talking about their personal experiences of religious faith, telling of insights they had into their faith experiences, expressing confusion, or asking further questions. When each of the questions had been explored and the discussion wound down, the leader called the group to prayer, lit a candle, invited spontaneous petitions, and then led the recitation of the Our Father. Members would chat informally when the session ended, with a few in the group sometimes going out for coffee afterward.

Through this process, faith-sharing groups at Saint Brigitta provide a structure that habituates participants to particular practices of religious reflection. During faith sharing, group members relate their beliefs to life experiences, a skill also practiced during the dialogue homily. In participants' sharing of unique faith journeys bound by common beliefs and traditions, faith-sharing groups express the church as community. By their conventions, they cultivate listening, informal, and spontaneous dispositions in their members.

During my group's Lenten faith-sharing sessions, conversation often centered on participants' images of God and Jesus. One participant, Maria Callahan, was particularly articulate about how she thought about God and reflected opinions and sentiments common at Saint Brigitta. A tall, thin woman with an angular but pretty face framed with thick and wavy graying brown hair, Maria had not gone to church for a long time during her young adult years and had been drawn back to church through Saint Brigitta. Maria spoke during one meeting about having to "get over her religious education, get over her early childhood training of thinking and imagining God," a Catholic training that had often portrayed God in terms of judgment. Eventually, she said, she arrived at an image of a more loving and accepting God.

In speaking about the Gospel story of the Samaritan woman at the well[37] at another meeting, Maria explored the contrast between images of God as just and merciful, saying, "Jesus just accepted the woman at the well. That is such a profound thing, and an effective one, too. More effective, I think, than John the Baptist. I think of John as passionate, but he's unforgiving." When she said this, others in the group affirmed her view; one participant remarked that she had never seen much good or much to look forward to in John's message, that it was "all hellfire and brimstone and pretty bleak." Maria continued,

> I grew up in a loving family. My parents didn't yell at me to try to make me change when they thought I was moving in the wrong direction. The parenting books I read are always saying not to do that! But through my parents' acceptance of me, and their example, I would end up seeing myself differently and then I would change myself. I think that this is what Jesus was doing with the Samaritan woman at the well.

Maria's story reveals her own faith journey as one of struggle with her beliefs about God learned during her Catholic upbringing: her present knowledge of God and Jesus as merciful and loving stand for her in stark contrast to the God of judgment she learned of in the Catholicism of her childhood. She reflects an abiding sense of ambivalence about her feelings of belonging to a church that represents a God of judgment prior to a God of love. Although the details of her story are unique to her own biography, the sentiments she expresses about the church and the general pattern of her story are common at Saint Brigitta. Her story reflects how these church members, acting within its norms, strive to treat each other: with acceptance that allows autonomous decisions for change. This is a flatter ideal of authority than is emphasized at Assumption.

The group's structure, moreover, facilitates self-disclosure, since participants strove to abide by the basic group rule articulated at the first session: members were not to interrupt or disagree, even if they did not appreciate the beliefs or experiences expressed by participants. Some who participated in permanent groups spoke of how faith sharing with those with whom they had developed friendships and come to know well sometimes made them painfully realize the religious differences that existed between them. But in the Lenten groups, shared sentiments and beliefs became grist for comment and discussion, and emotionally expressed stories were opportunities for empathetic response.

Because they are explicitly understood as expressions of community, faith-sharing groups provide a window into how people at Saint Brigitta think of community—or, at the very least, the kind of community they believe to be realistic and achievable. Their structure and rules place emphasis on the articulation of individual experience and do not ask participants to come to agreement or consensus

surrounding the context of their faith; in fact, they assume that people will disagree and require members not to voice disagreement but merely respect one
another's experience. Thus faith-sharing groups at Saint Brigitta are engaging in
practices that primarily emphasize individual autonomy, which serves as a locus
of religious authority. They do not practice a communitarian style of authority
relations that happens, for example, in consensus-based or democratically organized formal groups, although consensus-based decision making does happen in
some parish venues. This emphasis on expressiveness and individual autonomy
is similar to late-modern communitarian groups such as the Bruderhof. Like the
Bruderhof, whose members' motivations Benjamin Zablocki describes to include
"reconstitutions of the extended family and the desire to be free,"[38] Saint Brigitta's
faith-sharing groups strive to provide both autonomy and solidarity for participants. Affective ties, autonomy, and ambivalence toward institutionalized forms
of authority are also common to both Saint Brigitta and groups like the Bruderhof.

To some extent, the practice of faith-sharing groups at Saint Brigitta represents
the result of negotiating desires for different styles of community—some more
communal, others more autonomous—among Saint Brigitta's members, in a
surrounding capitalist culture that institutionalizes autonomy and privacy. Some
parishioners spoke reflectively about the achievability and limits of community
in this broader social context. For example, John Maloney-Jones, who lived at a
Catholic Worker House for a time when he was single, seeks a more communal
expression of the church at Saint Brigitta. He explains,

> Some of us have a hunger to deepen [a community lifestyle], to live it
> out, to make it more significant. We have plans to do something more
> radical about co-housing, taking on our living situation a little bit more
> cooperatively. On my part, even financially. But I think that's a little bit
> much [for most people]. Not everyone has come from something like the
> Worker....[And] having kids brings up the most elemental issues of secu-
> rity—how much you can really share.

John's experience aligns with what we know historically about the formation and
success of intentional communal living: accommodating nuclear families can be
quite difficult and often limits the success and continuation of intentional communities.[39] However, the limits John sees in the style of community at Saint Brigitta
do not impede the passion with which he and others pursue a more intense ideal
of the church as community, attempting to deepen alternative ways of living out its
fundamental tenets. Despite a practiced model of the church as community that
John perceives as imperfect, he and some of his fellows yet strive to inform their
everyday lives with this image of the church.

Disposing Oneself to the Sacred Ordinary: Reflection, Recognition, and Contribution

The sense of sacredness produced at the Sunday mass in the St. Brigitta gym coheres with, and can be understood as a further embodiment of, the model of church as community enacted in its worship. The dominant sense of the sacred in the gym is distinctly immanent and incarnational. Although responses to transcendent sacredness are occasionally practiced—for instance, when numerous congregants bow their heads and make the sign of the cross during the consecration—the settings and ritual practices at worship mostly express an immanent sacredness in the ordinary objects, events, and experiences of everyday life. The casual dispositions practiced during mass emphasize personal warmth and welcome, and the authority relations supported by this worship are grounded in the same ethic of self-reflection and personal contribution that characterizes its style of community.

Habits of the sacred ordinary

An immanent sense of the sacred is produced at Saint Brigitta in many different ways, but its logic is first noticeable in the locations for Sunday worship since, by contrast with Our Lady of the Assumption, masses are held not only in the church, but also in several other locations within the parish boundaries. The four Sunday masses held in the church take place in a Gothic-style building that was completed in 1929 but renovated shortly after Vatican II. Following the mid-20th-century style of *l'art sacré* that emphasizes simplicity in church appointments,[40] there are relatively few statues or paintings in the church. The altar rail has been removed so that the nave flows into the sanctuary, and the back pews have also been removed to make room for a large gathering space and baptistery.

In addition to the mass in the gym, a satellite Sunday mass is held in the atrium of a grade school near a cluster of seniors' residences, and the rectory chapel houses daily mass and communion services. All of these spaces are simply appointed and serve multiple purposes; for instance, although the rectory chapel was built as a sacred space, the pews have been removed, and the chapel now doubles as an art gallery for parishioners' paintings and drawings. The use of multiple spaces for worship stems in part from the pastoral staff's sense of practicality: they provide nearby mass locations for less mobile seniors and reduce the church's heating bills by having small worshipping congregations celebrate masses in smaller spaces. But the use of secular spaces also sacralizes ordinary spaces within its physical plant and in locations throughout the parish's boundaries in a transitory way.

The Saint Brigitta gym is a versatile worship space, and indeed the physical arrangements for congregational participation are often changed. Organizers decorate the gym for Sunday worship, but with few religious representations of the sort so abundant in Assumption's church: there are no anthropocentric religious images, no stained-glass or paintings. Besides the quilted banner behind the altar—whose design changes with the season and normally has familiar Christian symbols such as a cross, bread and wine, or a tree of life—the only decorations in the worship space are the flowers, candles, and other seasonal decorations arranged in front of the altar, helping to construct the immanent sacredness produced in worship. Lay organizers also use the flexibility of the space strategically when they want to set a mood or ritualize a spiritual experience; for instance, during Lent, the semicircle was turned 90 degrees, and the altar was placed at the far end of the gym, with a long space in between. After the homily, worshippers were asked to walk slowly to the altar in a ritual expression of the Lenten spiritual journey.

A sense of the sacred in the ordinary is also produced by the manner in which priests, homilists, musicians, and readers perform their ritual tasks and by the casual dispositions of ordinary worshippers. For example, the style of music at the gym mass is distinctly contemporary and combines country, folk, and gospel styles of music. Between six and ten musicians sing and play instruments each week, and depending on who is present, instrumental accompaniments can include piano, guitars, mandolin, and violin. The musicians are in worshippers' direct line of sight, and they gesture generously to encourage congregational singing. Worshippers sing enthusiastically during the Sunday service; even when solos are being performed, members of the congregation sometimes sing along as one would at a folk or soft rock concert.

Along with these practices, particular dispositions are expressed, supported, and cultivated at worship. These dispositions include enthusiasm for active participation, informality and personal warmth, and the capacity for spontaneity and improvisation. Congregational participation happens through ritual vocal prayers, gestures, and improvised speech—with this last happening especially during the dialogue homily. Not only do the organizers of the gym mass invite lay leadership but also they encourage active and generous participation in worship. These conventions in the gym make a particular style of active participation in worship normative. Moreover, by contrast with the dispositions of humility and reverence formally expressed during Assumption's Sunday mass, Saint Brigitta encourages expressions of personal warmth and individual self-expression through the informality of its worship style and ritual actors, including the priest presiders. Priests minimize the social distance between themselves and the congregation through personal self-revelation, and the physical distance by peripatetic meandering during homilies. Homilists nearly always bring the secular world explicitly into their preaching, along with notes of spontaneity and even drama. For example, we saw in the vignette at the beginning of this chapter that Joe Moran borrowed from his world of school administration in using a flip chart in his homily. And Father Theo shared his love of James Joyce in one gym mass homily by reading passages from *Ulysses* and then recounting a vivid story of his participation at events that honored Joyce in the free flow of drink and merriment late into the night.[41] Both lay and ordained preachers often relate personal anecdotes of work or family and tell jokes and stories, striving to entertain as much as inspire. One Sunday, a homilist even burst briefly into song to illustrate a point.

All these dispositions, moreover, are normative in the exercise of community throughout the parish, as is evident in the practice of its faith-sharing groups. But the informal dispositions of warmth and welcome, spontaneity, and improvisation have a place in daily life as well, especially as parents guide their children to imagine their own relationships with God in prayer and to develop these dispositions as personal qualities as they grow.

At the same time, regular worshippers can sometimes find the informality and noisy ambiance in the gym wanting. Christine Todd-Aikens acknowledges that she finds the mass too noisy sometimes, explaining, "What I don't like is that it's distracting, and if I'm really agitated and I need to get settled, it's not a good place to be. [Then] I'd rather be in the big church where I can isolate and withdraw and have a quieter prayerful experience." Several others expressed similar sentiments, saying that they sometimes missed worshipping in a church, but valued worshipping with their intimates more. Bryan O'Lear observes, "I have mixed feelings about the gym mass. I go there and like it, but it's too loose. It seems sometimes as if there's a loss of the sense of the sacred there." Bryan's comment suggests that some worshippers have ambivalent feelings about an expression of sacredness that is at times too ordinary—that worshippers don't always experience the sacred ordinary as sacred. And yet, the immanent sense of the sacred practiced intensely at the gym mass, and congregants' accompanying dispositions, characterizes the dominant sense of the sacred at Saint Brigitta, not only in the gym mass, but in its other worshipping congregations as well.

Sacredness and authority relations

The immanent sense of sacredness practiced at Saint Brigitta is intertwined with, helps to produce, and supports authority relations that are relatively egalitarian and, in many respects, flatter than those practiced at Assumption. These authority relations are embedded in the congregational sensibility of lay participation and leadership practiced at worship. Parishioners, Louis Beltrami explains, are mobilized by parish staff and lay leaders who "find indigenous leaders" and "sniff out the talents here and get them in front of the parish," rather than by merely fitting parishioners into prescribed roles. Louis and his peers work actively to encourage this ethic, which perceives personal contribution as both a responsibility and an opportunity for parish members, and which reflects a style of religious authority that primarily resides in individuals' competencies and relationships with God. To illustrate, Louis drew a parallel between eucharistic worship and a fellowship meal in everyday life, saying, "Look into the congregation, and say: 'I'd like to have her as the hostess of a party, so why wouldn't she be the logical person to have at the table, welcoming and gathering?'" Louis is here describing a communion service celebrated in the church during the midsummer feast of Saint Mary Magdalene where women preside and preach, an opportunity to give women leadership roles in worship—ones that he understands to be parallel to their societal roles and, not incidentally, ones that challenge hierarchical and institutional models of church.

The homily and dialogue are another illustrative expression of these relations because, in allowing laity to preach, Saint Brigitta's leadership flattens hierarchical authority and resists rules of the institutional church. In Catholic canon law, only someone who is ordained is permitted to give the homily during mass, but when the homilist invites dialogue and laity preach, the priest's homiletic role is shared with the congregation. Parishioners are not just invited to speak; they are actively encouraged to do so, reflecting a moral sense of the social body that hierarchical authority should be flattened and shared, and laity empowered. And the preaching team, comprised by resigned priests and theologically trained laity who give Sunday homilies on a rotating basis along with priests, plays an active role at Saint Brigitta.

In fact, the image of the church as community at St. Brigitta stands in contrast with, and in resistance to, a model of the church that emphasizes the hierarchical structure of institutional Catholicism. When Father Theo explained the significance of the gym mass and its role in the parish during an interview, he did so in terms that acknowledged this aspect of Saint Brigitta's self-understanding.

> It [the gym mass] was started about 15 years ago as a "jazz mass," and a core group of lay leaders, many of whom were once a part of the Catholic Charismatic movement, kept it going. Today, the gym mass is a place for returning Catholics who might be skittish about actually reentering a church building.

Some parishioners did associate church buildings with a style of institutional church practice they consciously reject. This sensibility is widespread enough at Saint Brigitta that Father Theo publicly acknowledged it one Sunday in the gym when, after singing in, *Gather Us In*, the opening song, "Not in the dark of buildings confining," he commented, "We're not in a confining building here," referring to Saint Brigitta's church building on the street corner opposite the gym.

Several regulars in the gym have spent time away from the church out of anger, frustration, or apathy generated by consternation over institutional teachings and practices surrounding these issues—although priests there are generally held in high regard by parishioners, because they encourage lay leadership and a sense of church community of equal members. Parishioners are often quite critical of the institutional church, especially concerning its stands on women's roles, mandatory celibacy in the priesthood, human sexuality, and its hierarchical authority structure. These issues, especially those involving women and human sexuality, are interwoven with parishioners' stands on public debates concerning family-related issues. In these instances, parishioners often draw boundaries not only with other groups involved in these debates but also with the hierarchical church. This is a key difference with Assumption, one that plays a role in constituting polarizing tendencies among Catholics.

Additional practices at Saint Brigitta also challenge the rules and practices of the hierarchical church. For example, the parish offers seasonal services during Advent and Lent where general absolution is offered. Participants during these services make brief individual confessions to a priest—or to Louis, as the pastoral associate—and when everyone is done, a priest gives absolution to the entire congregation together. Saint Brigitta conducted these services two or three times during the year of my field research, even though the bishop of the diocese had expressly and repeatedly forbidden the practice of general absolution. Louis, who is not ordained, hears confessions, also pushing at the boundaries of church rules. So does one of the resigned priests in the parish. All of these practices resist institutional rules and the church's authority to proscribe particular religious practices. These practices, in which many congregants express pride and clearly support, not only reveal the flattening of authority relations at Saint Brigitta, but also a relation with the institutional church that Richard Sennett has described as "disobedient dependence."[42]

In an essay exploring widespread ambivalence toward authority in modern Western societies, Sennett describes the ways in which people at once build bonds with those authorities they reject. Calling into question Max Weber's link of authority and voluntary obedience,[43] Sennett observes that people in modern societies both need and fear authority, and they often obey authorities they do not consider to be legitimate. Disobedient dependence is one manner in which people do this, with defiance of authorities—whether they are parents, teachers, or the church—and dependence on them occurring together. Sennett explains, "Bonds of rejection are the way we admit the need for authorities who are not safe to accept....A bond is built to the people we are rejecting; they are the point of departure."[44] The results of these authority relations are that "These bonds permit us to depend upon those whom we fear....The trouble is that these bonds also permit the authorities to use us: they can exercise control of a very basic sort over those who seem on the surface to be rebelling."[45]

The resistance that lies at the heart of authority relations of disobedient dependence is observable in the practices previously described and is sometimes explicitly articulated at Saint Brigitta, especially among regular attenders at the mass in the gym. A particularly good example of a discourse of resistance to the institutional church is evident in a narrative of an event surrounding the formation of Saint Brigitta's preaching team. This story, which was referred to frequently by parishioners and told by a few different people I interviewed, was told by one parishioner in this fashion.

> The presence of all these resigned priests was really the genesis of our preaching team. When the associate pastor (a priest) left…we needed at least two priests for six Sunday masses, but Father Theo was the only priest here. And there was a question, anyway, about whether orders and Eucharist need to be linked so tightly.
>
> So we gathered the resigned priests and said, "What do you think?" And they said, "Let's give it a try." The plan was for one of the resigned priests to preach one week, and then preside the next. But the bishop got wind of it, and he intervened.
>
> He told us, "You can't do it. I'll shut you down if you do." "Okay," we said. "We know you have to say that. But we'll do what we have to do and see how it goes." Then he sent a courier and said, "I think you misunderstand me. That may be true of some things, but in this case I'll have to suspend Father Theo." Well, that was not going to help our presiding situation because then, instead of having one priest and needing one more, we're down to none. So we decided not to do that. But it had raised a valid point about having these other voices in the pulpit.

As Sennett notes, Saint Brigitta's actions in this case took as their point of departure the rules and structures of the hierarchical church, against whom they rebelled but to whom they had to ultimately submit. But this story was told with a mixture of pride and matter-of-fact disappointment, communicating the perspective that, although the organizers of the preaching team would have liked to completely implement their plan, in this event they were able to challenge diocesan authority and achieve a partial success. Moreover, they exercised a form of principled resistance that brought the parish into conflict with hierarchical church authorities, taking a stance and articulating an argument that posited multiple loci of religious authority, and the bishop's responses confirmed in a partial way their position—that authority resides in the individual and the religious community, as well as in the church's hierarchy.

Louis further illustrates the importance of the individual as a locus of authority and an ethic of principled resistance to institutional authorities—which is
expressed and acted on in relation to both ecclesial and social injustices perceived
by parishioners—in speaking of the values he tries to instill in his children. He
explained, "I try to teach my daughters to give of themselves—as much as we can,
we give of our time and effort and our material resources. But I also try to teach
them that it is important to give of yourself in resistance to something."

Not all resistance at Saint Brigitta is dependent resistance, of course, but many
practices of resistance are explicitly directed at church rules. Some practices—
such as the general absolution services—serve more than one purpose, in that
they draw disaffected Catholics as well as enact the social body's resistance to the
church's authority. But significantly, these practices have also elicited responses
from hierarchical authorities, thereby engaging officials of the institutional
church. Although parishioners often talk approvingly of the parish as being somewhat distant from the church hierarchy, these practices, and the responses they
elicit, reflect a complex and intimate relationship with the institutional church
that is not often explicitly spoken of at Saint Brigitta. This complexity reflects one
way in which controversial ecclesial issues, including moral issues, are constituted
at Saint Brigitta—one that informs polarizing tendencies at the progressive end of
the spectrum of Catholic practice.

We see, then, that Saint Brigitta's collective practices of common prayer at
Sunday worship and in other group settings create and support very different
Catholic identities than the ones practiced at Our Lady of the Assumption. Families
find themselves incorporated into a church whose central metaphor of community
is one that both emphasizes the uniqueness of its members and values their fundamental equality with one another. The parish practices this central self-image
through the cultivation of informal, spontaneous, and improvisational dispositions; encouraging individuals' contributions and leadership; and structuring worship in an informal and participatory fashion that minimizes status distinctions.
These practices produce an immanent sense of the sacred where worship and
everyday life are intertwined and reflect one another and which embodies authority relations that emphasize individual autonomy and charismatic leadership and
resists forms of hierarchical social organization. In the imagery of community,
intimate ties are forged with self, with other parishioners, and sometimes with the
wider church—where sentiments of both unity and distance reside.

Conclusion

Worship is a particularly important locus of religious belief and practice for families, not only because it is most believers' central experience of church but also
because, as Penny Edgell notes, families with children in the home are often too

busy to attend church programs, especially among the growing number of dual-earner U.S. households.[46] In this analysis, I have shown that Sunday worship is, in fact, an especially important touchstone for Catholic families. Worship is not only a vehicle for religious socialization but also encodes church authority relations and social structures and provides resources for the internalization of the dispositions of the self that facilitate these social relations. The enactment of central ecclesial metaphors in parishes, especially in constituting local cultures with different authority relations, sets up a complex relationship among Catholics that helps to constitute polarizing tendencies among them, not only through two different visions of the social organization of church and family but also through different perceptions of how individuals make decisions about moral issues.

I have argued that in the cultivation of dispositions that underlie relations of religious authority, parishioners both exercise agency and participate in reinforcing the social constraints in which they operate, which limits their freedom. That is, they creatively exercise choice in ways that are relatively free but participate in reinforcing its limits. For example, at Assumption we see that the familial social relations expressed in worship emphasize the paternal obligations of priests toward parishioners; these relations both encourage parishioners' agency in initiating particular relations of pastoral counsel in confession and acknowledge and cement the force of pastors' moral authority, whereby they largely accept this authority's constraints on them, especially when pastors are perceived to be holy. By contrast, Saint Brigitta's relatively autonomous authority relations, encouraged by priests and pastoral leadership and embodied in worship, characterize social relations not only within the parish but also in parishioners' and leaders' agency in relation to the wider church, in which they fashion creative responses of resistance to authorities who impinge on the autonomy or charisma of members, while at the same time cementing ambivalent bonds to the church.[47]

Moreover, in analyzing the central ecclesial metaphors practiced at Assumption and Saint Brigitta, we have seen how different images of the church are expressed and supported in worship and devotional life. This happens through the combination of many distinct elements: through speech and song, but also through the material cultures and environments of worship, and through gesture and bodily comportment. In so doing, I have presented a first step in understanding how the images of the church as family at Assumption and the church as community at Saint Brigitta are linked to family practices and the habituation of dispositions that people draw on in everyday life in the wider world. In part II of this book, we will see how these central images of the church have affinities with and are transposed into family life, becoming a tool of support, meaning making, and problem solving in the negotiation of marital relationships, effective parenting strategies, and issues of work-family balance.

Before resuming this examination of how the different religious schemas at Assumption and Saint Brigitta become resources in families' everyday lives, I first examine another social process in these parishes important for understanding the relation of religion, everyday life, and cultural conflicts surrounding the family: how parishioners understand their religious identities and teach their children to be Catholic through their connection to churches of memory from childhood. Exploring the dominant churches of memory at Assumption and Saint Brigitta will allow us to understand more fully how their different styles of worship and devotion are related to the church more broadly and help us situate the domestic and public politics of family life in the contexts of institutional Catholicism and recent Catholic history—contexts that are critical for understanding moral polarization among Catholics.

2

Belonging

Our Lady of the Assumption
A cold and blustery day. Jim and Dana Jaszewski's city
apartment.
Jim Jaszewski, 33, is an entrepreneur. Dana, his wife, is in her
early 40s, and she is an event planner. When I met them, they
had been parishioners at Assumption for about a year. Initially,
Dana, and then Jim, began going to church there before they
joined the parish. Today they are active parishioners, helping
with the RCIA program and leading the Legion of Mary.

The Jaszewskis live in a spare second-floor flat in a city neighborhood where houses and Victorian era two- and three-flats are densely packed, and the streets are lined with parked cars. The apartment is fresh looking, sunny, and neat. A few small objects are scattered about—a pacifier and a baby bottle—reminding me that their newborn daughter sleeps in an adjoining room as we speak. We sit in the living room on a cane sofa and chairs with white cushions. The room is beautifully decorated with tropical floor plants and an abstract, earth-toned tapestry hanging above a brick fireplace. Like Dana's stylish appearance, the room reflects a careful sense of modern style.

As Jim and Dana tell the story of their meeting and marriage, they emphasize the common elements in their life histories that drew them together and cemented their relationship. Both had been previously married and divorced before they met each other, and they speak of upbringings and experiences with the Catholic Church that are in many ways similar. Dana begins, "We were raised in Catholic families. We fell away from the church for a while, and then came back. But in making that decision to come back to the Catholic Church, we said, you know, well, we're going to do it all the way. Or why do it at all? So in both our families now, we're very orthodox in comparison."

Jim explains, "We were pretty much born into 'mixed' religious families. Dana's mother converted from Episcopalianism to

Catholicism to complete the marriage. My father is Methodist, Presbyterian, something like that. Neither my grandmother nor my father went to church on a regular basis, and he actually had a very, very negative view of the Catholic Church. I don't know how that developed, and it's something I try to argue with my father. But he almost never went to church with us. My mother brought us to church every Sunday and on holy days of obliga-tion, and we went to Catholic school up until eighth grade.

"But what we didn't do, and what we have noticed in being close to a lot of very devoted people, is that we didn't have religion, oftentimes, in our home. We really never prayed together as a family. I have no recollection of going to special events at the church, unless it was a social thing like a spaghetti dinner, noth-ing like the Holy Name Society.

"And even the Catholic school—what's strange is there didn't ever really seem to be religion classes in Catholic school. Then I got to high school CCD classes. Compared to regular religion classes, they were very social—it was like, 'Be nice to people.'"

Dana then speaks of childhood experiences of family and the Catholic parish she grew up in that are both similar to and dif-ferent from Jim's, in part because she has memories of the church before Vatican II. She says, "I remember through first grade, the altar before it was turned around to face the people and every-thing in Latin. In second grade was when it changed. I remem-ber a lot of the very traditional parts of the mass, and that is why I love Assumption so much.

"My dad was a professional, and my mom stayed home with five kids. It was great, but religion was the same as in Jim's family. Other than when we were little kids, when we prayed before going to bed, there was no prayer in the home, there was no religious study in the home, and we didn't go to church for any other func-tions or volunteer work. Jim, your family wasn't involved in vol-unteer work having to do with the church—"

"Only for Confirmation, and stuff like that," Jim clarifies. "I just assumed it didn't exist. If there was any religious practice that I had or any catechism, I can't remember a thing. I think I blocked it out. I've told people who went through CCD classes that they got a lot more out of CCD than I got through Catholic school. Maybe they just figured that the Holy Spirit would filter through our heads through church. I don't know.

"I can say that, if both of my parents had been involved in the faith, things might have worked differently, at least at a younger

*age. I have in mind a number of couples who go door to door
doing home visits in the parish. They do what they call 'conversion calls,' they go to mixed couples and talk to them about the
faith. If there's one spouse that is not Catholic, their hopes are
that they'll understand that being of the same faith and being
unified there, that's important. It amazes me that people don't
think of spiritually being with each other in that way. Same with
my parents. Mixed marriages have obviously had an effect on
both of us.*

"But to me, conservative Catholics are people who go to benediction, Eucharistic adoration, basically fill a good percentage of
time in prayer and worship. It seems like there is a lack of that,
and service, in the church—people not wanting to get involved
in their religion."

*Then Dana picks up the story to speak of how their relation-
ship became intertwined with a spiritual and religious search.*
"For me as a teen coming out of the late 1960s, I studied other
religions, like Hinduism and other Eastern religions that were
popular at the time. I was always fascinated with other religions
and why, why, why?" *She continues,* "As a teenager, I saw a lot
of hypocrisy in the Catholic Church. Because I wasn't well educated in doctrine and so forth, I didn't understand that there was
a difference between what people do, what individuals do, and
the church's doctrine. As I got older, I was busy and working,
and I wasn't involved at all. I was married and went through a
very difficult divorce and a difficult period after the divorce. And
as a lot of people do, I went through a lot of soul searching and
reassessing my life and got things back in order. It's at that time
that Jim and I met."

Jim chimes in. "The bells were a catalyst. I like to tell people
that Assumption's bells kept calling us over there. Dana actually
made the initial decision to start going to church there. I was still
fighting it. Maybe because of the lack of attention given to catechism and theology and things like that, I didn't see the church
for what it really was when I was younger. I had stopped going to
mass when I was in college." *Jim explains that, as a young adult,
he searched for answers to questions of meaning in existential-
ist philosophy. During his 20s, he married and later divorced.
He left college before receiving his business degree, and in young
adulthood struggled with his career.* "I struggled with a lot of idi-
ocy, up to the point, really, that I met Dana."

They met in a professional setting, started dating, and then began to live together. Jim explains, "We've only known each other three years. We were living with each other, we were unmarried, and things weren't that great. We weren't looking too good in the eyes of the Catholic Church, but there was a start there, and one thing led to the next." Dana interjects, "I would get up and go to church. After a few weeks of him staying in bed, that was the end of that."

Jim continues, "And because of the interest and my looking into it and wanting to understand more about the faith, it was a rather quick process. My feelings were that I could no longer live with this woman and choose to be walking into the Catholic Church and saying, 'I have faith in this.' To me that was being unfaithful to God and my religion. So we sat down and I said, 'Dana, I want to get married to you, I've decided I want to be with you for the rest of my life. I've decided that I want to be Catholic.'"

As a part of their return to Catholicism and their preparation for marriage, they ceased living together. "We decided to let faith into our lives. So we talked to the priests, went through the whole process of confession, and came back to the church. It was an awakening."

Saint Brigitta
Midafternoon on a bright summer day. My home.

Father Theo considers Rick and Maggie McNeill to be among the new core of the young adult leadership in the parish. They are both in their mid-30s and parents to Robbie, who is two years old, and Rachel, his baby sister who is just about to walk. Rick and Maggie are among the hundred or so regulars who worship in the Saint Brigitta gym on Sundays with their family and friends. They spend a great deal of time with the many families they have come to know at Saint Brigitta, and especially with the group of college friends they followed there, most of whom now also have small children. Their college friends form the nucleus for a prayer group with whom they meet frequently; they exchange babysitting and rely on one another to talk through family and work decisions.

On the day that Rick came to my home for our interview, he talked about how his values have emerged gradually out of his Catholic upbringing and his subsequent life experiences. Sitting on the sofa in my living room, he appeared intent upon telling his story precisely, staring at his long legs stretched out before him.

His long face, framed with short brown hair that wants to curl, was animated with intensity and concentration.

Rick grew up in a white-collar family living in a diverse near-suburb of an eastern city. About his family's religious practice during his childhood, he says, "We said grace at meals, and in the home we had a priest who would come and say masses once in awhile. My parents had more faith than most people I knew growing up. They weren't proud about it, or thought about in one way or the other. They weren't articulate about their faith in the way that I have learned to be, but they were extremely faithful people. They weren't lukewarm, but they weren't extremely devotional, or extremely liberal, or conservative. They were just people of solid, strong faith."

He speaks about his experience of the church during his childhood. Rick is old enough to remember the reforming church after Vatican II but too young to remember the Council or the liturgical changes that took place in its immediate aftermath. "During my childhood, we had some nuns that were the old style, and some nuns without habits in our grammar school. I think that the church was softening noticeably by the time that I was growing up. There still was strictness to it, but not nearly what my older brothers and sisters experienced."

Rick connects his early experiences of faith with his present practice. He looks up at me across the coffee table, his large brown eyes sparkling as he says: "The three most important gifts my parents gave me were life, love, and faith. Faith is very central to me. During my time at Saint Brigitta, the local church and the worldwide church have come to have a meaning for me that I can articulate. I lean on that. I would not have predicted that a parish would be as central in my life as this parish is in my life."

"Was there ever a period of your life when you rejected religious practice?" I ask. He responds, "Oh yes, definitely. I was a relatively rebellious teenager. I didn't do anything terrible, but I did stupid things in high school that my parents were not equipped to deal with. I thought they were old-fashioned, even though they really weren't. So yes, there was a time in college when I really rejected religion. I just thought, why do people sit through this ritual over and over again? It didn't speak to me for a long time. But by the time I graduated from college, I was a regular church-goer again."

Rick relates his experience to that of his many brothers and sisters. "I think that all of my brothers and sisters would say now that they're people of faith. So I think that my parents have a lot to be proud of. My parents did a wonderful job."

Rick is trained as a lawyer and works in development with a church-related group; in his position, he meets a lot of people of his parents' generation. *"Working where I work now, I see that one of the great pains of my parents' generation is children that have fallen away from the church. My brothers and sisters and I all had that phase where we rejected the church and we rejected our parents' values. But by the end of my mother's life, she recognized that she had done a darn good job in that category. And I would say that if I can do half as good a job as they did in any number of categories, I'd be more than happy.*

"As a kid, you focus on the side of the church that is clearly unjust—like its treatment of women and homosexuals. How can I belong to an institution that would possibly do that? It's ridiculous and indefensible. But now I am able to articulate all the things that are good about the church when it does the right thing, and how it touches people's lives. I'll tell you, it's not always easy. But I know that the diocese, if you put it on a scale, there's ten times more good coming out than evil. And I feel the same way about the city and the U.S. I disagree with umpteen government policies, but the nation itself—I still believe what I heard in fourth grade about the highest ideals of the country. And that goes for the church, too. When I was a younger person, I used to talk more about spirituality, but now I've also come to realize the value of community."

Rick speaks about the relation of his religious practice to his political views, describing himself as difficult to pigeonhole. *"There's a lot of ways to express your faith, so I don't like to draw the dividing line too strongly between liberal and conservative. It's not a very important dividing line for me—although if Father Theo retires and we get an extremely conservative pastor here, it might become important to me. I am probably more moderate than a lot of people I know, and sometimes I feel labeled as a conservative, but I don't consider myself one. I like to be able to think what I think, and believe what I believe, without having to think that I'm necessarily in one camp or another.*

"I don't believe in abortion. Does that put me in a camp of people that I don't necessarily gravitate toward? I find more people that I want to be with, in my free time, at a place like Saint Brigitta than I would in other places. My friends all know and agree that there's injustice in the world, and we're not pretending that this

consumer society that we all participate in is somehow the way
things ought to be. I would have a hard time if my only friends
thought differently about such a core issue.
"But the funny thing is that I find Saint Brigitta frustrating for
exactly the opposite reason. I think the church is a big house for
everybody. But sometimes, when a homily or statement is made
at the gym mass, it's as if this is the mass for people that have
liberal points of view. I do probably agree with the underlying
point of view, but I don't like the assumption that we all agree.
I mean, it's not a black-and-white thing, but there is still a real
sense here that we should all agree, and I do agree—but what
if I didn't? How comfortable would I feel, how welcome would
I feel at the table?
"The folks that I work with now are older and Catholic—and
they're so devoted, and they're so good, and they're so generous.
I may not share their politics, but I can respect their faith, their
selflessness, and how they stick with something. So I think as
I've gotten older, I've come to wish for less polarization. At the
same time, I still find myself more at home at Saint Brigitta than
I probably would be at most other parishes."
Then Rick weaves together the significance of his upbringing for
what he hopes for his children. "My own family—Maggie, our
children, and me—is different than the family of my childhood,
but if the outcome can be the same, I will be very proud. I would
like to give my kids an example, tools, and encouragement to
have a relationship with their God.
"To learn to love the rituals of the church, the mass; for me, that
was very late in coming. Not until the last few years. It wouldn't
have come if it was forced on me. It came because I witnessed it
in my parents."

Catholic Belonging, Families of Origin, and Churches of Memory

These narratives of how individuals' Catholic belonging is intertwined with experiences of family disclose important similarities and differences in the Catholic
identities dominant at Assumption and Saint Brigitta. Although the details of
these narratives, and some of the perspectives, are particular to their narrators,
they also bring to light some of the general characteristics of Catholic identities that are supported and shaped in these parishes. In this chapter, I show that
these contrasts in Catholic identities are significant because they reveal a second

local-level social process that both supports and shapes family life and also fosters polarizing tendencies among Catholics surrounding the family, since the bonds and boundaries of identity in these settings are constructed in ways that bring these Catholics into opposition to one another over moral issues and church practices. Moreover, because individuals' most intense emotional investments originate, at least in part, in their sense of close connection to others and to themselves, these religious biographies—which reflect how their narrators understand themselves, their families, and their faith commitments—can help us understand the emotional resonance they feel with particular positions in cultural conflicts over the family.

This chapter therefore analyzes the ongoing process of Catholic identity construction at Assumption and Saint Brigitta with the particular aim of showing how Catholic identity boundaries are constructed in ways that provide a basis for polarization over moral issues related to family life. Identity narratives in both settings reveal three overarching similarities that point to a common social process in the construction of Catholic identities, but one that results in substantive differences between the identities practiced in each group: the importance of choice in their religious journeys, the significance of experiences common to the generation in which they came of age, and the importance of experiences of the church in their families of origin for their religious and familial trajectories. Examining this process in each setting provides groundwork for showing, in part 2 of this book, how people's religious identities matter in family life: in their choice of marriage practices, in their negotiation of work-family balance, and especially in parenting and the religious socialization of children.

In so doing, I pay particular attention to patterned differences in the stories at Assumption and Saint Brigitta, which are evident in how narrators describe their attachment to Catholicism today and what it means for them to be "good Catholics." For example, in the vignettes that begin this chapter, Jim Jaszewski defines Catholicism in terms of sacramental and devotional practice, but he does so within a broader context of the meaning and morality of intimate relationships and marriage. By contrast, Rick McNeill focuses on the Catholic Church as a broad community of faith, in which he expects both group commonalities and in-group differences to be respected. Moreover, while both Jim and Rick articulate criticisms of the church, their criticisms are focused quite differently: Jim focuses on the lack of "religion" in the parish church of his childhood, whereas Rick focuses on the larger church's injustices and cultural irrelevance. Such differences reveal that the bonds and boundaries of Catholic identity at Assumption and Saint Brigitta not only reflect different central ecclesial metaphors but also draw on different experiences of Catholicism.

Following Nina Eliasoph and Paul Lichterman's theory of culture in interaction,[1] I analyze the narratives in this chapter as discourses that are constructed through norms of speech that define a group's boundaries as well as its bonds. Although these stories of religious identity were only occasionally gleaned directly from contexts of group interaction, they are an ideal genre for examining religious cultures from an interactionist perspective since, like conversion stories, their construction involves pieces that are unique to the narrators' individual histories as well as elements that have been created or reworked in processes of interaction with others. These stories are not merely factual accounts of life journeys and the role of religion in them; rather, narrators are refracting their past life experiences through the lens of their present practice of Catholicism. As they tell their stories, they make sense of their experiences of a church and a society undergoing social change. They do so, in large part, in terms of their relationships with their parents and their parents' experiences of these same societal changes. These discourses both create in-group solidarity and establish how these groups distinguish themselves from others, including from other Catholics.

I focus on the narratives told by those at Assumption and Saint Brigitta who were raised Catholic, not only because they are majorities in these churches but also and especially because they present an opportunity to examine both continuity and change in members' relationships to Catholicism during a time of turbulence in both Catholicism and the family. Before turning to this analysis, I briefly explain why the three fundamental similarities in the stories in the two settings—choice, memory, and generation—are central categories for illuminating the bonds and boundaries of Catholic identities in contemporary American contexts.

A Culture of Choice

Although one common historical image of the Catholic Church is that of a monolith, Catholicism is actually pluralistic—a pluralism that has been historically comprised in the United States by ethnic and class differences, with the demographic composition of various ethnic and class locations of Catholics having changed over time but still salient among Catholics today.[2] At the same time, newer differences among Catholics today are like those we see illustrated in the stories here—ones that explicitly focus on different aesthetic and normative styles of Catholicism but often occur in similar class locations. These are not differences based in ascribed identities like class or ethnicity. Rather, these differences are chosen—they are achieved identities.[3] Such differentiated religious expressions among Catholics can be situated in what scholars have referred to as a "culture of choice" in contemporary American religion.[4]

According to survey researchers such as Dean Hoge and his colleagues, recent cohorts of American Catholics increasingly evidence a "more selective sense of a 'consumer' Catholicism than a practicing or institutionally validated one."[5]

Whether they practice or not, Catholics today tend to make up their own minds in accepting or rejecting particular church positions. But younger cohorts tend to have fragmentary knowledge of doctrine, tradition, or Catholic institutional life generally, and therefore many younger Catholics have difficulty articulating what is distinctive about Catholicism. Although those involved at Assumption and Saint Brigitta tend to be knowledgeable about their faith—knowledge fostered by the relatively intellectual religious cultures of each parish setting—parishioners, especially young adults, are at times not completely unlike their peers who have difficulty identifying Catholicism's distinctiveness. Moreover, as Jim's and Dana's stories illustrate, many are drawn to these parishes as seekers, with reflection on the implications of religion in their daily lives being a part of the process of achieving a Catholic identity. In so doing, individuals tend to emphasize particular beliefs and practices over others, although the great majority of those at Assumption and Saint Brigitta would certainly eschew the description, "cafeteria Catholic."

This process of the creation of achieved religious identities reflects Catholics' participation in a religious culture of choice, one that has become increasingly important in American life in the last several decades.[6] Scholars tie the notion of religious choice historically to a Protestant form of religious individualism where there is no mediator between the believer and God, and where an individual's acts of conscience and commitment are the ultimate repository of his or her faith. Some scholars, exemplified first by Peter Berger, worry that the contemporary culture of choice trivializes religion. They interpret the growing importance of choice as a negative development linked to secularization, which is ultimately destructive of the ties of community that animate and strengthen civic institutions.[7] In fact, survey research suggests that, if not a causal factor, this culture of choice is associated with a decline in religious practice among American young people broadly and among younger cohorts of Catholics in particular.[8]

But other scholars, including Christian Smith, assert that religious choice is not *necessarily* secularizing and that choice, rather than weakening religious belief in the ways that secularization theories hypothesize, can actually strengthen religious faith.[9] Smith notes that recent studies by Lyn Davidman, Nancy Ammerman, and Mary Jo Neitz demonstrate that among those who actively choose religious identities, the act of choice validates, makes vibrant, and confirms for them the rightness of their religious practice.[10] According to Smith, this is the case because, for modern Americans and other Westerners, "authentic" or legitimate identities of any kind are fundamentally grounded in individual choice—therefore, to personally choose them *is* how Americans legitimate their identities. This is an important aspect of American expressive individualism: ascription alone cannot validate identity, and one owns an identity and makes it personally meaningful through choosing it.[11]

Although it is possible that, depending on the context, religious choice may well contribute either to the strengthening or to the weakening of religious practice, the following narratives show that choice strengthens religious identities at Assumption and Saint Brigitta. Parishioners' choices, moreover, enter in a foundational way into processes of religious identity construction.

Churches of Memory and the Importance of Generation

Danièle Hervieu-Léger also recognizes achieved religious identities as an effect of Western modernity and similarly suggests that their strength is tied to its cultural conditions. Her account of the appropriation of these identities has an institutional basis that adds helpful insights to how Catholics actually construct identities in a culture of choice. Hervieu-Léger believes that religion in modernity has declined because of scientific rationality and the autonomy of the self but argues that the desire for experiences of sacredness is pervasive today because life is fraught with uncertainty, especially with the accelerated pace of life and rate of change in people's social environments. She concludes that religion has not disappeared in modernity but has been transformed: religion is now a mode of believing that practitioners legitimate through an appeal to a religious tradition in a "chain of memory." But because collective memory is both superficially homogenized and fragmented in modernity, religious memory has to be recovered and is often reinvented. Hervieu-Léger asserts that being religious therefore involves people making use of religious narratives—often fragmentary ones—to connect their beliefs and practice to a tradition.[12]

Hervieu-Léger's theory of religion is helpful for understanding Catholic narratives of religious belonging because the appeal to a tradition, or traditions, in a chain of memory is demonstrated in the varied ways people understand and practice Catholicism and evident in how people actually speak about their religious journeys. The involved Catholics at Assumption and Saint Brigitta choose among strands of Catholic tradition as they reconstruct churches of memory locally. These choices vary not only by the characteristics of the parish settings in which they practice but also by parishioners' childhood experiences of the church, their religious trajectories, and the problems they encounter in marriage and family life.

Churches of memory that are more or less collectively constructed at Assumption and Saint Brigitta (and in their networks of like-minded others) are revealed in parishioners' narratives of religious identity. These narratives define aspects of religious identity that together constitute the bonds and boundaries of group identities that place them vis-à-vis their Catholic peers. In their stories, which evaluate childhood experiences of the church, they articulate what they believe to be authentically Catholic, and what is not.

Moreover, because churches of memory are bound to individual life histories, they involve a generational component. According to Karl Mannheim, generation is significant for individuals' outlooks and life trajectories because similarly located people of the same generation have similar experiences of the world—of historical events and developments and of the social effects and environments created by such events. The different constellations of attitudes that members of a generation develop, especially during their young adult years, become the locus of what Mannheim calls different "generation units."[13] The impress of generation, and different generation units, is exemplified in the narratives of belonging explored in this chapter. Generation matters in the stories of Catholic identity not only as a reflection of narrators' early experience of church but also because it is a part of the construction of a church of memory that is in dialogue with these remembered experiences. In other words, these memories form a basis for identifying with a particular Catholic lineage—that is, a church of memory—in the present. The outlook and attitudes of a particular generation dominates the shared perspective at each congregation, with different generation units of other cohorts finding their place within this dominant perspective. At Saint Brigitta, the dominant narrative is that of the Vatican II cohort of Catholics, whereas at Assumption, the narrative is that of the post–Vatican II generation.

In what follows, I show how members of Vatican II and post–Vatican II cohorts at Assumption and Saint Brigitta who were raising families and had children in the home spoke about the churches of memory that form their religious lineage and the boundaries and bonds of Catholic identity in these settings. For each, the boundaries of faith include a critique of the churches of parishioners' childhoods, with people in both congregations focusing, at least in part, on criticism involving the practice of Catholic worship. The bonds of faith are narrated largely in discussions of people's experiences of religion in their families of origin, through which they explain their current choices for religious participation. Especially in defining their criticisms of the church, which tend to oppose social relations and values that the other group espouses, these narratives comprise identity boundaries that play into polarizing tendencies surrounding public conflicts regarding the family.

Catholicism and Belonging at Our Lady of the Assumption

Narratives of belonging at Assumption focus on why people adhere to the retraditionalized Catholicism practiced there. In these stories, parishioners emphasized that some of their beliefs—especially church teachings surrounding human sexuality, such as those on contraception—were ones to which the majority of American Catholics do not adhere, in this way creating boundaries with other Catholics. The importance of adhering to church teachings on sexuality at Assumption is a primary way in which the parish positions itself in cultural conflicts surrounding the family. But this was by no means the only way that parishioners articulated the boundaries and bonds of Catholic identity. Identity was also expressed in relation to particular experiences of the church, especially worship practices and childhood socialization into Catholicism. Parishioners told narratives of the churches of their childhoods as churches in crisis and saw the efforts of their pastors and lay leaders as rebuilding a "true" church of memory grounded in liturgical and doctrinal traditions preceding Vatican II reforms. Those in post–Vatican II cohorts also tended to emphasize the discontinuity between the faith of their parents and their current practice of a newly traditional Catholicism. The bonds of faith that tie parishioners to one another were often, though not always, contextualized in conversion narratives that spoke of return or "reversion" to a retraditionalized Catholicism, especially among those in post–Vatican II cohorts.

The Boundaries of Faith: Post–Vatican II Catholicism, Crisis, and Secularization

Through discourses surrounding particular worship practices, both remembered and in the present, Assumption's parishioners created a symbolic boundary with other Catholics. To be a serious Catholic at Assumption—one who, as Jim Jaszewski said, "want[s] to get involved in their religion"—constitutively involves regular worship and devotions, including older devotions considered traditional, and recovered practices, such as Eucharistic adoration, that are practiced less frequently today than they were prior to Vatican II. Many younger parents, even some raised in homes they described as devout, spoke of childhood churches that lacked meaningful worship, and the large majority talked of similar experiences in the more recent past. Nearly all of the Vatican II and post–Vatican II generation Catholics at Assumption defined their Catholic belonging in opposition to experiences of childhood and present practices of the post-Conciliar church, with worship figuring prominently among them. The following analysis demonstrates how, through discourses of remembered and present experiences of Catholic worship, Assumption's parishioners define authentic Catholic practice according to a retraditionalized sensibility and against a more common sensibility and practice developed in the post–Vatican II reforming church.

One example of how parishioners differentiated Assumption's Catholic practice by reference to worship at other churches came from Ron Reyes, who is in his early 40s. Ron first came to Assumption with his parents about ten years ago because he and his wife were not happy at the parish they were attending. He drew a distinction between the parishes near his home and the preaching and practice that attracted him to Assumption. "I have always been religious," he said, explaining that Catholicism had been a consistent part of his life from childhood.

"I was raised to think of religion simply as a part of life." Ron described his parents as involved Catholics who understand the teaching of religion to children as a primary parental duty; his mother taught him the Baltimore Catechism as a child at home. He and his brother went to daily mass with their parents while growing up, and he never went through a phase of not wanting to go to mass in his childhood or adolescence. But about the parish near his home, he said, "At the church we were attending, Saint Margaret Mary, the sermons would be like, 'I had this insight the other day on the ninth tee'—the sermons were bland. They did not have the Catholicism I knew from my upbringing."

Maria, his wife, who is in her late 30s, grew up in a less learned Catholic home than Ron, but she also contrasted the practices of her childhood parish church with that at Assumption. When Maria was a young adult, her church, Saint Thecla, was renovated. She explained that, at that time, "The priests at Saint Thecla reconfigured the pews and took out the kneelers. You could only sit or stand during the mass. It was more difficult to participate." She left Saint Thecla and did not go to church regularly for a long time, until she began attending Our Lady of the Assumption.

Both Maria and Ron find the worship at Catholic churches they attended in the past to be less adequate than what they now experience at Assumption—and each understands their choice to belong to Assumption, and their Catholic identities, in light of the contrast between their previous experience of other churches and their present practice at Assumption. Ron is old enough to have experienced the church prior to Vatican II as a small child and has memories of a reforming church from his youth. Even though he thinks of the church of his childhood as primarily continuous with his adult practice of faith, the homilies of his early adulthood did not evoke for him the strength of the Catholicism he had practiced as a child. He describes the homilies he heard at Saint Margaret Mary critically and with irony, implying that how homilists there related daily life to faith was weak at best. In Ron's view, these homilies were filled with material that was not relevant or inspirational and did not challenge him to live a better life. In these respects, homilies at Saint Margaret Mary neither reflected the Catholicism of his childhood nor inspired him as an adult, as they do at Assumption.

Maria similarly explains that the church of her young adulthood did not facilitate or fit with her expectations of Catholic practice that would nurture her faith or suit her religious sensibility. She did not explicitly say why she stopped going to church as a young adult, but it was after finding that Saint Thecla's renovation made it difficult for her to participate in worship that her attendance dropped off. The difficulty in participating for Maria was that she could no longer kneel during prayer but could only stand or sit. Before Vatican II, the typical practice in U.S. Catholic churches was to kneel for the consecration, but during the 1980s and 1990s, some churches recovered the ancient practice of standing for the

Eucharistic Prayer, as did Saint Thecla. For Maria and her peers, kneeling during the Eucharistic Prayer was a routine practice with which they had grown up (as had nearly all those I worked with in both parishes) and to which they were accustomed. Reverence is embodied at Assumption through kneeling, genuflection, bowing one's head, and other gestures, and Maria finds this sensibility more reflective of her faith and more conducive to participating in worship than the Catholic practice at Saint Thecla.

Ron and Maria emphasized that they do not differentiate themselves from other Catholics, but understand their practice simply as Catholic. By asserting this, they articulate that they strive to practice an authentic Catholicism, one bound to the universal church, and they understand their Catholic identities within this framework. They express their concerns about the quality and content of homilies and expressions of reverence at worship as practical concerns: elements of public prayer that can either inhibit or facilitate their own prayer. But although Ron and Maria do not want to differentiate themselves from Catholics as a whole—to make their desire for a particular kind of worship a marker of identity against other Catholics or other Catholic practices—they are more comfortable with a certain style of worship than with others. At the same time, worship practices are symbolic of *what* is inspiring and *how* one is prayerful and are thus constitutive of a particular way of being Catholic. Even if they do not see these practices as sharply distinguishing them from others, they still comprise a retraditionalized religious identity.

Others at Assumption do more clearly articulate worship as a part of a package of practices that mark their identities over against others, even (or perhaps especially) other Catholics. Adele Dunning, 50, also came to Assumption with her husband and children because of her dissatisfaction with their neighborhood parish, which they joined when they moved from the East Coast to the Midwest. Her description of this neighborhood parish was distinctly critical. Like Ron, she criticized the preaching at her previous parish, saying that the "homilies were so bad they were almost blasphemous." And in a way similar to Maria, she described distracting worship practices at daily mass, such as holding hands during the Eucharistic Prayer, saying,

> It doesn't have to be the Tridentine mass, but there's a limit! I suppose I should be a better person and be able to look past this stuff, but I can't. Daily mass, that's my time to talk to God. My 20 minutes, half an hour, just me and God, we get to chat. I don't want butterflies or a lot of distractions. Just plain, old, unadorned mass.

Here Adele is contrasting pre-Conciliar worship, which she is old enough to have participated in into her teens, with worship practices initiated after Vatican II and practiced during the experimental period of liturgical reform following in the wake of the council. Adele makes it clear that she doesn't need the church to return to the style of worship practiced before Vatican II, but she also finds some aspects of liturgical reform problematic. She characterizes some practices, like standing joined around the altar at the Eucharistic Prayer, to be trivializing and inauthentic. They are so irritating to her that they inhibit her ability to pray. Adele connects this experience of worship at her previous parish with other problems she perceives to have been created by Vatican II reforms, including the problematic religious education her children received at the parish school. In this context, Adele spoke at length about her experiences of the church in the Midwest and used a vivid analogy to illustrate what she believed had happened within the church after Vatican II.

> Here in the Midwest, I know some really good Catholics who tolerated a whole lot more than I ever would. And the reason was that they were always here. [They were like a] frog sitting in the pot, and the heat was turned up, and they never knew that they were being boiled! Whereas with me, I was living in the Northeast, where everyone was orthodox and everything was fine, and I got here, and I hopped into that hot pot and I hopped right out again.

Because Adele comes from an area of the country where Catholic parishes often emphasize older Catholic traditions, she sees a sharp contrast in how Catholicism in the Midwestern United States has changed, inappropriately in her view, since Vatican II. Like a frog in a pot that is slowly being boiled, Adele understands the Catholic Church as progressively changing in detrimental ways over the course of her adulthood. The worship practices that bother her in Catholic churches like the one near her home are just one symptom of a set of problems that she perceives within U.S. Catholicism, problems that also include inadequate teaching and socialization of children into Catholicism, religious illiteracy among Catholics, and inadequate and sometimes misguided church leadership.[14] For Adele, an insistence upon Catholic orthodoxy, symbolized in but not limited to worship practice, is not only an expression of Catholic identity but also a clarion call in a contest over the right direction of American Catholicism as it moves into the future.

Adele is a Vatican II–cohort Catholic, and others of her cohort also criticized the direction in which the church had moved since they were young adults. But members of post–Vatican II cohorts were most consistently critical of Catholicism in mainstream parishes—an interesting finding, because this generational group has no experience of the church before Vatican II. The churches of their childhoods consisted entirely in post-Conciliar Catholic practice, and yet, this group was most articulate about the rightness of a retraditionalized practice, comparing this practice favorably with the practice familiar to them from childhood.

Pam Williams, 35, gives an illustrative example of how this cohort uses worship and parish practice to draw a symbolic boundary between their Catholic identity and that of others. Pam vividly narrated experiences of Catholicism in her family of origin that, she says, contributed to her adoption of a conservative Catholic practice as an adult. An excerpt of that story is included next, together with her thoughts on how Assumption differs from the Catholic Church nearest her home, Saint Barnabas.

> The church that we went to [when I was a child] had a guitar mass, and all these horrible "run with your head up in the wind" songs from the 1970s, and not a single crucifix anywhere. I don't even remember there being a tabernacle, no kneelers—and that is how I grew up.
>
> As for the church [today]—I've had problems at Saint Barnabas. I just can't go there. I think they're almost Anglican in their worship of the form without substance. They have a great choir. It reminds me of Anglican churches and concerts. I think they are, like their ads in the local paper, "Not all things to all people, but we're trying!" Thousands of little clubs and stuff they're doing—and not that much emphasis on the sacraments.
>
> They would never say you should go to confession. At Assumption, Father Aidan will say, "God is so happy you're in church, and so are we— but if you haven't been to confession, stay away from that Eucharist." The point is that it seems that they're willfully ignoring the rules.

With these observations, Pam refers to some of the boundaries that encircle Catholic identities at Assumption, and she fleshes out some of the characteristics of the church of memory that resides within these boundaries. She describes the church of her childhood as one where worship practices lacked reverence; music lacked elegance, taste, and meaning; and perhaps most important, the church lacked the abiding presence of the Eucharist and even the central Christian symbol of Christ on the cross. In other words, this church lacked the very heart and substance of a shared and historically grounded Catholic faith, symbolized in the absence of the crucifix and tabernacle.

Similarly, Pam's criticism of Saint Barnabas hinges on religious practice that she understands as watered down, stripped of meaning, and, by implication, not authentically Catholic. Worship at Saint Barnabas is more Anglican than Catholic, according to Pam, in such a way that emphasizes the trappings of worship without enough attentiveness to the faith that underlies it. Moreover, although worship at Saint Barnabas is beautiful, Pam perceives that it lacks some of the essentials of sacramentality, which is a distinguishing mark of Catholicism. In "willfully ignoring the rules" to reach out to a broad range of people, they gut the Catholic doctrines of sin and penance. And even its activities and programs are misdirected. Pam does not see these as elements of faith, but as a form of busyness that dilutes Catholicism's central message.

Pam describes Saint Barnabas as a church that is in many ways similar to the church in which she grew up. In fact, like many of her peers at Assumption, she explicitly draws boundaries, not only against other Catholic parishes but also against the church of her childhood. Inside these boundaries we find a "true" church of memory that she understands to be more authentically Catholic than her childhood church and other contemporary Catholic parishes, even though she is too young to have experienced that church. This church is sacramental, displays visible symbols of fundamental beliefs, and respects its institutionalized formal rules—recovering traditions in a chain of memory that stretches back before Vatican II in ways that other Catholic churches do not. How is it that Pam, and others like her at Assumption, has arrived at a church of memory so tied to a past she has not experienced?

The Bonds of Faith: "Reverting" to Orthodoxy in a Culture of Choice

If parishioners at Assumption establish the boundaries of their Catholic identities and differentiate themselves from others, at least in part, through the symbolic content of particular worship practices, they bond themselves together not only as we saw in the last chapter—in the sensibility and habits they cultivate and the image of the church they enact—but also in the church of memory through which they ground their Catholic identity, the historical church that legitimates their believing and establishes their belonging. This church of memory is experienced at Assumption and learned in religious practice there: not only in worship but also in formal adult catechesis programs, in preaching, and in informal interactions and at parish events. And while parishioners alternatively named their practice and this church of memory as "orthodox" or "traditional," it is in the term *reversion* that we can best understand how Pam and her peers come to embrace a church of memory that they did not experience as children.

Several members of post–Vatican II cohorts at Assumption referred to themselves as "reverts,"[15] and Pam Williams explained that a friend of hers proposed the term as fitting because "We are returning to a kind of Catholicism we never experienced as children." For Pam and her friends, *reversion* contains the meaning of returning to Catholicism after a period of absence or of engagement with other religions. But this identity fuses return with conversion, both because this is a new experience of Catholicism for adherents and because its practice has accompanied a felt change of heart among them.

These parishioners related their reversion to a retraditionalized Catholic practice to their families of origin in varied ways. The stories of their families of origin and churches of memory sometimes reflected continuity and attachment to parents; at other times, they reflected discontinuity with childhood or less intense religious practice during childhood. This latter pattern was often accompanied by feelings of disconnectedness with parents and is the one we saw in Jim's and Dana's stories in this chapter's introduction. Among Pam's group of friends, most told stories of religious upbringings that, although not usually as stark as Jim's story of overt conflict with parents over religion, often contained both elements of conversion and a sense of discontinuity with their parents' practice of Catholicism.

In answering the question of how younger cohorts at Assumption arrive at this church of memory, let us examine more closely the relation of their experience of their parents' faith and religion in the home to their present religious practice, for it is here that we can pull together how their generational experiences of the church play a role in their attraction to a retraditionalized church of memory whose referent is found in the pre-Conciliar church. In order to do this, let us first return to the story Jim Jaszewski told at the beginning of this chapter.

Like several of the stories Pam and her friends told, Jim's story has elements of a conversion narrative. Jim turned from an adult life in which religious faith was essentially absent and, like Pam and her friends, reverted to a serious form of Catholic practice he never knew as a child. With this turn, he made a commitment to a different style of life than he had lived previously. Significantly, this turn involved serious choices in his personal life, including his decision to marry Dana, to cease living with her, and to be sexually abstinent until they married. Like other reversion stories told by Assumption parishioners, Jim's turning included serious life changes—changes in his routines, in the ordering and use of his time, and in the rules by which he lives.

Jim, like others in the post–Vatican II generation of Assumption parishioners, sharply contrasts the religious practice he knew as a child with the Catholicism he adheres to today. Specifically, Jim speaks at length of a religious practice in his family that was relatively uninvolved and uninvolving and of a childhood church that was uninspiring. This is the case even though Jim's mother brought him and his siblings to church each Sunday, sent him to a Catholic grade school and a high school CCD program, and participated with him in parish sacramental programs such as confirmation. Somewhat ironically, Jim understands his childhood Catholic upbringing as inadequate, and yet, the sum total of the involvement he and his family did have with the church likely would be interpreted by survey researchers as indicators of relatively strong familial involvement with religion. Jim believes his religious upbringing to be wanting, in part because his father rarely went to church with them and regards the church negatively. But perhaps more important, he describes his childhood experience of the institutional church as lacking what he understands to be essential to religion: he describes his experience of Catholic schooling, religious education, and parish life as primarily social, as opposed to religious. Saying that he may have "blocked it out," he doesn't remember having religion classes at his grade school, even though religion classes are standard in Catholic schools. In fact, he asserts that religion "didn't exist" in his childhood Catholic parish, nor did he experience religion in the home. He believes that, as a result, he suffered from a religious illiteracy that prevented him from understanding the importance of religious faith for moral and effective living.[16]

Despite the fact that the post–Vatican II generation of parishioners like Jim find most reform-minded Vatican II Catholic practice wanting, their parents' views were more mixed, and some told of parents who have quite different perspectives on Catholicism than the ones that they now espouse. Pam Williams's story reflects this pattern. Her experience of the Catholicism of her childhood and her parents' practice of faith is mixed in that it contains elements that have contributed to her serious religiousness as an adult; however, it is dominated by a form of practice that her parents embrace but that she rejects. In fact, the church of memory she today considers to be most authentically Catholic was, during her childhood, disconnected from her family's practice and is largely disconnected from her parents' faith perspective today. She explains,

> [My dad] thinks the church is crazy on sexual matters, he thinks there should be women priests, and he is extremely in love with the hagiography of the saints and the cathedrals over in Europe. When we were young, we were taken all over Europe to see cathedrals and so, for me, growing up there was this disconnect.
>
> My dad would not go up for communion. But my mom…had very devout parents. She's one of those recovering Catholics. She practices, and we went religiously.
>
> So for me personally, when I grew up there was this disconnect between what we did every Sunday, which was go to this crazy guitar mass, and my memory of going to Chartres and seeing all this great art and all this stuff. Culturally, it's the most beautiful thing, just seeing the European cities where the cathedral was the biggest building in the city, and clearly people paid a lot of attention to that. The church had a huge influence.

Pam's parents are from the pre–Vatican II generation of Catholics. They grew up in the church before Vatican II and came of age at a time not too distant from Vatican II. Pam describes her father as deeply attached to the church, but despite this, he disagrees with some of its doctrines, especially its teachings on human sexuality and women in the church. Her mother is a "recovering Catholic," someone who left the church at some point but now practices. It is significant that, as Pam describes them, her parents sound similar to many of the pre–Vatican II generation of Catholics at Saint Brigitta—just as there is similarity in the sensibility of the style of worship in the church of Pam's childhood and that at Saint Brigitta. Pam articulates a Catholic identity that, while sharing much in common with her parents and those at Saint Brigitta, creates boundaries with them in worship and parish practices that symbolize the recovery of what she perceives to have been lost in the post–Vatican II church.

Pam understands her parents' attitudes and practices to be at odds with another aspect of the church she values, and that they apparently value, too: a church that has continuity with centuries past, a church of the saints, a church embodied in the cathedrals of Europe. She does not explain how her parents may have integrated the church with which they disagreed and the church they loved, but she experiences these two aspects of their Catholicism as disconnected. This aspect of her parents' church—the church of cathedrals and the church of the saints—is the one that is connected to her practice today. It is the primary link in the legacy of a church of childhood and the church of memory she now espouses.

Pam's description of the disconnect between a church of memory characterized by its symbolic societal centrality and authority and the post-Conciliar church of her childhood and adolescence both evidences the generational sensibility of post–Vatican II Catholics at Assumption and also helps us situate parishioners' comments and criticisms of other Catholic churches. For post–Vatican II Catholics at Assumption, most churches are fraught with uncertainty, blandness, religious illiteracy, and an experience of parish life that is more social than religious. By contrast, these cohorts find their religious identities not in the practices of the reforming church, but in ones that were often left behind or de-emphasized with reforms.

This is what is meant by reversion; people return to a different version of Catholicism than the one in which they were raised. Not only does worship constitute the church as family but also the way it is practiced and the social relations that underlie it are symbolic of the substance of religious beliefs emphasized at Assumption and legitimated in a chain of memory. These stories thus make a strong connection between "right worship" and a church that promotes knowledge of Catholic teachings about human sexuality and church authority. This Catholicism is represented by the very practices that were not only de-emphasized with reform but also, before Vatican II, considered most distinctively Catholic in the American context: devotional practices such as novenas, Marian devotion, and Eucharistic adoration; a ritual style that communicates transcendence and demands reverence; and religious education that depends on and is codified in a catechism. Such practices are claimed as central in the retraditionalized Catholicism practiced at Assumption, which is grounded in the institutional church and seeks to reestablish the distinctiveness of Catholic identity. In these characteristics—particularly in the normative sensibility, social relations, and the importance of Catholic teachings on human sexuality—retraditionalized Catholic identities constitute a basis for moral positions at one pole of cultural conflicts surrounding the family.

Catholicism and Belonging at Saint Brigitta

By contrast with Our Lady of the Assumption, narratives of belonging at Saint Brigitta tended to focus on sentiments and experiences of connectedness to the Vatican II church, often despite parishioners' disagreements or difficulties with particular aspects of church teachings and practice. In fact, at Saint Brigitta the boundaries of Catholic identity are expressed frequently in opposition to aspects of the church often identified with the period before Vatican II, such as its emphasis on the hierarchical constitution of the church, the prevalence of sin and guilt in popular piety, and the prominence of church teachings on human sexuality in its moral discourse. At the same time, parishioners expressed appreciation for the church and emphasized the continuity of their present faith with that of their families of origin, rather than its disjuncture. They spoke of their parents' faith in positive terms and communicated a sense of appreciation for their practice, even if they understood their perceptions and practice of Catholicism to differ from their parents' practice.

Criticisms of the church, especially those surrounding church teachings on human sexuality, stand in stark contrast to Assumption's orientation to Catholic identity and are implicated in varied ways in how Saint Brigitta's parishioners perceive cultural conflicts surrounding the family. In what follows, I show how these foundations of Catholic identity at Saint Brigitta contribute to moral polarization, and I foreground their implications for analyses of domestic and public politics of the family in chapters 3 through 5.

Boundaries of Faith: Worship and "Culture Two" Catholicism

As at Assumption, people's stories of how they came to belong to Saint Brigitta often involved worship and parishioners' churches of childhood, but they focused these discussions quite differently than did their peers at Assumption—especially in enumerating different criticisms of the church. In fact, whether they spoke appreciatively or with ambivalence about their childhood churches, discourses surrounding worship practice allowed parishioners to situate themselves vis-à-vis the institutional church, and in this sense, worship served a symbolic role as they articulated Catholic identities.

Rick McNeill's story at the beginning of this chapter captures some of the most significant differences in narratives of Catholic identity at Saint Brigitta, compared with Our Lady of the Assumption. Although some of Rick's criticisms of the church concern its relevance to everyday life, these are not focused on a lack of meaning or muscularity in post-Conciliar Catholicism, but rather on the ways he perceives the institutional church to be unjust, the ways he perceives it to lack a strong witness within the world, and how he believes it has damaged some people's lives.

Rick says frankly that he did not find Catholic worship to be meaningful to him for a long time, although he now connects his attachment to the church's ritual life to the example of his parents. He describes his parents as seriously observant Catholics with whom he now shares a religious sensibility, though this was not always the case. He credits their religious practice as eventually leading him, as an adult, to learn to love the church's worship tradition. Rick's description of his parents' faith and its eventual effect on him illustrates the positive way the majority of those interviewed at Saint Brigitta perceived their parents' religious observance and its effects in their lives.

Rick speaks of his attachment to the church's rituals in the context of a church of memory that is both grounded in the support and friendship of others at Saint Brigitta and contained within the Catholic Church as a "big house," that is, a community of inclusion. In these comments, he addresses the broad moral polarization he perceives in the church. Rick's views on women and homosexuality are consonant with the sensibility practiced at Saint Brigitta. But he describes himself as politically moderate and cites his belief in the immorality of abortion as an example. In fact, a large group of leaders at Saint Brigitta take this stance; while I knew there to be parishioners at Saint Brigitta who were pro-choice, all of those interviewed there who spoke about or mentioned abortion described themselves as pro-life.

Rick locates the issues of women, homosexuality, and abortion as polarizing but points to a larger sensibility at the poles, constituted in local cultures, as particularly salient to the divisions in the church. He views himself as one who does not fit firmly on a side of the polarization he perceives, nor does he want to locate himself there, and he finds problematic the aspects of Saint Brigitta's local culture that support these tendencies. As we have seen, the moral demand to include diverse others in the church is constitutive of the parish's central image of the church as community, but Rick's vision of inclusion moves beyond that of many who belong there. His definition is one meant to stretch the boundaries of Catholic identity at Saint Brigitta. Although he shares a religious sensibility with his peers there, he is critical of attitudes that do not embrace the church's catholicity. He resists the idea that the gym mass should be just for those with "liberal points of view."

For Rick, then, the rituals of the church are an important symbol and practical manifestation of the church's universality, especially its tradition of embracing difference. This emphasis on inclusion is constitutive of Rick's sense of his identity as a person and as a Catholic. Like Ron Reyes at Assumption, he sees himself as Catholic in a larger sense than can be captured in more polarized identities, but unlike Ron, he frankly acknowledges and criticizes this polarization within the church. He does not invoke worship style as a marker of difference; instead, he emphasizes that he is at home in the milieu at Saint Brigitta because it emphasizes religious values he holds dear.

Rick's view of worship was neither uncommon nor wholly shared at Saint Brigitta. In fact, parishioners expressed a range of diverse attitudes toward worship, especially in some of its more traditional forms. A different view, though one common at Saint Brigitta, is found in Christine Todd-Aikens's story of how the church's rituals are related to her faith. She explained,

> To this day, I don't have a lot of need or affinity for the institutional church, the hierarchy—I don't know much about it, and I'm bored by my friends who think it's exciting to file around. I don't get off on following all that stuff; it's not where my energy goes.
>
> I go for the coffee hour more than for the mass. I could go to any church. I'm not an incredibly Catholic person but Catholicism is familiar. It rings deep. It's tradition. I probably don't have too much hearkening to traditional things, but pull out a piece of music (it's probably the modern stuff anyway)—it touches me. "Create a clean heart in me, O God"; just one phrase can do it.

As she spoke of her relationship to Catholicism and its worship, Christine explained that the foundation of her appreciation for Catholicism stemmed from the church of her childhood and early adulthood. Although she and her family members were the only Catholics in their neighborhood when she was growing up, the church played a central role in her family of origin. Her parents were regular churchgoers, and they were involved in the life of their parish and friends with its priests, who were often dinner guests in their home. When she left home for college, Christine says, she still connected with Catholicism, although

> I went through a couple of years of really not believing. Yet I stayed attending Catholic masses at the Newman Center infrequently. It was enough to know that I was always Catholic at heart.
>
> After graduate school—I got a social work degree after college—I was living on my own and lonely, so I got myself out on Friday night to bingo at Saint Ambrose Parish and met people who are still good friends. I knew

I'd met a community. I got back involved in a parish. It was a home base, a familiar feeling. I went there for social needs, but found a lot of meaty substance that began to feed me and develop my faith again in a mature, deep, adult way. What that community gave me as a single person was important, and those are the kind of things I value in a church.

In Christine's story, we hear common themes of belonging at Saint Brigitta that touch both the bonds and boundaries of Catholic identity there. For Christine, the boundaries of Catholic identity are somewhat narrower than they are for Rick; we see this most clearly in the first of these excerpts, in which we hear Christine saying that she does not pay much attention to the institutional church and that she doesn't particularly connect to the church's tradition. But she values the church's familiarity, sociability, and spiritual resources and what these contribute to her everyday life.

Christine's perspective, one that many at Saint Brigitta share, is one that psychologist Eugene Kennedy has described as the second of two contemporary religious cultures dominant within American Catholicism. In reflections upon the post–Vatican II American church, Kennedy suggests that these two distinct cultures each contain different foci, different points of reference, and different loci of religious authority.[17] And though Kennedy speaks of these two cultures as more or less objective realities, I want to suggest instead that we understand them as Weberian ideal types that can help us characterize variation within the population of involved parishioners at both Assumption and Saint Brigitta.

According to Kennedy, Culture One Catholics can be oriented either in more progressive or more conservative variants of Catholic belief and practice, but what distinguishes them from others is an intense orientation toward and involvement with the institutional church. In fact, Kennedy says, those who minister and work within the institution are, almost by definition, Culture One Catholics. They *really* care about the church as an institution, and they work to preserve it, whether through tradition or reform.[18] They fight with one another over the content of its most authentic expressions. Culture One Catholics are present at both Assumption and Saint Brigitta. For example, Louis Beltrami's story, recounted in chapter 1, about the genesis of Saint Brigitta's preaching team and the parish's encounter with the bishop over their plan to have resigned priests preside at mass, suggest that Louis is a Culture One Catholic. Similarly, the story Assumption's Adele Dunning told in the previous section of this chapter, describing her Midwestern Catholic friends by analogy to a frog boiling in a pot, locates Adele in Culture One.

By contrast, although Culture Two Catholics are also highly connected to the church—they practice intensely, and Catholicism is deeply implicated in their identities—the institutional church matters much less to them. For Culture Two Catholics, the locus of religious authority lies within the individual, not the institution of the church. As we saw in chapter 1, at Saint Brigitta this form of authority relations is closely connected with the central image of the church as community. It is this characteristic that Christine demonstrates in her narrative and that makes her an exemplar of Culture Two Catholicism: she is deeply committed to her faith, she practices regularly, but she is not heavily involved in the Culture One Catholic world of the institutional church. By contrast with the importance of the hierarchical church in the retraditionalized practice at Assumption, this part of the church doesn't command Christine's attention or energy. For her, although Catholic worship can strike an emotional chord of faith and inspire her personally to prayer, it also evokes an image of the institutional church that she finds uninvolving and relatively irrelevant to her everyday life.

Importantly, and by contrast with some of the criticisms of Catholic churches articulated at Assumption, Catholicism is for Christine a familiar place to connect to others socially—and that sociability is not divorced from or antithetical to faith. In a way similar to Rick McNeill, Christine learned from her family of origin that she could find resources in Catholicism that pertain directly to her daily life, and this is where her church of memory is located. Although it is also the case that Assumption's parishioners find that Catholicism enriches their daily lives, the two settings tend to access different Catholic traditions, different parts of daily life, and different values surrounding the issues of everyday life that their religious practice most often addresses. Saint Brigitta's parishioners credit having learned this relation between Catholicism and everyday life in their families of origin—something that was less uniformly the case among Assumption's members.

Some at Assumption exhibit characteristics of Culture Two Catholicism, but the emphasis on church teachings at Assumption makes Culture One beliefs more central. By contrast, aspects of Culture One and Culture Two Catholicism are more mixed and varied at Saint Brigitta, and like Christine, several of the parishioners I worked with there tended more toward Culture Two perspectives. A good example of how Culture One and Culture Two perspectives are mixed, and how these perspectives are related to a church of memory whose boundaries are symbolized in worship, is Bryan O'Lear's story of belonging. In speaking about how the church of his adolescence has led to his present practice, Bryan describes feelings of ambivalence toward Catholic worship. His adolescent experience was one of

> Catholic guilt. About sex being a selfish thing, about needing to be a nice person and not be angry. There was a lot of inner conflict in me. The church was emotionally stifling around identity, about sex and anger. How do I fit the rest of myself into being a Roman Catholic?
>
> I had a sense of something deep and important here, and the Paschal Mystery deeply moved me, but it's hard to describe. I [associated ritual]

with an area of emotional and sexual repression related to the Catholic Church.

Later on, in speaking about his mother, Bryan similarly connects passion—or the lack of it—to Catholic worship. He described her as a "passionate, live-it-up kind of person" and described her perception of the big stone Gothic church his family worshipped in as a child as "cold and lifeless," a perception he shared. He explained,

> [My mother] is loose, soulful, and passionate—not stuffy, stilted, or controlled. That's often my criticism of the church. For example, religious music tends to feel sort of stuffy and insipid.
>
> I experience myself as a marginal Catholic now. But I'm a member of this local church community, part of a group of people, with whom who I feel very connected.

Bryan explicitly connects his adolescent experience of church, and worship in particular, to the emotional issues of sexuality and anger. Like Christine, Bryan expresses ambivalence—attraction, disinterest, and even repulsion—toward the aesthetics and practices of traditional worship. Experiencing the church before Vatican II as a child, he located himself as being in the first class of altar boys to shift from serving the Latin mass to the *Novus Ordo* mass in English. As a child, he internalized guilt and repression that he today connects directly to the church and understands to be symbolized in its worship. Although Catholic worship is an expression of the Paschal Mystery, and in this respect moves him deeply, Catholic ritual is for him also symbolic of repression and therefore sterile, dull, and vapid— the very opposite of life and passion. Thus he struggles between a Culture One vision of the church as containing authority and truth and the Culture Two perspective of the truths of his everyday life, his inner self, and his conscience, whose authority at times seems antithetical to the church's institutional vision. This ambivalence is characteristic of nearly all of those I worked with at Saint Brigitta.

Bryan fleshes out his struggle a bit further in describing the church of his childhood. As he told his story of belonging, Bryan described himself and his family as involved with Catholicism, even though he had "fallen away" a number of times. He and his older brothers were heavily engaged with the church, with two of them becoming priests and later leaving the priesthood. Bryan described his religious journey from the time of his youth as inner, personal, and spiritual:

> I was a devout Catholic boy, concerned with being good and with Jesus' suffering. I had that old Catholic theology of the nuns. My sins were like

pounding a nail into Jesus' hands. I was guilty a lot, going to confession. This was more mine than my parents. I didn't talk with my parents about religious or spiritual matters. I struggled on my own.

When I started high school, I would ditch mass—go, pick up a bulletin, and find a place to hide. I did it myself. I'd go to a quiet park. Eventually I "came out" to my parents. I felt guilty, but there was no big parental reaction.

I had cool teachers at the Catholic high school I attended, and I idealized them. They taught me never to throw the baby out with the bathwater, but I held the church at arm's length. I always knew I was a spiritual person, even if I wasn't participating in organized ritual.

In charting his adolescent experience of the church and his response to it, Bryan gives an account of how he currently manages the contradiction between the church of memory he adheres to and the Culture One Church with which he struggles. Sensitive and guilty as a child and rebellious as an adolescent, Bryan felt connected to the church despite his infrequent participation. Like others at Saint Brigitta, he resolved this tension by "not throwing the baby out with the bathwater," that is, by embracing what he perceives to be truest about the church, including the Paschal Mystery and a church of memory enfleshed in community, and paying less attention to aspects of its institutional authority that he perceives to be distorted or opposed to his experience of growth and feeling in everyday life.

These stories of belonging, although possessing specific elements unique to the individuals who tell them, together reflect the major themes of the stories told by parishioners at Saint Brigitta. Their stories of belonging demarcate a local culture in which Catholic identity is centered in a Culture Two Catholicism whose boundaries are drawn variously, but one that engages the institutional church in their construction—whether in strategies of inclusion that honor the diverse traditions within Catholicism or in ones that minimize or respond with ambivalence to the roles played by the institutional church. In some respects, these Catholics contain polarization in the church within their religious identities.

Bonds of Faith: Continuity with the Past in the Faith of Our Fathers (and Mothers)

The church of memory encircled in the varied boundaries of Catholic identity at Saint Brigitta is one with which only its youngest members are unfamiliar because the dominant church of memory there is the reforming church of the decade or two following Vatican II. That church of memory contains within it memories of pre–Vatican II and Vatican II generations of Catholics and also carries through younger Catholics' memories of their families of origin and their parents' stories of the church before and during the Second Vatican Council. In these ways, three generations of Catholics at Saint Brigitta are tied together in a common experiential knowledge that spans the pre- and post-Conciliar church and interprets the pre-Conciliar church through the lens of older generations' experiences of difficulty, excitement, and engagement with the reforming church. Thus, family members of different generations tend to share a common outlook on the church, agree on many of their criticisms of the church, and appreciate the faith lives of their peers and family members across generations, even when they differ from their own. Their common outlook tends to crystallize their orientations toward the church at a pole of Catholic practice opposed to that toward which parishioners at Assumption gravitate.

We see a glimpse of this church of memory and its connection to the faith of parishioners' families of origin in Rick McNeill's introductory story. Rick describes his parents as solid, faithful Catholics who passed on their appreciation and love of Catholicism to their children through education and example. Although he describes them as not being exceptionally devotional, they practiced regularly and were engaged enough with their parish to know priests who would come and say masses in their home. Rick describes a church of memory and a Catholic identity that are profoundly intertwined with those of his parents; like them, he is neither liberal nor conservative, neither devotional nor lukewarm. Like his parents, he espouses a strong faith embedded in a church that is both local and universal. And though he remembers the church on the heels of the council as strict but "softening," his criticisms of the church are rooted, not in these older images, but in the present injustices he perceives within it. Despite its problems and imperfections, he is willing to bear with the institutional church as his parents did and as do the older people with whom he works—and whose selflessness and endurance he admires. Rick's parents and their peers serve as models of forbearance with a church that has the capacity both to inspire and to disappoint and frustrate.

Some of Saint Brigitta's Culture Two Catholics spoke of learning this perspective in their families of origin. Monica Maloney-Jones, 36, told of a similar experience of her parents' sense of belonging and their relation to the church, adding an additional dimension to how the generation who experienced the church before and during Vatican II provides modeling for the post–Vatican II generation and their sense of Catholic identity. She explains her parents' influence upon her faith as follows:

> My father was married young, married for six months and then divorced. He always felt he was a good Christian, but wasn't sure if he was a good Catholic.
>
> I didn't grow up with a moralistic Catholicism. The church is an ideal, but people are human. There was never shame. My mom's a little more

into the authority thing, but their views are basically similar to mine. They think they ascribe to the church's authority, but underneath they don't really agree, especially about sexual things being sinful. My parents never talked like this.

Although she describes her father as not entirely confident of his relation to the institutional church because of the implications of his early divorce, Monica's parents practiced Catholicism regularly and sent her and her brother to Catholic schools. And like Rick, her parents dealt generously with the church in what they perceived as its strengths and weaknesses, understanding the church's moral demands as ideals that flawed human beings often fail to reach. Although tacitly accepting the institutional church's importance and authority, they yet communicated to Monica their Culture Two Catholic perspective—the assertion of an internal locus of authority, especially surrounding the church's association of sin with sexual expression in arenas other than that of marital chastity. In so doing, they, like Rick's parents, showed Monica an example of fidelity to the church through forbearance with institutional practices and teachings that did not fit well with the authority of their lived experience.

Others spoke less about parents' ability to tolerate and accept any gaps between institutional beliefs and practices and their internal sense of authority, and more about their parents' struggles or difficulties with the church during and after Vatican II. Responses of these sorts ranged from coping with disappointment to outright anger with and rejection of the institutional church. At the same time, in these patterns of response, like those previously discussed, parishioners largely identified with and drew upon their parents' experience and perspectives in explaining the trajectory of their own identities as Catholics. Beth McGivern, 36, gives one typical example in explaining her parents' differential reception of the reforming church and its relation to her own church of memory.

Growing up, parish was central to our [parents'] life—their friends were there, a community of people. They had breakfast with the other daily mass goers. I grew up with this atmosphere. As things changed, my parents held on to the conservative view, but welcomed Vatican II changes, and thought they were good, especially lay involvement and the use of English in the mass. But the changes in leadership in the church and the decline of the priesthood—they see it as a loss for the church. I think that it's not always going to be this lost situation.

In college, I came with a pretty narrow view of the church, but then I questioned everything—politics, religious views—I didn't go to church but found a different way of connecting with faith in informal masses, for instance. I was rebelling against everything and went pretty wild, but after a couple of years that was tempered. I started to connect with a group [of students] and we shared views and asked the same questions. I got hooked into campus ministry—and they taught me I didn't have to throw the baby out with the bathwater. It was helpful.

Beth's parents weathered Vatican II changes and held on to much of a perspective strongly supported by the church before Vatican II. They retain their practice of attending mass each day and staying highly involved in parish activities. They view the post-Conciliar church as a mixed bag: as involved Catholics, they welcomed the vernacular liturgy and the renewal of the laity's role but have been disappointed in church leadership—and Beth seems to agree that something important has been lost in the post-Conciliar church. Beth's parents model a way of preserving the continuity of their Catholic identities by, on the one hand, feeling entitled to take stock and evaluate the reforming church, though without rancor, and on the other hand, maintaining the devotional practices and parish involvements that are meaningful to them.

Although her parents' religious beliefs and practice are more conservative than hers, Beth doesn't criticize or dismiss their practice. And although she and her siblings rebelled against her parents and the church of her childhood, there is not a lot of negative emotion driving her words. Instead, her story is matter-of-fact and focuses on what she shares with her parents. In this way, her story emerges as one of integration of continuity and change into her Catholic identity through a church of memory largely shared with and mediated by her parents, even though she locates herself somewhat differently within that church of memory than they do.

Bryan O'Lear's description of his parents' relationship to Catholicism represents a final but still more ambivalent perspective, although it is also one that reflects continuity between their participation in Catholicism and his own. He describes his parents' faith in this way:

I always had the sense that my mom and dad were cultural Catholics. We never said grace or the rosary at home, except for holiday dinners. They've fallen away from Catholicism in old age. They are critical of the church. It started when both my brothers left the priesthood, because there were no laicizations [happening then].

They got involved at Saint Brigitta because of Lyn and me. They go to mass fairly regularly. My mom is very verbal, and critical of the pope [John Paul II], saying, "He's a disaster—why don't they get someone new?" She's indignant about patriarchy in the Catholic Church.

Bryan describes the actual practice of Catholicism in his home during childhood as less involved than that of many of his peers. And yet, he and his siblings have all had intense connections to Catholicism, even if their practice has tended to wax and wane throughout their lives. Similarly, he describes his parents as practicing in his youth and connected less regularly with the church—more or less holding it at arm's length—as they have aged. At present, they are openly frustrated with a church whose disciplines have had very concrete consequences for their family, especially because the church did not allow their sons who were priests to be laicized, thus impeding their ability to marry in the church. Moreover, Bryan's mother is frankly critical of Pope John Paul II, the institution's system of all-male leadership, and its delineation of women's roles in church and society—issues that play into larger public conflicts surrounding the family. He describes his mother as openly angry with the church. Despite this anger, Bryan's parents have not left the church, and any estrangement they may feel does not prevent them from practicing regularly. In fact, they travel to attend Sunday mass in the gym with Lyn and Bryan, and one of his brothers also attends with his wife. In the Saint Brigitta gym, principled resistance to the church coupled with regular practice can literally be a family affair.

As these narratives illustrate, the church of memory dominant at Saint Brigitta bears the impress of a historical and familial coherence through pre–Vatican II, Vatican II, and post–Vatican II generations. And while many parishioners clearly stand closer to one end of the spectrum of Catholic practice than others who strive to be closer to the center, their difficulties and disagreements with the hierarchical church locate the parish generally at one pole of ecclesial practice opposed to that espoused at Assumption, one imbricated in parishioners' stands on moral issues of cultural conflict surrounding the family. The ethic at Saint Brigitta tolerates a diversity of approaches to Catholic identity that makes room for a Culture Two sensibility that, while deeply attached to Catholicism, openly struggles with Culture One.

Conclusion

In the stories presented in this chapter, I have shown how people at Assumption and Saint Brigitta construct different Catholic identities. These narratives, of course, are retrospective constructions whose sociological significance lies in their usefulness for interpretive analysis, for understanding how their present Catholic belonging matters for their religious identities, and in comparative analysis, how identity bonds and boundaries contribute to polarizing tendencies among Catholics. In their narratives of belonging to a church, parishioners draw on distinct churches of memory whose boundaries and bonds can be identified in their criticisms of other churches or the institutional church, and stand in different relationships to their religious practice and socialization in their families or origin. In these ways, the local parish cultures in which they are embedded support and shape religiously informed worldviews that have the capacity to affect many life arenas, especially their relationships with other Catholics, and how they approach cultural conflicts about the family in the public sphere. Most Catholics would recognize the contours of Catholic identity at Assumption and Saint Brigitta as reflecting ecclesial polarization within Catholicism, especially around church authority and particular teachings about human sexuality.[19] This is, in fact, an important dividing line for understanding moral polarization surrounding the family among American Catholics. These parishes show the axes of difference in these arenas to be subtler and more complex than often portrayed.

As we have seen in these narratives, parishioners most often arrive at Assumption or Saint Brigitta with already existing religious identities previously fashioned in other contexts, such as schools, campus ministries, or other Catholic movements. For cradle Catholics, these identities are generally both ascribed and achieved; for others, their religious identities are grounded in other denominations or are generalized or seeking identities without a basis in a particular tradition. People are often attracted to these parishes because they resemble their previous religious contexts or signal an orientation to Catholicism that fits an identity crafted in other contexts. Once at Assumption or Saint Brigitta, individuals participate in religious identity processes as they maintain and fine-tune their religious identities, as well as in some cases actually constructing or reconstructing them. And people often integrate their religious identities in new ways when their life experience or life status changes.

As illustrated mainly through the example of the post–Vatican II cohorts at Assumption and Saint Brigitta, different generation units tend to be attracted to each church. The dominant church of memory in each setting is shared, but it is one most associated with a particular generation. At Assumption, the dominant church of memory, though drawing on pre-Conciliar church traditions, is a retraditionalized one particularly responsive to the concerns and experiences of the post–Vatican II generation. At Saint Brigitta, the dominant identity is one embedded within the Vatican II generation of Catholics and passed on to the next generation through a perspective that privileges continuity between the pre- and post-Conciliar church.

The variations we see in the Catholic identities between the two settings are compatible with, and perhaps even largely made possible by, the contemporary American culture of choice that these Catholics must negotiate. The cradle Catholics whose narratives we have explored reveal the lingering power of ascribed religion by showing how ascription still matters in a culture where religious authenticity entails choice. In fact, because Catholicism is a particularly well-embedded ascriptive religious identity in the United States, given its historical intertwining with ethnic, class, and gender identities, it reveals processes involving the achievement of chosen Catholic identities with particular clarity. Viewed from the perspective of the stories of arrival told at Assumption and Saint Brigitta, personal commit-ment rather than ascriptive belonging defines one's religious identity—and yet, those who tell these stories also closely link their commitments to ascribed aspects of their religious histories. Thus they fashion achieved identities "chosen" from Catholicism's rich storehouse of traditions. These choices, which we shall explore more deeply in part II of this book, have consequences that are not trivial but are often profoundly implicated in the shape of their families' trajectories and daily routines.

PART TWO

The Families

3

Marriage

Our Lady of the Assumption
Assumption Church, a Tuesday in February at 7:00 p.m.
It is a Lenten meeting of the Assumption Young Adults Group,
and about 40 young men and women pray at a benediction ser-
vice in the church to begin the evening. When the prayer is fin-
ished, the group convenes in a rectory meeting room for dinner
and the evening's speaker. The long rectangular room is arranged
with a table and lectern across one long side and rows of folding
chairs placed opposite the lectern all the way to the back wall.
Young adults gradually fill the room, greeting one another and
conversing. A few at a time, men and women walk to the room
next door, where a simple buffet dinner is laid out. They come
back with food and drink.

After dinner, we crowd into rows of chairs to hear the evening's
presenter, Chris Schweickert. Tall and thin, Chris is tonight
dressed formally; he wears creased khaki pants, a dress shirt, and
a tie. One of the leaders of the Young Adult Group introduces him,
highlighting his involvement as a parishioner at Assumption, his
roles as husband and father of four, and his educational work
with an organization promoting church doctrine on human sex-
uality. Tonight Chris is speaking about marriage and Catholic
teachings on contraception. As he begins, some in the audience
pull out their day planners and begin to take notes.

Chris is an engaging speaker who lacks the reserve characteristic
of parishioners at Assumption. He speaks frankly about mar-
riage and sex, beginning by saying, "Contraception is an ancient
practice, one that has always been prohibited by the church—not
because people shouldn't plan their families, but because of the
nature of men and women, and of sex and marriage."

He presents the reasons the Catholic Church continues to pro-
hibit artificial contraception as "against human nature," even
after decades of argument from high-profile Catholic theologians,
entreaty from laity, and the doctrine's rejection by most American

Catholics. Chris tells the group that Pope John XXIII established a commission to study the issue of birth control in 1959 and explains why, in 1967, Pope Paul VI accepted the commission's minority report instead of the majority report that recommended allowing artificial contraception. "Humanae Vitae," he asserts, "rejects artificial methods of contraception because they are violations of the procreative nature of sex."[1]

He explains. "Basically, our nature, the nature of human beings, is to be self-giving, like Christ. In marriage, sex has the meaning of self-giving with one's spouse, and the openness to give life to children. Because of human nature, and the nature of marriage, every sex act should be open to the creation of new life. To have sexual intercourse the way human beings were meant to, without artificial contraception—to do this is to recognize that it is God's prerogative to decide when a new life will begin and when it will not. Every child deserves to be conceived by an act that is open to its life, not an act that humans have tried deliberately to thwart. "The church recognizes that the purpose of sex is not solely the creation of children, but also the fostering of intimacy between husband and wife in self-donation. In the Theology of the Body,[2] Pope John Paul talks about sexuality as intrinsic to human nature." Chris quotes from Genesis. "'In the divine image he created them, male and female he created them'[3]—we are created as sexual beings," he asserts, "in God's image."

Chris explains that natural family planning[4] is allowed by the church, since it works with human nature and doesn't thwart it. He says, "Married couples should make decisions about planning their families; they just shouldn't use artificial contraception to do so. At the same time, there are good and bad reasons for planning children and limiting family size. Wanting to have three SUVs or a houseboat are bad reasons for putting off having children! Psychological or economic limits in families might be good reasons for limiting family size."

A brief discussion ensues. A few men in the audience challenge the notion that married couples should plan their families at all. One asks, "Don't you mean that couples should have grave reasons for limiting the number of children they have? That is what the catechism says."[5] Chris replies that the unofficial version of the catechism says "grave," but the catechism's final translation from Latin does not use the word grave. It says "just," acknowledging that couples can have good reasons for family planning.

Chris goes on. *"I want to be clear,"* he says, *"that the church doesn't teach that contraception is wrong because of its effects, but because of what it is: a violation of human nature. But contraception does have negative effects!"* Chris appeals to his audience's experiences of social disintegration of the family—divorce, child abuse, abortion—and suggests that these are some of contraception's effects. *"It increases divorce, it increases adultery, it destroys the fabric of intimacy between husband and wife! All these things are rooted in the 'contraceptive mentality.' Don't we see these things around us? Don't we know this to be true in our experience?"*

Chris acknowledges that he fights an uphill battle in promoting the church's teachings about contraception and explains how life experience convinced him that the church's teachings were indeed the truth. He tells his personal story: how he rejected Catholicism in college and how it was through the practice of natural family planning with his wife that he returned to the church. Eventually, Chris explained, the practice of natural family planning increased their *"openness to life,"* and he and June began to desire more children. *"I have a special love for my two-year old son, Zachary, and my baby on the way,"* Chris explains, *"because they owe their lives to my becoming a Christian and being convinced of the truth of the church's teaching on contraception."*

He moves on to talk about the quality and character of Christian marriage as a relationship of self-giving to one another and to one's children. He picks up the Bible he has brought with him. Opening it, he quotes Ephesians 5: *"Wives, be submissive to your husbands, as to the Lord.... Husbands, love your wives, as Christ loved the Church...."*[6]

As Chris reads this passage, the group's mood shifts; the audience still listens attentively but becomes tense and silent. Some women put on poker faces. Others visibly strive to repress emotion. Still others are not quite so circumspect; several women dressed in business attire look at one another and collectively roll their eyes. Sensing the tension, Chris acknowledges that in these times it is not politically correct to talk about this passage of scripture. Then he perseveres to make his point. *"Our Holy Father uses this scripture,"* he says, *"to point us toward a spiritual way to think about marriage."* As he speaks, he shifts his language away from the controversial discourse of submission and onto the more familiar terrain of conjugal love and sacrifice.

Several women's faces soften. As the young adults meander through the topic of sacrifice in intimate relationships, the turbulence of the previous moment gradually recedes. It is not mentioned again.

Saint Brigitta
The Maloney-Joneses' residence, a morning in early December,
10:00 a.m.
On a bright day at the beginning of the winter, I fought rush-hour traffic to get to Monica Maloney-Jones's house for a mid-morning interview. When I arrived, Monica opened the front door looking as if she had hurried to reach it and yet appeared prepared and professional. She was neatly dressed in slacks and a sweater, and her shoulder-length sandy hair had been tamed to frame her oval face and hide a brow often creased in concentration.
Monica greets me with a smile, and she shows me around her newly remodeled home as we chat. Monica and John have two young boys, but Daniel, who is seven, is at school this morning, and John left the house a short time ago with five-year-old Sean. The house is quiet. After we walk through her home, Monica invites me into her living room. The furniture is casual and ample, with dark wood frames hewn in simple lines and stuffed with big cushions. Monica settles her slight frame into the sofa. I take a seat, turn on the recorder, and place it between us on an armchair. Animated and articulate, she begins her story. She talks about her family of origin and her childhood, narrating the journey that has brought her to this urban home, her marriage to John, the family she has created with him, and her career as a psychotherapist.
Monica speaks of the extended family that surrounded her as a child and about parents who were practical, caring, and unfailingly supportive. The Catholic Church figures prominently in the story she tells. She distinguishes her family's perception of the church from that of other families she knows, explaining that she grew up without the "moralizing" Catholicism she perceived in many of her peers' families and that her parents understood the church as holding up ideals for people to reach.
Monica describes her parents' hard work and her family's eventual economic success. She takes a moment to talk about the Catholic high school she attended, where she ranked second in her class and where she "did a lot of volunteer work, with a lot of nuns. In high school, it was kind of cool to go to mass, just like it was at Georgetown." Then she enthusiastically describes her

college years as a time of life that she still considers to be pivotal in how her future has taken shape. She went to Georgetown as a pre-med student, intending to be a doctor, and also pursued a second major in English; eventually, she decided on a career in psychology instead of medicine.

Monica met John in college. She found him attractive then, but they didn't start dating until they reconnected when they were both doing volunteer work after college. They were drawn to one another by their common passion to do religiously meaningful work in service to others. Even today, they integrate that passion into their marriage by creating space for each of them to pursue careers animated by service: Monica works part-time as a psychotherapist, and John does ministry-related work for a local university.

Monica describes how she and John still work to structure their lives with the religious principles that inspired their work and their relationship in earlier years. Now that they have children, they self-consciously try to define their familial roles in ways that allow them both to pursue careers. The group of friends surrounding them at Saint Brigitta considers their arrangement to be ideal. "Me and John are fighters," she says. "It's how we resolve things. We negotiate, like, everything! In some ways, if there are definite sex role stereotypes, some things are easier. You don't have to negotiate everything. But at this point, I think I'm happy with our negotiation. A lot of our friends look at us and think we probably do share more things in terms of child care [than we actually do]—they think we have this great thing worked out. But they don't realize how much we fought about it.

We were the first in our cohort to have kids, so my friends didn't have children. That was hard.

"This is an interesting time because we're getting back to our roots in the last two years or so. We met as Jesuit Volunteers and worked at the Catholic Worker House together. We were in love with changing the world, as well as being in love with each other. We felt that we were where we were supposed to be. It was hard, but it felt very alive."

She contrasts her marriage to John with their parents' marriages. "Now that we have kids, we make a point of going out to the movies or dinner together. Recently we went for a weekend away, just the two of us. We also do wholesome stuff as a family, like going out to dinner with the kids. We do that a lot.

"Our parents both sacrificed their relationships for the good of the kids; neither couple has been good tenders of their marriages. Their primary mission in life was their children. I don't feel that way. I think about what we're going to do when they're gone. John and I are very companionable. When we get away, we get along; we like to do the same kind of things."

Catholic Marriages: Constructing Coupled Intimacy

The stories told by Chris Schweickert and Monica Maloney-Jones in these vignettes create two different portraits of married life that exemplify some of the dominant beliefs and practices surrounding marriage at Assumption and Saint Brigitta. These contrasting styles of married life are significant because they reflect local cultures of marriage in the two settings—cultures that, though containing some similarities, reveal fundamental differences in how marriage relationships as the substrate of family life are to be envisioned and constructed. In this chapter, I analyze these different styles of married life and show how they are supported and shaped by social processes involving the enactment of central ecclesial metaphors and constitution of Catholic identities. In so doing, I show how these two models of marriage contain opposed ways of understanding and practicing love, intimacy, and gender relations and how these differences help to constitute cultural conflicts about the family among Catholics.

My aim in this chapter is to elaborate these different understandings of marriage by identifying and explaining the particular ways in which Catholicism contributes to them.[7] At Our Lady of the Assumption, marriage is tightly coupled with church teachings concerning human sexuality, especially those prohibiting artificial contraception. As we see in Chris's talk to Assumption's young adults, this understanding of marital intimacy is grounded in sexual expression and necessarily honors its procreative potential. The project of marriage and marital identities in this setting, moreover, are fundamentally constituted around family life. The parish supports this understanding of marriage, as well as the retraditionalized gender relations that spouses tend to practice, in its central self-image as a family and in social relations and identities that affirm the church's role to teach authoritatively about sexual intimacy. By contrast, although the project of marriage at Saint Brigitta also involves family, couples instead tend to ground marital intimacy in romantic love, on the one hand, and in actively forging equal partnerships through negotiating roles and tasks in everyday life, on the other. These negotiations are frequently shaped by couples' desires to accomplish outer-directed and religiously informed work in a career or other service activities, desires that were often initially animated in them through experiences of lay empowerment and vocation in post–Vatican II church settings. This style of marriage practice draws principles and skills from Saint Brigitta's central metaphor of the church as community. An emphasis on autonomous authority relations supports a loose coupling between church teachings and marital sexuality and the compartmentalization of sexuality in the private sphere.

How, concretely, does parish life matter to the distinctiveness of these plural Catholic marriage patterns? As the contrast in these styles of marriage suggests, the analyses in this chapter reveal that the organization and meanings of marriage at Assumption and Saint Brigitta are related to their different styles of organizing the church, which we have previously observed in their worship, in patterns of parish discourse, and in parishioners' self-understandings of Catholic belonging. In addition, the ways in which the affinities between the logics of church and marriage play out in these settings is significantly shaped by two larger contexts, which I discuss next: first, recent sociocultural and economic changes in the organization of marriage and family in the United States, and second, previous patterns of marriage and family life among Catholics that inform present patterns. These contexts are mediated differently at Assumption and Saint Brigitta and therefore are important for explaining how Catholicism supports and shapes both the domestic politics of marriage and its relation to polarizing tendencies surrounding the family in public politics.

The Individualized Ideal of Marriage and Family Change

As Chris's and Monica's stories illustrate, the most pervasive contemporary concern surrounding marriage for men and women at Assumption and Saint Brigitta is one they share with their peers generally: they must negotiate intimate relationships in a societal context where definitions and norms surrounding marriage are in flux. This larger context comprises a climate in which commonsense understandings and social supports for marriage prevalent in earlier decades—including father-breadwinner and mother-homemaker gender roles, the indissolubility of marriage, and the stigma upon divorce—are publicly and privately contested.[8] The norm of heterosexual marriage is itself contested, as intimate relationships take a plurality of forms. Cohabitation, both as a transition to marriage and as a lifestyle choice, has become commonplace. Same-sex relationships are more socially accepted than in previous generations.[9] In response to these widespread social changes, some people have recovered traditional notions of marriage; others simply dismiss them as remnants of a bygone era. And at the same time as the models and meanings of marriage are being transformed, couples today generally have higher expectations for relational intimacy than those of their parents' generation. By contrast with those married even a generation or two ago, today's couples take for granted a richly intimate partnership as a marital ideal and an intense marital work ethic as a way to achieve such a partnership.[10]

In analyzing these changes in marriage, some scholars have observed that the new pluralism in family life is linked to the structures of coupled intimacy in what scholars term *companionate* and *individualized* forms of marriage; others more sharply distinguish this pluralism as an outgrowth of individualized marriage. According to Andrew Cherlin, companionate marriage is constituted by father-breadwinner and mother-homemaker roles and values couples' emotional satisfaction.[11] This model of marriage reached its zenith in the 1950s. Along with Judith Stacey, Robert Bellah and his colleagues, and others, he observes that the companionate presuppositions of marriage, which initially developed with modernity, helped to construct the modern nuclear family.[12] But as Stacey observes, the contradictions inherent in its premises weakened its structure: the importance of couples' emotional satisfaction entailed voluntary commitment, and the fragility of that commitment implied the necessity of divorce; its structure separated young families from kin; and marriage became less anchored in patterned roles and social institutions. It is more or less taken for granted that in this ideal, what people hope for in intimate relationships is based on the sharing of autonomous individuals—what Bellah calls a "therapeutic ideal of love"—in freedom, not obligation, and based on the assertion of authentic selves.[13]

People's talk of romantic love is likewise based on this ideal of the intimacy of autonomous selves, but as Ann Swidler points out, Americans are ambivalent about romantic love.[14] They often argue against romantic meanings of love and emphasize the prosaic qualities of intimate relationships, but they also commonly apply the trope of romantic love to marriage, especially to explain lasting marriages. Swidler asserts that this ambivalence arises from a social structure where marriage is a "yes or no" ideal and an enduring commitment, but one that is difficult to maintain. According to Cherlin, Paul Amato, and others, this is precisely the bind in which contemporary couples find themselves, and it signals the emergence of individualized or "soulmate" marriage, whose primary emphasis is on emotional intimacy and expression, self-development, and personal fulfillment.[15] Individualized marriage prizes these above—and sometimes at the cost of—marital permanence.

Versions of this narrative of companionate marriage and its transition to individualized marriage are told by scholars who often disagree about the best answers to contemporary public contests and questions over marriage. How much normative value do we give to the permanence of marriage, in the presence of plural family forms and the real difficulties people experience in marriage? What is, and what should be, the legacy of the companionate model of marriage for the significance of gender roles and relations in marriage today? These are key moral questions for society, the academy, and churches, as well as for married couples—and they are played out in different ways among Assumption's and Saint Brigitta's Catholics. In the first part of the following analysis, I argue that each parish responds to these questions by religiously transforming individualized and companionate models of marriage. In so doing, they at once distinguish these models from and mesh them with religious meanings and practices, just as couples blend narratives of prosaic and romantic love predominant in the broader culture with religious meanings of intimacy. Thus each church redefines spousal love in religious terms but in different ways.

Religious Responses to Changing Family Contexts

A second significant context that helps to shape marriage patterns at Assumption and Saint Brigitta is that of U.S. Catholic history, especially the recent history of marriage patterns among Catholics.[16] The Catholic tradition has shaped and supported particular patterns of marriage in previous historical eras and now provides a legacy from which contemporary Catholics draw, intentionally or unintentionally—often through their experiences in parish settings and in their families of origin. This context is of particular importance in shaping and informing gender relations and sexuality in Catholics' contemporary marriage patterns.

Recent historical studies of Catholics have shown the importance of the legacy of Catholic teachings and practices regarding marital sexuality and intimacy. Leslie Tentler chronicles an important piece of this history in *Catholics and Contraception*, detailing how a positive theology of marriage promoted through pre-Cana programs, the Cana Conference, and the Christian Family Movement (CFM) in the post–World War II United States both supported the church's teachings prohibiting contraception and unintentionally highlighted their difficulty for Catholic couples as they formed and raised families.[17] These movements celebrated the vocation of marriage as sanctified, the symbolic and practical ideal of spousal self-donation in sexual expression, and the self-giving of the noncontracepting couple in their openness to children. Fertility was high among couples in these groups in the post–World War II years, and as Tentler explains, couples participating in Cana and CFM either embraced natalism or struggled with their excess fertility, with the latter response leading to arguments from experience by married couples for the moral rightness of limiting family size through contraception. These arguments were rejected by Pope Paul VI in *Humanae Vitae* but were largely accepted by American Catholics.

Equally important to understanding contemporary marriage practice among Catholics is how particular gender roles and relations in marriage have been religiously supported historically. For example, Ann Taves has shown how prayer books promoted and supported the ideal of the devoted, pious mother and her role as religious educator in the Victorian household.[18] Kathleen Cummings has shown how Catholic women—married, single, and religious—responded to the "new woman" of the progressive era with the model of the "true Catholic woman,"

who combined women's self-assertion into the public sphere with more traditional religious notions of womanhood and domesticity.[19] And Robert Orsi has
shown how early-20th century Marian devotions in Italian Harlem shaped and
constrained women's roles vis-à-vis their husbands, as well as how devotions to
saints such as Saint Jude and Saint Gemma Galgani helped women cope with
mid-20th century gender role constraints.[20] These and other studies show how
U.S. Catholicism has responded to historical trends in gender relations through
processes that both incorporated women's changing roles in American society
and brought elements of Catholicism's traditions and teachings into dialogue with
changes in women's societal positions.

Because marriage practices are fundamentally concerned with intimacy and
identity, these Catholic legacies are emotionally laden and symbolically rich
ground where connections between domestic and public politics are anchored.
In what follows, I explore how teachings on human sexuality and their historical
legacies of lay response today play crucial but often ambivalent roles in Catholic
marriages, as do practices surrounding gender. In the second part of each analysis, I examine how each parish interprets and responds to church teachings about
premarital sex, contraception, and divorce, revealing subtle but important differences in how Catholicism figures in marriage at Assumption and Saint Brigitta—
ones that are in several respects opposed to one another in ways that constitute
moral polarization among Catholics.

Marriage at Assumption: A Redemptive Partnership in a Sinful World

Chris Schweickert, in the talk to the Young Adult Group described at the beginning of this chapter, reveals how understandings of marriage at Assumption are
intertwined with Catholic doctrine, especially with church teachings on human
sexuality that prohibit artificial contraception. This doctrine plays a particularly
important role in Catholic identities at Assumption. Teachings on contraception constitute a linchpin for religious meanings of love and marriage in two
distinct ways.

First, they are a part of a web of religious understandings that redefine secular notions of love and ideals of marriage in ways that are distinctively Catholic.
Sexual expression is given particular importance in marriage, both practically
and symbolically, not only as a primary site for human happiness in its capacity to unite couples but also as creating the possibility for the work of spiritual
redemption to take place in families and in the church. Significantly, since in this
view the integrity of sexual expression is threatened by contemporary societal
attitudes and practices, it is also an arena where problems are often perceived
to arise for young adults as they seek intimate relationships. Church teachings

create a strong impress upon identities at Assumption because these perceptions of sexuality, itself a dimension of human existence central to social identity, are tightly coupled with bodily existence, interpersonal intimacy, and what it means to be human.

Second, teachings about contraception are a particularly important aspect of Assumption's integration of church teachings because, according to parishioners, adherence to them is a "litmus test for orthodoxy" and thus a crucial practice around which group boundaries are drawn and identities constituted. We saw in Chris's talk that the importance of this teaching is intertwined both with life experience and with strong institutionally oriented authority relations in a retraditionalized church family. Crucially, this teaching is also central to Assumption's model of marriage. It helps to shape an understanding of marriage that prizes prosaic love and permanence. Assumption's integration of church teachings on contraception is consistent with its central ecclesial metaphor, coherent with parishioners' responses to living its consequences—which include an increased desire for children and the possibility of unintended pregnancies—and consistent with their responses to other aspects of church sexual teachings, which concretely define their Catholic identities in everyday life. Moreover, as they prescribe conditions for moral sexual intercourse, teachings about contraception also tend to privilege particular gender relations for men and women.

Stories of Marital Intimacy: Sexual Expression and Forging Partnerships

At Assumption, parishioners' narratives of love and marriage were often interwoven with explanations of how church teachings about marriage and sexuality helped them find satisfying and enduring partnerships or solve problems of relational intimacy. The religious definition of marriage entwined with these teachings is one in which sexual intimacy is the paradigmatic expression of married love, and in this respect, we might consider it part of the private sphere, if not individualized. But because marital intimacy is grounded in its God-given purpose in the establishment of family life—the couple as embodying the potential to have children—this model of marriage is an integral part of the dialogic relationship between families and the image of the church as a family and is in this respect institutionally oriented.

Julia Flaherty's story of young adulthood and marriage exemplifies the importance of sexual expression in married love and how the church's prohibition of artificial contraception plays a role in a definition of marriage at Assumption that is quite different from secular models. She told a story about problems with sexual intimacy encountered during her young adulthood and how, in her search for a solution to these problems, she also recovered her Catholic roots.

Julia, 37, began her story by describing her Midwestern upbringing, the Catholic family in which she was raised, and the importance of her educational experiences at a girls' Catholic high school. She explained that as a young adult, she grew distant from the Catholic Church after finding herself confused by discussions at her upper-middle-class parish that appeared to dismiss church teachings. She said, "You know, I did not know that my faith was fragile. I just thought maybe they changed things and I didn't know about it....I thought if I prayed enough I would get this. But I ended up falling away."

At the same time, Julia was not satisfied with her job. She was working as an economic analyst in a world of young adult professionals where she felt she did not fit, either personally or professionally.

> I started my job along with another Catholic girl from the Midwest. She slept around all over the place, and her career just absolutely skyrocketed. And she was really good at what she did....I could see that my career was not going that well....I just wasn't cut out for the job that I was doing, and as hard as I tried I was never going to be good at it. And that was humiliating for me.

She began to reevaluate both her professional life and her personal relationships. Julia wanted to find a relationship that would lead to marriage, and she wanted to have children. She was dating someone, but she felt conflicted about that relationship, especially about its sexual dimension. She explained,

> Things were getting hot and heavy with my boyfriend. And then he had a condom. And that was it—okay, well then, there's no reason not to do this. And I didn't feel right about it, but he wouldn't have a relationship if there was no sex. And so there [was] just a real tearing at my soul.
>
> When I was with him, the condom broke a couple of times. I was advised by this doctor friend of his just to get a D and C and not tell anybody that it was for abortifacient purposes and not for female problems. I'd never cried so much....Here I was, a shell of a person, and I thought, What does this guy want? He wants me for sex, he doesn't care about me as a person.

It was around this time that a friend, Sam, introduced Julia to Catholics involved in Opus Dei. At first she told Sam that she wasn't really interested. But eventually, Julia said, Sam "opened up this world of intelligent Catholics that I'd never met [before], people that *read* things. I never knew about *Crisis* magazine or *First Things* or the Liturgy of the Hours, and so it was a really great experience." This group gave her needed support when she decided to break up with her boyfriend and played a large role in Julia's reconciliation to the church.

She eventually met her husband, John, through this Catholic group. In choosing John, she chose a different kind of relationship than the one that had previously caused her so much pain and internal conflict. Julia and John found that they shared not only a common faith but also common expectations of love and marriage. In embracing church teachings about love, sex, and marriage, she found a way of living out intimate relationships that was profoundly different from that of the young adult professional world in which she moved. She explains that she now experiences church teachings on human sexuality as truths because

> Contraception is perceived by so many women as being a real liberating thing, because it addresses so many problems. They don't want to have kids, they think kids are commodities….[But] if you practice natural family planning, your husband's respecting who you are. I don't think that women are cherished if you're expected to be sexually available [all the time]. If you're not going to be open to life. So I just think there's a real integrity in the Catholic faith.

In explaining why she now accepts church teachings on human sexuality, Julia argues both against artificial contraception and for a married love that cherishes women by respecting their fertility. Linking the satisfaction in her marriage to the practice of NFP, she affirms the Catholic teaching that sexual expression belongs only in marriage and, correlatively, the crucial role of sexual intimacy in creating marital intimacy.

For Julia, then, finding a good marriage was the result of finding Catholics who introduced her to a Catholicism that was partly familiar from her youth and partly new to her. In the process, she was able to make personally persuasive connections between her experiences of difference from her professional peers, career dissatisfaction, desire for family, and religious heritage—welding these into a newly coherent and fundamentally religious sense of identity. Her embrace of church sexual teachings prohibiting premarital sex and the story of her reversion constitute a trenchant critique of the young adult world in which she moved. Her story specifically links these mores to career success and failure: though she was not doing well in her career, another Catholic woman who "slept around all over the place" did much better. And in her practice of NFP with John, she finds a satisfying married love that confirms the rightness of observing church teachings. Julia's account is not merely an explanation of how she got from her young adulthood to her present family life; it is also a moral tale and a conversion story that makes experiential arguments for adherence to Catholic teachings on human sexuality. Through a recovery of her religious faith, Julia resolved problems of negotiating competing societal models of intimate relationships. Thus, the retraditionalized Catholicism she practices has provided "old" answers to contemporary problems of intimate partnerships. They cement Julia's reversion to a new and strongly held Catholic identity.

Julia's story is typical of those told at Assumption in some important respects, especially in its critique of the secular world and contemporary sexual norms. It illustrates concretely how the church's teachings on human sexuality are involved in parishioners' Catholic identities: through both experiential and intellectual rationales, Julia has come to affirm these teachings, which most Catholics reject and which many "reverts" at Assumption also rejected before reclaiming Catholicism. Julia's story also vividly illustrates the power of retraditionalized Catholicism's marriage practice: because it is so intricately tied to the practices of the sexual self and desires for lasting spousal partnerships, these identity narratives have emotional power for those who tell them and for those who find resonance in their narrators' desires.

Moreover, because the rejection of artificial contraception, the practice of NFP, and an attitude of openness to life have religious authority in this milieu, parishioners perceive them as a countercultural but viable way to form and sustain family life and as supplying a firm ground for the permanence of their commitments. Even if, as Chris implied at the young adults meeting recounted at the beginning of this chapter, all young adults drawn to the parish might not share them fully or may contest some of their details and implications, these perceptions were widely shared at Assumption.

This way of conceptualizing love and marriage is countercultural not only in the content of its sexual practices but also in the ways in which couples perceive and express married love. Although married couples grounded their intimacy in a religious understanding of sexual expression, they tended not to talk about romantic love—which forms an important dimension of interpersonal intimacy in the broader culture, even though, as Ann Swidler notes, American couples approach romance with ambivalence.[21] To be sure, this relative absence of a focus on romance at Assumption did not indicate an absence of affection; in interviews, couples often expressed affection nonverbally or talked appreciatively of one another—acts that were far from the dispositions of reserve parishioners displayed publicly at church. But they told stories of romantic love or courtship only rarely, instead more often talking about prosaic love in marriage. Why is it that couples at Assumption talked so rarely about romantic love in marriage, which Americans so often use to explain why their marriages last and which appears to be compatible with, and even complementary to, its firm grounding in sexual expression?

In answering this question, it is important to observe that "true" notions of married love at Assumption were often explicitly contrasted with romantic love, which was perceived as a problematic basis for marriage. In a lecture given to the Young Adult Group about the sacrament of marriage, Father Bernard Cabot, a visiting priest, illustrates how Assumption's couples come to understand the experience of romantic love as an insufficient foundation for marriage.

> Love is not a feeling. Love is self-giving. It's self-donation. Two people become one. That means that people in marriages should not do their own thing, because they become one. They are a community in marriage. This is [one] reason [why] marriage is indissoluble.
>
> Feelings of love aren't the goal of marriage; in fact, sometimes they can be distracting. Real love is love for a lifetime, or it was never love to begin with. Unless you can commit yourself to another person—unless you know that you can love this person for a lifetime—it cannot be a marriage. That is the nature of marriage.
>
> It is a misunderstanding, that Paul says that marriage is a remedy for concupiscence. Rather, marriage is a healing of humanity itself, with its pledge of self-giving love. This is something a person can do only for one other person.

Father Cabot articulates several aspects of an understanding of marriage and married love that, in fact, conflict with common understandings of romantic love. First, this understanding of married love reflects back to the mid-20th-century theology of marriage that grounded the pronatalism of the 1950s: married love is about self-giving, especially sexual self-giving to one another and a couple's openness to the possibility of creating a new life. Thus, love is not about romance, but fundamentally about self-donation and procreation. Second, in this definition of love as self-giving, real love is profoundly prosaic. Third, love is defined as a commitment enacted toward others in everyday life: at its root, it is not a feeling about another person. Father Cabot goes so far as to say that feelings can distract from loving another person. Therefore, romance alone can only be an illusion of love, since love requires a lifelong commitment. The fact that marriage is a "community" precludes individualizing behaviors, that is, partners "doing their own thing." Importantly, by this definition of love, the model of individualized marriage is *not* marriage, since it does not require that love last a lifetime. And in rejecting individualized marriage, parishioners at Assumption establish a boundary that delineates their Catholic identities against others who practice this model of marriage.

This identity boundary is profoundly emotional, in that lifelong commitment in marriage is a church teaching in which Assumption's Catholics firmly believe and one that married couples (and those who hope to marry) seek to accomplish in their lives. Moreover, the lack of social supports for marriage in the broader culture, which makes achieving this ideal difficult, heightens anxiety regarding the prospect of divorce. As we have seen, Assumption provides multiple supports for marriage in the very self-image of the parish, in the structure of its social relations, and in its authoritative teachings. These supports are at least in part a response to perceived secular threats to marriage and the family, which parishioners experience in the circumstances of their lives and those of friends and family. Most involved parishioners have been married only once, but some have been divorced, and some have divorced parents. In fact, the parish as a whole comes close to mirroring the plurality of intimate relationships found in American society broadly; Father James explained that he and Father Aidan encounter many cohabiting couples and marriages where partners have been previously married and divorced. Much of his work involves assisting couples by "regularizing" marriages—that is, helping couples take the steps needed for sacramental marriage—and at the same time safeguarding the sacrament and providing support for marriage in parish programs.[22] Despite these efforts, the realities of divorce were a subject of particular anxiety among parishioners. This anxiety surfaced during Father Cabot's talk about marriage, when nearly all of the questions after his presentation were about divorce, annulments, and the causes of failed marriages. The questions asked showed great concern about the tenuousness of marital commitments in society generally and how the causes of instability in marriage affected their own marriage prospects.

A story told by Steve Donigan, who was in the audience for Father Cabot's lecture, vividly illustrates both the depth of the reach of marital failure among parishioners' family and friends and the energy and anxiety with which young adults approach their own prospects for a successful marriage. During a conversation with Steve, we discovered that we had a common acquaintance, Jan Smith, who had been actively involved in the pro-life movement. Steve said, "It was so sad, what happened to her, her husband just left...." After Jan and her husband married, they had one child, and then she became pregnant with a second. The pregnancy was difficult, and doctors determined that the baby had a fatal birth defect. Doctors recommended a medical abortion, but believing that abortion for any reason was immoral, Jan chose to carry the child to term. At birth, the child died, and she and her husband grieved. A few years later, Jan once again grieved when her husband asked her for a divorce. Steve expressed consternation, saying, "It's scary, that can happen to someone like Jan." I responded, "It's difficult to think that divorce could happen to a person as good as Jan," and Jim said,

> Yes, that's my concern! I think faith is really important in sustaining a marriage, and if two people share their faith, you're less likely to get divorced. And I would not choose to marry someone who was not as committed as me. But I hope I would know someone well enough to see them clearly.

Jan's experience was consequential for Steve and his friends at Assumption because in their eyes, her decision to carry the baby to term was both morally right and heroic. Her husband had stood by her, and to all appearances, theirs was a model of a good marriage—and yet, her marriage failed, and she had no choice in its ending. Young adults at Assumption therefore worry about the difficulty of sustaining marriages despite their belief that religious faith gives them a better chance of success than otherwise. In this uncertain marriage culture, the stakes are especially high, and they search for knowledge and skills that will help them make wise choices and build solid relationships that will last in a society where divorce is common.

In so doing, they explicitly reject narrowly individualistic perspectives in marriage while affirming the institutional grounding of marriage in the church. But they also appeal to the authority of one's experience, an individualized act, as justifying evidence for the rightness of this perspective. Thus, although marriage at Assumption rejects the individualized model of marriage, it brings along with it some individualizing assumptions and practices from the broader culture. In addition, in arguing for the authority of church teachings on the basis of their life experiences, couples at Assumption helped to shape, and even subtly reinterpret, the significance of these teachings, their meaning, and their practice—for in this local discourse, these teachings are no longer solely grounded in church authority or official doctrinal logics; they are also grounded in the variability and multivocality of life experience. On the one hand, this discourse invests these teachings with more authority, since the sources of authority for them are now dual. On the other hand, life experience and its interpretation are more mutable sources for religious authority than hierarchy and logic, and they potentially introduce the capacity for variation and change. Nonetheless, the principles on which this vision of marriage is grounded—in authority centered in the church and experientially confirmed, and in a critique of romantic love as insufficient for marriage that affirms a religiously informed prosaic love—establishes marriage in an institutional model that helps to constitute one pole in cultural conflicts about the family.

Marriage and Catholic Doctrine: Gender, Sexuality, and Orthodoxy

Following church teachings on marital sexuality both helps to constitute Catholic identities at Assumption concretely and places particular constraints on married couples. First, eschewing artificial contraception necessitates that couples deal with constraints in the possibility of unintended pregnancy. Second, as the meanings of love and marriage intertwined with these teachings are defined in dialogic tension with models of marriage in the broader culture, they further constitute Catholic identities in gender relations that focus on maternal and paternal roles. The rejection of contraception and the sacralization of gender roles are, in fact, concrete sites where the religious culture of marriage at Assumption not only

supports particular ways of everyday life among families there but also often significantly shapes them. In so doing, these practices strengthen the particularity of
parishioners' religious identities around one pole in cultural conflicts about the
family, with their adherence to church teachings on human sexuality and especially abortion constituting an identity boundary with others.

Unintended pregnancy and providence

The acceptance of Catholic teachings prohibiting artificial contraception has definite consequences for family life, with the capacity to shape couples' trajectories in
very particular ways.[23] When a couple practices NFP, routines such as taking and
charting a woman's basal body temperature makes women and men aware of their
sexuality and fertility every day; those who spoke about such practices emphasized
their capacity to improve a couple's communication and increase their awareness
of the sexual dimension of their relationship. But deciding not to practice artificial contraception also shapes marital partnerships with an acute awareness of
the possibility of having to accept and adjust to some of life's unexpected turns,
especially those involved in childbearing. Thus adhering to church teachings on
contraception can both circumscribe lives and open up heretofore untried possible ways of living. Husbands and wives adjust themselves to the possibility of
unintended pregnancy, as well as to the idea that one or both of them may come to
desire more children as a result of being "open to life." These couples live with the
relative uncertainty of not depending on contraceptive methods that allow couples
to feel a greater degree of control over when and how often they will be pregnant.
This can provoke worry, but Assumption's religious milieu also provides spiritual
attitudes, habits, and disciplines that couples use to cope with this uncertainty.

Pam Williams articulates the uncertainties involved in practicing NFP and how
she and Rob cope with them:

> When I had my third kid I really started thinking about it [NFP] because
> I realized, I didn't know whether we would be able to stop at three. When
> I got pregnant with the fourth I got really depressed. Rob was convinced
> [that we should use NFP] and I said okay, we'll try it, and I got pregnant the
> second month we were using it. I thought, how are we going to do this? It
> was the worst time to get pregnant, [with Rob] right between jobs, but luck-
> ily everything worked out. In a way, it's been a lot of this "abandonment to
> divine providence" thing.
>
> [MEK] It wasn't that you and Rob wanted a lot of children?
>
> Not at all. We never talked about it. I've always loved big families,
> though. Both my parents came from big families. We're lucky. Rob's got
> this job that pays well, and we haven't felt like we have too many children
> to support financially. We're just sort of playing it by ear.

Although Pam worries that the decision not to use artificial birth control will result in their having more children than they might desire or be able to manage, especially since they have used NFP to avoid pregnancy without success on at least one occasion, Pam accepts this uncertainty and relies on religious belief in God's providence. And in fact, she sees their situation as a fortunate one, even providential: though they didn't plan to have a large family, she is comfortable with the idea, and Rob's salary minimizes the financial stress that might otherwise accompany this possibility. Similarly, Julia understands NFP to involve risk, and she goes even further than Pam in seeing the uncertainty involved in not using artificial forms of contraception as a positive thing. She explains, "I don't want a secure life, not taking any risks." She admits that being open to life means encountering the financial burdens a large family brings, but this risk is meaningful—since as we have seen, following church teachings on contraception is intertwined with feminine, marital, and religious aspects of Julia's identity.

Although both men and women at Assumption spoke about adhering to church teachings prohibiting artificial contraception, only women talked of feelings of worry about the uncertainty of controlling their fertility and the possibility that they may have more children than they desire or can afford. I maintain that this is the case because, although marriages are modeled as partnerships and men can be highly involved in parenting, the elevation of women's roles as mothers and nurturers encourages practices whereby the primary responsibility for children falls on women. Thus, in some respects, the growth of their families and the uncertainty about the number of children they will have weighs more heavily on women, even if they desire a large family. In addition, women at Assumption usually take on management of the home as a primary task, and most women of my acquaintance who had more than three children did not work outside the home unless their economic needs required it—placing a further responsibility on them. For those who want lives that move beyond the domestic sphere to public, civic, career, or religious activities, the size of their families and the uncertainties of unplanned pregnancy may limit or constrain them; and although their spouses are also constrained, as primary breadwinners, they are already active in the public world. Moreover, those women who do not work outside the home, or those whose paid work is supplemental to a husband's income, are dependent; they have less personal control, in the sense of being an actual earner, than their husbands do over the generation of income for the family economy. Therefore, while the women I worked with at Assumption expressed a high level of satisfaction with their marriages, they were actively aware of the uncertainties entailed in the style of partnership they practiced.

Nevertheless, in the practices and consequences involved in adhering to church teachings prohibiting artificial contraception, the religious ethic at Assumption provides supports for marriage that are particularly valued by parishioners. The

benefits of adhering to this litmus test for orthodoxy include marital strengthening in practices that can foster communication, create shared understandings of
intimacy, elicit trust, and bind couples to each other and to their peers in their
difference from a broader society in which smaller families are normative. And
although the possibilities of unintended pregnancy and unexpected desire for children entailed in this practice can provoke worry, religious resources of belief and
practice, such as the doctrine of divine providence, as well as the support, companionship, and modeling of their peers, provide couples with ways to allay anxiety
and cope with uncertainty. At the same time, this relinquishment over the control
of one's fertility heightens the stakes for couples, contributes to their moral commitment to this particular way of living out marriage, and cements their engagement in public positions that protest family decline and promise to provide greater
societal support for marriage and the nuclear family.

Gender relations

The choice to practice NFP introduces an element of uncertainty into couples'
family planning, but the uncertainty and contest over gender relations in the
broader culture is one that couples do not choose. This uncertainty is evident in
Julia's story and in the Young Adult Group meeting described at the beginning of
this chapter. For Julia and for many others at Assumption, the solution to problems of interpersonal intimacy and marriage involves models of gender relations
whose underlying logic defines men and women in terms of the Catholic sexual
morality that they have come to accept. While men and women at Assumption
work out gender roles and work-family balance in varied ways within the normative framework of the nurturing mother and protective father, these images
are reinforced through couples' experience of sexual intimacy and its religious
meanings.

To illustrate this, let us return to Chris Schweickert's references to his personal
experience of marriage in his talk to the young adults presented at the beginning
of this chapter. In an interview, Chris filled out the marital history that he alluded
to in his talk. When in college, Chris left the church over issues of sexuality. He
met June at that time, and they became sexually involved early in their relationship. They experienced relational turbulence from early on, but when their birth
control failed and June became pregnant, they decided to marry. June gave birth
to Jeremy, and in the few years following, they had two more children. As Chris
recalls, "There was a lot of fighting between my wife and me about sex. [There
were] a lot of tensions—angry, in the middle of the night fights. Horrible things
said on both sides. There was a lot of tension there." It was in this tense marital
climate that Chris and June began practicing NFP, a decision motivated by June's
negative experience of taking birth control pills. Chris explained that, because of
the modeling of the couples they met at an NFP class and the experience of a new

closeness developing in their marriage through their daily practice of NFP, Chris eventually returned to the church.

> What led me back to the church is partly personal, partly marital, and partly familial. Between the Gospels and NFP and the desire for religion in the family, before long I realized that something was happening. Our family life changed. My wife quit her job, we ate meals together, there was no work on the weekends, and we said prayers at meals. It was a discovery of what the church really is.

In this portrayal of marriage and family, Chris evokes the domestic church, an image that is supported and mirrored in Assumption's central ecclesial metaphor of the church as family. But it is also one that is structured along the lines of retraditionalized gender relations: as a stay-at-home mother, June now homeschools their children, and Chris is the family's sole breadwinner. Chris attributes this change to improved marital communication, other couples' modeling, and most important, religious faith.

Moreover, June and Chris both attribute their renewed intimacy to their religious conversions and, subsequently, the reordering of their gender relations. June explained how church teachings figure in this process:

> Now I understand that virginity is something to be protected, both for a man and for a woman. The church has these rules to protect people from dangers like having a child out of wedlock....Now I look back on it and see what it did to me, how hard it was on our marriage. We have friends who did save their virginity for marriage. They seem to have had an easier time of it. Saving that spiritual intimacy for marriage is protecting both of you, preserving it for that relationship of marriage—where you're not going to leave each other and you have time to work things out.

Church teachings, together with the knowledge of other couples who have been observing them longer than she and Chris have, help her to explain, for herself and for us, why her marriage to Chris was initially so difficult. Their religious conversions are intertwined with feelings of protection and security arising from following church rules involving the exclusivity of sexual expression in marriage and a strong commitment to marital permanence—antidotes to the turbulence they had experienced previously. But even with this renewal, Chris felt a need for more structuring in their marriage and thought that further plumbing religious teachings about gender relations might be helpful. This, in fact, was his motivation for reading the passage on wifely submission from Ephesians at the Young Adult Group meeting; in a later conversation, when I asked him why he read that

passage during his talk, he explained, "I'm looking to the church for more guidance about marriage." Having experienced that the church had wisdom to offer
that had improved the quality of his married life and changed the structure and
substance of his marriage, Chris wanted more assistance—in particular, clearer
gender norms—than secular society currently offers. Chris was looking to further
strengthen his own marriage, perceiving that the passage from Ephesians was one
whose logic might conceivably enhance the religious basis of their marriage and
deepen his and June's companionate practice.

Chris's attitude is by no means univocal at Assumption, as was evident by the
body language of the women who attended his young adult talk; they appeared
unwilling to consider gender relations that suggest inequality, even the largely
symbolic ones that emerge in the interpretation of Ephesians 5 in some evangelical Protestant groups.[24] Instead, there is a range and subtlety of practice in how
men and women deal with gender relations in marriage at Assumption. Although
masculine protection and feminine nurturance are dominant ideals expressed in
its central ecclesial metaphor, references to submission like Chris's were rare, and
married partners generally seemed to assume that an equal partnership underlies
the complementarity of women and men in marriage as mothers and fathers. At
the same time, these partnerships are understood to be forged in gendered difference and related to capacities like protection and nurturance that are typed either
male or female. This view is recognizable as a sensibility that is often aligned with
the conservative pole in public cultural conflicts about the family. But its roots in
this case are distinctively Catholic, intertwined with church teachings about contraception instead of a doctrine of women's submission.

Significantly, both women and men at Assumption spoke of these gendered
capacities as empowering and related to their lived experiences of marital sexuality and intimacy. For example, Julia articulates this connection of partnership and
power in her story; through the practice of NFP and the rhythm of fertility and
sexual unavailability, Julia found not only an explicitly feminine dignity affirmed by
cooperation, respect, and her husband's self-control of sexual desires during periods when she is fertile but also an affirmation of her power as a woman. Rejecting
what she perceives to be an unconnected and impoverished view of women's equality with men, Julia describes her understanding of women's power as follows:

> I respect the *strength* of women—it's different from feminism. The women's
> movement is so radicalized! You shouldn't want husbands or families—it's
> as if men are evil. Women have to basically *be* men. It's not appreciating
> what it is to be a woman.

Julia finds womanhood literally embodied in her experience of marital sexuality and intimacy because of their practice of NFP. Because she perceives that

feminism does not allow for marriage and family life, she rejects it. But like the women in Christel Manning's study of how conservative religious women respond to feminism,[25] she does value women's power and identifies women's strength *as women* as its source—a perception of womanhood that is embedded in the desire for heterosexual spousal love and motherhood. Here, too, this critique of feminism resonates with those who take positions on the conservative or traditional side in public cultural conflicts about the family. But once again, Catholic identity and practice constitute this critique in a way that is distinctive: locating it in an understanding of feminine power that confines sexual expression within marital permanence, but one in which feminine power is experienced in a noncontracepting spousal relationship.

Similarly, Chris also experiences masculinity in terms of strength, not as machismo or power over another, but in the power of controlling oneself and the effects that self-control has had in his marriage. When Chris told the story of his and June's first experiences practicing NFP, he said, "I found to my amazement that I was actually able to exercise self-control. The tension in my marriage was greatly reduced by the demands of chastity." Chris discovered of a sense of masculine strength in the sexual self-control involved in marital chastity, and he communicates his respect for his spouse through sexual self-control, since during times when they are not ready to have another child, they abstain from sex when they know conceiving a child is possible. His self-control was an important catalyst in the renewal of their marriage because it communicated to June his respect and care for her. In this practice, his experience was one of successful self-control that was efficacious and therefore powerful in two ways: he experienced the power of mastery of his sexual self and also the power of being able to effect positive change in his marriage.

Moreover, experiences of gendered power are often emotionally laden, but because these particular experiences involve interpersonal intimacy and sexuality, they are all the more likely to have a highly emotional dimension. When such experiences become symbolically connected to related issues in larger social settings, as in public conflicts over the family, these emotions become implicated in the issues to which they become connected. Julia provides us a good example of how this happens with the public politics of abortion. Like the women Kristin Luker wrote about in *Abortion and the Politics of Motherhood*,[26] Julia's perception of the efficacy of her maternal identity has become implicated and symbolized in the politics of the abortion debate. Consider how she explains her changed views on abortion:

> I believed intellectually in women's right to an abortion when I was in law school and it was talked about so much. But after what I went through, I came back full circle to what the church taught about the sanctity of life

from conception. I remember praying the rosary and thinking, "How cool, how prescient of God to make the Visitation happen, when John the Baptist leapt in the womb. There is a person hanging out in there!"

For Julia, the vision of womanhood that emerged from her life experiences coheres with church teachings on abortion. She contrasts her previous intellectual approach with the visceral experience of pregnancy, in the experience of feeling a baby move in the womb, and in speaking about how she changed her mind about abortion. But she also directly connects her experiences of confusion and pain in an intimate sexual relationship and her subsequent experience of religious and relational conversion to her beliefs about the sanctity of life. And in fact, the religious and sexual identities she now inhabits originate in deeply emotional experiences that have led her to see abortion not only as morally wrong but also as a symbolic issue highlighting women's distinctiveness from men.

Julia's account suggests that Jon Shields's recent survey study reevaluating Luker's argument that the abortion issue is symbolic of traditional views of motherhood is partly correct yet also highly problematic.[27] Shields has recently argued that polarization over abortion cannot be explained by a politics of the family revolving around motherhood and women's roles in society because those opposing abortion have become both slightly more numerous and more gender egalitarian over time.[28] Therefore, Shields concludes that pro-life views cannot be explained by a gender traditionalist worldview and that Luker is wrong that the contest over abortion is merely a symbolic contest over women's roles and gender relations. Instead, Shields argues, those who are pro-life really care about protecting the unborn and see abortion as a profound injustice. He further concludes that polarization around this issue is not about culture, worldview, or gender ideology but, instead, simply about the embryo's moral status—and it is here that religion matters.

However, my account shows that polarization around issues like abortion is related to *both* the cultures of family life and religion and that the two are intertwined. Furthermore, Julia's story exemplifies how experiences and perspectives surrounding motherhood, and its intertwining with family life, are deeply implicated in beliefs in the importance of protecting the unborn. For Julia and those in her milieu, abortion is not *merely* a symbol of a particular image of motherhood and gender relations, but it is not divorced from it, either. For Julia, abortion is wrong because it is the killing of a person. But she has come to this view through an experience of motherhood, one conditioned by the details of her life journey to marriage and how her Catholicism helps her to make sense of her past and present experiences of family life.[29] In this way, then, the public politics of abortion becomes connected to people's experiences of gender and power and to the *ways* in which they live in intimate relationships. Julia's way of perceiving womanhood imparts strength to women and is ultimately a deeply felt source of her value as a person. Thus, abortion is repugnant to her not only because she has come to believe in the sanctity of human life and personhood from conception but also because women's role in the creation and nurturance of human life is deeply implicated in her marital identity. Moreover, her experience of the rightness of church teachings surrounding sex and marriage generally confers legitimacy on its teachings about abortion. Julia's story, then, demonstrates how and why these Catholics' pro-life positions on abortion become symbolically connected to people's everyday lives and their domestic politics in deeply emotional ways. Her story, therefore, can help us to understand why polarization surrounding the family among Catholics, if not a culture war in the sense of a rigid and overdetermined moral polarization among the American public at large, can still be intractable— not just in the public sphere or in the media, but at local levels.

Marriage at Saint Brigitta: Equal and Passionate Partnerships of Faith

The culture of marriage dominant at Saint Brigitta is characterized by a constellation of three emphases upon which marriages are ideally built: a style of romantic love intertwined with religious commitment; the negotiation of spouses, so that both have opportunities for service in the wider world; and the infusion of marriage with religious meanings that draw from some strands of Catholic tradition while existing in tension with others.

First, as Monica's narrative illustrates, couples at Saint Brigitta highly value marital intimacy and work hard at creating a vibrant family life. And like marriage at Assumption, religion plays a central role in marital intimacy, but by contrast with the discourse of marriage at Assumption, romantic love, not sexual expression, is the facet of intimacy most talked about as intertwined with religious convictions and commitments, as it is in Monica's story in the vignette that opens this chapter. This first characteristic of marriage at Saint Brigitta is linked to the second: couples perceived marriage, especially when shared religious convictions ground their romantic love, as anchoring and making possible their involvement in the wider world. This was a defining discourse about marriage at Saint Brigitta that was absent among couples at Our Lady of the Assumption. Despite quite a bit of variation in marriage styles among Saint Brigitta's couples, ideal marital partnerships—which is how friends perceive Monica and John's marriage—involve mutual respect for each partner's autonomy and individual pursuits, especially their careers and works of service for others. The parish plays an important role in encouraging this outward-looking orientation of marriage partners, particularly through speech and action expressing its central ecclesial metaphor as a community. Third, shared religious belief and practice is a significant spousal bond for many couples at Saint Brigitta and is exemplified both in common religious observance and also in service to the wider world. However, church teachings and practices surrounding human sexuality and gender were more often considered an obstacle to religious belonging, rather than a bond to the church. And yet, these teachings, especially those on contraception and divorce, were also creatively integrated into marriages and parish life. These tensions in the local culture of marriage at Saint Brigitta support perspectives in cultural conflicts about the family that tend to settle around the pole opposed to Assumption's, though not always along the lines that culture wars proponents describe the religious divide, especially concerning abortion. In what follows, I discuss these aspects of marriage culture at Saint Brigitta in turn.

Stories of Intimacy: Romance, Vocation, and Negotiating the Everyday

Stories told by Saint Brigitta's couples generally were narratives of two types: courtship stories, which centered on romantic love and the role of faith in a couple's attraction to one another, and stories of negotiating marital partnerships, in which prosaic love was central and partners assumed the task of transcending aspects of previous generations' gender relations that they did not want to reproduce. Both types of stories reveal how religious beliefs are involved in creating and sustaining marriages at Saint Brigitta, but couples' stories of how they negotiate marriage on a daily basis show how the parish's central ecclesial metaphor, its organization, and the social skills that complement it are transposable onto, and help to structure and support, its marriage practice.

Romance, religion, and vocation

Models of marriage at Saint Brigitta are often substantially and consciously informed by religious beliefs. However, the role religion plays in marriage is in important respects quite different than at Assumption. So are secular models of marriage, especially individualized marriage. Rather than a rhetoric that expresses resistance to individualized marriage by minimizing the importance of romantic love, couples at Saint Brigitta instead integrate and nurture romantic love in marriage. This is particularly evident in couples' courtship stories, which they often told at length. In so doing, they borrowed from tropes of romantic love linked to individualized marriage, but they gave them a religious inflection by discussing how faith drew them together and now forms a substantial part of marital intimacy. In so doing, couples rework and subtly transform individualized marriage.

Although this approach to marriage was dominant among involved parishioners at Saint Brigitta, marriages varied in the intensity to which couples shared the same religious perspective. And even for those who did not share faith with their partner as fully as they might have liked to, discussions of religion figured in explaining their draw to one another and the expression and limits of intimacy. Thus, in exploring courtship stories, I examine these different types of narratives, some representing the dominant or ideal model, and others demonstrating the diversity of marriage models at Saint Brigitta through its important variations.

The first story, Ann Burke's, exemplifies the dominant model. Ann, 49, elaborates some of the common themes present in Monica's story at the beginning of this chapter. Ann and Kevin have been married a little more than ten years and live with two children, seven and nine, in a single-family house near Saint Brigitta Church. Ann described a lifelong connection to the church, which provided her with support during in the many years when she remained single. From early on in life, she knew she wanted to marry but did not marry until age 38. Because she longed for marriage, being single was a struggle. But during that time, she thrived professionally as a nurse. About her training, she said, "I loved learning the information that would help me help people, I craved it. I couldn't wait to get out of school to help people and save the world."

Ann had grown up in a tight-knit, working-class Catholic family, one with immigrant roots and strong connections to the church. When she left home, she found friendship and spiritual support in the post–Vatican II church settings of her adulthood: at a college Newman Center and later in the parish near where she lived. Through these churches, she grew in her understanding and practice of nursing as a ministry and eventually took clinical pastoral education (CPE) courses to credential and learn more about that work. She eventually met and married Kevin, a community organizer and a resigned priest. When they met, she said,

> We clicked immediately; it was special. He had been in the process of leaving [the priesthood]....I wasn't part of that in any way. It was nice. He was really listening to where the Spirit was leading. I was making my decision, [moving from a Midwestern college town a few hours away to the city where we met], listening to the Spirit. There was a synchronicity of the Spirit guiding us together. Once he left [the priesthood], we decided to date and married about a year after that. We feel very blessed.

Ann describes their meeting and marriage as almost destined, but this is not merely a romantic story involving fate. Rather, it is one constituted in religious faith. Ann and Kevin had been on professional and personal trajectories that were significantly shaped and informed by their experiences of religious practice from long before they met. Close in age, both are members of a Vatican II generation that came of age in a reforming church, where they learned an outer-directed spirituality to which they responded vocationally, and experienced parish and other church groups, where they shared stories of faith and life struggles on a regular basis. When they met, both were practiced at welding their personal and professional lives into meaningful coherence by grounding the self in religious identity. This common perspective is a key aspect of how Ann describes their meeting, romance, and decision to marry. Her story is explicitly constituted in religious faith, especially in how she and Kevin accessed the resources of spirituality in discerning their next steps and in their common passion for religiously inspired service to others. She elaborated: "We were engaged on Holy Thursday. It was symbolic for us, of our shared desire for ministry, to care for and to serve people." Although Ann is not at present working in the nursing profession and works instead as a stay-at-home mother, she still speaks of her marriage as grounded in their common ministerial vocation of service to others.

Ann ties passion for a service-oriented religious lifestyle with passion for a partner. In this respect, her story is similar to Monica's, and in fact, in both these cases and several others, Saint Brigitta's couples described meeting, falling in love, and marriage in the terms of a religious experience—even *as* a religious experience. But in addition, Ann's courtship narrative also draws on the model of individualized marriage: in the importance of their experience of romance, in emphasizing their individual vocational journeys and connecting through them, and in their separate decision-making processes. Nevertheless, this story of marriage and the marriage model underlying it is infused with religious meaning, transforming an individualized model of marriage into one that is partly fused to Catholicism and its institutions. And perhaps because couples like Ann and Kevin share an intense, outer-directed religious commitment as a basis for marital intimacy, they do not worry that the romantic quality of their love might reflect its possible insufficiency, as those at Assumption might.

Although there are many couples like Ann and Kevin at Saint Brigitta, some others are not as intensely outer-directed or explicitly romantic about the shared religious perspective that undergirds their marriages. Sharon and Andy Winkowski are a good example of such a couple: Andy and Sharon both work in the business world, where they met and cultivated a friendship. Eventually they realized that they attended the same church and began to meet one another there. Their friendship grew into something more, though this did not happen quickly for Sharon. And by contrast with most couples at Saint Brigitta, she did not describe their courtship as involving romance. Andy

> Proposed within a year and a half, and I said no. After he asked me, I started thinking, if it's not Andy, who is it going to be? What am I waiting for? Andy has it all. He has these qualities—integrity, a good father, a good provider—and he loves me, and that's the most important thing of all. Everything I wanted, Andy had. Commitment and love—I could give

that back. He could give it to me. I thought we had a good relationship going. Even though it wasn't a hot and stormy romance, he was a wonderful person. And I knew it.

Sharon emphasized prosaic love in her story, but it is still a love that grew between them in their mutual connection to the church. And in fact, the Winkowskis also share an orientation to religious service; they are involved together in evangelization activities, Marriage Encounter, liturgical ministries, and faith-sharing groups. Although they are involved in activities that are somewhat closer to home than some others at Saint Brigitta, whose Christian service often reaches beyond neighborhood and church, they are similar in their grounding of marital intimacy in religious service.

As these stories suggest, the feelings and experiences linked to habits of a shared spirituality can contribute to marital intimacy in unifying and supportive ways. Discussing the role of religion in marriage, Kevin Christiano[30] notes that there is a link between prayer and happiness and a relation between a couple's practice of shared prayer and happiness in marriage. Christiano quotes Andrew Greeley,[31] who observes that whether married couples "pray often together or not is a very powerful correlate of marital happiness, the most powerful we have yet discovered." Assumption's couples also share prayer—but along with worship and formal prayer, many of Saint Brigitta's couples also place shared extemporaneous prayer, on the model of faith-sharing groups, in the routines of their religious practice. This practice provides a structured vehicle for interpersonal intimacy that involves self-disclosure of and reflection upon everyday life events.

Other couples at Saint Brigitta do not share prayer in this fashion, and some do not share a common religious perspective or style. In these cases, the church can still play a supportive role but offers fewer obvious resources. For example, Maria Callahan and her husband, Dan, discovered when they met that they shared a common Catholic upbringing, but today they practice different styles of Catholicism. Maria explained that, after they married, she had a spiritual awakening that brought her to a sense of intense involvement with her faith and with the community at Saint Brigitta. Although they go to church together each Sunday with their children,

Dan doesn't feel the connection that I do. He doesn't like being with other people very much. For a long time he saw [my involvement with the church] as something that took me away from him....He is conscious of his relationship with God, but [his faith] is more traditional; for instance, he says the rosary. He is where I was [when we married], living a good Christian life, but with no sense of community. He likes to go to mass by

himself....I regret that he's not with me, that we're not this couple who is
a part of the community [together].

While Maria believes that Dan's style of Catholic practice is in part related to per-
sonality characteristics, the most crucial differences between them are explicitly
religious and involve the divergence between traditional faith and the sense of the
church as a community. Both have perceived this difference as an obstacle to marital intimacy, with Dan perceiving Maria's religious involvements as drawing her
away from him, and Maria wishing that he could share them. Their religious difference reveals that religious homogamy is not merely sharing a denominational
affiliation or even a pattern of church attendance. In fact, this is a type of religious
difference that survey research on religious homogamy tends to miss: a couple's
homogamy of religious *style* and *identity* can enhance intimacy, perhaps more
than affiliation or attendance, whereas its lack may constrain it. Evelyn Lehrer
and Carmel Chiswick hypothesize, "Marital companionship is enhanced when
individual spirituality can be shared and is inhibited when the partners must look
outside the marriage for religious intimacy."[32] Maria and Dan's story demonstrates
how marital intimacy can be shaped by couples' religious commitments. Their
story also shows concretely how one partner's change in religious practice can be
challenging for a spouse who does not share a similar experience or image of the
church to which they belong. These differences matter not only to marital intimacy but also to a church's capacity to support couples in their marriages.

Importantly, Maria and Dan's marriage also gives us insight into how people
with different understandings of the post–Vatican II church and different preferred religious practices react and respond to one another. Dan's Catholicism falls
somewhere between Maria's progressivism and the retraditionalized Catholicism
most typical of Assumption's families, but Dan's difference from Maria—and
from the dominant norms at Saint Brigitta—shows how church organization and
the dominant metaphor for the church matters to parishioners' perceptions of
everyday life. Moreover, while they do not have explicitly opposed Catholic identities, they show how people, even those who care deeply for one another, can fail
to connect when they do not share a style of religious identity, even though they
participate in the same religious tradition. Between groups, this failure to connect
might be considered to be a precondition for the development of the opposed
identities that undergird polarization.

Marital intimacy as negotiation

While courtship stories at Saint Brigitta emphasized romantic love, the prosaic
love of everyday life dominated stories of marriage negotiation. Instead of problems of sexual and interpersonal intimacy, Saint Brigitta's couples most often
talked about the kind of intimacy involved in working out the nitty-gritty details

of everyday life as they forged partnerships and tried to transcend the constraints of older gender role patterns reflected in their parents' marriages. As couples told stories of working through the everyday difficulties of work-family balance, faith often played a role, and so did an image of an ideal marriage as a negotiated equal partnership.

We first saw this in the story at the beginning of this chapter. Monica talked about how she and John had worked intently at negotiating a partnership that works for both of them. Their friends at Saint Brigitta perceive their marriage to be ideal because they routinely communicate about the sharing of household responsibilities and work out arrangements that free each other for work and volunteerism outside the home. John explains this intensive communication style as having grown out of his dual desires for family and community:

> [For me,] wanting to be part of a family was in conflict with the value of wanting a community that keeps faith and tradition at the center of its life....I think it's only because I had been with Monica in community at the Catholic Worker that I looked at [the possibility of] our life together as partners with a family. [Our partnership involves] partly feeling like having the experience of community and feeling like the radical consensus we have and the sharing of responsibility, and in some ways an equal voice. [It's] not a democratic thing, [but] continually coming to a common mind.

John describes their partnership not as embodying an autonomous or therapeutic companionate ideal, but as one that is communitarian in the sense that it is grounded in religious expressiveness and negotiated through consensus. He explicitly talks about marriage as an emotional project in which the work of achieving consensus is intimate and enduring in virtue of the continual work it requires. As he continues, John talks explicitly about the importance of the small details of marital work, emphasizing how he and Monica work at not unduly constraining their partnership with traditional sex role stereotypes.

> This would be the hardest thing: in what way are you radically partnered in life and raising kids? The details!...If you see husband and wife, mother and father, as a real, mutual partnership, then it should be evident in everything you do.
>
> My parents were not really like that. My mom takes care of everything in the house. Not in terms of a partnership, really. But certain things Monica and I take on in terms of ability and interest. I do more of the work around the house, fixing up the house, but I'm not as good a cook...but she's a really great cook. Realistically, three times a week I need to cook for me and the boys. So I think things fall into areas of what you're good at and what

you like to do, but always explicit discussion to feel like we're both in this equally and together.

John describes marital negotiation and partnership as an intimate form of his image of community. He understands marital partnership, like community, as achieved through the work of negotiation. John understands the radical partnership of marriage to be mutual and rooted in the intimacy created by shared values, goals, and responsibilities. John and Monica self-consciously seek to create their marriage differently than their parents' marriages, supporting each other's professional pursuits—"This is no nine-to-five kind of life," Monica remarked—and explicitly distinguishing their marriage from their parents' marriages and the traditional gender roles of the modern nuclear family. Instead, they understand themselves as negotiating household tasks by taking each one's personal choices into account. Nevertheless, in falling back on learned habits and skills, some of the areas each chooses for household responsibilities also reflect common gender patterns present in wider societal contexts. John is explicit, however, that their practices do not reflect the traditional images of gender presented in the modern nuclear family. They are different, John believes, precisely because they are mutually negotiated and take account of each one's individual desires and skills—although he does not discuss here how these might be themselves socially shaped.

Louis and Patricia Beltrami have struggled similarly with creating an equal partnership that transcends the constraints of older gender role patterns. Louis highlights how, when he and Patricia became parents, his outer-directed sense of vocation initially made achieving such a partnership difficult.

> It really took a lot of working out, especially having children. I was coming out of, "What do I have to contribute to the world?" and I was looking right past my house! My wife's life changed dramatically 180 degrees when our first child came along. It really didn't seem to change that much for me...my impression was, oh my gosh, this is really something—but day to day, I [would] go to work, I [would] come back—I did feel I was creating more outside effort, but it probably seemed that way [that I was not doing as much as she]. That took a lot of discussion...lots of conversation, frustration, we needed to talk about this.

Louis confesses that when they had children, it took time and discussions with Patricia for him to realize that the brunt of childrearing had inadvertently fallen on her. But this portrait of their marriage is one whose ideals are similar to John's and Monica's: both couples desire a negotiated partnership, and both work intently at communicating with one another about household duties, working out an arrangement that satisfies each partner as best they can. This is an intimate emotional project, which finds support and modeling in Saint Brigitta's image of the church as a community. In this image, equal and mutual communicative relationships are highly valued, and thus the social relations that embody community at Saint Brigitta provide a template, a normative climate, and social supports for these couples' efforts.

It is important to note, however, that although this ideal of marital partnership is widespread at Saint Brigitta, it is not the only model practiced there. Some couples talked more about strategies of marital accommodation than negotiation. For example, when she was a stay-at-home mother, Maria Callahan balanced work and home not by negotiating with Dan, but by accommodating to his needs and the needs of their children. She said,

> I stayed home for five years. I was always doing something—[like] the booklet [of the art in Saint Brigitta Church]. I was creating this booklet on my own, and I had two kids. I sensed it right away [that it would be a problem if it intruded into family life]. My primary responsibility was kids and house. It was very important to me that [my work] could never be thrown back in my face.

Maria and Dan each adjust to the other in accommodating their differences without necessarily communicating about them or explicitly working them out together. Maria's management of her family life with Dan corresponds to how she manages their different religious styles; Maria continues to nurture her marriage while at the same time exercising autonomy, albeit in ways that respect her husband's need and limits. But this way of managing difference within their marriage does not depend on or draw imaginatively on Saint Brigitta's metaphor of the church as a community—although it is not completely divorced from it either, since the church as community seeks inclusion of difference and fosters the authority of autonomous selves.

Thus, in fashioning marriages, couples at Saint Brigitta generally reveal a domestic politics where newer gendered patterns, especially those related to women's work in the world, figure prominently, whether through couples' negotiation or accommodation. These domestic politics emerge in the midst of practical everyday struggles, but they are also supported by the ecclesial metaphor of community at Saint Brigitta—at least to the extent that couples' models of marriage reflect its norms. In these cases, the image of the church as community imparts moral weight to equality in partnership and skills for marital work that ultimately serve family life. These are religiously supported moral stances that conflict with a public politics of the family that elevates the gender relations of the modern nuclear family (even when they are combined with a practical egalitarianism). They thereby help to shape a local culture of marriage that contributes to polarization among Catholics in its firm rejection of ideologies of gender role traditionalism.

Church Teachings and Intimate Relationships

The negotiated and individually oriented style of marriage practiced at Saint Brigitta presents a sharp contrast to the more institutionally oriented style of marriage practiced at Assumption, especially in how church authority and teachings about human sexuality are coupled to marriage: at Saint Brigitta they are loosely coupled to actual marriage practice, whereas at Assumption they are more tightly coupled. However, it would be mistaken to think that this means that Saint Brigitta's couples do not engage Catholic teachings on sexuality and marriage, for many do, sometimes in affirming ways and often critically. This local culture of marriage provides an environment where tensions surrounding church teachings on human sexuality often play out in ways that locate Saint Brigitta's public politics of the family at a progressive pole, but one that is much more nuanced than is usually portrayed in the culture wars literature, especially around the issue of abortion.

Saint Brigitta affirms the ideal of marital permanence presented in Catholic teachings, and the sheer prevalence of modern nuclear families at Saint Brigitta accentuates the importance of continuous marriage to family life as an element of couples' social status and belonging. But the parish is also welcoming of people practicing other family forms and explicitly welcomes those who are divorced, single parents, blended families, and GLBT families. In fact, it successfully creates worship environments that attract these different constituencies, as well as others who value tolerance and openness to them. The presence of relational diversity in the parish signals these values; for instance, Sarah McFadden, a single heterosexual young adult, casually remarked about her belonging at Saint Brigitta, "I knew I'd found the right community, when I saw this lesbian couple in the gym!"

Tolerance and openness toward a plurality of family forms is maintained by making a strong distinction between public and private life in marriage and intimate relationships. This distinction is reflected in Saint Brigitta's worship practice. Although preachers often speak about situations and stories from family life and childrearing, they seldom discuss marriage publicly. Moreover, despite a proliferation of groups and committees at Saint Brigitta, except for pre-Cana and Marriage Encounter, there are not many formal groups designed to support couples, although discussions of marriage can take place in settings such as men's and women's prayer groups. By contrast with Assumption, there were no parish meetings where marriage was the advertised topic during the period of my field research.

In a parish where marriage and intimacy is situated firmly in the private sphere and where preaching and catechesis about marriage is not routine in public

settings, how the parish actively supports married couples is an open question—
one of concern at Saint Brigitta, at least among the parish staff. Louis Beltrami
publicly articulated this question in a bulletin letter on a Sunday in the late spring
of my field research, just after Rev. Jesse Jackson Sr. had announced publicly that
he was the father of a child of a woman who was not his wife. Louis wrote,

> It seems that somewhere along the line [Jackson] failed to heed some very
> sage advice—"Whenever you wonder if something you are doing could be
> considered 'unfaithful,' ask your spouse." We married couples can't hear
> this advice too often apparently, since some studies show a very high inci-
> dence of "cheating" by husbands and wives alike.
>
> Can our parish play a positive role in keeping marriages strong? Can
> Saint Brigitta be a place where the struggles as well as the joys of couple-
> hood are shared and lightened? If Rev. Jackson were a member here, would
> he have found a listening ear and a compassionate but clear voice urg-
> ing him to stay the course, to remain faithful? This is the gift we offer to
> each other when we bind ourselves together as a community grounded in
> faith—to accompany one another through the times of courage and temp-
> tation, reminding one another who we are and whose we are.

Louis's question to the parish about its role in strengthening marriages was one
of only a few times during my fieldwork when someone expressed concern about
married couples' needs for support in sustaining marriage or referred to how the
church could provide support for marriage. Here, musing on how Saint Brigitta
can provide support to married couples specifically around issues of fidelity, Louis
identifies the image of the church as community as a context and vehicle that can
keep marriages strong by providing couples support and a moral voice. He envi-
sions that the social bonds of the faith community have the capacity to support
the more intimate bonds of marriage through its presence—thereby reminding
couples of their common religious identities and commitments. Louis's challenge
implies a more active and more public vision of the parish's role in supporting
marriages than the dominant sensibility of marriage present in Saint Brigitta's
discourse, in which issues of marriage and divorce are primarily private domains
of life.

Similarly, even though the parish sought to welcome, support, and make
comfortable those who had experienced a divorce, responses to divorce at Saint
Brigitta were largely private ones. Saint Brigitta does not deal with divorce pro-
grammatically, but its intentional community provides informal support for
those who have experienced divorce, as well as space to heal and re-create their
lives. Moreover, Saint Brigitta's parishioners articulated different feelings, concerns, and approaches to divorce than those at Assumption. For example, Vince

Palumbo, 62, who eventually remarried after his divorce, explained the breakup of his first marriage this way.

> We brought in a [foster child] who was seven years old. We had him for
> 11 months, and we reached a breaking point. We were so devastated. The
> school couldn't handle him, I was working, and the other kids were in
> school. That was the beginning of the [end of our marriage].
>
> Gina went through a midlife crisis, where [she thought] somehow our
> marriage was a total failure. Her parents had been very controlling, and
> I always thought that when our older children were teenagers that she
> would have difficulty with them. I had to get out of the house, so we ended
> up divorcing. She's been through hell emotionally.

It seems clear from the tenor of his story that Vince has grieved his divorce and come to terms with the emotional issues surrounding the breakup of his first marriage. And while he communicates the extreme emotional difficulty their entire family suffered at that time, as well as empathy for his ex-wife, he expresses an honest evaluation and acceptance of his divorce. His attitude was typical of the way parishioners approached divorce at Saint Brigitta. By contrast with those at Assumption, parishioners did not search for the underlying causes of divorce in society at large, or worry as they spoke about it. Instead they analyzed marital failure in interpersonal and psychological categories. And while the fact that someone had obtained a church annulment would sometimes come up in an interview, no one ever brought up church teachings about divorce.

Similarly, when people at Saint Brigitta discussed other church teachings surrounding marriage and sexuality, they generally expressed the view that these were private topics in which autonomous authority should play a large role. This was especially the case regarding teachings on contraception. For instance, when asked explicitly about how she regarded church teachings surrounding sexuality, Maggie McNeill said that she agreed with the church that abortion is wrong. Yet, she also described her struggle with church teachings on human sexuality as a whole.

> This isn't smorgasbord Catholicism, at least, I don't think so. I think that
> what I believe can all fit together. We're pro-life, and it's always a struggle,
> finding your place in that. I think of abortion along with issues like the
> death penalty, as a part of a consistent ethic of life. It's not as cut and dried
> for us as church teaching. [Using artificial] contraception is just not an
> issue for us.

Maggie only briefly discusses contraception, seeing it as a settled private issue where she exercises autonomous authority. But significantly, Maggie and Rick do accept church teaching prohibiting abortion. However, they do not understand the immorality of abortion in the same way parishioners at Assumption do; specifically, they do not talk about abortion as one of the signs of family decline. In fact, Maggie expresses her difficulty in finding a place for her stance among pro-life Catholics—probably because she does not link her opposition to abortion to other family issues, but instead to a broad spectrum of life issues that includes the death penalty and other concerns. In fact, she and Rick explicitly reject the perspective that abortion should be linked to church teachings on human sexuality generally; by contrast with those at Assumption, she decouples contraception from abortion. Her view on abortion is instead informed by a "seamless garment" or "consistent ethic of life" approach, developed and publicly articulated by Joseph Cardinal Bernardin of Chicago during the 1980s and 1990s.[33] This stance is congruent with what Elfriede Wedam describes as a contextualist style of moral reasoning about abortion, which is grounded in an ethic of justice and considers the ambiguities of women's structural positions in society.[34] This perspective enables Maggie to define abortion and contraception as distinct moral issues instead of ones that are intertwined, allowing her to stand with the church in opposing abortion while minimizing the importance of church teachings prohibiting artificial contraception.

Most parishioners at Saint Brigitta who spoke about abortion did so as Maggie did. While acknowledging the issue as one grounded in the church's teachings on sexuality, they decoupled the issue of abortion from teachings about marriage and family life and instead articulated their pro-life stance as a fundamental issue of justice and human dignity. But generally, people at Saint Brigitta spoke much less often about abortion than people at Assumption, and during the period of my field research, there was almost no public discourse about the issue in the parish. Nor were there any pro-life events advertised at the church. A Respect Life committee was listed in the parish directory, but there was never an advertised meeting of the committee, even though justice-oriented events, including those regarding other life issues such as anti-death-penalty campaigns, were routinely advertised in the bulletin. Father Theo said that, in the first few years that he was pastor, some parishioners, most of whom eventually left the parish, would occasionally ask him to incorporate the issue into parish activities. But he didn't do so. He explained that he tended to avoid the issue.

Although Father Theo didn't explicitly articulate his rationale for avoiding the issue beyond linking it to his personal ministerial style, I believe that the decoupling of abortion from the politics of the family, the disagreement parishioners would voice about issues of church authority and women's roles, and the silence about abortion in the parish's public discourse together constituted a climate in which those who did not accept church teachings about abortion could quietly disagree. In fact, people holding diverse views about cultural conflicts surrounding the family generally appeared to coexist peacefully by avoiding these disagreements.

This is precisely the climate that Rick McNeill describes in this chapter's introduction: he has grounded himself in a community where his moral convictions about abortion are a flag of his conservatism, but his views are respected. Moreover, pro-choice parishioners at Saint Brigitta never speak about their views publicly; nor did anyone discuss pro-choice positions in the context of private interviews, although I was aware that there were people at Saint Brigitta that were pro-choice. In fact, this climate at Saint Brigitta likely reflects the current practice of public discourse among Catholics about abortion generally: with the exception of groups like Catholics for Choice, those in the pews who are pro-choice are largely silent in church contexts, despite the fact that Catholics are divided on the issue largely in the same proportions as Americans generally, although churchgoing Catholics are less likely to be pro-choice than others.

By contrast to the silence surrounding abortion, parishioners were publicly critical of other church teachings surrounding human sexuality. Some explicitly sought to engage, criticize, and reinterpret church teachings, especially on homosexuality, premarital sex, and contraception. For example, John Maloney-Jones accepts the premise that marriage should be open to life but justifies artificial contraception with both practical and theological argumentation. He explained,

> I'm theologically orthodox. Catholic teachings on birth control just don't work for most Catholics today. I see the value of them, and I am pro-life. But I believe that the implementation of these teachings undermines the values that the church is trying to protect. I think of marriage and sexuality as a commitment of fidelity. Being lifegiving [should be about] a whole lifetime, and not every instance of sex. I think that the church should trust laypeople to make those decisions on our own. NFP is an ideal, but it doesn't always work out.

John accepts the theological argument that marriage and sexuality should include openness to children, and he agrees with those who practice NFP that couples should plan their families. But he redefines being open to life as an attribute of marriage generally, criticizing the doctrinal requirement that every act of sexual intercourse must remain open to procreation. His criticism originates in the practical experience of everyday life: following church teachings has created great difficulty for those who need to limit the size of their families. John is exceptionally articulate about this issue and demonstrates both a critical engagement with church teachings and a creative approach to authority relations, one supported by the social relations imagined in Saint Brigitta's central eccesial metaphor.

Others also engage church teachings on contraception through the benefits they see in them—but like the public silence at Saint Brigitta surrounding abortion, parish practice requires that this engagement is primarily a private endeavor.

Andy and Sharon Winkowski practice NFP and have talked to other couples about the method in different church contexts. They explain why NFP has a low profile at Saint Brigitta in the following way:

> Sharon: We don't talk about NFP at Saint Brigitta. We have a Respect Life Committee in the parish, which we were involved in for a long time. And one of the couples that participated, they were similar, and [had been practicing NFP] for a long time. . . .
>
> Andy: But the parish doesn't want to come off being too dictatorial as far as sexual matters go, because it's divisive.
>
> Sharon: We have a Marriage Encounter; we are the coordinators, and in our group, we have talked about [NFP]. But it's not something we make presentations about in church. Father Theo, because he's been a part of our pre-Cana, knows we have experience with NFP. I would imagine if anybody asked him—
>
> Andy: But we've had no references from him.

As Sharon and Andy explain why they don't talk publicly about NFP at Saint Brigitta, they give the impression that NFP is a sensitive subject not only because people there have varied and often negative responses to some of the church's teachings on human sexuality but also because publicizing NFP might unintentionally constitute an act of explicit agreement—or perhaps more properly, a squelching of individuals' private disagreement—with church teachings surrounding contraception. Because Saint Brigitta welcomes those who feel at odds with institutional Catholicism and seeks to provide support and space for parishioners to safely air any disagreements with the church, information about programs like NFP that potentially imply support for teachings that groups within the parish find uncomfortable or unconvincing is provided privately, not publicly. The way in which Saint Brigitta handles NFP demonstrates the extent to which marital sexuality is treated as a private domain in the public life of the parish.

Others at Saint Brigitta either simply rejected church authority to teach about sex—emotionally, rhetorically, and/or rationally—or, like Maggie, walked a fine line whereby they incorporated some church teachings while criticizing or rejecting others. Many at Saint Brigitta shied away from talking about issues of sexual intimacy altogether. When asked about how couples regarded church teachings on marriage and human sexuality, people would often reply with a brief statement and then change the subject. For example, when I asked Ann Burke about the church's teachings on sexuality, she said,

> I had [romantic] relationships, but except for two long-standing ones, [contraception] wasn't really an issue. The part of the church that was alive for me was more about how my life was in relationship to other people. When

it got down to some of the rules, I just didn't pay much attention. It just didn't make an impact on my life.

In a way similar to how people at Saint Brigitta responded to the abortion issue, Ann shies away from talking about issues of sexual intimacy, considering them to be part of a private sphere inappropriate to public conversations about religion and family, even one-on-one interviews. This orientation is supported in the social relations of the church as community, which elevates autonomous authority; we see this in how Ann makes a distinction between the church as a site for relationships and the church as providing rules for life conduct. For Ann, the church is primarily about relationships with others—essentially, it is about the church as a community. Moreover, her comment about rules reflects the flattening of religious authority, with the result that the authority of church teachings is not as central as in more institutionally oriented models of church. In this regard, Ann represents and expresses the Culture Two Catholicism that, for some, defines the bonds and boundaries of Catholic identity at Saint Brigitta.

In sum, while Saint Brigitta's self-image of the church as community provides a model for a particular kind of marriage, its flattening of authority relations allows a diverse set of family forms. Unity in this diversity is achieved through relatively strict boundaries between public and private life and by social norms of silence about particular cultural conflicts surrounding the family, which allow the church to avoid polarization *within* the parish, coalesce around the common aspects of its Catholic identity, and position itself at odds with Catholics at an opposed pole.

Conclusion

Both Assumption and Saint Brigitta provide social and religious supports for married couples. Couples in each setting spoke from explicitly and uniquely religious understandings of intimate relationships and marriage, and each transforms secular models of marriage—especially individualized marriage—religiously. However, although some of the social structures and parish programs are similar in the two congregations, the very character of marriage in each congregation and the routine supports each parish provides are quite different. These local cultures of marriage tend to support polarizing tendencies surrounding family-related issues, as their central ecclesial metaphors provide support for different marital relations both through the affinities between their social relations and also their constitution of authority relations vis-à-vis the institutional church.

At Assumption and Saint Brigitta, the relationships between the problems of marriage and religious practice suggest a particularly important role for congregational images instantiated in worship in supporting particular ways of being married. In each setting, worship helps to constitute and reproduce worldviews and images that make particular understandings of marriage not just plausible but normative. The central sacred image of the church as family at Assumption is interlaced with congregational understandings and values surrounding marriage, and its authority relations and gender roles are intertwined with the centrality of church teachings on contraception. By contrast, the central religious image of the church as a community at Saint Brigitta especially supports marriages that strive to enflesh a partnership of equals, while allowing space for diverse models of interpersonal intimacy and varied responses to church teachings. These affinities between religious practice and the practice of marriage reveal the contours of congregation-level social processes that have the power to support, reinforce, and even shape complementary patterns of relationship within families. The resultant models of marriage in each setting perceive and address different life problems, and address them through different social organizations and religious identities. Thus, while leaders in both congregations were concerned with keeping couples together, each church is better equipped to address some problems in marriage and not others.

Moreover, couples' stories of marital problems and negotiations reveal patterned connections between domestic and public politics. In stories of marriage told at Assumption, men and women emphasize church teachings on sexuality in healing intimate relationships and sacralizing motherhood. These stories dovetail with the public politics of sex at Assumption, which preaches church opposition to divorce, abortion, and homosexuality. By contrast, stories of marital conflict and problems at Saint Brigitta revolve around negotiating explicitly egalitarian relationships and creating space for each spouse to make contributions to the world outside the home. These stories mirror the congregation's public politics, which centers on concerns about gender, not sex; are embodied in public discourse and action around social justice; and are often paradigmatically enacted in supporting equal roles for women in church and society.

The issue of abortion is a particularly useful example of how moral polarization occurs among Catholics—importantly, even among those who *agree* on the immorality of abortion. As we have seen, people in both parishes take pro-life positions, but they do so from different logics. Just as important, these congregations' social norms about *how* one should deal with disagreement over the abortion issue are quite different. Assumption's pro-life stance is univocal and spoken of publicly and frequently. It is grounded in church teachings on sexuality and intimately related to them, to the constitution of the family, and to women's experience of marriage and maternity. By contrast, at Saint Brigitta, parish leaders do not mention abortion publicly, and parishioners with pro-life and pro-choice positions coexist while maintaining public silence about the issue. Those who are pro-life approach the issue in a consistent ethic approach, emphasizing human dignity and justice rather than the morality of sexuality and family.

To what extent do these parishes reflect the attitudes of American Catholics generally and help us to understand polarization among Catholics beyond these local contexts? We know that Catholics are polarized around abortion; a 2009 Gallup report found that 40 percent of Catholics, compared with 41 percent of non-Catholics, found abortion morally acceptable,mirroring the broader American population in their views.[35] However, a 2005 study by James Davidson found that regular churchgoers, such as those interviewed at Assumption and Saint Brigitta, are far less likely to view abortion as morally acceptable; only 24 percent of churchgoing Catholics do, compared with 52 percent of those who do not attend church regularly.[36] There is also a generational trend: younger Catholics are on average more inclined to think that one can be a good Catholic without agreeing with the church on abortion—89 percent of millennial Catholics said this, as well as 59 percent of Catholics overall, up from 39 percent in 1987.[37] In addition, while Davidson's study found very limited support for the consistent ethic approach articulated at Saint Brigitta, it also found that this approach was more common among those who attend mass weekly and pray daily.[38]

These statistics suggest that the portrait of polarization among pro-life Catholics at Assumption and Saint Brigitta may well reflect a more general state of affairs among churchgoing Catholics. Although Catholics generally are divided on the abortion issue, churchgoing Catholics are more strongly pro-life—and we have seen that, in these two settings, the divide is not only between pro-life and pro-choice Catholics, but also between those whose pro-life stance is embedded in moral concerns about the family versus those who take a consistent ethic of life approach and are willing to coexist with those Catholics who do not share their pro-life views. These differences among pro-life Catholics show that polarization is not just about being on one or another side of hot-button issues in the public sphere. Rather, polarization is predominantly grounded in cultural worldviews and everyday life choices of particular social groups—and then reflected in particular issues.

As we have seen, contests over issues such as abortion are not merely symbolic; people really do care about these issues as ones of justice and human dignity. But also, as the issue of abortion illustrates, the domestic politics of marriage in each setting finds echoes of the problems around which it is structured in the public political debates each church cares about and actively engages. At both Assumption and Saint Brigitta, the profession of moral ideals around issues of public conflict surrounding the family reflect not only concerns about how society should be structured but also congregants' different desires for particular supports for the everyday practice of marriage and the practical resolution of difficulties.

4

Children

Our Lady of the Assumption
Nine o'clock in the morning. My home.
June Schweickert is right on time this summer morning, wait-
ing at the front door. Of average height and small build, June is
dressed casually in a navy blue, square-necked sleeveless tee and
white cropped pants. Caramel-colored curls frame a placid heart-
shaped face, made vibrant as she smiles a shy "hello." June's hus-
band, Chris, is caring for their four older children this morning.
June has brought the baby with her; Caroline is two months old.
She is bright and active and smiles easily.
June places Caroline's carrier on the floor and looks about her,
saying, "What a lovely house! It's so big!" This is surprising to me
because the Victorian rooms of our four-bedroom house have felt
increasingly small and cramped for a family of four these days.
What is her house like? Chris has said that he had painted their
living room bright orange, "to stimulate the children's learning,"
since the Schweickerts homeschool.
A few moments later, we settle ourselves in my living room.
I ask June to tell me about herself, her family, and what brought
them to Assumption. June speaks for a long time without much
prompting—calmly, but with intensity.
"I think there is a feeling about Our Lady of the Assumption,
but I don't think I could pinpoint it. The priests there are very
reverent, the people who go there are, for the most part, a little
more conservative and more serious about the faith. And more
'straight line.' They support the pope in everything. There are a
lot of big families there. You feel comfortable bringing a crying
baby to mass. There are always other crying babies.
"At Saint Barnabas, people turn around and look at you." *Saint
Barnabas is the parish nearest to both our homes.* "People seem
surprised at Saint Barnabas that we have a large family—five,
these days, that's a lot. We met one family there that had five
children. Other than that, I've never noticed a lot of big families."

In fact, there are many large families that belong to Saint Barnabas, some bigger than June's. I explain, "Families at Saint Barnabas often don't go to church all together—"

"Why don't they?" June asks.

I am puzzled momentarily. "I don't know...." Why don't large families at Saint Barnabas come to mass all together, as they do at Assumption? Having been immersed at Assumption for almost a year, I find it natural that June would ask this question. Later, I remember that at Saint Barnabas, parents attend Sunday mass with one or more of their children but leave younger ones at home with their spouse, who attends later in the day. It is easier for parents to be attentive at mass if they don't have to care for small children.

June goes on. "At Assumption, I felt comfortable with the kids and felt people were more complimentary. 'Oh, you have such a beautiful family,' people will say there. At Saint Barnabas, you get, 'Oh, wow, you have a lot of kids!' or 'Oh, you have your hands full!' I don't see any other large families, and I feel out of place."

She moves on to talk about her family life and why they decided to homeschool. "I love having kids from nine down; it's really fun. I love seeing my older kids have the experience of a baby. It's something I didn't have. For instance, Jeremy, my oldest child, can pick up Caroline, and he feels special, to help me out. I like it, too. Our younger children have the older ones to learn from.

In a larger family, siblings are a real gift to each other.

"It's a challenge for me. I have to be organized with cooking and shopping and things like that. But because I have the older ones to help out, it's no harder having five than two. The ones I'm really taking care of are the toddler and the baby. The older kids are off playing a lot, and I don't have to do as much for them at those times.

"I was interested in homeschooling because of Montessori, where the philosophy is that each child is an individual and that children should learn on their own curve." June had been a teacher in a Montessori school for several years before she and Chris decided that she should stay home with the children. "I was prepared for homeschooling in that way. I wanted my children to thrive, to learn at their own pace. If I sent them out of the home to school, they would have to learn at the pace of the class.

"Jeremy went to pre-Kindergarten for a while. He was frustrated because he hated writing letters. 'I don't want to go! It's so boring.

I know how to do it,' he would say. At a traditional school, he would be bored and frustrated. I don't know if he's gifted, but I just want him to learn at his own pace and not place him in a situation where he has to learn what the teacher says they have to learn that day.

"I went to a good school, but I remember feeling bored a lot. And there's the social structure. How important peers become! Fitting in becomes the most important thing: clothes, popularity, crushes on boys. Sometimes I think, I don't want to be overprotective, to keep them from the real world. On the other hand, I do want to preserve their innocence."

As she is speaking, Caroline starts to fuss. Fists ball up, arms move in the air, and a little tongue searches in hunger and discomfort. June picks up Caroline and discreetly breastfeeds her, helping Caroline along while she speaks about her motivations and the particulars of schooling her children. June and Caroline remind me of the many images of the Madonna that have drenched my consciousness this year—in churches and homes, in visual representations and in discourse. It is easy to think of this mother and child as another.

I ask, "What do you want to do after you've finished raising your children?" She responds right away. "When the kids are older, I would like to be more involved in community service somehow. I would prefer not to work for money unless I have to. I hope always to be available to babysit for grandchildren, to help my children out, and to have time to read—I love novels—but I'd like to do pro-life work.

"Growing up, I was pro-choice. 'It's woman's body, and she should have the right,' that argument made sense to me. But with the experience of pregnancy, I had such feelings of protectiveness toward my children. And with abortion, there's no one protecting this baby. I don't think that's right.

"Modern feminism focuses on women as victims. I don't like that. It's very negative on motherhood. It's damaging! The message of feminism is that you're only free if you're unencumbered by men and children. I think it's freeing to be a mother and wife. I grew up in an environment where I was raised to think that I'm entitled to free time, not to be dragged down by housework. But I've found that only by immersing yourself are you free. The culture says, 'Indulge yourself,' but it doesn't make you happy."

As June is articulating thoughts about motherhood and freedom, Caroline finishes nursing. She comes away sated, milk ringing *her small mouth. Her eyes open and close sleepily several times. Still in June's arms, Caroline drifts into sleep.*

Saint Brigitta

Sunday morning. The Saint Brigitta gymnasium.

In the gray midwinter when clouds plug the sky and hide the shortened day's sunlight, the Saint Brigitta gym mass community is bathed in dank and glaring artificial light. But the large crystal punchbowl, set on a tall pedestal in the middle of the assembly, sparkles and shimmers. The water within it ripples and shines; colorless, yet it is full of light. It brightens the pallid surroundings.

Today the church in the Saint Brigitta gym commemorates the Baptism of the Lord, but this is not the only baptism being celebrated here. This day, Joey's baptism will be celebrated, too.

Seven-year-old Joey Smith is the foster son of Andy and Sharon Winkowski. Andy and Sharon have faithfully brought Joey to the mass in the gym since he came to live with them about a year ago. Joey's attention span is brief, but he does not wander the gym or play with the other children at its edges. Instead, he sits with his foster parents and pays attention to the mass. When Joey gets fidgety, Andy picks him up, sits him on his lap, and soothes him. Not too long ago, Joey asked Andy and Sharon if he could be baptized. Andy and Sharon were surprised but delighted.

Father Francis presides at the gym mass today. After the Gospel, he invites the congregation to take their seats and tells us proudly, "Joey has asked me to be the one to baptize him." Over the last several months, Father Francis has worked with Joey, taught him about the church, and helped him prepare for this day. "Now," he says, "Joey is ready to be baptized."

But first, Father Francis preaches a homily in the style of the Saint Brigitta gym. "Do any of you have tattoos? Do you know people who have had tattoos applied?" he asks, and quickly gets to the point. "Tattoos define people. They are painful to apply, and difficult and painful to remove. And they are a statement about yourself, a statement of your identity.

"Baptism is like a tattoo—or, at the very least, it should be. Once you're baptized, you can't really get 'unbaptized.' You just become inactive as a Catholic. Someone actually called the rectory once, wanting to be unbaptized, but I had to explain to them that it can't be done. Being baptized Christians, our faith should not be something that happens to us just on Sundays, but it should be suffused

*throughout our lives. Our faith should be like a tattoo, a mark of
our identity—our identity in Christ, as followers of Christ."*

Today's event takes the place of the customary dialogue, so when
Father Francis finishes his homily, he moves directly to the improvised baptismal font and invites the Winkowski family to join
him. Andy, Sharon, and Joey leave their seats in the first semicircular row of steel folding chairs and walk forward a few steps
until Andy and Sharon are shoulder-to-shoulder with Father.
Francis, and Joey is standing encircled by the adults. Joey is short
and lithe and itches with energy. He is very excited today. He has
an elfin face, big brown eyes with a slight tilt, and dirty-blond
hair styled in a brush cut with a prominent widow's peak. He
is dressed in a plain but formal manner, wearing a short-sleeved
white button-down shirt and black dress pants. Andy stands at
Joey's right, and Sharon stands on Joey's left.

Father Francis begins the baptismal rite with a water blessing.
As he prays, six or seven children leave their seats and gather
at the back of the main aisle of the semicircle, directly in the
line of sight of the font. One by one, they sit down on the floor
to watch. Others follow suit. Soon, nearly all the congregation's
children, about 15 of them, have gathered together there. Some
of the children are school-aged, but many others are toddlers or
preschoolers.

A few parents intrude into the group to sit with their children. As
the service proceeds, one or two whisper in a child's ear; another
directs a preschooler whose excitement has brought him a little
too close to the proceedings. The service is long, but the children
don't appear to be bored or distracted. They sit contentedly or
strain to see, intent on what is taking place.

Father Francis asks the question prescribed in the baptismal rite,
"What do you ask of the church?" Andy replies somberly; then
Joey, with a twinkle in his eyes, softly replies that he wants to be
baptized. The priest then leads the Winkowskis and the congregation in a profession of faith: "Do you reject sin so as to live
in the freedom of God's children?" "We do," the congregation
replies. "Do you believe in God the Father, creator of heaven and
earth?" "We do," and the prayer continues. Then, scooping up
some baptismal water from the font in a small pitcher, Father
Francis tilts Joey's head awkwardly over the punchbowl and
pours water over his head three times, saying, "I baptize you in
the name of the Father, and of the Son, and of the Holy Spirit."
The water splashes.

*The rite continues. Joey is given a lighted candle and then a
white stole that Sharon has decorated. The children crane their
necks to see. A couple of them shout and applaud their approval,
and the rest join in, creating a high-pitched cacophony. Then the
congregation applauds its congratulations.*

*When the rite is over, the children disperse. A few at a time, they
resume their usual activities during mass: some draw, others
play with toys. Toddlers clatter and chatter at the edges of the
gym. But a few pay attention to what is happening at the altar
as the Eucharist commences. Their curiosity has been piqued by
the baptismal service, which has been so obviously an event for
children.*

Childhood and Parenting: Revealing Christian Anthropologies and Catholic Identities

June Schweickert's ruminations on how she raises her five children and the story of how the gym mass community at Saint Brigitta celebrated Joey Smith's baptism present common concerns and practices of these parents as they raise children, but importantly, they also give us a window into the differing logics that underlie their parenting approaches. In this chapter, I show how Catholicism is implicated in these different logics, particularly in the different religious perceptions of human nature—that is, religious anthropologies—that underlie their conceptions of childhood. These anthropologies, which also reflect aspects of each group's Catholic identity, help to constitute local religious cultures that emphasize particular parenting strategies and thereby embody distinct visions of moral living that, while sharing common concerns, also oppose one another in ways that support polarization among Catholics.

This chapter therefore examines the Christian anthropologies expressed in constructions of childhood and the practices of parenting at Assumption and Saint Brigitta. Significantly, both local cultures strongly believe in human goodness, especially as it is embodied in childhood, and both are fundamentally concerned to appropriately protect, nurture, and educate children as they grow. But they have different strategies for accomplishing parenting that are supported and, at times, even rooted in the differences in their religious anthropologies. The culture of childhood at Our Lady of the Assumption is underlain by a religious anthropology that is highly cognizant of human sinfulness. This impels parents to strongly emphasize their role in protecting their children from harmful influences that have the potential to disrupt or destroy their development as moral individuals and to concertedly cultivate and guide them in habits of religious practice while providing them an integrated education that promotes growth in virtue. By contrast, the culture of childhood at Saint Brigitta is grounded in a perception of humans that emphasizes their developmental capacities throughout the life course, the psychological and spiritual importance of self-knowledge for forging happiness, and the fundamental connectedness of humanity. Parents exercise dual strategies of appropriately protecting children and gently exposing them to social settings beyond their own, also trusting that in raising them within the religious community, they will develop naturally into moral individuals.

The choices and routines parents practice in these different styles of parenting comprise two subtly different domestic politics of childhood that, despite similarities, support how parishioners in each setting perceive cultural conflicts surrounding the family and help to crystallize polarizing tendencies at opposed poles in the two settings. I elaborate this thesis in what follows by first briefly discussing how previous research informs the relation of religious belief and parenting practices. Then I explain how Christian anthropologies inform local cultures of childhood in ways that support and shape practices that, in turn, can foster polarizing tendencies among Catholics despite many similarities in their basic childrearing goals.

Religion, Childhood, and Parenting: The Role of Belief in Practice

How do religious congregations matter to parents as they rear their children? Although much general sociological research on congregations reveals how they meet families' needs throughout the life course—often, for instance, through congregational programming—focused research on parenting suggests a strong role for religious beliefs in the relationship between religion and parenting practices.[1] Beginning with Gerhard Lenski's research, sociologists have found correlations between individuals' religious characteristics, such as denomination, and their valuing of obedience and autonomy in children.[2] Over time, Protestant-Catholic differences in these values have more or less converged, while intradenominational differences have emerged.[3] Starks and Robinson have shown that, while denominational differences have not disappeared, especially between evangelical Protestants compared with mainline Protestants and Catholics, differences in the valuing of obedience and autonomy in children occurs across denominations according to moral cosmologies.[4] Those espousing religious orthodoxy, for whom moral decisions take place in a communitarian fashion whereby believers subject themselves to God's laws, tend to value obedience over autonomy in children, but Starks and Robinson's "modernists," for whom moral choices occur in contexts and whose choices occur in an individualistic framework, value autonomy over obedience.

Other studies examine specific views of human nature that underlie such broad moral cosmologies. For example, one illustrative set of studies involves the relation of evangelical Protestantism to the corporal punishment of children. Using survey data, Christopher Ellison and his colleagues show that conservative Protestants are more likely to endorse and use corporal punishment than other parents and explain this finding as a consequence of religious beliefs: beliefs in biblical literalism, the idea that human nature is inherently sinful, and the belief that sin demands punishment.[5] Related research, on topics including general childrearing practices and parental values of obedience versus autonomy, similarly connects conservative theological Protestant beliefs with particular childrearing styles and valuing obedience in children. John Bartkowski, Brad Wilcox, and their colleagues fill out and build on this research by demonstrating that theological views are likewise related to strict discipline, together with warmth and expressiveness, arguing that they comprise an authoritative parenting style, not an authoritarian one.[6] Each of these studies theorizes how religious beliefs about human nature are intertwined with ideas about childhood, and they demonstrate a close link between parenting practices and religious beliefs.

This chapter engages this tradition of scholarship by closely examining the relation of parenting and religious beliefs and practices at Assumption and Saint Brigitta to trace out when and how religion is salient in childrearing. I maintain that in Christian churches, perceptions of childhood can often be informed by beliefs about sin, grace, and the human condition, with the practical problems of parenting perceived through religiously supported lenses. The bulk of the examples discussed in this chapter are, in fact, based in parents' solutions to such practical problems. However, beliefs and perceptions about children and childhood are not only practical; they also have the capacity to symbolize adults' concerns, worries, and hopes. Thus, while children are the focus of parents' many practical concerns—such as providing stability for them and monitoring unwanted or unsafe influences—they also symbolically embody broader worries and hopes in the lives of the adults who care for them. Because childhood itself is culturally constructed, children not only embody a set of shared experiences that we call childhood but also can represent other meanings, values, and concerns about the world they inhabit and the adult worlds parents negotiate, including those linked to morality and to conduct of life generally.

We see this, in fact, in the first vignette, when June locates her feelings of protectiveness toward children in motherhood. These feelings of protectiveness are not only a practical response to the worlds of childhood that her children must negotiate but also are constitutive of her identity as a mother, and they symbolize her sense of self. Moreover, they have become symbolic of, and symbolized in, her feelings about the morality and public politics of legalized abortion, since her feelings of protectiveness toward children aroused in motherhood have transformed her beliefs about this issue. Her Catholicism offers an interpretive lens whereby she connects emotions anchoring her maternal identity to the issue of abortion, fusing religion with life experience in ways that view cultural conflicts over the family from one deeply felt pole. Similarly, Joey's baptism is the culmination of a practical process through which he has joined the Catholic Church, but it is also much more: at his baptism, the congregation engaged and symbolically enacted shared beliefs about the importance of people's connectedness to others and the naturalness and capability of children's faith. At Saint Brigitta, the emphasis on connectedness and individual autonomy, even among children, contributes to a religious culture that supports individuals' choices and the expansion of people's options—and this sensibility supports positions often opposed to Assumption's in various cultural conflicts surrounding the family, although as we have seen, these positions, though tending toward one pole, are more varied. At Assumption, the problems of childhood come to symbolize and express family breakdown in society, and children's religiousness presents hope for a restoration of the values and structures of faith and family espoused there. At Saint Brigitta, children are also a sign of hope, but it is a hope for people's closer connection to God and a widely inclusive connection with others that stretches especially to those with little social power.

Thus the following analysis focuses on how children are perceived, cared for, and situated in relationships with the adults in their lives, rather than on children's own subcultures. Moreover, in foregrounding this analysis, it is important to acknowledge that despite their differences, the ways in which parishioners at Assumption and Saint Brigitta approach childhood and parenting have important similarities; in fact, these congregations are more similar in their perceptions of the practical problems of childhood than in many other areas of family life. They are both concerned about appropriately protecting children from adult realities for which children are unprepared, such as sexuality and violence. They are each concerned to give children tools for attaining happiness and successful living according to the standards of their class cultures, which includes passing on their Catholic faith to their children. But although families in each parish, by virtue of their common class location, confront similar challenges in childrearing, and both groups perceive at least some of the same problems, they differ in their interpretations and relative emphases of these problems, and they tend to solve them differently.

How do they differ? Although the cultures of childhood at Assumption and Saint Brigitta both enunciate belief and hope in human goodness, especially as it inheres in children, the dominant culture at Assumption also emphasizes the human capacity for sinfulness. Parents at Assumption thus especially strive to preserve their children's innocence through parental protection, and they guide their religious and moral impulses through habitual devotional practices,

intellectually oriented religious and academic learning, and the creation of balanced routines for children. Acutely aware of the reality of human weakness, parents at Assumption emphasize character and virtue as desirable human qualities
that must be molded in children, first through parental influence but with the help
of teachers and pastors. The dominant culture at Saint Brigitta instead emphasizes persons' capacities for spiritual growth and human connectedness. Parents
at Saint Brigitta strive to protect children, but by contrast with Assumption, they
also intentionally expose children to some of the grittiness of urban living and
familiarize them with members of groups vulnerable to the effects of local and
global social problems. The parish extends the reach of community bonds beyond
the borders of the church to teach children to seek moral solidarity with those who
are different from them, and especially with the poor. In addition, they emphasize
the distinctiveness of children's faith and largely leave its development to children
themselves, while presenting adult models of faith by enfolding them within the
religious community. The basic outlines of these differences involve parents' often
conflicting impulses toward children's protection from and exposure to the wider
world, as well as the amount and kind of control they believe they should exercise
over their children.

Cultures of Childhood and Christian Anthropologies

Underlying each of these approaches to parenting is a particular culture of childhood and a related Christian anthropology. To see how these are related, we must
first analytically organize each local culture's beliefs and dominant perceptions
about childhood by asking: What does it mean to be a child in each setting? How
do congregants think children are "naturally" disposed? How do parents and
other adults perceive the challenges that children face within the larger society,
and how do they see their roles in dealing with them? In answering these questions, I draw on the insights of scholars who have shown the impact of cultural
constructions of childhood in shaping the lives of children in varying social and
historical contexts.

Through historical investigation, scholars have demonstrated that childhood is
not an unchanging, natural, or simply biological stage in the life course, but rather
that cultures of childhood have changed over time with changing social conditions. In particular, aspects of childhood ranging from parental and peer relationships, to children's participation in schooling and work, to children's passage into
adulthood have undergone great change with modernity.[7] Scholars have observed
that the notion of childhood is itself a modern invention, and even long-standing
understandings such as the notion of childhood innocence are primarily modern ideas. Steven Kline notes that medieval children were much more involved
in the economic tasks of adult living than children are today,[8] and Philip Aries

demonstrates the absence of perceptions of childhood innocence in the open and even ribald attitudes with which 16th-century European adults regarded prepubescent children's sexuality.[9] By contrast, moderns understand childhood as a distinct phase of life generally characterized by vulnerability, physical growth, and the need for nurture and play.

The different ways in which childhood has been perceived in modernity varies by many factors, including class contexts, people's perceptions of gender, and groups' perceptions of the wider world generally.[10] Some of these factors are discernible in the cultures of childhood at Assumption and Saint Brigitta, but except for each parish's dominant perceptions of the wider world, these factors did not appear to yield great differences. However, each congregation's ideas about human nature and its relation to childhood vary significantly.

Anthony Synott provides one model for understanding this relation by showing how cultures of childhood vary historically by their relation to ideas about human nature and by showing that particular ways of conceptualizing human nature lead to distinct parenting behaviors.[11] For instance, humanist and romantic views of childhood focus on children as basically or intrinsically good and entail that parents should treat children openly and without violence. By contrast, a Calvinist view of childhood perceives children, and humans generally, as prone to evil, requiring guidance and punishment. Similarly, an environmental approach to childhood understands children as primarily shaped by their environments and advocates the importance of education and nurture in shaping children into productive adults, whereas a contrasting view understands "nature," either biological or God-given, to be determinative of how children—and human beings in general—will develop.[12] Synott's work both demonstrates the importance of ideas about human nature generally and suggests the importance of religion, among other factors, upon those ideas. However, his characterization of religious views of human nature is far from complete, and in fact, Calvinist anthropologies differ significantly from Catholic ones.

Thus, in the following analysis, I extend this work, as well as the work of survey researchers on religion and parenting, by focusing explicitly on how distinctively Catholic understandings of human nature matter for local religious cultures of childhood in parishes. I explore Christian anthropologies and Catholic practices at Assumption and Saint Brigitta to show how and when they align with parenting practices. I claim that churches, as moral communities grounded in particular worldviews, are settings for the development of dominant group cultures around childhood that connect particular perceptions of childhood to religiously informed beliefs about the human person. Since many Catholic churches contain more internal variation than at Assumption and Saint Brigitta, other parishes may contain competing cultures of childhood. But because these parishes are closer to ideal-typical, the local cultures of childhood in each setting were not generally sites of struggle—although in what follows, I portray relevant variations in each.

The group cultures at Assumption and Saint Brigitta contribute to polarizing tendencies around family-related public conflicts in ways that both confirm and elaborate Georg Simmel's observations about the intensity of conflict among religious groups because of their basic similarity or historical unity.[13] In this case, arguably small differences in emphasis regarding each group's beliefs about the human person underlie their ideas of childhood and thereby support important differences in the childrearing practices in the two settings, despite the fact that many parents' concerns and goals for their children in these settings are essentially similar. These different practices create everyday routines that contribute to differences in the larger religious cultures in the two settings, and the boundaries of Catholic identities encoded in these differences are linked to polar views around public cultural conflicts surrounding the family. We see this especially in direct mentions of opposition to abortion and homosexual sex among Assumption's parishioners in discussions of childhood, which represent one pole and are opposed to the sensibility at Saint Brigitta that affirms individual autonomy and tolerance of particular differences in childrearing. Just as importantly, these two cultures of childhood express competing moral visions that in themselves represent polarizing tendencies among Catholics, which help to constitute a foundation for the ways in which they participate in cultural conflicts about the family in society generally.

The following analysis has two parts. The first examines the relation of cultures of childhood in each parish to Christian anthropologies, as I have described. The second explicitly examines its practical effects in parents' accomplishment of childhood religious socialization; here I examine what parents in each setting believe children need to learn and why, and how parents, along with other adults, teach them what they need to know. In each part of the analysis, I demonstrate how each congregation's central ecclesial metaphor figures in, and shares affinities with, the definition and tasks involved in children's religious socialization, as well as how Catholic identities are reflected in the Christian anthropologies observable in each congregation's perceptions of its children.

Childhood and Parenting at Our Lady of the Assumption

Assumption's dominant culture of childhood reflects a belief in human goodness, especially in the perception that children possess a natural curiosity that most often leads them in the right direction as they seek to learn about the world, if protected from adult realities and properly guided. However, children's innocence makes them vulnerable, and with little experience of the world, parents believe that the sober realities of adult living have the capacity to influence them in undesirable ways, especially in a society in which older supports for the nuclear family have diminished. Thus children need protection and strong guidance. Moreover, for these parents, protecting and guiding children in a society rent by family breakdown is doubly difficult because of the perceived dearth of Catholic contexts, especially schools, that can support parents' efforts at protection, guidance, and the teaching of a strong doctrinal faith. Therefore, counterintuitively, parents find themselves operationalizing the boundaries of their Catholic identity against particular Catholic institutions. These boundaries are discursively constructed in ways that support the polarizing and even antagonistic tendencies in Assumption's Catholic identities.

The perceptions of childhood that ground this approach to childrearing are underlain by a Christian anthropology that calls for attentiveness to human sinfulness, in the self and especially in the wider world, and a notion of sin that has qualities of a disease, including the potential to infect others by contact with it. This further implies the need for protection of children from arenas where sin and its effects are evident, as well as building up virtue in children as protection from sin and its ill effects. Moreover, along with the emphasis upon sin, the central metaphor of the church as a family works to delineate the boundaries of the social worlds to which children should be connected and those to which they should not—for Assumption itself is a protective milieu for children as they cultivate the virtues necessary for successful negotiation of the wider world.

A Culture of Childhood: Children's Innocence, Sin and Weakness, and the Need for Protection

Although June's reflections on childhood at the beginning of this chapter depend on her personal life story as much as her religious orientation, her perspective on children and parenting is one that has resonance with the shared perceptions and practices surrounding children in Assumption's religious milieu. In the vignette, June talks about childhood innocence as something to be preserved in children, reflecting a common sentiment often expressed by Assumption's parents. June's concerns about preserving children's innocence emphasize a portrait of a child who needs protection to thrive in his or her daily routine. The arenas in which children are perceived to need protection include aspects of the adult world considered to have age-inappropriate contents for children, such as various forms of media, and also the social environments of children in schools and neighborhoods. Although parents at Assumption were concerned to protect their children in a general way and mentioned a variety of concerns, they were particularly invested in preserving their innocence about adult sexualities.[14] Perceived improper sexual conduct was both an adult reality from which children should be protected and a metaphor for disease among individuals and society more generally.

First, in explaining why she homeschools, June talked about childhood innocence, together with her concerns about broad patterns of social learning that usually occur in school contexts.[15] Here she worried mainly about the effects of children's peer cultures. She focused not on academic learning, but social learning, saying that she wanted to preserve her children from having to learn to fit in with their peers at an early age. June doesn't want her children to experientially acquire practical knowledge about informal peer-driven socialization and social hierarchies, about "popularity and clothes and crushes" that most children encounter when they go to school. Preserving childhood innocence, therefore, involves limiting children's exposure to and knowledge of particular kinds of social relationships. In protecting them from the environment of the school, June is protecting them from the structuring of children's peer groups around social and prepubescent romantic relationships. Others are similarly concerned to protect children from the negative effects of childhood peer cultures; for example, some choose private school environments, where they hope these effects will be mitigated.

But in the interview, June moved beyond these broad concerns about children's peer cultures to talk about their effects, and those of other social settings, on children' knowledge of sexuality. Families at Assumption are explicitly concerned to preserve their children's innocence regarding sexuality. June gives examples of exposure to sexual images, bodies, and practices that she believes to have profound effects on children if they encounter them. She believes this in part because their lack of experience makes them vulnerable to the negative effects of viewing sexual images and in part because she perceives that contact with adult sexual practices may lead to the development of unhealthy and immoral sexual habits. When asked what she found to be most difficult about raising her children, June said,

> The most difficult thing is protecting their innocence. With Internet access, we have to watch closely because of pornography. I really worry about that. Early exposure to porn can have a big influence on [boys'] psyches for the rest of their lives. Seeing images of women like that can change how they see women—as objects for your own pleasure.
>
> Girls, too, how they're supposed to look and act. One of the things that bothers me about them playing with the kids on our street is that we have three girls a couple of doors down—I love the family—but I see girls acting inappropriately, like Britney Spears, suggestively. They're not aware of it, they don't know the ramifications, how it's affecting them, growing up in an oversexualized culture. It bothers me. I know I can't hide that from

them. It's all over the place, in billboards and commercials, even without television.

June believes that societal messages about sexuality have the capacity to profoundly affect children's psyches and the way they see themselves. She fears that viewing sexual images and engaging in suggestive behaviors can affect children even at very young ages, regardless of whether they understand the significance of what they are doing. June's general concerns about the availability of sexual images are, of course, common complaints, and in fact, parents at Saint Brigitta expressed similar concerns. But at Assumption, these concerns about children's exposure to adult sexualities in the broader culture are spoken of in ways that are intertwined with religious beliefs and logics.

As we have seen, church teachings on sexuality are authoritative among Assumption's parishioners. They therefore resist a broader social climate that condones the disjuncture of sexual expression from marriage and procreation in premarital sex, homosexuality, artificial contraception, and abortion—aligning themselves at one pole in cultural conflicts over the family with religious arguments for the rightness of this view. Moreover, they not only view permissive sexual norms in the broader society as sinful but also believe that exposure to them can lead to children's moral degradation. In other words, sexual sin has the qualities of a disease—it weakens the individual, it weakens society, and it can be transmitted even by incidental contact or exposure to others affected by it, even indirectly. Therefore, parents see the need for diagnosing and avoiding environments ripe for exposure.

How does one recognize a setting in which children's innocence is likely to be threatened? Which environments are potentially problematic, and why? Here is June's identification and diagnosis of one such abnormal environment and its effects on a friend of her daughter's:

> Two years ago, a six-year-old boy was interested in getting our daughter, Beth, who was four at the time, to take her underpants off. I told him that he had to leave, and I didn't let him in the house after that. He must have had exposure to porn! A brother with Internet access, his mother was depressed and on painkillers—they let them watch anything on cable, see anything on the computer. I *know* they were getting into that, because that's not normal to be that interested, and persist and persist. But Beth didn't know.

June does not talk about how this incident affected Beth, but she does speculate on how unsavory influences in this boy's family of origin might have caused his behavior. June tells us that this boy lives in an environment of family problems and insufficient supervision, a world of adult problems and freedoms where children can view things they shouldn't, and she fears that Beth's exposure to him will result in her unhealthy contact with age-inappropriate sexual knowledge. In June's view, this boy's environment is antithetical to the preservation of childhood innocence; his behavior is a product of insufficient protection. Families should protect children, but they often do not, at least in part because of insufficient judgment or an inability to do so—for example, a mother who is "depressed and on painkillers." Although June does not explicitly say it, she implies here and elsewhere, as do others at Assumption, that such problems are a result of family change, breakdown, and decline in contemporary society. Thus in these cases, childhood exposes the *consequences* of family change wrought by sexual sin and shows its negative effects. Not only do children become a barometer of family breakdown and a symbol of its effects but also they make evident the acute need to protect children in such contexts.

Children's exposure to unwanted sexual images can also come from consumer culture. In discussing the limits she places on her children's exposure to sexual images, Julia Flaherty discusses the boundaries she draws for her children but acknowledges a range of attitudes toward such exposure among Assumption's parents.

> I won't give my girls Barbie dolls, because they're too sexualized...at the same time, I don't think it's a mortal sin to watch a movie like *Meet the Parents*. Some people at Assumption are probably watching out for their kids' souls more than I am. I don't think you can have kids be hothouse flowers. They're going to be all over the place.

Although she perceives that even toys can have negative sexualizing effects on children, Julia believes that it is impossible to completely protect them. She tries to guard her children against possible emotional harm but perceives her standards to be less stringent than some other Assumption parents' standards—specifically, less religiously stringent standards. Indeed, other parents had stricter standards that some talked about, as Julia does here, in terms of sin. Concerns about children's contact with adult sexuality, therefore, are not only about their psychological health but also about the constitution of their moral life.

Although Julia believes that it is neither desirable nor possible to completely protect her children, when her first grader, Gabe, was ready for Tiger Scouts, she was conflicted. Julia likes the breadth and structure of scouting, but she was concerned because of media attention over homosexuality and the Boy Scouts. She worried that if Gabe became involved in scouting, he might encounter gay scout leaders. She explained, "I don't want that. I don't want my kid thinking that's okay. I've known some nice gay guys in my life, but as a parent, I have reservations about that kind of thing. They go off on a camping trip—it would really bother me." Significantly, Julia begins with practical concerns about what Gabe might learn about gay lifestyles and not wanting him to think that she morally approves of homosexuality. But then she appears to conflate homosexuality with pedophilia in worrying about sending Gabe on a camping trip with the Tiger Scouts. In a way similar to her concern about the effect of certain children's toys, scouting is a children's setting but one that possibly exposes her son to an inappropriately sexualized atmosphere, even a dangerous one. Moreover, the issue of homosexuality is not just a moral judgment of right and wrong behavior, nor is it just a symbolic issue related to family decline; rather, it is also one that is implicated in how parents rear their children and construct routines for them.

In fact, in many of the comments Assumption's parents made about their concerns over children's exposure to sexuality, moral concerns and danger are conflated, and immorality is perceived as diseased and dangerous. These concerns are obviously practical; they are about shaping children's behavior and preserving their well-being, since immoral sexual behavior is perceived to be a cause of individual and social problems and implicated concretely in family breakdown.

But issues of sexual behavior are even more; they are also a metaphor for the results that contact with immorality can engender in young people. This symbolic dimension of sexual morality is reflected in Adele Dunning's words as she talks about the problems that she has seen in her own children's peers.

> I look at most kids today, and they are walking wounded, hurt by divorce and other kinds of family problems. And schools do all the wrong things. We [i.e., as a society] are raising a generation of smart, educated kids who can't think clearly, who are fornicating themselves. They are not happy, not satisfied, not functional.

Here sexual immorality is employed as a striking metaphor for young people's unproductive and misdirected actions. Adele succinctly summarizes the ill effects of family change with this metaphor, using the imagery of fornication to express concern over how the current generation of young people hurts themselves because of the habits they are learning in the very social institutions that are supposed to protect them—the family and the schools. Thus immoral sex, as it is defined by the church's teachings, and its perceived relation to social problems and disease of the self is so much a matter of urgent concern at Assumption that it is an easily available and pointedly vivid image for what happens to children when their innocence goes unprotected and their character development is not properly guided.

Adele believes that in spite of their intelligence and the intellectual training children receive, in "fornicating themselves," they are not thinking clearly; despite the pleasures of the lives they are living, they are neither happy nor functional because their moral compass, which should be instilled and strengthened by school and family, is instead misdirected or broken by these same institutions. In fact, Adele criticizes not only the society that tolerates this situation but also, perhaps surprisingly, the Catholic school that her children attended before homeschooling.

> I never intended to home school. But Saint Norbert's was not what
> I expected. The religious character [of the school] was opposed to what
> I wanted to teach my children. It was very touchy-feely. For instance, during my kids' first communion preparation, the teachers edited the Ten
> Commandments to eight, and they changed them. "Thou shalt not bear
> false witness" became "Be sincere." When they came home from school,
> I felt like I had to hose them down.

In extending her criticism of problematic environments to Catholic schools, Adele marks the boundaries of Catholic identity narrowly. Not all Catholic education is equal, nor is all of it authentic. The boundaries enclosing "authentic" Catholicism oppose those expressions perceived to be inauthentic because they threaten her children's spiritual health. Adele elaborated that, by contrast with Saint Norbert's School, "virtue and objective truth" are the qualities of emphasis in students' character formation she finds in good Catholic schooling. Her emphasis on virtue hearkens back to an older approach to building character in children, one that she believes is necessary in a contemporary society that presents acute problems for children as they approach adulthood.

> Today is worse in a lot of ways than the 1960s....I don't think my kids have
> any trouble understanding how wrong the world is, but if you want to be a
> good person, it's really tough. I hope they hold out....We live in a culture
> that undermines the family and that undermines decency! There is not
> a good sense of family in our society....But family is the *only* salvation.
> Family is the salvation of the country. That's what I believe.

In a society that Adele perceives to be rent with moral turpitude, families are the only institutions that she believes are able to turn society back toward wholeness and decency. Despite the woundedness of many families, Adele therefore also sees the family as the primary cause for hope, and her work within her own family is one small step in that direction. In fact, Adele talks about the family—the modern nuclear family—as *salvation*, that is, as a particular religious solution to the country's problems, one intertwined with and emphasized as central to Catholic identities practiced at Assumption. Although Adele states her concerns from a particular viewpoint on family and American culture, many Catholic parents—including many at Saint Brigitta—would find resonance in the worry of "how wrong the world is" and in the assertion that children encounter a societal culture that contains insufficient supports for them as they strive to grow into mature and ethically oriented adults. But in refusing to acknowledge Saint Norbert's as sufficiently Catholic, she parts ways with her Catholic peers. Perspectives and sentiments like Adele's, especially when linked to Catholic institutions such as schools, contribute to heightened stakes and, correlatively, parishioners' positions at one pole in cultural conflicts over the family. Her remarks explicitly define the boundaries of religious identity against other Catholics and Catholic institutions that make different assumptions or emphasize different—and in her view, gravely mistaken—values and practices around the family, and challenge their authority. Although expressed in terms of doctrine, this is primarily a moral concern arrived at through pedagogical and cultural differences with Saint Norbert's—that is, through her approach to moral education—prompted by the perspective on childrearing in the culture in which she is embedded.

In addition, the definition of the good family has observable characteristics and norms that allow its recognition and helps us to understand why, in the vignette that begins this chapter, June expresses feeling uncomfortable at Saint Barnabas, even though Saint Barnabas understands and markets itself as a family-oriented Catholic Church. When June discussed the dearth and invisibility of large families there compared with Assumption, it was not only the size of families that bothered her but also the particular ways in which family identities and habits, especially religious habits, are expressed and practiced at Saint Barnabas. June's comments show that it is not merely the presence of many children that distinguishes Catholic families at Assumption, but their presence together: their habits of thinking of themselves as religiously faithful families, embodied in their presence together at church on Sunday and in other public settings. This way of being a family entails a particular way of seeing and living in the world—one that shields children from harmful elements in the broader societal fabric, in part, by their family's presence together in the many walks of public life.

The central metaphor of the church as family, then, expressed at Assumption at Sunday mass and embodied in this particular way of family life, has both practical affinities with childrearing and broader symbolic ones. The family in symbol and practice preserves children's innocence in an oversexualized, intensely interconnected, and often invasive broader culture and fosters a strong sense of familial belonging that allows parishioners to retain considerable independence from that culture. In fact, this image of the family is not only a symbol for right living but also an implicit critique of Catholic identities that are perceived to be "insufficiently" Catholic, as well as those that signal the legitimacy of contemporary family forms that do not cohere with the content of church teachings.

Religion and Parenting: Children's Capability and the Inculcation of Virtue

Despite the recognition of human sinfulness, in ways similar to historical conceptions of childhood in humanistic and romantic traditions, children at Assumption are perceived to be basically or naturally good. But at the same time, adults at Assumption understand parental guidance to be essential for children to achieve their potential and realize their promise. Like traditions that view the child as a *tabula rasa* ("clean slate"), children are also in need of guidance as they grow to preserve and nurture that goodness. This may seem contradictory, but it is not. Not only is this approach consonant with middle-class norms—especially the impulse to guidance, which is similar to what Annette Lareau terms "concerted cultivation"[16]—but also it can be understood from a religious point of view through the Catholic principle that grace builds upon nature.

The perception of the capable and curious child is especially resonant around issues of schooling and around children's religious and moral education—two concerns that are often practically intertwined in the choices of parents for their children and in children's everyday routines. The image of the capable and curious child is exemplified in June's story of how she homeschools her oldest son, Jeremy. For June, children are capable because of their individuality; their curiosities and learning styles result in natural impulses to learn that best flourish in child-centered styles of learning. In daily life, parents nurture children's capabilities, especially their moral and religious growth, with two strategies: by fashioning safe and supportive home and school environments where they can accomplish personal growth by following their own impulses and interests and, at the same time, by creating or taking advantage of structures for academic, religious, and moral learning. For Assumption's children, then, the structures of schooling and the freedom to pursue their curiosities and interests ideally go hand in hand.

This approach to children and childhood is undergirded by assumptions that children are naturally good and that education matters, echoing historical romantic and humanistic conceptions of childhood, as well as the idea of the child as a clean slate, ready for the impress of education.[17] This perspective also reflects parental sensibilities of natural growth and concerted cultivation that Lareau identifies among working-class and middle-class parents, respectively.[18] But unlike the parents in Lareau's study, Assumption's parents combine these strategies; they are at least partially uprooted from the class embeddedness Lareau describes. Assumption's parents concertedly cultivate moral, religious, intellectual, and physical skills in their children, but this cultivation is tempered by the perception that children, even with their shortcomings and the human tendency toward sinfulness, will grow morally and in other ways because of a natural proclivity to goodness.

The perception of the capable and curious child is resonant at Assumption especially around the religious and moral education of children. Parents at Assumption—and adults in the congregation generally—highly value the intellectual content and doctrinal arguments of Catholicism, and parents take care to be sure that their children are well schooled in Catholic doctrine and habituated in virtue. Echoing a general concern of Assumption's parents, Denise Wood, 41, who with her husband, Dan, has four children from ages eight to 15, explains, "My husband loves to say, 'If we're paying for a Catholic education, darn it, we want one.'"

But parents do not necessarily expect doctrinal education to take place in a classroom or a religious education program. This is partly the case because of the difficulty of finding religious education programs they judge to be adequate for their children in Catholic schools and churches and also because parents believe that religious education begins in the home and the church, where parents act as children's first teachers. On the one hand, on Sunday mornings at Assumption, it is easy to see why children are perceived to have natural religious sensibilities, for these children display serious interest and self-discipline during mass from the time they are very young, practicing the arts of quiet concentration or quiet play from the age of three or four. On the other hand, parents assiduously encourage such behaviors at mass and teach during mass, so that by the time they are school-aged, children are fully participating: they sing, pray orally and silently, kneel, sit, stand, and genuflect at the appropriate times and places, practicing adult habits of worship.

Mothers and fathers take seriously their responsibility as their children's first teachers in the Catholic faith, though they most often also see themselves as working in concert with trusted others. Denise, whose four children have attended both private and public schools, explains, "I do think first and foremost that we want to make sure our children are trained in the Catholic faith [in a way] that's really sound. When you're [able] to get that at school, those schools realize that we are the primary educators and they are going to help us teach our kids the Catholic faith." Thus, parents at Assumption understand doctrinal education to be fundamental to living good and effective adult lives and therefore partner with teachers at Catholic schools that share this emphasis in order to equip their children with these tools.

In religiously encouraging and guiding their children to learn and grow in faith, parents are also often personally assisted by priests, especially in determining children's preparation and readiness to receive the sacraments. For example, Father Aidan and Father James sometimes help them in determining when a child is ready for First Communion or First Confession by assessing his or her faith and understanding of the sacraments. In one of the stories a father told about Father James's assistance, the priest had approached him when his son was not much more than five years old and told him that he thought his son might be ready to receive his First Holy Communion, even though the customary time for the reception of First Communion is in second grade, about seven years of age. Father James then sat down with the child to ask him what he knew about the mass. Despite the boy's lack of formal religious education, he had absorbed enough knowledge about the Eucharist from going to mass and family religious practice to correctly answer everything that Father James asked him. Father James determined that the boy was ready.

Father James's practice of noticing when children are ready to receive the sacraments and telling them so affirms parents' perceptions of their children as naturally capable and self-driven learners who actively seek knowledge of God and the church. At the same time, parents' cultivation of religious habits in the home—including such practices as grace before meals, bedtime prayers and examinations of conscience, family recitation of the rosary, reading religious books, and viewing religious videos and films—no doubt makes it more likely that children will seek out religious knowledge and show evidence of religious progress, perhaps especially at young ages when their social circles are likely to be more limited and homogeneous than they are later in childhood. And in fact, although this father made it clear that neither he nor his wife had tried to teach their son about the Eucharist—and was proud that he had shown the sensitivity, interest, and initiative to learn about his faith on his own—this family, like others at Assumption, regularly engaged in daily practices that cultivated a sense of the importance of, and attentiveness to, the religious dimension of their lives.

Other Catholic parishes often assume that they will do the lion's share of the religious education of their parishioners' children and use sacramental preparation programs to provide parents with updating and religious education opportunities. But at Assumption, even though priests pay close attention to families where parents are religiously knowledgeable and provide them with help, they actively encourage all mothers and fathers in their role as their children's primary religious teacher. And although many priests in Catholic parishes encourage parental involvement in children's religious education as Assumption's priests do, not all are as personally involved as at Assumption. Involved parents at Assumption appreciate—and in some cases even appear to expect—that priests will play a personal role in children's religious lives. Chris Schweickert's experience with sacramental preparation at another Catholic parish illustrates this point. Chris told of having asked one of the priests at Saint Barnabas, where he and his family sometimes attend mass, to help him in preparing his son Jeremy for his First Confession by speaking to his son. Father Jeff, however, surprised Chris by referring him to Saint Barnabas' director of religious education. To Chris, this priest's response seemed disinterested and abrupt; Chris's experience of religiously educating his children, and his experience of priests at Assumption assisting him, had led him to believe that this should be a priest's role even if others, including a parish director of religious education, also participated in his child's religious education.

Chris's story also reveals something about expectations concerning the religious education of children and religious knowledge more generally at Assumption. As we have seen, many of Assumption's adults seek doctrinal knowledge of Catholicism, and priests and lay leaders develop parishioners' religious knowledge in doctrinally based homilies, young adult meetings, Rites of Christian Initiation for Adults (RCIA), pre-Cana, lecture series, Evenings of Reflection, and Cooperators' Circles. Parents' religious knowledge thus acquired increases confidence in their ability as their children's first religious teachers.

In addition, the parish also provides a family mass one Sunday each month that assists parents in teaching children Catholic practice through habituation. Small but significant changes are made to the mass on these Sundays to highlight children's participation and leadership. A few older girls and boys are chosen to read the first and second scripture readings from the lectern, which they do quite seriously and solemnly, and others take turns reading the Prayers of the Faithful. Children, accompanied by their parents, bring up the gifts at the offertory. In the homily during the family mass, the priest mentions children or directs remarks specifically to them. On Sundays when the family mass is scheduled, one sees more children in the congregation than usual; many of the families whose children attend the parish school come to the family mass instead of the Spanish-language mass many of them usually attend. The family mass is a resource that helps parents socialize their children to habits of adult religious practice at mass at young ages.

As parents spoke about their efforts to build on children's goodness by religiously habituating them through worship and Catholic education, virtue was repeatedly named as a primary goal. Parishioners spoke about virtues in the context of classical and scriptural referents and counted charity, honesty, self-discipline, self-sacrifice, purity, patience, fortitude, and courage among the virtues they valued.

Parents encourage virtue in children especially through religious devotions. For example, several parents described bedtime routines of examinations of conscience during night prayers. Through this practice, they teach their children to identify bad or sinful behavior and resolve to correct it. Denise describes how she and her husband taught her children to do this.

> The first thing we taught the kids is to make an examination of conscience every night, and when they were little, while they were in their beds,

I would ask them to do their own private little thing; hey everybody, ask God, think of three things, what you did that was good, what you did that was not so good, and how you're going to be better tomorrow.

She also describes other spiritual practices she teaches and encourages in her children:

We have the vocal prayers, the rosary—we have a rule, if it's going to be after eight o'clock that everyone gets home, then you're responsible for saying your own rosary....And then early on, we've done three Hail Marys for purity and then "Blessed Mother, help me to be pure and good."

Through regular devotional practices like the rosary, Denise's family prays together every day. She and her husband connect these practices to moral behavior in directing her children to ask the Blessed Mother for goodness and purity. As Denise's description illustrates, parents at Assumption teach their children formal prayers, simple extemporaneous prayers, and how to reflect upon the morality of their daily behavior, all from the time they are very young.

This concerted cultivation of moral and spiritual formation in the home is complemented with a rigorous academic education that is both intellectually and morally oriented. One mother who sends two of her children to schools sponsored by Opus Dei fleshes out a classroom philosophy explicitly designed to inculcate virtues; she explains, "Day to day, the classroom philosophy is charity, order, patience. These are things that they bring up in the classroom." Similarly, Adele emphasized the importance of character education in the homeschooling curriculum she uses, explaining that it emphasizes patriotism, respect for authority, and "pro-family, pro-normal family, pro-mom and dad." In this view, education is incomplete if it does not explicitly provide both a religious worldview and the ethical precepts that flow from it.

Denise brings these concerns together in describing the small independent school that she and her husband helped to found—and which her ten-year-old daughter attends—as follows, reflecting her thoughts about what schooling should provide.

The school focuses on the main things: of course, a solid Catholic education, character or virtue formation—character education, which is the current term, I guess—and solid academics. I think the families that come to this school that are not Catholic, I would venture to say—and I've heard and I've known enough [parents] to know—that they are mainly coming for the character formation and the academics. They go hand in hand. You've got to have the Catholic faith, and then academic excellence. That's

what we're looking for, all three of those: Catholic doctrine, character formation, and academic [education].

Significantly, Denise mentions the presence of non-Catholic families in the school,
several of whom are Muslim, who value the combination of intellectual rigor and
moral formation that are distinct from, but intertwined with, Catholic formation
and education. Involved parents at Assumption generally look for academic rigor,
formation in the virtues, and religious education grounded in Catholic doctrine
in schooling. In so doing, parents hope to build on children's natural goodness
by providing guidance, especially moral guidance, so that they can, as Adele said,
"bend the reed the way you want it to grow."

However, in social environments of childhood among the middle classes,
where the tasks of concerted cultivation seem ever present, making sure that there
is time for academic, moral, and religious education is not always easy. Therefore,
a final important quality parents at Assumption seek to instill in their children's
lives, and in their own, is a healthy balance: between children's activities and family time, between work and recreation, between achievement and worship. Denise
explains,

> The Vicar of Opus Dei gave a talk to women and said, "We can take our
> kids, sign them up for things that are formation activities, but we have to
> do it at home." How many times in the past month have I brought my kid
> to a sports event, versus asking them to pray for five minutes?

Knowing the busy schedules of middle-class soccer moms and their children, this
priest admonishes mothers to help children keep their lives in perspective through
regular prayer in the home, even amid the busyness. Similarly, another mother
spoke of methodically regulating her children's activities so that their schedules
provided some activities that intellectually stimulated them, others that physically
challenged them, and still others that allowed relaxation and personal attention for
both her children and herself. Such routines allow mothers to nourish children's
curiosity, intellect, and capacity for discipline—and in all of these things, combined with religious formation in the family and at church, they cultivate virtuous
habits and dispositions in their children.

At their most optimistic, Assumption's parents hope that their children will,
through their own future practice, improve society in ways that better support, and
not subvert, this vision of childhood and the human person, as well as the tenets
of faith and family that accompany it. One parent observed that the cohorts of
Catholics who are parenting children right now were raised to practice their faith
privately but that their children talk about their nascent faith publicly in ways that
these parents never have. Assumption's parents see in their children a hope for

the future, in that these naturally capable children already show signs, in talking of their faith to others, of adult qualities of religious and social leadership. They hope for an evangelizing generation capable of recovering this vision of faith and family among Catholics and in society broadly, one whose lives and words will convince others of the rightness of their religious and familial convictions and result in social and religious change. In other words, their hope for change in the midst of ecclesial and societal polarization is not for rapprochement or dialogue with others, including other Catholics, whose convictions differ, but conversion—a conversion that several of these parents have experienced themselves.

At the same time, these parents are keenly aware of the social limitations that impinge on their present efforts, especially amid the societal family change and religious polarization from whose effects they seek to shelter their children. Joanna Fitch, the mother of two teenage daughters and a school-aged son, was realistically cautious and even pessimistic at times about her capacity to protect her children. Along with her daily efforts, prayer provided a divine recourse for her, in asking for grace and protection for her children when things seem especially difficult. At Assumption, this sentiment is widely shared.

> Raising children is very tough, very hard. I tell them, I want to prepare them, to be ready for the fires they will face out there in the world. I try to teach them, and I pray for them—keep them safe with my prayers, until the time that they can do it for themselves on their own.

Childhood and Parenting at Saint Brigitta

Like parents at Assumption, those at Saint Brigitta also believe in children's fundamental goodness. But instead of emphasizing the threat of sin in the self and in the wider world, the dominant Christian anthropology undergirding perceptions of childhood at Saint Brigitta is a view of the human person that emphasizes humans' psychological developmental capacities on the way to adulthood, individuals' need for self-knowledge, and their fundamental connectedness with others as a participation in the life of God. By contrast with Assumption, childhood faith is less something to be channeled than it is to be affirmed and allowed to grow on its own. In Lareau's terms, childhood faith at Saint Brigitta is the object of natural growth, not concerted cultivation.[19] Following the psychological orientation in its Christian anthropology and by contrast with perceptions of childhood at Assumption, children's faith is understood to be distinctive to childhood and fundamentally different from adult faith. Parents therefore give great weight to children's experience, recognizing its fundamental difference from adult faith, and patiently allow the capabilities of children to grow developmentally.

Moreover, the importance of one's connectedness to others in Saint Brigitta's Christian anthropology has both pedagogical and moral consequences for childrearing. In terms of teaching, while parents strive to protect their children, they also value the lessons gained from experiences of cautious exposure to some of the difficult realities of life, especially the circumstances of people different from and less economically advantaged than they are. They encourage their children to care about and care for others beyond their immediate neighborhood, teaching them that caring for others is a fundamental moral response to the human connectedness that originates in God and is central to their religious identity as Catholics. Thus in childrearing, the central metaphor of the church as community is transposed onto the neighborhood and even beyond, extending families' reach beyond the church to the neighborhood as a setting for children's growth. The roots of childrearing strategies at Saint Brigitta are found in this vision of God and the human person, which emphasizes that all people have fundamental goodness in them, that all deserve care, and that the church's mission is to help improve all lives, especially those most in need. These emphases result in the practice of a largely different religious culture of childhood at Saint Brigitta than at Assumption in ways that intertwine with and support perspectives on several family-related public issues opposed to those embraced at Assumption—despite the fact that parents in both settings have many common childrearing concerns.

A culture of childhood: human goodness and therapeutic models of parenting

In the event of Joey's baptism, we can see some of the varied ways that children in the Saint Brigitta gym respond to worship. On many Sundays, worship is primarily an adult activity. However, when children are focal actors during worship, such as at Joey's baptism, or on special occasions when children perform liturgical dance or enact the Gospel, the congregation's children move from the periphery of the gym and become enfolded within it. At those times, children participate in congregational roles as they did at Joey's baptism, with responsory prayer, song, enthusiastic improvisation, and even applause. On these occasions, they participate in worship as active members of the Saint Brigitta community, yet still clearly as children.

The ways in which children are included in the mass in the Saint Brigitta gym reflect a dominant view of children as basically good and spontaneously oriented toward God and in this respect is similar to people's understanding of children at Assumption. But by contrast with parents at Assumption, Saint Brigitta's parents never talked about teaching their children to practice examining their consciences and turning daily from sin to virtue; they instead utilized the language and skills of psychotherapy with the goals of modeling and teaching children to become conversant with both the psychological and spiritual dimensions of the interior self. At Saint Brigitta, then, human psychology and faith are closely related and intertwined. And more broadly, since understandings of childhood are informed by psychological views of human development, childhood is understood as a distinct stage of life that is profoundly different from adulthood, with unique expressions and tasks that children must move though. Ideally, children move through childhood in warm, appropriately protected, and supportive environments, but where they are mostly allowed to follow their own inclinations. Parents think of the Saint Brigitta gym mass, and the community of the parish, as one such environment.

Thus three aspects of the Christian anthropology underlying religious practice at Saint Brigitta are vividly revealed in its culture of childhood: a belief in the goodness of humans as children of God, a belief that connectedness to others is fundamental to human nature, and a developmental psychological view of the human person that emphasizes the importance of self-knowledge for human flourishing. This Christian anthropology is similar to Assumption's in its belief in human goodness, but it otherwise differs. It has implications not only for the practical work of parenting at Saint Brigitta but also for how this culture of childhood is implicated in polarizing tendencies in cultural conflicts about the family, especially in its beliefs and practices surrounding human connectedness, on the one hand, and individual autonomy, on the other.

How these principles of personhood shape perceptions of childhood at Saint Brigitta becomes evident as Maggie McNeill articulately describes how children's religious capabilities are intertwined with their capacity for human connection. Her children, Robbie and Rachel, were two of the children gathered at the edge of the congregation on the Sunday of Joey's baptism. A few weeks earlier, Maggie had talked about how these children, even at their very tender ages, behave in ways that she understands to be instinctively religious.

> Raising my children, their faith lives—I've been amazed at how early it starts. It seems instinctual, and makes me think, what a deep level we all operate on! Because I really think there's something going on for both of them. Robbie perceives going to church as a part of his routine—he sees his closest friends there, and he has a sense that we're all in it together, and no one can move!
>
> In our prayer group, we've tried to do something with families once a month, with simple prayer, and the kids are included as a part of that. And we've been praying with Robbie. We keep it really simple for him right now, with grace before meals and prayer before bed. We started when he was a year old. We ask who we're going to pray for, and we pray for whoever comes to [his] mind. Maybe he's thinking of it on a completely different level, but I think there's something to it.

The nascent faith that Maggie observes in her children is something that she identifies as deeply inscribed in the human person, already evident in toddlers, and
reflective of their basic goodness. Importantly, her perception that Robbie and
Rachel practice an instinctive faith is similar to Assumption's parents' images of
children as naturally religious. But by contrast with Assumption's parents, she
does not describe this sensibility explicitly as sacramental; moreover, it is one in
which God is implicit. Instead, incipient childhood faith is identified primarily in
children's recognition and desire for human connectedness. The church is a place
where one sees one's friends and where even very young children perceive and
respond to the centrality of the church as community.

When Robbie says his bedtime prayers, Maggie says, he most often prays
for his small group of friends. With their friends, she and Rick foster their children's religious practice in prayer group family gatherings, keeping the children's
prayer "really simple." Instinctive childhood faith at Saint Brigitta and the practices Maggie describes as fostering it—church attendance, fellowship, and simple
petitionary prayer at meals—reflect the assumption that this faith is grounded in
human connection. Like the adults who parent them, children perceive the immanent sense of the sacred in the church community and in the human connectedness it entails. In Maggie's description, childhood faith differs from adult religious
practice primarily in its simplicity. Maggie continues,

> I don't even know what our own prayer life is, but calling to mind, letting
> them know that you go with things—the good things and the hard things in
> your life. You go to God and keep it simple. I think what we do every night
> is helping them to ask God to hold people in their hearts, and...when put-
> ting them to bed, singing whatever, *Be Not Afraid* or *Amazing Grace*, that
> kind of stuff will hopefully [stick]. They'll be kind of mortified at some
> point. But Monica and John's Sean is in first grade, and it's very sweet to
> see how normally—how he does not do that.

Like parents at Assumption, many of Saint Brigitta's parents also first teach their
children to pray when they are very young. But the practice of prayer that Maggie
and Rick teach their children is different from that taught in Assumption's homes.
There is no emphasis on formal prayers or on examinations of conscience. Instead,
Maggie describes prayer mainly in the simple act of going to God with the joys and
difficulties of one's life and keeping other people in one's heart. Thus, Maggie and
Rick teach their children to pray in an extemporaneous, unstructured, and fluid
way. Giving their children a relatively large space in which to move when establishing the practices of prayer, they let their children shape much of its content.

Moreover, prayer is a ritual that Maggie believes her children may be uncomfortable with at some stage of their development. This assertion reflects both a

developmental perception of childhood and an awareness of adolescent rejection of church practice—an event that was common among adult's life stories, both at Saint Brigitta and at Assumption. At Assumption, however, while parents sometimes alluded to the possibility of adolescent rebellion against faith, they did not expect such events in their own children's lives, as Maggie does here. At the same time, Maggie is heartened to see that her friends' child is not—or is not yet—inclined this way, but instead responds "normally" to the practice of prayer.

Adults' perceptions of an instinctive faith in children that reflects human goodness and the parenting strategy of loosely guiding children in learning to pray are also observable in the general ambiance of the gym mass. In fact, parents take this approach to childhood in many arenas of life. The clear distinction between childhood and adult faith that is observable in gym mass practices is accompanied by an acceptance of children's distinctive needs and developmental trajectories; therefore, parents in the gym focus on the rite and allow their children or teens to choose their own level of participation in the mass, rather than instructing them or monitoring their behavior. But parents interact with their children more substantially after mass, by socializing while caring for a young child, shooting a few hoops with a son or daughter, and otherwise drawing their children into the sociability of community. In fellowship activities where the sociability of community is foremost, then, children and adults share a kind of social commonality, participating in an intergenerational setting and interactions, whereas at worship, children's practices and interactions are distinct from those of adults.

Christine Todd-Aikens explains the distinction between childhood faith and adult religious practice as she talks about how she and Brent perceive and channel their two teens' religious practice:

> We drive the kids to church. They hate going to church. We don't [always] make them go. They can have one skip a month; it gives them some freedom. These days I'm saying, "There's teen mass, if you think this is boring, go to the teen mass. I didn't make you come to this mass [the gym mass]." Because I don't disagree that it's boring. Why should they be interested? There's nothing there for them; it's not a banquet for them. It's not that there's nothing there—I think receiving communion is a powerful spiritual experience—but it's hard when you're a teenager. If you look around [the gym], are there any religious things around, [things] that they see? Symbols?

Christine's comments reflect the perception that faith development is part of the transition from childhood to adolescence to adulthood and that adult faith and adolescent faith are grounded in different interests and different needs. She believes, then, that the gym mass is boring for young people because the mass is essentially designed for adults. Her children need things other than those provided in the gym for worship to be a meaningful experience for them: they need symbols and perhaps people their own age. Interestingly, Christine thinks that part of why the gym mass might be unattractive to children and adolescents is because of the lack of explicitly religious and symbolic material in the aesthetic appointments of the space—a perception with which Assumption's parents would heartily agree. And in fact, the Saint Brigitta teen mass takes place in the church, where at least some of these appointments surround worshippers. Christine and her peers let their teens intentionally choose this option, with relatively minimal control on their church attendance compared with Assumption's parents.

This way of parenting is grounded in habits of exposing children to religious practice by taking them to church, enrolling them in CCD, and praying with them but without the devotional training and strong guidance of religious parenting strategies at Assumption. At Saint Brigitta, parents believe that by surrounding children with adults who share their perceptions of childhood, their philosophy of parenting, and their religious habits, their children will grow into adulthood with similar habits. In other words, they trust in the development of children's faith through its natural growth, nurtured in the context of Saint Brigitta's community. This natural growth strategy is coherent with the shared aspects of Catholic identities there that are founded on engagement with and critical distance from the institutional church, beliefs in the importance of connectedness of community, and authority relations grounded in the autonomy of the self—some of the very principles that are either de-emphasized or rejected at Assumption.

Saint Brigitta parish provides a number of ways of involving children in parish life that are consonant with these perceptions of the nature of childhood faith. For example, when organizers intentionally incorporate children into Sunday worship, they keep it simple by assigning to children activities that are already familiar to them from school or home life. They take routine practices in the gym and reshape them in ways that children can perform them, as when a group of six or seven children in the primary grades danced during the opening rite on each Sunday of Advent. They danced with long, brightly colored ribbons tied to their wrists that floated and spun through the air as they moved, with one of them stopping to light the Advent candles toward the end of the dance each week. Other activities are based on children's play, such as when, at Eastertime, four or five children dramatized the story of the empty tomb while Father Theo read the Gospel. Sean Maloney-Jones and Robbie McNeill played stunned disciples, while another child, wearing a set of silk wings pinned to her back, acted the part of the angel announcing Jesus' resurrection. These examples show how children's faith is perceived to be different from adult faith at Saint Brigitta, but they also show that children's religiousness shares its adult sensibility in the emphasis on individuals' performances as a model for public religious practice.

The same logic of difference in children's and adults' religious sensibilities is evident at the Saint Brigitta family mass, which is held weekly in the main church. When I observed the family mass in the spring, the church was nearly filled with parents and children. The family mass regularly features a "kids' word" segment: when the scripture readings are about to begin, kids' word is announced, and the children are invited forward. That Sunday, when the announcement came, about a hundred children, toddlers to preteens, rushed past the priest and toward the sacristy door and unceremoniously exited the nave. The children went to a meeting room where catechists led them in a children's version of the scripture readings and homily and then returned to the church after the homily to join the adult congregation for the rest of the mass. Kids' word separates children and parents so that children can worship *as* children—and their parents can worship with other adults, without having to keep an eye on young children as they play and wander about. This respect for the uniqueness of children's faith development reflects parents' stories of their own religious journeys, especially the sentiments of appreciation for their parents' religious practice despite the ways in which their own practice differs—as we have seen, their accounts emphasized the importance of discernment and choice to their adult appropriation of religious faith.

At the same time, family participation in worship at Saint Brigitta allows parents opportunities, as Jenny O'Mara says, to "surround kids with a communal sense of faith—so that they're not just getting it from us." As the parish staff emphasizes the bonds of community that comprise Saint Brigitta's central ecclesial metaphor, they explicitly work to bond families to the church. Maria Callahan takes on this task in a personal way. Maria believes that "families need advocacy" at Saint Brigitta, and she makes a point of bringing their needs to the attention of the parish staff on a regular basis. In her responsibility for providing sacramental preparation programs for children and parents, Maria spends time with school and CCD children and their families. She has also initiated several activity- and service-oriented programs specifically geared to families, such as the Elizabeth Ministry, where experienced mothers mentor new mothers from the time they are pregnant, and holiday sharing programs, in which she facilitates families' contributions of time and goods. Institutionally and informally, the parish strives, in Maria's words, "to connect children with other caring adults besides parents" in accomplishing religious training and in acts of compassion and service.

This approach to childhood at Saint Brigitta, grounded in perceptions of children's developmental trajectories and practiced in the strategies of patience, loose guidance, and provision of a community of adult models, was accompanied by a keen sensitivity to the possible pain that children could sustain in family relationships. This approach once again contrasts with parenting strategies and the anthropological assumptions that underlie Catholic identity at Assumption, where parents assumed children's basic competence and the family's goodness but were keenly concerned to ameliorate the effects and reach of sin in contexts beyond the family. By contrast, during interviews, parents at Saint Brigitta did not articulate their concern about relational pain in terms of sin at all, and instead of concerning themselves exclusively with problematic influences outside the family, they also emphasized the connection between good parenting and their own abilities to curb actions that might inflict pain on their children. Parents explained this focus as a mixture of reactions to and learning from their own experiences of being parented themselves. Moreover, while many talked primarily about their upbringings with satisfaction and gratitude, some explained that they had experienced pain within their families when they were children—sometimes in part as a result of their parents' experiences of the church—and wanted to provide their own children with something better. Regardless of whether they perceived their own childhood experiences of being parented as primarily nurturing or painful, parents at Saint Brigitta were clearly concerned to mitigate the effects of their weaknesses as parents and to teach children how to deal effectively with their feelings. For example, Christine Todd-Aikens tells a story of the pain she experienced during childhood and its effects into adulthood in explaining how and why she and Brent parent as they do.

> Being good parents is more important than anything Brent and I do....Even though we both come from very strong religious family backgrounds, both of us feel that, like many people in our generation, our parents weren't that great at being parents. So we feel like we have injured selves that want to figure out how to do it right.

Christine's and Brent's childhood experiences have resulted in their mutual desire to shield their children from distress within the family, and Christine portrays their motivations for their parenting styles as strongly related to the pain they experienced as children. Importantly, Christine goes on to locate the source of her parents' inadequacies in the Catholic Church's prohibition of artificial birth control. She explains that her family was too large for her mother to care for adequately.

> Both our parents had more kids than I think they should have had....In my case, my mother could have handled two or three kids, but five was too much, and I was the fourth. I wasn't really sure I was loved! And to this day I will stand by that fact. I didn't want it that way. My mom was angry at the Catholic Church.
>
> She would have used birth control if she'd felt it was okay. I think to have children when you don't want them is wrong, really wrong. Women took a lot of [expletive] about being sacrificial. And human beings are born that aren't even loved. So those are some core issues that I grew up with.

These issues explicitly engage a Catholic identity that is opposed to Assumption's expression of Catholicism and orientation to family-related issues in important respects, especially in rejecting the church's teachings on contraception. Identifying these as "core issues," this narrative grounds a religious identity that both critically engages and distances itself from institutional Catholicism. Her personally painful experiences of childhood, and the convictions emerging from them that today Christine enacts in particular parenting practices, are a part of a discourse in which she connects Catholic images of sacrificial motherhood to her mother's inability to limit the size of her family, to the detriment of her emotional health and that of her children—and rejects this discourse and church teaching on birth control because of the damaging effects they had on her and her mother.[20] The autonomous authority required to take this stance not only reflects Saint Brigitta's central ecclesial metaphor but also gives insight into how this view, opposed to church authority, develops for her specifically around family-related issues and also opposes views of Catholic milieus like the one found at Assumption. Poignantly, Christine's experience of her mother's struggles and inadequacies were clearly painful—but they have resulted in a desire to avoid some of the weaknesses she experienced in her own parents. In this effort, psychological counseling has played an important part in helping both Christine and Brent come to terms with their childhood experiences and incorporate what they have learned from them into the ways they parent.

> By the time we decided to have children, I'd been in therapy for a few years and felt really like I'd be a good mom. And then, when our kids were little, it was so overwhelming and tiring, we entered into therapy...figuring out how to put a line down the middle of the table and say, "This is yours" and "This is yours" and "If you want to share, you'll figure it out, but you're both going to be whole about this"—and we have incredibly healthy kids. There's been a lot of talking about issues, a lot of work.

Here Christine presents a psychological perspective on parenting that moves beyond Saint Brigitta's perception of adult-child differences to engagement with therapeutic methods as a resource and a tool for creating the type of family bonds that assure children that they are loved and for producing children who are, in Christine's words, "healthy kids, strong kids, with interesting opinions, children who are honest and accept their feelings." Christine focuses her social work career in counseling, so the therapeutic perspective integral to her professional background is familiar to those in her household. Nonetheless, she represents a common perspective among parents at Saint Brigitta, especially in the principle that good relationships require mutual work. Because she sees the church—specifically, church teachings on birth control—as integral to experiences in her family of origin that caused her to feel unloved as a child, Christine does not rely on the resources of the church in this case, but looks outside of it, although to a resource that she identifies as being connected to humans' spiritual capacities. Her experiences in her family of origin and her experience of the church are intertwined and parallel; she is connected to her parents as well as to the church, but both cause her pain. This reality shapes both her Catholic identity *and* her parenting practices, not only in their therapeutic design but also in the way she fosters faith in her children—both keeping her own critical distance from particular institutions within Catholicism and encouraging her children to stay connected to their faith as Catholics.

Other parents, like Bryan O'Lear, spoke in more positive terms about their parents, but Bryan and his wife, Lyn, also rely on psychological tools as they parent their two-year-old daughter, Sara. When asked what he hopes to teach Sara, Bryan told the following story to illustrate his sense of what it means to parent effectively. He and Sara were home alone together one evening. It had been a long day at work for Bryan, and both he and Sara were tired and irritable. Sara was wandering around the flat, playing with toys and some household things. In her wanderings, she found an electrical cord plugged into an outlet. When she started tugging on the cord, Bryan spoke to Sara sharply, saying, "Sara, *NO!*" Bryan then reflected,

> It's okay to be frustrated, angry, and firm with a child—but one thing I can do for Sara is to teach her how to handle anger, through being restrained and firm with her. I think I got a little too personally mad at her because I was in such a bad mood that day. That wasn't necessary for the lesson— which is probably okay—but I could have modulated myself better.

Bryan expresses a sensitivity to teaching Sara how to manage her emotions and avoiding wounding her, sensitivity grounded in a psychologically oriented sensibility that values self-awareness and well-developed communications skills. He reflects a style of parenting that is widely shared among Saint Brigitta's parents, in which psychologically oriented parenting practices are perceived to play nurturing and protective roles in childrearing. Parents are concerned to protect their children from some of the same things as Assumption's parents worry about, such as too early exposure to sex and violence, but at Saint Brigitta, the tasks of parental protection explicitly begin with avoiding bad habits and thoughtless actions that might lead to pain in the intimacy of the family. These efforts at nurture and protection involve cultivating parents' and children's self-awareness, practicing self-critique, accepting help, and doing mutual psychological work. Parents monitor themselves and teach similar skills to their children, with the goal of protecting and equipping them psychologically.

At the same time, parents did not strongly connect psychological and religious practices in talking about childrearing, even though the connection between psychology and religion often figured in adult faith. It appears that, like the instinctive faith they perceive in children and the rejection of faith they expect among adolescents, parents at Saint Brigitta expect their children to eventually move back toward a chosen and therapeutically informed adult faith, as they did themselves.

But for these parents, the realities of their children's waning interest in religion can be jarring, even with the expectation of adolescent resistance or rejection of church practice. For instance, Jenny and Tom O'Mara have given their children routine exposure to prayer at meals—even when, as Jenny said, they "look at you funny"—as well as Sunday mass and the practice of their weekly adult prayer group. But Jenny has found herself perplexed when her older children, now young adults, no longer go to church.

> I think it's odd, now that they're young adults. There's not a whole lot of indication that faith matters that much [to them]. We were just discussing it this weekend, because one of our older daughters has romance troubles. You could see she was so hurt. It would make a big difference if she would know that it would all be okay, no matter what happens. Life is in such turmoil [in the young adult years]. She would very much like to meet somebody. Her friends are changing, you're not quite interested in what you were—so it would be nice to have faith. I forget which kid I said this to, "You could try praying about it." They went along with that here. We weren't real hard core, but they always came to mass with us every Sunday. I think it's very clear how important it is here [in our home]....I don't think the other two go to mass. And it's a big joke. Like when we would call them in college, Tom would yell out, "Go to church! Go to mass!"

Although Tom is at least superficially sanguine about their young adult children's lack of interest in religious practice, Jenny expresses consternation and concern. She represents parents at Saint Brigitta who spontaneously shared such feelings over their adult children's falling away in ways that Assumption's parents did not. Jenny's consternation is mirrored not only by other Catholic parents whose children stop attending church but also by scholars who report that adolescent indifference to religious practice is widespread; this is at least in part a life course response, since adults often return to religious practice once they marry and have children.[21] But in a survey of emerging adults, ages 18 to 23, Christian Smith and his colleagues found that only about 30 percent of emerging adults attend church more than once a month, and 35 percent don't attend church at all.[22] Smith and his colleagues report that those most likely to engage in religious practice as emerging adults are those with strong religious upbringings: they tend to have highly religious parents, practice personal prayer, and consider faith to be very important.[23] At the same time, Smith found that levels of religious practice among young adults have decreased in recent decades and that Catholic young adults are among those least likely to engage in religious practice; less than 15 percent of emerging adult Catholics reported going to mass weekly in 2006, compared with 25 percent in 1972.[24] Jenny's concerns, then, reflect the broader perceptions of uncertainty about this current generation's return to religious practice.[25] Like Jenny, parents at Saint Brigitta want to pass Catholicism on to their children, and they want them to experience religious faith as life affirming, morally shaping, and mission driven, as they do themselves. Despite the critical attitudes that many at Saint Brigitta hold toward the institutional church, they value Catholicism, especially the religious resources of prayer and community, which for them proved to be vehicles for the development of rich faith lives as adults.

Jenny is practiced at a style of parenting in which she gives support and nurture in a way that allows children their own space to shape their worlds and make their own decisions in multiple arenas of life. However, she has found that it can be difficult for her to cope with this gentle accompanying of children when they experience trials and disappointments and, like many at both Assumption and Saint Brigitta, relies on her relationship with God to cope with the disparity between what she can give her children and what they seem to need. She says,

> I believe that, in many ways, it's out of my hands. I do what I need to do to the best of my ability, and after that, I have to trust....Not to push you into doing all these other things to prove that you're an extraordinary person because you're getting straight A's and a star athlete—I can from the heart appreciate who they are, just as they are. I think a lot of that probably stems from worrying that unless you're something super, what's going to become of you? I have felt that way....My faith tells me that I can trust it to the hands of God, even with my weaknesses.

Reflecting the perspective of children's natural growth, Jenny's faith helps her to resist broader middle-class pressures to push her children to excel from the time they are very young, instead focusing on appreciating her children as they are and without placing undue pressure on them to conform to weighty social expectations, in order to raise children who "will be the kind of persons who have a big heart."

Religion and parenting: preparation, exposure, and the community beyond the church

As Saint Brigitta's parents aim to protect children from emotional pain, they also seek to protect their children from undesirable influences in the surrounding environment, especially from violence, excessive consumerism, and adult sexualities.

But they place considerable weight on a different strategy than Assumption's parents to combat some of these problems and familiarize their children with other aspects of life they believe they need to know about: they prepare children for meeting undesirable influences, and the problems they can cause, through teaching about and cautious exposure to these problems. This strategy, which is geared toward inculcating moral behavior in children and helping them to craft a meaningful life, is interwoven with both Catholic identity and the church as a community at Saint Brigitta. Closely examining this parenting strategy, which involves expanding the boundaries of identity and community at Saint Brigitta, can help us better understand how childrearing practices are implicated in the everyday constitution and support of responses to cultural conflicts over the family that crystallize around a pole competing with that predominant at Assumption. Despite a concern for the integrity and strengthening of families, families at Saint Brigitta generally eschew practices that create high boundaries with families that don't conform to the modern nuclear family model; in fact, they instead explicitly foster the inclusion of a plurality of family forms through their parenting practices.

Before analyzing how Saint Brigitta's parents employ strategies of exposure and connection to others in parenting their children, let us first briefly explore how they think about protecting children. Louis, for example, voices concerns similar to those expressed by Assumption's parents and assesses some aspects of this problem similarly—for instance, he is concerned about his daughters' exposure to sexualized images of women—but interprets and solves this problem in a somewhat different way. He explains,

> We don't watch much TV, and we regulate it for our kids—but I often swallow hard and say, "Why does that person dress like that? Why is that commercial on?" It's about defending our way of life.
>
> For me, it's offensive language and immodesty of dress—it brings down your spirit, it doesn't lift you up, to expose yourself to that. You need to be prepared for that, you need to understand. What kind of conversation, how to prepare [our 13-year-old daughter] for that exposure? We're not naive. We know that she will be exposed.

Like parents at Assumption, Louis wants to protect his daughters from sexually immodest images, offensive language, and sexually suggestive styles of dress. But his perspective is different from Assumption's parents in important respects: he does not talk about his children explicitly in terms of their innocence, but instead talks about parenting as preparing his children for exposure to these images.

> We let her see PG-13 movies; we're not "strict-strict." And she's not way out, but she is interested in romance and relationships. We have friends down

the block, dear friends—but their kids watch every movie from every age. To me it's maddening—no filter. What am I going to do? Say something about their parents? It's frustrating. But we can hold the line, more or less, and the girls don't watch stuff at [our friends'] house—they're sensitive, at least, that our kids don't watch that.

Like parents at Assumption, Louis knows neighborhood parents who have a more permissive set of rules for their children than he and Patricia do, but the particular neighbors he talked about are also friends—a friendship they maintain despite their different approaches to parenting. This family is able and willing to accommodate the Beltramis' rules when Louis and Patricia's girls are at their home. Parents at Assumption generally had stricter boundaries with such families than those at Saint Brigitta. Rather than limit their children's contact with their friends and friends' families, parents at Saint Brigitta engaged and negotiated with their parents. Other parents at Saint Brigitta also negotiate understandings with families with whom they might not always agree, as well as form coalitions with like-minded families, in protecting their children. For example, Maggie McNeill asserted, "For us, it's no Nintendo and no guns. We all want to be on a similar page in terms of values when it comes to raising kids." Like Louis, Maggie and her peers rely on other parents and friends who share common values to help protect their young children when they believe it to be necessary.

Besides sex and violence, Louis sees additional elements of contemporary Western social structures and cultures that lessen the quality of family life and make childrearing more difficult. Yet he retains his optimism, largely because of his experience of peers who perceive the same problems and are willing to work on solutions. He explains,

I'm very pleased with the discovery of a number of parents that have hit this wall—the cultural influence that seems so negative. I really find this is getting stronger. Even if everybody hasn't figured out how to manage it, at least we're asking the same questions—easy McDonalds, movies, TV shows, materialism, constant consumption. Let's find a different way than, "I'm too busy, so here's another toy."

Parents at Saint Brigitta focus not only on sexuality and violence but also on other arenas of the broader culture, especially those connected with consumerism, that can negatively affect children. Louis's concerns have both cultural and structural origins in the present contexts of dual-earner households, increased average working hours, increased costs of living, and contemporary consumption habits.[26] He and his peers seek parenting solutions—ones buttressed with communal support—that will provide for the emotional needs of their children and strengthen family interconnectedness.[27] As with other issues, parents at Saint Brigitta rely heavily on the resources of community—the community of the church, as well as other communities to which they belong.

But also, despite undesirable influences in the larger society, parents at Saint Brigitta do not only or uniformly seek to shelter their children from the wider world; instead, they remain resolutely connected to it. In fact, they believe that children can benefit from exposure to some of the more hard-edged and difficult realities of life in the diverse experiences of culture and social class contained in city life. In these experiences, children can grow in maturity, competence, and poise in handling difficulty and can learn compassion for others who live in fraught circumstances that they would not ordinarily encounter otherwise. While the aims of children's growth in competence fits the logic of the developmental and psychological aspects of their perceptions of childhood and the human person, their children's growth in compassion is a goal that has explicitly religious roots in a Christian anthropological view of the person as intrinsically connected to others. An illustration of how people at Saint Brigitta perceive the former aim is provided by Rick McNeill, who explained that he and Maggie decided to remain in their urban neighborhood once they had children instead of moving to a suburb because

> It made a difference to me, meeting people [here in the city at Saint Brigitta] 10 or 15 years older than me who had these wonderfully integrated teenage kids. And also meeting people in the suburbs with teen urban wannabe jerks—it made me realize that it is possible to raise kids in the city. They see a lot more stuff, they're not as immature. The O'Maras have these wonderful kids—seven of them—and Bryan O'Lear's sister has these two integrated, composed kids. Kids benefit greatly from the city.

In comparing the teens he knows, Rick has come to believe that raising children in an urban context gives them a more expansive set of experiences than suburban living, because childhood lived in the city necessarily creates more exposure to diverse people and experiences than their suburban counterparts experience. He perceives a causal connection between the exposure to diverse people and ways of living and the development of maturity in adolescents. The teens he knows who have been raised in the city are focused, "integrated"—that is, psychologically healthy, self-aware, and poised, and thus better prepared for adult life. In other words, at Saint Brigitta character development is accomplished in children explicitly through a lifestyle that exposes them to varied and diverse life experiences. This strategy and the outcomes it hopes to achieve are very different from the religiously grounded character formation that Assumption's parents favor, but with this strategy, Saint Brigitta's parents are likewise aiming for character development in their children.

The neighborhood in which Saint Brigitta is situated is in many respects ideal for parents who desire that their children have exposure to diverse subcultures, classes, and styles of life. Although the neighborhood surrounding the church is gentrifying, some of the surrounding neighborhoods are predominantly working class and working poor. Immigrants populate lower-middle-class and middle-class neighborhoods contiguous to those in which the church is located. Racial and ethnic diversity characterize all of these neighborhoods. And at the same time, this is not an atomized urban life. Monica explains,

> It's an integrated community. The people you go to church with are the people you play with. We socialize together, the whole neighborhood. We had an ecumenical service last year, and the whole neighborhood was there. And at the school, it's racially and culturally diverse, just as the neighborhood is.

For those who live in the neighborhood around Saint Brigitta, city life is not an isolated anomic experience of *gesellschaft*, despite the neighborhood's considerable cultural, racial, and class diversity. In fact, as Monica describes it, life in this city neighborhood mirrors the experience of the church as community in its communal sensibility and solidarity despite differences. Although the neighborhood is more diverse than the church membership in its racial and class composition, the neighborhoods surrounding Saint Brigitta are places where children can learn solidarity amid difference, find their life experience enhanced, and grow in a sensibility that emphasizes interconnectedness with others.

City living also gives parents ample opportunity to expose their children to different ways of living than their own, as well as broader societal problems of social injustice. In this way, living in the city allows Saint Brigitta's parents to expose children to people, experiences, and social structures through which they can teach religious values of interconnectedness, responsibility for others, and compassion to their children and mirror the church as a community. Parents use life in the city both to educate children about the importance of and reasons for charitable giving through routine life experiences and to create intentional service learning experiences focusing on groups living in extreme poverty. Both sets of experiences reflect a Catholic identity that values service to others.

For example, Ann Bernardo and Kevin Burke have found ways to integrate the diversity of city life into daily family routines that teach children an outer-directed religious morality. They work at fostering in their children a value-oriented sense of connectedness to others through exposure to nearby poorer neighborhoods in the city, which they combine with global education and family prayer. They engage their children in giving money, clothing, and household items to charitable organizations. They make a point of taking their children with them when they drop off used toys and clothing at a neighborhood center in a nearby poorer part of the city. As a family, they donate money to relief organizations. They name their daily good deeds when they pray at the dinner table. Ann explains that they build these works into their family routines to teach their children that the whole world is not like their own placid and ordered middle-class home.

> Kevin and I feel that it's important to teach our children to care for other people. It's a big part of what we focus on. We took some of the money we made at our garage sale—it was a family project—and joined Bread for the World. We talked about it with our kids. We do a lot of outreach: taking clothing [that] the children outgrow to a shelter and making sure that they go with us, just to see that the whole world isn't like [ours]. That there are people with greater needs.

In this way, Ann and Kevin, along with their peers at Saint Brigitta, teach children that the sense of connectedness they have experienced from the time they were very young—what Maggie identified as children's instinctive faith—goes beyond family and church and extends the church's central ecclesial metaphor in relationship with, and even to encompass, the society beyond the parish's boundaries.

Some parents also explicitly seek out opportunities to educate their children about the world beyond the city, teaching them a religious perspective on social and political problems across the globe through events, discussion, travel, and activism. For example, along with some of their peers at Saint Brigitta, Monica and John teach their children about poverty and war through witness and protest. Monica explains,

> We'll probably take our kids to El Salvador next summer. They know there's a war going on now. They know what we think of that. After the bombing [of Afghanistan following on the events of September 11, 2001], we took them to a protest downtown. John takes them to things [social justice events and programs] at the university all the time. Daniel wants to know how God feels about the war on Afghanistan. We say that God is very sad. I hate war—and so does God.

Monica and John and other parents make efforts to expose children to issues of justice grounded in the Catholic Church's social doctrine, emphasizing a religious ethic of human dignity and the interconnectedness of all humanity. Such efforts exemplify how parents at Saint Brigitta morally form children in an outer-directed ethic grounded in religious convictions. Monica explains,

> The most important thing I can teach my kids is that your faith should dictate how you live your life. This is where we are in our family right now.

What do these things that we *know*, say about how we *live*? And [I want them to believe] that how you live is essentially, intrinsically, intensely connected to how other people live. We work on that a lot. It matters—how we spend money, how we act.

Monica says here that the connection between religious knowledge and moral living—that is, between a worldview and an ethic—should be critical and reflexive, and it is at the heart of childrearing. Parents in both parishes would agree with Monica on this point. But among the consequences of this approach is the everyday living out and reproduction of values at Saint Brigitta that locates them in a religious culture that fosters tendencies at a pole opposed to that which prevails at Assumption. The connection of this religious culture of childrearing with polarizing tendencies surrounding public cultural conflicts regarding the family is less direct than at Assumption in the sense that Saint Brigitta's parishioners less often explicitly connected family-related public issues to their discussions of childrearing. But the Christian anthropology underlying these practices, especially the beliefs surrounding connectedness with others and the psychological and developmental view of human nature, supports and shapes these practices in ways that lower boundaries with those whose family practices differ from theirs—therefore supporting responses to debates over family-related issues at a pole that is uncomfortable with diagnosis and protest and against "family decline" and supports a plurality of family forms and practices, rather than arguing against them.

Father Theo supports and encourages these efforts at moral education, family and community connectedness, the gentle support of children's religious practice, and parenting efforts in other life arenas. One Sunday in the gym while addressing parenting in a homily about the costs of discipleship, he explained that people who show intense commitment—in work, in the public sphere, and in private arenas of life—are often not respected, and sometimes they are resented or even hated for their commitment-inspired actions. Some parents, he told the congregation, fall into this category.

Take parenting as an example. Who are the very best parents among us? What do they do, those who are very, very committed to being good parents? They know and do things like, "it takes a village," and that you must give children both "roots and wings," but they do much more. Who are these people in our parish?

More often than not, I think, they are the parents who are criticized. I will hear others say about them, "They don't have tight reins on their kids." These people struggle with teaching their children, but not so confining them that they mess them up. They give them enough space to find their own way. They struggle with their children's struggles, and with how much control of their children is enough. This approach shows their commitment as parents.

Father Theo acknowledges the variation in parenting that exists at Saint Brigitta, while affirming and encouraging children's natural instincts toward connection with others in exposing them to the broader world and to other adults in their orbit. He emphasizes the value of interconnectedness and community in the practice of parenting. At the same time, he affirms the therapeutic and autonomy-encouraging parenting strategies that these parents favor; like Jenny, he links faith-based commitment and trust to struggling along with children in their struggles. In this statement, Father Theo sums up the dominant sensibility surrounding childrearing at Saint Brigitta, taking an affirmative stand within it.

Conclusion

As we have seen, parents at Assumption and Saint Brigitta want many of the same things for their children, identify some of the same aspects of the larger social world as problematic for children and childrearing, and perceive many of the same challenges in raising children. Some of their beliefs about children, and their responses to the perceived negative situations in their class context and the broader cultural trends of American society, are similar. Parents at both parishes imagine children as naturally religious and naturally good. They identify some similar boundaries and limits of children's acceptable exposure to sexuality and violence. Parents in both settings conceive of prayer as a place of solace and a source for wisdom and judgment when experiencing difficulties in parenting. And they seek to not only bond their own families tightly but also reach out to like-minded others to accomplish the project of parenting.

But the differences in parents' perceptions of childhood, parenting goals, and strategies in the two settings are fundamental and constitutively related to religious belief and practice in each setting in ways that inform and support competing tendencies surrounding cultural conflicts about the family among Catholics. These local religious cultures of childhood are shaped by each group's conception of the human person and the relationship of God and the self in ways that are intertwined with the social relations represented in each group's central ecclesial metaphor. For example, the reality of human imperfection in individual selves is understood in terms of Catholic beliefs about sin at Assumption, whereas at Saint Brigitta people's weaknesses are interpreted with a spiritual and therapeutic idiom. Differences in childhood prayer in these settings reflect a differential emphasis on the awareness of human imperfection and personal sin, more evident at Assumption, and the broad bonds of interconnectedness and social sin emphasized at Saint Brigitta. Images of human nature are thus represented—and confer religious meaning upon—people's perceptions of childhood and the domi-nant parenting goals and strategies undertaken in each setting.

Thus, parenting styles and orientations toward cultural conflicts surrounding the family are intertwined. Regarding parenting styles, at Assumption, parental protection of children is emphasized more acutely, especially around issues of sexuality. At Saint Brigitta, parents protect children but emphasize exposing chil-dren to ways of living different than their own and educating their children about social problems and issues of social justice. Parents at Assumption believe in the need to give strong guidance to children, whereas parents at Saint Brigitta believe in giving children a great deal of room for their own self-determination. These different parenting styles reflect, on the one hand, an authoritative approach to parenting at Assumption, similar to one documented by Brad Wilcox and his col-leagues among evangelical Christians,[28] and on the other, a more therapeutically oriented approach at Saint Brigitta.

Similarly, the differential marking of boundaries in childrearing practices in the two settings—seen most clearly in identity boundaries with other Catholics and with the wider world—supports similar boundaries that distinguish each par-ish's dominant perspective on public cultural conflicts surrounding the family. Assumption defines itself with high boundaries against the wider world primar-ily in its concern over family decline and children's safety, and it defines its local religious culture of parenting against other Catholics and other Catholic institu-tions that it perceives to inadequately morally educate its children. By contrast, in defining itself in opposition to social injustices in the wider world, Saint Brigitta lowers and expands its boundaries to create a more inclusive notion of commu-nity in which to enfold and educate its children, while expressing its ambivalence toward church teachings and hierarchy as it educates its children in the faith. The assumptions and practices that help to constitute these local cultures of chil-drearing thus incorporate opposed tendencies in the underlying principles they espouse and in their resulting boundaries with others. Everyday practice of these cultures thus supports two different sets of assumptions, worldviews, and ethics, into which polar tendencies around family-related issues in the public sphere fit logically, and reside.

5

Work

Our Lady of the Assumption

July, nine-thirty a.m., a suburban hamlet ten miles from Assumption Church.

It is not yet mid-morning on this first Thursday in July, and I am on my way to the church where Pam Williams and her friends are meeting for a gathering of their book group. I haven't had time to reread more than a few pages of the book being discussed today—C. S. Lewis's Out of the Silent Planet.[1] *My memory of the book is fuzzy.*

Pam invited me to her book group a week or two ago. She and some of her friends had attended Opus Dei cooperators' circles, but they found that the meetings didn't allow them to participate as much as they would have liked. Supernumerary members do most of the speaking at these meetings, "which is formation for them, I guess. And in this way," Pam explained, "they try to avoid all the crazy pop psychology and sociology out there." Momentarily I wonder what Pam means by "pop sociology." She continues, "I've enjoyed the circles I've gone to, but it's a lot of listening."

So about a year and a half ago, Pam and Julia decided that they should start a group themselves, independent of Opus Dei but with similar purposes of spiritual formation and companionship. They started their reading with the writings of Saint Teresa of Avila and some papal encyclicals, but they found these texts turgid and difficult to understand. One group member suggested reading novels with religious themes, and they found these books more in line with their sensibilities. For more than a year now, they have enjoyed their reading, gaining insight from their discussions and support from their monthly fellowship.

The church where the group meets is a gray, Gothic-style building that dominates a residential corner of a busy street. I park my truck and walk around the building until I find the entrance to the basement. Hearing clatter and the high-pitched voices of children, I follow the sounds to the nursery. Toys ring about half of its perimeter, and half a dozen children are already playing at one end of the room. They climb into its bright plastic play-houses, serve up imaginary breakfasts in its miniature kitchen, or choose from the games piled high in a corner. The mothers in the group have brought along only their youngest children; the older ones are occupied in summer camps or other programs this morning. A couple of babies sleep in carriers or sit on a mother's lap. The women are gathered in a corner opposite the play area, seated on child-sized chairs around a low table.

Saying hello, I pull up one of the small chairs and join them. I know most of the women, but there are two I don't recognize, so Pam introduces me to Donna and Joanne. Then we launch informally into the book discussion. Joanne takes the lead. She starts us off by telling us some details of the life of C. S. Lewis. As she speaks, members of the group occasionally interject or ask a question.

Then Joanne opens up the floor for discussion. Donna speaks first. Saying that she was able to get only about halfway through the book, she asks what happens as the story progresses. She engages Joanne about the significance of some of the characters, their actions, and the meanings that lie behind them. Joanne answers her questions and then starts to speak with enthusiasm about what she liked best about the book. When she mentions the characters' attitudes toward death—she explains that cohorts die all together and feel no anxiety about death—Julia picks up on the description.

"I liked that people were peaceful in the face of death. I wish I was there," Julia says, "but I'm not. I'd like to face death with equanimity, but I just am not there." Donna nods and consoles her saying, "That's because you have kids—you have responsibility." As if to prove her point, one of the toddlers approaches his mother. She lifts him onto her lap for a minute and snuggles him, and then he runs off to play again.

The group continues on, moving from topic to topic, parsing the meaning in the book's plot and its characters. Every now and then, a child interrupts the discussion, wanting to satisfy a curiosity or a need. After an intense discussion, there is a lull in the conversation. Julia launches into a different topic. "What do you call yourselves?" she asks us, and then clarifies, "What do you say you are—a housewife, a mother, something else?" Several of us look at her quizzically. She explains, "I'm asking because

John and I purchased a new computer and we just got it this week. When I was registering it, I had to pick from a list of occupations. But there was nothing on the list that described my work as a mother! I didn't know what to register as, or what to write in 'other.' So when people ask you, how do you usually describe what you do?"

The women bat this question about. "I don't usually call myself anything." "That's a difficult question. I really don't like the term 'housewife.'" "I know someone who calls herself a 'professional housewife,' but I don't like that. It sounds too formal, too uptight." "How about 'home manager?'" "I usually just say that I'm a 'stay-at-home mom.'" Lightheartedly, I pitch in, "My mom always used to call herself a 'domestic engineer,'" but no one seems amused. I feel awkward, realizing that I am the only person at the table who could easily find herself on Julia's computer registration list.

June repeats an earlier suggestion. "I think 'stay-at-home mom' is the easiest way to describe what I do. It's what I usually tell people." And having exhausted other options as too formal, too traditional, not encompassing enough, or otherwise inadequate, the women agree that "stay-at-home mom" is the best way to describe what they do every day—it is an occupation, a job title. We move on to other topics. The children, now fully occupied in the rhythm of play, leave us undisturbed to visit for quite some time.

Saint Brigitta

Mid-May, late morning, the neighborhood around Saint Brigitta Church.

Beth McGivern's prairie-style two-story home looks as if it could use some new paint, but even in its imperfection, it is angular, sturdy, and emblematic of Midwestern solidity. On the broad front porch, a baby carriage and a fold-up stroller occupy a convenient corner near the door. I walk quickly up the steps and ring the bell. After a moment, Beth appears at the door, motions me inside, and whispers, "Come on in. I've just gotten Alex to sleep." I know Alex from church; he is a plump toddler, with bright blue eyes and wisps of blond hair framing his face. He has just turned two.

Beth and I exchange greetings and chat quietly for a little while. Then she invites me to take a seat in the living room on an earth-toned sofa beside a red-brick fireplace. It is a bright and sunny

*room with a long band of windows facing the sun porch; it looks
as if one can almost touch the spring foliage beyond the clear
glass. Straight ahead, a photo gallery lines the wall framing the
stairway to the second floor.*

*I give Beth the usual introduction to my study, and I tell her in a
general way what I would like her to talk about. She takes a few
moments to collect her thoughts, and then she begins, still speaking softly so as not to wake Alex.*

"Our family is large and Irish, and my siblings and I grew up in
a strict environment." *Beth's physical features—her abundant
auburn hair curling at bobbed ends, a pale freckled complexion,
and a delicate but determined jaw—reflect her heritage.* "When
we got out [of our house], we all went a little crazy. I went to
a Catholic women's college, and I rebelled against everything.
I partied a lot, and I went pretty wild for a couple of years.

"But then," *she continues,* "after I'd been at Rosary for a while,
I started to connect with a group of people at school who shared
my political views. We were all asking the same questions. I was
questioning what I was raised with, and I was searching for my
life, for my path—for meaning—and the church was a part of
that. I was involved in a peace group and in the hunger coali-
tion. But I backed away a little from more overt religiosity. It
didn't fit for me. It was 'too good.'" *Instead, Beth got increasingly
involved in service learning and volunteerism, and in this way
she stayed connected to the church.*

"Around that time," *she says,* "I started to think that maybe
law was a way to do something socially conscious. My uncle is
a lawyer, and he has a real sense of justice. I was getting a sense
that law might be a way to make an impact. I thought I might
make a career in public interest law. But then I wasn't sure, so
I decided to do volunteer work after college.

"I wanted to connect, to reach out, be a part of the solution in
some way. So I lived at a Catholic Worker house. I worked in a
soup kitchen. I did direct service. I'd lived in a sheltered, privileged environment my whole life. Having the experience of being
around people who were struggling—I had to find a way to help
out there, to be a part of the solution. That's where my thinking
was. And yet, I didn't feel a call to make that my life's vocation.
But I wanted to explore faith more. Priests and seminarians had
theology to help them make sense of what they were doing. It was
what I wanted to do. In retrospect, I'm not sure if it was the right
path or not."

After her time at the Catholic Worker, she moved to the city where she still lives, found an apartment with friends from college, and went back to school to get degrees in theology and social work.

"I was struggling—a woman, not ordained, not a religious— what would I do in the church? I didn't want to be in a male-dominated environment with a lot of seminarians and priests where I would be always struggling, asking, 'What is my role?' I thought maybe counseling work: making a personal connection and helping on a personal level. What will my role be? I started focusing on the MSW. A lot of people at school weren't keen on mixing social work with a theology degree; there wasn't a lot of support there. But I thought, 'This is something I can do. It's income. It's some definition.'"

As she speaks, we hear Alex starting to fuss in the nursery, gulping and sighing. We pause to listen for his waking, but he grows quiet again, and Beth continues her story. "When I finished school, I got a job at a social service agency that offers a crisis program for kids. It was intense. I felt called to this. I found that I could touch people on a personal level and make sense of my work with my faith. But in terms of processing that with people on the same page, I didn't have that, so that became lost for me. I stayed at the agency because I needed a place to work, I was treated well, and learning a lot. But I couldn't quite figure out how I could make this merge back into church stuff. I still struggle with that. *It's not integrated.*

"But Peter and I were in our mid-30s, and it was time to start having children. We didn't want to wait forever. And soon I got pregnant. Do I work? Do I stay at the agency? Do I go part-time? At the time, I was directing a child and adolescent program, I was on-call every day, and there were 24-hour on-calls. There wasn't a part-time option for my job. I could have maybe *found another position with the agency part-time—*

"But then I sort of weighed everything, and I decided to leave my job. I felt that I didn't want to be divided and harried. I know people who can do that, who can do the juggle. I didn't feel I could do that, because I felt very immersed in my job. And I thought, at this point in my life, maybe this is my chance to *make my impact with a little child.*"

Beth talks about what it has been like to make the transition to staying at home with Alex. And soon we hear him fussing again. He cries—he is fully awake now—and Beth goes to the nursery, returning a few moments later with Alex in her arms. She sets

a blanket and some toys on the floor between us and places the
toddler upon it. As he plays, she picks up her previous train of
thought.
"The first year of having a child, I was buried in that. But then
I started feeling, I wish I was finding a way to do something
outside of home. While I feel happy and there's a great commu-
nity here, a parish we love, a neighborhood we love, and family
nearby—I am still searching. I wish, part of me, that I was doing
something more to make an impact. I value what I'm doing right
now, but professionally I'm feeling a little lost and directionless
and ill-defined."

Work in the Family, Work in the World, and Women

As these vignettes portray, both the women in Pam Williams's book group at Assumption and Beth McGivern and her stay-at-home peers at Saint Brigitta are challenged by their relationships to the professional world, and they struggle with how to adequately communicate their present work vis-à-vis those who work in the professions. But the two groups perceive this task differently, since the stay-at-home mothers at Assumption have largely left their professional identities behind them, while Beth and her peers at Saint Brigitta still feel connected to career identities. This is the first of a number of important differences in the ways in which mothers at Assumption and Saint Brigitta, whether they stay at home or work in the world, approach work-family balance. Such differences are important because the social problems underlying cultural conflicts about the family in the contemporary United States, especially those surrounding work, are often most acute for women[2]—and therefore, investigating these challenges in women's everyday lives constitutes a final promising venue for understanding how moral polarization surrounding the family is sustained in local religious settings.

This chapter thus explores women's attempts to resolve problems in balanc-ing work and family, how their congregations provide support for their solutions, and how their symbolic and practical roles in congregations are intertwined with polarizing tendencies among Catholics. I will show how such differences reflect local religious cultures that, in response to the pressures parishioners experience from the wider world of work, practice different perceptions and norms of work—especially women's work. In what follows, then, I demonstrate how the religious meanings and social relations of work at Assumption and Saint Brigitta are under-lain and supported by each church's central ecclesial metaphor and its practice of Catholic identity. I further demonstrate that the different cultural frameworks surrounding women and work in these two settings represent opposed and competing visions of work and family and that these two visions contribute to polarizing tendencies surrounding the family among Catholics.

In so doing, I aim in this chapter to add to scholarly knowledge of how women in U.S. congregations generally manage the strains of work and family life. Extant studies have focused mostly on how conservative denominations support women's traditional motherly and domestic roles through religious gender ideologies in solving problems of work-family balance. They have shown that beliefs and practices within conservative congregations help women to prioritize domestic life and give legitimacy to solutions that are countercultural or contested, while supporting these choices through congregational networks.[3] This scholarship further demonstrates that congregations often both uphold these ideologies and at the same time accommodate women's need to work outside the home for financial or other reasons.[4] Since Catholic women are responding to the same societal context as their religious peers, perhaps it is not surprising to find a retraditionalized gender ideology at Assumption that is in many respects similar to that found in other denominations. But while a few studies explore how religious institutions can instead support women's desires for public and/or professional pursuits, we know much less about how progressive religious groups help women negotiate work-family balance while pursuing career goals or stay-at-home motherhood.[5] Thus, analyzing women and work at Saint Brigitta promises to contribute to knowledge about how progressive churches' gender ideologies and practices help to form and support mothers' work-family balance strategies.

This chapter also illuminates some of Catholicism's distinctive contributions to how women balance work and family. We have seen in previous chapters, especially in the discussions of gender relations in marriage in chapter 3, that while some of these patterns are similar to those found in other denominations, gender relations at Assumption and Saint Brigitta are each intertwined with Catholic teachings and therefore inflected with Catholicism in ways that distinguish them from other denominations, particularly in the ways in which they explicitly link gender and sexuality. But whereas marriage and childrearing directly involve the relation of public politics with domestic politics in Catholic doctrine surrounding human sexuality—in the issues of abortion, homosexuality, and proper use of one's sexuality generally—the relation of women's work-family balance to moral polarization rests on more complex underpinnings. Solutions to the problem of work-family balance at Assumption and Saint Brigitta shed light on how their gender relations are distinctively Catholic, not only because of their recovery and use of particular gendered beliefs and practices from the rich storehouse of Catholicism's traditions but, crucially, also because of the ways in which their images of gender are fitted with different strands of Catholic thought about the significance of human work. In showing this, I will contend that these different traditions of work afford only incomplete solutions to women's efforts at dealing with the pressures of work and family. Women embedded in the local religious cultures at Assumption and Saint Brigitta are ultimately confronted with a forced choice between maternal and career identities—a choice often urged in the larger culture and reinforced in churches. Their struggles, moreover, illuminate how incomplete resolutions to this problem figure in polarizing cultural contests over women's roles in family and society.

I elaborate these claims first by discussing contextual studies that show why focusing on women's negotiation of work-family balance is particularly helpful in understanding their roles in cultural conflicts over the family. Then I discuss how religious ideas of work are implicated in women's solutions to problems of work-family balance, thereby concretizing particular configurations of gender relations, both practically and symbolically.

Contemporary Strains: Achieving Work-Family Balance among Middle-Class Families

Like their professional peers, mothers and fathers at Assumption and Saint Brigitta face constraints and pressures in achieving work-family balance that have grown steadily in American society over the past four decades, with the most pervasive pressures involving women's allocation of time. Although average working hours overall have remained relatively constant since 1970, women's labor force participation has increased such that the family workweek rose from 53 to 63 hours per week between 1970 and 2000—meaning that families have less time for household labor, childrearing tasks, and leisure.[6] And since 1970, the average working time put in by professionals has increased substantially, with professionals and managers putting in the longest working hours of any group.[7] Between 1970 and 2000, the percentage of professional and managerial men working 50 or more hours each week increased from 21 percent to 27 percent, and that of professional women increased from 5 percent to 11 percent. More than one-third of professional men and one-sixth of professional women worked at least 50-hour workweeks in 2000, up from one-fifth of men and less than one-tenth of women in 1970.[8] As working hours for professional men and women rise, the impact on dual-earner professional couples with children is particularly acute—and there are many indications that time allocation is especially problematic for women.

Similarly, this also tends to be true about women's time allocation for housework relative to other activities. Although family time spent in housework has fallen over the last four decades, and the time that women and men each spend doing housework has partially converged, women still spend substantially more time performing household duties than men. According to Suzanne Bianchi and her colleagues, in 1995 women performed 17.5 hours of housework each week, while men spent 10.0 hours on housework.[9] Marriage increases time spent in housework for women but not for men, and the presence of children increases housework time for both, but three times more for women than men.[10] Perhaps, then, it is not surprising that with so many claims on women's time, full-time work is losing its attraction for many of them. Although families have become increasingly dependent on women's earnings—about 75 percent of American women now participate in the paid labor force—a decreasing proportion of mothers with children at home, about 21 percent in 2007 (down 11 percentage points since 1997), think full-time work is ideal for them, compared with 72 percent of men.[11] Together, these statistics reveal why issues of work-family balance are acute for women and likely to be most problematic for professional women.

Scholars have observed that men's and women's time allocation in work in the world, housework, and other activities is partly due to their available time but also a result of the relative amount of power each spouse has in the marriage due to education and income—as well as to cultural expectations of gender performance, which are supported and shaped locally by religious practice. Therefore, we should ask: How are these societal pressures perceived in religious settings and how do congregations respond?

Religion, Work, and Family

Penny Edgell reports that religiously involved men and women tend to seek a lifestyle that places a premium on family time; in fact, religiously involved women are more likely than others to be stay-at-home mothers.[12] Moreover, for churchgoing women who work in the paid labor force, work-family balance is especially taxing, whereas religiously involved men find it easier than their secular peers. For men, church involvement itself allows men more family time with children than they would otherwise have and tends to support them in scaling back work time to have more time for family. But for churchgoing women who work for pay, the more hours they work, the less frequently they attend church—and the more they experience work and family life in conflict and as personally draining.[13] These findings suggest that churches support stay-at-home mothers and bolster men's efforts to balance work and family but provide less support for women who work for pay, for whom work-family balance is already difficult.

Edgell also finds that, while women generally take on more caretaking duties than men, Catholic women are more likely to be regular caretakers than other women and are also more likely to spend more time on household tasks than other women.[14] We have seen that such choices are religiously supported at Assumption through gender images, such as those embodied in the Blessed Virgin Mary, that valorize women's nurturing roles and provide religious legitimacy for stay-at-home motherhood. But do Saint Brigitta's women also find religious support for such choices, and, if so, what forms does that support take? Moreover, what religious supports do mothers in each setting who must work outside the home, or choose to do this kind of work, find in their churches? What moral and practical resources do parishes offer families, and women particularly, as they prioritize the tasks of work in the world and work in the family? And how do dominant cultural and religious frames for women's work shape churches' attempts at supporting women's efforts in balancing work and family life?

As I demonstrate in the analysis that follows, the gender images dominant in each parish setting, while necessary, are in themselves insufficient to explain how Assumption and Saint Brigitta inform women's experience of and responses to problems of work-family balance. Rather, each parish makes sense of these problems by employing both religious images of gender *and* religious understandings of work drawn from different Catholic traditions. These religious understandings conceptualize work in terms of vocation, that is, as a religious calling. These understandings in themselves do not reference gender, but they complement each parish's fundamental presumptions about gender in ways that best support particular gender norms in each setting. However, each of these approaches leaves some of the tensions that surround women's work-family balance unresolved, and each emphasizes some aspects of women's identities at the expense of others.

Religious understandings of work at Assumption and Saint Brigitta are similar in that both congregations emphasize the importance of public work, see larger purposes in life beyond work, and understand the goal of human work in the context of salvation. However, the central religious understandings of work in each congregation are otherwise different, especially in the religious meanings of work in the family and work in the world that they most emphasize. Whereas the religious meanings of work at Assumption more or less equally emphasize all forms of human work, Saint Brigitta emphasizes religious meanings of work in the world. These two approaches support different solutions to women's problems of balancing work and family in each setting. As we have seen, at Assumption the central sacred image of family elevates motherhood; this reinforces women's decisions when they leave the workforce to stay at home. In addition, Assumption's religious discourse surrounding work emphasizes work both within and outside the home, lending further support for mothers who choose to stay at home with their children but doing little to ameliorate any felt tensions about having left work in the world. By contrast, the central sacred image of community at Saint Brigitta contributes to discourse and practices that sacralize social contribution through work in the world. This sacralization of work in the world supports women in their professions, but it is a double-edged sword for mothers at Saint Brigitta, since religious supports for motherhood are not as explicitly emphasized or as well developed as religious meanings of work in the world. Thus, whether they decide to combine professional work with childrearing or take time off to be stay-at-home mothers, balancing career identities with maternal ones requires a form of support that can be difficult to find at Saint Brigitta.

Because the professional families in these two settings have more resources at their disposal than many American families, women can choose between full-time or part-time work in the world or choose to leave the paid labor force altogether. The very fact that they are able to choose requires them to make meaning around these choices and thus fosters the symbolic potential attributable to their actions. In solving practical problems of work-family balance, then, women's symbolic positions in both congregations are brought into relief, as their actions come to express each group's discontent with the socioeconomic pressures placed on the middle class and the cultural uncertainty of women's roles. Ironically, this is a problem of privilege, one that women's recent gains in the U.S. labor force have largely made possible. The practical choices of mothers at Assumption therefore symbolize not only the congregation's maternal ideals but also its protest against family decline. By contrast, the activities of mothers at Saint Brigitta express congregational vexation at the lack of complete societal and ecclesial equality for women, and they come to represent for their peers the quandaries of marginalized minorities generally. Thus through their practical problems and activities, women in each local culture represent struggles against different societal problems, and they offer competing solutions—which incorporate often opposed, and sometimes polarizing, conceptions of the social organization of gender and work.

Work and Family at Our Lady of the Assumption

At Our Lady of the Assumption, the primary religious significance of human work is as a vehicle for accomplishing individual salvation and practicing evangelization—conferring equal dignity on women's and men's work, as well as on work in a career and work within the family. But these meanings of work, combined with the sacralization of family roles in the church's central ecclesial metaphor and in practice, provide strong religious support for fathers' breadwinning, parenting, and spousal roles and for mothers' work and maternal identities. In practice, regardless of whether women at Assumption worked outside the home, they spoke about motherhood as a religious vocation. By contrast, they never spoke of work in the world as vocational. Moreover, many mothers, especially stay-at-home mothers, expressed ambivalence toward the professional world: a mix of feelings of frustration with that world's inability to adequately accommodate mothering, recognition of their diminished status in the eyes of that world, and yearning to reclaim their place in it. And for both stay-at-home mothers and those who worked for pay, the primary problem of work-family balance involved their ability to pursue their maternal vocation most fully in the midst of countervailing socioeconomic and cultural pressures and lack of societal supports. Therefore, women's responses to their experience of work-family tensions and their embrace of maternal identities are practical, but their actions also symbolically embody Assumption's protest against contemporary threats to the modern nuclear family and the possibility for recovery of supports for this way of life. These experiences and responses, moreover, confirm for them the rightness of their positions on public cultural conflicts surrounding the family and place them in opposition to Catholic peers like those at Saint Brigitta.

Religious Belief and Practice and the Meanings of Work

To understand how the central religious meaning of work at Assumption supports maternal identities without fully resolving the tensions women experience concerning work in the world, let us examine how the parish perceives work and especially how work is intertwined with the twin goals of salvation and evangelization.

Father Aidan and Father James frequently preached at Sunday masses about work as an important arena for the practice of faith, explaining that one's daily work in the world, in whatever capacity, is the primary arena where, through virtuous action, the faithful cooperate in accomplishing their own salvation and the salvation of the world. In this understanding, which is heavily informed by Opus Dei's theology of work, there is a sense in which all work, including the hidden work of the private sphere, is public. Father James's homiletic exegesis of the parable of the unjust steward, preached on an autumn Sunday at Assumption, exemplifies how pastors challenged the congregation to engage the world on its own terms when at work but with religious goals in mind.[15] In the Gospel story, the steward, learning that he is to lose his job because he has administered his master's affairs poorly, lowers the amount his master's debtors owe his master, thereby putting them in the steward's debt. Father James tells the congregation, "The steward is praised by the master not because he is unjust, but because he shows ingenuity and the ability to negotiate the everyday world in an effective and creative way." Similarly, Father James recommends that Catholics should approach the world shrewdly on its own terms but for otherworldly ends:

> As Christians, we should not be comfortable just with living comfortable lives and going about our daily tasks. Rather, we should engage the world on its own terms, in order to do what small good things we can. By doing small good things for Christ we help to make the world a better place. We help in the work of the salvation and redemption of the world.
>
> But where is our sense of urgency?... Instead of coming home after work and watching television all night because we are exhausted, we [should] get out there and do something, do some small good work. All the little things we do will contribute to the good, in the battle with evil.

Father James does not recommend retreat from the world, but engagement with it, and he asks the congregation to consider the whole of daily life in contemplating what good works one might accomplish, since one's work in the world can contribute to the good.

Similarly, the workplace is an arena where congregants should seek to evangelize others, especially through example. When Father Aidan preached at Pentecost, he compared contemporary society to the historical time of the birth of Christianity, saying, "This time that we are living in is not so different from the early Church of the apostles. There was a lot of abortion and homosexuality in that time, too." But he explains that, because there is moral corruption in today's world, there is also work to do:

> We all have a duty to evangelize: first in the home, by creating a Catholic culture in our families; then at our place of work, whatever that might be, setting an example by our lives; then among our friends, to encourage them to come to church, to encourage them to live a Christian life; and among our other social groups and gatherings.

Father Aidan identifies moral corruption in the world directly with polarizing public issues that are often rhetorically linked to family decline in contemporary society—and to the need for the defense of the family. Conversely, the work of evangelization *begins* within the family; their religious observance should stand as an example for others. Parishioners should lead their peers both by the example of their own lives and by actively encouraging friends and colleagues to religious and moral life conduct. The three arenas of family, workplace, and friendship thus form a trio of social settings to which parishioners are encouraged to bring an evangelical Catholic practice.

The dominant understanding of work at Assumption coheres with these exhortations to parishioners' evangelical and salvific duties in the world in that it resists compartmentalization in favor of perceiving work, life tasks, and occupations generally as an integrated whole. This meaning of work encompasses *all* forms of labor performed in everyday life. Thus both work in the secular world of the professions and work within the family have religious significance at Assumption, as do all the good works that people perform in the course of daily living. This theology is central to Opus Dei and reflected in its name, which means "work of God." A cooperator's brochure enunciates this focus:

> Every honest human work, whether intellectual or manual, should be carried out by a Christian...with both professional competence and Christian perfection: out of love for God's will and in the service of mankind. When done in this way, any human work, no matter how humble or insignificant

the task may seem…is taken up and integrated into the great work of the creation and redemption of the world. Thus work is raised to the order of grace and sanctified, becoming a work of God, *operatio dei, opus dei*.[16]

This ethos of work coheres with the meanings of work practiced and preached at Assumption. It recognizes the dignity of all human work and does not privilege particular kinds of work, or even professional work as a whole, but perceives work well done as a good in itself. Thus parishioners from various professions, as well as women who do not work outside the home, easily find themselves in this religious view.

This perspective is reflected in the diverse professions represented among those interviewed and their spouses, many of whom are parish leaders, and all of whom are all highly committed Catholics (see table 5.1). Among men, five are in business, sales, and technical professions; three are attorneys; two do church work; and one is a former businessman and currently a high school teacher. Similarly, among women who worked for pay, there were two administrative assistants, an attorney, a businesswoman, a church worker, and a day care provider. Assumption's ethic of work, which holds up the dignity of all human work, thus has the capacity to mobilize religious identities within the secular world in various walks of life.

These meanings of work not only advocate public evangelization but also make permeable the boundary between private and public work. Parishioners understood their faith to be public in work; for instance, Ron Reyes explained, "Maria and I do not leave our religion at the door when we leave the church. We are called to be saints—the church calls us all to that—and I look in my life for the church to help me to be a better person, to be a better attorney, one who lives my Catholicism in my work." Moreover, he and Maria bring Catholicism into the workplace. Maria explained, "I will tell public officials what I believe about abortion. I will make my pro-life stand known. A lot of times, they just don't know [a lot about abortion]."[17] Since both work in fields of law that bring them into contact with political officials, they make known their political positions, informed by church teaching, even about the most polarizing public moral issues. These are public acts of evangelization.

Others at Assumption practice their religious faith in the workplace in ways that elide private and public practice. For instance, several parishioners go regularly to a priest who hears confessions in a downtown law office every Friday, so busy downtown workers who are members of Opus Dei can easily fulfill their obligation to practice weekly confession. This practice is a good example of the permeable boundary between public and private life at Assumption, since in this practice, parishioners bring the private practice of religion into secular arenas in a quiet but public way, by practicing it in a corporate conference room instead of a church confessional. Downtown confessions insert the practice of a private spirituality into the

Table 5.1 Professional and Occupational Training at Assumption
and Saint Brigitta

	Men	Women[1]
Assumption		
For-Profit/Business		
Sales/Business/Technology	5	3
Attorney	3	2
Writer	0	1
Nonprofit/Helping		
Teacher	1	3
Church work	2	1
Child care provider	0	1
Administrative assistant	0	1
Total[2]	**11**	**12**
St. Brigitta		
For-Profit/Business		
Sales/Business/Technology	3	1
Attorney	3	0
Journalist	1	0
Nonprofit/Business		
Church work	2	1
Teacher	0	1
Educational administrator	1	0
Social worker	0	4
Community organizer	1	0
Psychologist	2	1
Nurse	0	2
Total	**13**	**10**

1 The counts for both men and women in this sample reflect the careers for which they
trained, not their current employment situation. Some have jobs in occupations that are
different than the ones they initially trained for. Several of the women in this sample
were not working outside the home at the time of data collection.

2 In most cases, I interviewed both members of a couple. In the event that I did not
interview both partners, I asked for the occupational training of the noninterviewed
member of the couple and include these figures here, which is why the totals are greater
than the 38 I interviewed.

public world of work and reflect the sensibility of adult generations at Assumption who daily practice a private devotional religion in public settings.

Moreover, parishioners understand the work of the private sphere of the home to have public ramifications. Because work as a vehicle for sanctification of oneself and the world includes all human work, women's daily household and family work also is included as an arena for the accomplishment of sanctification and evangelization. But even more important, work in the household contributes not only to a robust family life and, through good works, to one's individual salvation and the salvation of the world but also to the public sphere—not only to the good of society at large but also particularly, and reminiscent of Alexis de Tocqueville's arguments, to the vitality of the American experiment.[18] In this way, the private sphere in some sense *becomes* public or, perhaps more precisely, comes to have public significance. As Tocqueville understood women's roles in the home as essential to the vitality of American democracy, so women at Assumption perceive their work in the home as a public contribution to society—as expressive of their Catholic identities but also public and evangelical. This is evident, for example, in Adele Dunning's assertion, "Family is the salvation of the country—that is what I believe!"[19]

Thus in spite of the seemingly sharp distinctions men and women at Assumption make between work in the world and family life, this religious view of work makes permeable any sharp boundaries between public and private spheres of life. Work in the private sphere is by definition a part of the work of salvation and therefore universal, and it has public secular ramifications, just as work in the world integrates a modest but public perspective on one's ostensibly "private" life of faith. In these ways, boundaries between public and private life are blurred; this local culture understands household work, predominantly conceived of as a private task, as a public contribution relevant to polarized contests about the family in society broadly.

Religious Meanings of Work, Motherhood as a Vocation, and Tensions over Work in the World

Because Assumption's religious orientation toward work encompasses mundane tasks like household work along with work in the world, those who do not work in the professional world, like many of Assumption's mothers, readily find their work included in a sense of religious mission. But the ways in which this theology of work combines with Assumption's gender ideology does not completely ameliorate the tensions between mothering and work in the world. Although stay-at-home mothers expressed strong commitments to their choice, they also expressed conflicted feelings about having left the paid labor force, feelings exacerbated by their religious peers who also work in the labor force. At the same time, for mothers who also work in the world, Assumption's orientation toward work creates tensions in entailing that their mothering should take priority over career pursuits, even when their jobs are personally meaningful or not wholly economically driven.

Stay-at-home mothers and tensions with the world outside the home

Like many of their middle-class peers, all of the women interviewed had worked in professional occupations—law, writing, administration, teaching—before they married. Once married with children, many left the professional world and took up the role of full-time mother and homemaker, while some continued to work or resumed paid employment after periods of full-time homemaking. A lower percentage of women in the Assumption interview group (45 percent) worked outside the home than that of women in the United States generally (77 percent), but their workforce participation was nonetheless significant.[20] Judging from numerous informal conversations I had with women and men at Assumption, the interview group more or less reflects women's workforce participation among the middle-class nonimmigrant portion of the parish membership. Women at Assumption expressed varied desires, attitudes toward professional work, and reasons for the ways that they structured their households—but whether they were full-time homemakers or worked outside the home, they expressed common perspectives about motherhood at Assumption. And although both women and men working outside the home spoke of efforts to balance the dual responsibilities of work and home, men never expressed ambivalent feelings about their negotiation of work-family balance, but women—especially stay-at-home mothers—often did.

Stay-at-home mothers at Assumption tended to have large families and husbands whose professions provided ample income to support the household. Because of the intensity of their professional lives, their husbands often spent significant time at work, even though they put a premium on family time and sought as much flexibility as possible. As a result, stay-at-home mothers at Assumption perceived that family obligations precluded them from staying connected to their professional work while childrearing, although most said they intended to pick up their career aspirations once their children did not need them as much. Stay-at-home mothers at Assumption evidenced many of the aspirations and challenges characteristic of their high-achieving professional peers who left the workforce to raise children full-time, but they differed from them especially in the ways they perceived and presented their maternal identities.

The distinctiveness with which they approach these identities is exemplified in the book group's response to Julia's question about what they called themselves. The discussion her question provoked reveals that women at Assumption who leave the workforce to become full-time homemakers encounter the standards of the professional world in their everyday lives and react to them with ambivalence, yet with resistance based in moral values that critique the dominant culture's lack of support for children's nurturance and family life. As the group's women responded to their absence from Julia's registration list, they actively tested options for how to present themselves in worlds outside home and church, recognizing that although their religious milieu affirms the value of their mothering work, other elements of U.S. society do not.

Their first instincts were to somehow professionalize their role in communicating it to the wider world, searching for words that fit their everyday routines while speaking in a language that conferred legitimacy on their work *as* work. But as they moved through the options for naming themselves, the group rejected professionalized descriptions as inaccurate to describe what they do, for these descriptions of homemaking and mothering neither fit their experience nor dignified the work they do. In settling on describing themselves as "stay-at-home moms," they acknowledged an identity and a social status that stands at a distance from the professional world—and in asserting motherhood to be an accurate description of their work and in refusing a professionalized description of it, they took a stance against broader social norms that confer status on professionalized and public work. Rather than trying to accommodate professional norms, they assert that motherhood is an important job that, while happening mostly in private, contributes to the public good. This resistance reflects one way in which mothers engage and try to resolve the contest over the value of mothering in contemporary Western societies. Their response differs from other high-achieving women who leave the workforce to raise children—who intensively parent but often describe their identities in terms of the work they have left behind.[21] By contrast, the women of the book group name their identities *as* mothers, not as former professionals. This choice is countercultural and represents a moral critique of the prevailing society.

The logic of how religious ideas about work, gender, and a moral critique of socially dominant family practices intersect in stay-at-home mothers' accounts of their choices to leave the paid labor force is articulated by Beth Bennett and evident in other women's words and choices. These perceptions and ideas sometimes also constrain women's perceptions of possible alternative ways of combining mothering with other pursuits.

Beth attributes her decision to leave the labor force to hers and Dean's increased involvement with Catholicism, which encouraged their sense of duty about the seriousness of childrearing and the need for parents to be present to their children. Beth said,

> We were married for five years before we had kids. Then we got more Catholic. I was an accountant, and I enjoyed my career. I took a maternity leave when my son was born, and I expected to come back to work. We had taken a vacation out East before I was to start working again, and we were driving back, listening to the radio in the car. Dr. Laura...was saying something about how important it is for parents to be with children, and it just clarified things for me. I knew that this was what I should do. So I quit my job when I came back home.

Beth presents her choice as a moral decision to be with her children because it is the right thing to do, despite the fact that she could—and had planned to—return to work. For Beth, religion and the desire for a certain style of family life are intertwined; becoming "more Catholic" preceded her decision to stay at home with children full-time. Women at Assumption generally put a high priority on their ability to spend time with their children, perceiving children's need for the presence of parents as needs that mothers are particularly responsible for, or desire to fill—a perception that is reinforced by the sacralization of maternal nurturance. In a certain sense, this simplifies women's decisions to leave careers when other women struggle with this choice because of the careers they leave behind; women take up a new identity in motherhood that is so religiously valued at Assumption that it can, for the most part, replace professional identities—something that secular high-achieving professional women who decide to stay at home do not necessarily have.

But at the same time, this sacralization, with the religious supports it provides for motherhood, is often intertwined with a discourse of women's sacrifice for their families, one that valorizes these women's choice but facilitates a "drift toward domesticity"—that is, a trajectory in stay-at-home mothers' activities and relationships that moves them toward traditional mother-homemaker roles and makes it more difficult for them to resume or reimagine careers.[22] A good example of the discourse about mothers' sacrifice comes from a Lenten Women's Evenings of Reflection, when a middle-aged mother named Jenny talked about the practice of confession with explicit references to women's routines as mothers.

> Confession is about you, not your husband's or your children's failings. Get to the point. Don't waste the priest's time. Be specific. Not "I was lazy," or "I was angry." Rather, "I didn't make dinner for my family five times last week." Don't make exceptions for yourself. Not "Because I have a big family and I'm tired, I didn't go to mass on Sunday." It's an obligation; you don't get an exemption just because you have a big family....Be sorry. Resolve not to do it again, and mean it, even if it means giving up friends.

Jenny articulates not only the perception that women serve their families through household tasks and that their doing so is a moral and religious obligation but also the conviction that women should strive to meet their obligations to church and family even if they have to renounce aspects of self in so doing. This discourse, and the sensibility from which it originates, both affirms mothers in their nurturing roles and encourages them to pursue this nurturing work sacrificially. Although it no doubt becomes more difficult for most mothers to find ways of combining work in the world and work at home as their families grow, for those at Assumption the practical results of this emphasis include constraints on women's perceptions of possible alternative ways of combining mothering with other pursuits, such as work, whose primary goal is their personal satisfaction.

For example, in choosing to stay at home, Pam Williams, a writer, has left behind a daily routine that includes the professional world, even though she still tries to practice her craft in the interstices of her family duties. Rob's job is demanding, and their four small children—her oldest is in first grade, her youngest is still an infant—need care. She retains her professional interest in writing, even though finding the time to write is difficult. Her husband makes a comfortable salary, but she says that she cannot justify paying for child care so that she can work. Her expression of constraint in this regard isn't a direct logical result of the religious convictions that lead to welcoming large families, but rather is related to the economic division of labor in the household and to norms about what it means to be a good mother, constraints that other stay-at-home mothers also experience. But these norms are also undergirded at Assumption by the sacralization of maternal roles and the sacrificial discourse that accompanies it. Pam is a particularly independent, confident, and self-reflexive thinker, one who was not afraid to assess the costs of her family's religious commitments. At the same time, these norms contribute to and reinforce her perceptions of the limits to her autonomy as she tries to balance pursuing independent professional projects with her family's needs.

Pam talked about her options for continuing her professional work despite her constraints in a very matter-of-fact way, but sometimes women at Assumption expressed explicit frustration at their circumstances. For example, one mother who has a graduate degree in the humanities and worked as a high school teacher before she had children spoke with intensity about her work as a mother and her devotion to her family. But in the middle of describing the routines of her everyday life as a stay-at-home mother of four young children, she stopped, turned to me, and said, "Don't you think I wouldn't want to be continuing my education, too? Don't you think I wouldn't like to be getting an advanced degree?"

This mother's emotional questions reveal the particular bind in which many mothers at Assumption find themselves, especially those with larger families. On the one hand, they spoke explicitly about the joys of childrearing and their commitment to raising their children intensively. But on the other hand, many have trained for and worked in a professional world that they find satisfying and stimulating, and in their work they internalized a professional identity that equates one's job with one's social status. Among a religious group that valorizes motherhood and yet allows a range of choices for women—choices that encompass but extend beyond the traditional roles of wife and mother—and surrounded by professionals in their neighborhoods and social circles, the professional world remains a presence around them, even though they do not work within it daily. Even with the religious supports that valorize their maternal identities, it is difficult for them to wholly remake themselves solely as mothers, since they have professional roots. Therefore, despite the fact that Assumption's women often expressed feelings of alienation from the professional world and actively appropriated a maternal identity that other women in similar social locations sometimes find more difficult to embrace, they still often saw themselves in its terms. This situation at once reflects the professionalism of Assumption's membership, its theology of work, and, at the same time, aspects of its religious ethic that do not easily dovetail with secular values and reinforce tensions between maternal and professional satisfactions and statuses.

One way in which some stay-at-home mothers dealt with these tensions was through the articulation of highly developed critiques of the professional world. These critiques cohere with the narrative of family decline more broadly but allow women whose experiences with the professional world were difficult to make meaning of them. For example, Julia Flaherty explained,

> Most men want working wives. But I don't like the way the working world is, in terms of the expectations it places on mothers. The working world is hostile to women, and to mothers in particular. My women friends who have successful careers don't have children—they have cats instead.

In elaborating some of the experiences that led her to conclude that the professional world is hostile to women, recall (from chapter 3) that Julia interwove her critique of the professional world with that of societal values generally. And in describing her first professional job as a researcher at an economics think tank, one of her complaints was, "Nobody seemed to want to have kids."

Julia was single when she worked at this think tank but hoped eventually to marry and have children[23]—and she first perceived the possible problems for women and mothers in the world of work at this job, which she also described as not suiting her demeanor, skills, or talents. But perhaps just as importantly, she viewed herself as having largely different personal priorities and practices in intimate relationships than other women with whom she worked. Although she didn't explicitly connect the relation between her lack of job satisfaction and her personal priorities, she made note of the correlation: the professional world requires a personal life where one's maternal and sexual self is subordinated to one's career. These experiences of the working world retrospectively give meaning and a rationale for why she has decided not to try to sustain a career while raising children. Like other women at Assumption who also used the phrase "cats, not kids" in assessing women's chances in the world of work, Julia perceives professional work and family more or less in terms of an either-or choice: either she can pursue career success, or she can raise a family—but given how her narrative unfolds, she concludes that she can't do both successfully at the same time. This construction of work as oppositional to family for women is societally common,[24] but the inclusion of intimate life more generally—an addition reflecting Julia's religious worldview—heightens the stakes.

Julia's critique of the working world is directed at its unwillingness to acknowledge and accommodate mothers, and in this respect, Julia's attitudes mirror those of women in some evangelical Christian settings who have felt disillusioned by the promises of feminism because of their experiences of difficulty in combining a fulfilling work life with an intimate spousal relationship and children.[25] As Julia's religious conversion led her to a satisfying marriage, so also it supports her decision to disengage from work in a career.

At the same time, Julia questions whether, if she had made different choices right out of college, she might have achieved more career satisfaction and success in work as her life moved forward. Her rationale for being a stay-at-home mother, in fact, goes beyond the sacralized, gendered, and relatively settled roles of husbands and wives at Assumption—it is a critique of women's experience of the professional world and yet tentatively but insightfully speculates about whether different professional experiences might have altered her subsequent decisions. In fact, despite her critique of the professional world, she hopes to reenter it down the road. She said, "I look forward to going back to work when my kids are grown. I would love to work for the church. But I am not sure what I could do. When the time comes, though, I think God will provide opportunities."

These stories, and those of other stay-at-home mothers at Assumption, suggest different trajectories for the role of religion in their work-family balance choices. In some cases, women came to Assumption with a desire for a marriage with traditional family roles, attracted by a religious milieu that supports and, in some cases, deepens these values and desires. In other cases, like Pam Williams's, religious observance actually changed their priorities. And Pam complicates the messages in narratives like Julia's, where there is an instrumental link between a desire for a particular lifestyle and Assumption's support for families, by explaining that she and her friends sometimes purposively conceal the religious reasons for their choices, especially the choice to have a large family. She explains:

> If I was saying to my family, and to other people we know, that we just wanted a lot of kids, and that we have the money to give them a good upbringing, this would be more acceptable to them than the truth, which is that we are doing this for religious reasons. My friends and I don't know what to say when people ask us about why we are having large families. Julia, for example, explains that she is from a big Italian family. But we don't like the reactions we get from our families and acquaintances when we tell them our real reasons.

Pam asserts that some of the constraints women feel in balancing work in the world and work in the family are grounded in religious convictions that lead them to eschew artificial birth control and live with an ethic that encourages a desire for large families and relies on God's providence. Pam did not present herself as having wanted a large family or wanting to stay home with their children; instead, she described her decision to have a large family to be rooted explicitly in religious beliefs. She directly underscores the importance of Catholicism in *how* she and her friends make decisions about work in the world and work at home. In asserting the importance of religious belief in family choices—even if she and her friends do not always communicate this to other family members or peers—she complicates any interpretation of the place of religion in family life at Assumption as wholly instrumental. Whatever other reasons Assumption's women and men might have, their choice to have large families has a strong religious dimension, and it is one that they do not always disclose to others. These religious principles eschew artificial contraception, value large families, emphasize women's roles as nurturers of children—and they magnify the drift toward domesticity for stay-at-home mothers as their families grow. Religion, then, is not merely a resource, but an ethic that has consequences for how families actually structure their lives. As Pam's musing about her limited options for balancing work and child care reveals, these consequences are often unforeseen by couples until they need to make specific choices surrounding work-family balance.

The ambivalent sentiments that stay-at-home mothers expressed toward the world of work are sometimes tinged with hope and at other times pessimistic. On the occasion that Pam spoke about the pluses and minuses of being open to having a large family, she rather pessimistically assessed the consequences of this choice for her future professional chances and those of her friends. Referring to the reality that she and her friends have been out of the workforce for more than a few years now, Pam said bluntly, if inaccurately, "We have no skills!" These words took me aback; as professionally trained, accomplished, competent, and energetic women, they could easily reinvent themselves whenever they chose. And yet, she did not emphasize or acknowledge their competencies. Instead, affirming other values, Pam went on, "But we have good marriages. You really have to trust your husband a lot to do this."

Mothers' work outside the home: mothers' vocation and work-family balance

Mothers who worked outside the home, whether they worked solely for economic reasons or for personal satisfaction, did not express the same ambivalence about the working world as did stay-at-home mothers, nor did they express the same tensions. Instead, they ordered their public and domestic lives in ways similar to how fathers negotiated them: they subordinated their work lives to motherhood and expressed their reasons for doing so in vocational terms. Men, even when they worked long hours, conserved time to devote to family work and considered fatherhood to take priority in their lives—making it a rationale for their work in the household as well as the work of breadwinning.[26] Whether their wives work for pay or not, men generally provided the most consistent portion of family income through full-time work in the professions. This meant that men's income alone often provided comfortably for the needs of these families through highly demanding and well-remunerated jobs. By contrast, most of the women in the interview group who worked outside the home worked in part-time positions. This was true of all the women interviewees who had more than one child. Some of these mothers had not planned on having a career, others chose professional work that involved children, and still others had moved out of their previous profession to seek flexible part-time work. Mothers at Assumption who worked outside the home therefore understood their careers, qua careers, to be secondary to their religious obligations to their families.

For example, when Dana Jaszewski was pregnant, she planned to build a life with both work and motherhood. When I first met Dana and Jim at a church lecture early in my field research, Dana was well into her pregnancy. She talked eagerly about preparing for her child's birth. When I asked if she planned to work after the baby was born, she said, "Oh, yes, definitely—I would be so bored if I didn't. I need something to do. I'll continue working, at least until I have a few children at home." Jim affirmed her choice.

> Oh, yes, she'll continue working. We need her income. Women today are different than they used to be. In the time of Christ, women didn't work—that's why it was so important to take care of widows and children—they had no income, they were poor, because they didn't work. But society today has changed.

Dana anticipates that eventually she will need to stop working outside the home; she privileges her childrearing responsibilities over her career, although she plans to work until she perceives that her responsibilities as a mother preclude her from working. Like her secular peers, she perceives work to be a psychological need and an antidote to boredom and says so explicitly—Dana *wants* to work in her profession. But Jim focuses on providing legitimacy for Dana's combining career and mothering by giving Dana's employment a practical rationale that is also religiously justifiable. He asserts that he and Dana are not violating religious norms or stretching the boundaries of acceptable practice, since in contemporary society working mothers can still be good mothers.

The privileging of maternal and household work as vocational work over work in the world is evident in how men and women talk about work in the world generally and about professional jobs in particular. One feature of these narratives is their inflection with gender. For example, Maria Reyes described her job as an attorney as follows: "I'm fortunate in my job. The people I work with know that my boss likes me, so I more or less keep the hours I want to. Ideally, my job is a man's job. There are really a lot more evening hours—a lot of meetings and fundraisers—than I am working right now." Maria's evaluation of her job as "a man's job" reflects the perspective that mothers and fathers have different roles in childrearing and that a mother's nurturing role entails the primary care for a couple's children. Even though men and women are equally educated and professionally competent, the local culture at Assumption thus entails that mothers and fathers approach the professional world differently. Even though she works full-time in a career position that she finds fulfilling, Maria views the evening hours required by her job as inappropriate for a mother and, therefore, more suitable for men. In fact, Maria's evaluation of her job shares commonalities with Julia's evaluation of the working world as "hostile to women," although Maria avoids the conclusion that Julia reaches. By contrast with Julia's experience of feeling ill-suited to her job, Maria not only likes her job but also is allowed to keep her own hours and avoid meetings that conflict with her duties as a mother. Maria works successfully at this job not only because her supervisor is willing to let her work flexibly but also because her husband's hours are flexible and he shares child care with her regularly—and likely also because they have only one child and therefore a relatively uncomplicated family routine. Thus, Maria is able both to fulfill the requirements of her vocation as a mother and to negotiate the professional world.

When we had this conversation, Maria had recently learned that she was pregnant with a second child. She was anticipating changes in her life and went on to talk about how she imagined her work would change as her family grows. She said, "I'm ready to stop working for a while. I will always find other things to do, with my background in organizing and community involvement. The issue here is flexibility and time." Maria emphasizes women's particular needs for flexibility once they are mothers, contrasting this need with the demands of her profession, which she has been able to negotiate until now but anticipates will be too taxing to continue once her family grows. And yet, although Maria perceives the demands of motherhood as more immediate, more important, and more central to her at this time in her life than her professional role, she still sees herself as retaining a public and professional identity. Even though she plans to leave the labor force to stay at home with children, she anticipates finding time for community involvement, too. In this, Maria's approach to stay-at-home motherhood parallels that of her secular peers who sustain their professional identities through volunteerism.[27] At the same time, her plans to do this as a stay-at-home mother who remains a public contributor, even though she has left the paid labor force, also recall a long tradition of women who have combined domesticity with volunteer service in community and church.[28]

Like Maria, most women at Assumption who worked outside the home did not present themselves as especially conflicted between family and profession, and most seemed quite comfortable in negotiating a balance between work and home. Most, however, presented this choice as a practical necessity: they worked for pay because their families needed the income. For example, although Don Dunning has worked two jobs through most of their marriage to make ends meet, while Adele's primary job has been the care and schooling of the children, she also works outside the home. Adele explained that if her family did not need her paycheck she would not, but her case is interesting because, on the one hand, she asserts that her work is instrumental for the family's economic welfare, but on the other hand, her paid work allows her to express her religious convictions around the publicly contested issue of abortion and about motherhood in society generally. Adele claims her vocation to motherhood as primary—but also expresses that vocation in public work in the world, which allows her to express a closely related professional identity.

Adele has two jobs. Her first job is a regular part-time job as an administrative assistant at an adoption agency. She is happy to have the job, she says, and strongly supports the mission of the organization that employs her, since the agency she works for explicitly promotes adoption as an alternative to abortion. Even though she does not claim this work as a part of a professional identity, the work itself is a contribution to a public issue closely interwoven with the religious beliefs about family that undergird her vocational identity. Her second job is just as closely related to the vocation of motherhood: Adele gives public lectures for Catholic organizations several times each year. These speaking engagements, which evolved out of giving talks for Right to Life organizations, include talks on faith and family, home management, femininity, womanhood— the "maternal heart of a woman," as she described it—the Madonna, the pope, homemaking, and the practical details of homeschooling. "When I'm asked to speak," she said, "we negotiate a little bit—I receive stipends and travel reimbursement when I do a talk." This public speaking affords Adele opportunities to give voice to her convictions as a Catholic and as a mother, homemaker, and teacher of her children.

Both of Adele's jobs affirm her identity as a mother. But in her public speaking work, she performs according to recognizably professional idioms, right down to negotiating her fees. At the same time, through this work, Adele assists and inspires mothers with similar convictions and socially elevates her choices and those of her peers, precisely by bringing her maternal identity into the public sphere where it can be scrutinized. Through her public speaking, Adele professionalizes her maternal role, although in a very different manner than one observes, for instance, in the activities of professional women who have left the labor force and intensively parent their children with the same thorough attention to excellence that they pursued in careers. And significantly, although Adele's adoption agency job and her public speaking both reflect her religious commitments, like most other women at Assumption, she did not talk about any religious meaning that these activities may have for her; rather, her reflections about the religious meaning of her work are concentrated around the substance of family, parenting, and marriage—sentiments of a grounded maternal identity that she is able to express in professional work.

Other mothers who worked for pay also talked explicitly about the meanings of motherhood as a religious vocation, by contrast with stay-at-home mothers, who rarely spoke about motherhood specifically in vocational terms. This was likely the case because, as women who work outside the home but find their primary sense of self in motherhood, it was more important for them to articulate the primary value of their work as mothers and to emphasize that their work in the labor force did not represent a conflict with the value they placed on motherhood. At the same time, they varied in the ways they understood their work in the world; although most, like Adele, saw their work outside the home as necessary but also satisfying, others perceived the necessity of their labor more negatively.

Anna Smith, who was raised in a practicing Catholic family, talked at length about both motherhood and work.

> I thought I would end up married with children, but I never knew that this was the vocation God had for me, I never thought of it in those terms. And if I had thought of it in those terms I would have done a lot of things differently.
>
>   You know, we were always told, you should get your education, you should have your career, you should travel, you should have all these experiences. And I did many of the things I wanted to do, and it sort of got me satisfaction, but now with my husband and kids I feel real happiness. I want to tell my girls that their happiness is going to be their husband and kids. Or if you're cultured and businesslike, that [you can have a career, but] your career is secondary.

Anna had encouragement and opportunity to pursue a career but suggests that, despite the advice of adults, she lacked firm direction from them. She now concludes that what was missing was a striving for a sense of vocation, which she identifies in the satisfaction and happiness she now feels as a mother. She therefore understands her maternal and spousal roles as essentially vocational and sees women's primary work in the home, even for married women who are oriented toward work in the world.

Anna works part-time for a pro-life advocacy group. As was the case with Adele, this organization expresses Anna's positions and religious ideals in public contests over the family. She says,

> I work for financial reasons. But we could get by without my work, so actually I don't work for financial reasons. I work so we can have extras, and also I enjoy getting out for a couple days a week. I enjoy the work that I do. I would not want to work full-time if I didn't have to financially. We do make financial sacrifices, because I wouldn't want to be away from my kids for that long. I don't think it's good for them if you can avoid it.

It's funny, you know, the work that I do is so removed from the actual girls going into the clinics. It's hard for me to feel that [I am connected to the girls], although rationally I think that I am [connected], and that God has put me in this little place, so that's what I do. I really admire the people who just pray the rosary in front of the clinic. But God calls us all to do different things.

Anna seems to think through her rationale for working outside the home as she speaks—her paid work is not strictly necessary to the family's economic welfare. She works in part for enjoyment, and she perceives her job in the pro-life movement not only to be imbued with religious meaning but also in some sense a calling. At the same time, she still clearly sees her work at the clinic as subordinate to her vocation as a mother, both in terms of how she allots her time and in where she finds happiness.

By contrast with Anna, Joanna Fitch, who works part-time in a doctor's office and also provides in-home day care for neighborhood children, interprets her work in the world as necessary but views her situation, and that of other mothers in the labor force, more pessimistically.

Feminism, which started out [advocating] equal pay and things like that, got distorted, and the monster got so big that it could not be controlled. It affected people's lives in that women now cannot afford to stay home. There are so many people in the workforce, such that so much money is required to support a family, and men are forced to compete with women. That makes their lives more stressful, and children are not being raised by their mothers anymore; they're being raised by surrogates like me... .

I believe that each of the sexes has their own power and strength and gifts that are strictly masculine and strictly feminine. Some of them, of course, cross over. I do think that women can rise to great levels of strength *on their own*. I do think that there are some dads who are better at mothering than some mothers.

We human beings, in order to get on with our lives and get on with our living, should get over these petty jealousies of the sexes and just do our jobs. Roll up your sleeves and do your job, what God wants you to do.

Joanna sees the structural conditions that propel women into the workforce as largely negative for women and their families. She locates what she perceives to be the present confusion about men's and women's roles historically in the second wave of the feminist movement. She sees the cultural legacy of feminism as the key engine for changes in economic structures that requires her, and women like her, to participate in the paid labor force. She is careful to say that she doesn't rigorously ascribe to an essentialist view of women's maternity. But neither does she see present gender relations, which she perceives to be competitive largely because of the feminist movement, to be useful or even moral. Like other women at Assumption, Joanna expresses ambivalence toward work in the world because of the lack of fit she perceives between maternal roles and the demands, drive, and inflexibility of the workplace. This was as true for the majority of women at Assumption who worked in the world as for women like Joanna, whose selves are more exclusively rooted in motherhood.

Assumption's retraditionalized gender relations perhaps play out most clearly in women's efforts at balancing work and family. Mothers' struggle with the larger world of work is not so much about whether they should work outside the home, but rather how their work within the home is to be regarded and valued. Since motherhood is profoundly vocational, women evaluate work in the world from the perspective of the extent to which it accommodates family life—especially childrearing—for themselves and others and by considering its social effects on the family generally.

The religious meanings attached to women's work, especially in the discourses of sacrifice and vocation, not only are a sense-making tool that mothers use to explain their work and family choices but also play roles in Assumption's interpretation and critique of the "decline of the family" in American society, and in this way they support their public politics in cultural contests over issues such as abortion and women's societal roles. The affinities between the central ecclesial metaphor of family and how women structure work-family balance, together with elements of Catholic identity at Assumption, contribute to this local culture of women and work, as do religious understandings of work in their intersection with gender. I have shown that in the ways that priests and parishioners invoke issues of cultural conflict over the family—especially the issues of abortion, homosexuality, and women's societal roles—in work-related discourses, and in women's choices for paid work that uses mothering skills or expresses maternal identities, religious understandings of work are deeply intertwined. In addition, we have seen that women's sacrifices and how they prioritize the work of motherhood symbolically embody protest against family decline. In these actions, the congregation both stakes its place at one pole in public conflicts over the family and creates a coherent vision of the importance of the modern nuclear family to the larger social world. Families strive to live out this vision and, in living it out, hope to impress it upon society broadly.

Work at Saint Brigitta

Leaders and parishioners at Saint Brigitta share with those at Assumption their affirmation of the dignity of all human work, perceptions of larger purposes in life beyond work, and an understanding that work is intertwined with world-saving activity. But these beliefs play out very differently at Saint Brigitta, where the religious meanings of work concentrate primarily on people's work in the professions, prize socially contributory work in the world, and sacralize the performance of this work as vocational. These definitions and values shape women's negotiation of work-family balance toward particular ends, since the parish prioritizes women's participation in the public sphere equally with men's and emphasizes both the personal satisfaction and economic benefits women gain from such work. Saint Brigitta constitutes women's roles in a way that is in some respects opposed to Assumption's local culture, with work in the world comprising women's vocations, not motherhood. Moreover, the parish's culture of work supports flexible family structures and plural family forms that increase women's options and their freedom for professional pursuits. The flexibility inhering in this logic therefore also makes room for a variety of positions on issues in cultural conflicts surrounding the family, but ones that focus at a pole opposite that to which Assumption tends.

Like those at Assumption, both mothers and fathers at Saint Brigitta often create a balance between work and family by choosing flexible jobs when they can, especially so that fathers can share parenting tasks when mothers work in the world. But by contrast with mothers at Assumption, at Saint Brigitta even most stay-at-home mothers retain the professional identities they internalized when they worked outside the home and still talk about themselves in those terms. Mothers who have devoted themselves to parenting children and care of the household often long for the professional work they have at least temporarily left behind, even as they perceive their role in the home as extremely important for their children's thriving. Saint Brigitta's culture of work strongly affirms women's professional identities but offers few religious meanings for motherhood. Women's commitments to motherhood are strong but not explicitly spoken about in terms of religious meanings; instead, the value of motherhood is seen in women's practice and constitutes an element of taken-for-granted or common-sense understandings of family life among them. This local culture protests lingering inequalities for women in society and church and as a whole constitutes an alternative vision of gender roles that in several respects conflicts with the one dominant at Our Lady of the Assumption.

Religious Perspectives on Work: Faith and Work in the World

Catholicism at Saint Brigitta serves to sacralize work in the world, especially in beliefs flowing from the church's social teachings and in practices, such as the dialogue homily, where the congregation hears parishioners' accounts of their experiences of work. The religious meaning of work at Saint Brigitta is informed by a notion of vocation that sees work ideally as service in the world to which people are called in virtue of their unique talents—talents recognized in one's competence, desire, and self-actualization as a person. Competence in work is highly valued, and contributory work is sacralized, making work in the world a moral pursuit.

This emphasis on contribution in professional pursuits was exemplified on a September Sunday in the gym, when Father Theo preached on the Gospel of the shrewd steward. This is the same Gospel that Father James preached on, discussed earlier—but rather than exhorting congregants to a sense of urgency in doing small good works to fight evil, as Father James did, Father Theo used the parable to problematize the right uses of money and, in so doing, evoked congregational reflections on the value of work. He began by telling his own parable:

> Two boys found a lady's purse. It had identification in it, and a ten dollar bill in the wallet. It was obvious from the contents of the purse that this woman was poor. They thought they shouldn't keep it. So they decided to return it to her, but before they did, they went to the store. They changed the ten dollar bill for ten one-dollar bills and put them back in the wallet. Were they somehow morally less than they should be for doing that, or just shrewd?

Father Theo poses a moral question surrounding the steward's, and these boys', shrewdness, focusing on the politics of relationships and the ways in which people get things done. But then he asks, "How do we decide on the right uses of money? How do we put concerns about money in perspective?" Congregants' responses involved how they earn their money, and making decisions about work central to morality surrounding money. Lisa's response is a good example:

> I know this man who has been transformed by the events of the last couple of weeks [since September 11th]. He is in his thirties, and he is a millionaire several times over. His entire life is money. But we were telling him, just recently, what a good teacher he would be. He lost a lot of money in the fall of the stock market. But he doesn't seem distressed or sad. He's happy. He's thinking about teaching. He's been transformed by these events.

Lisa defines work in the world through a vocational lens: she tells us that she and her friends urge this man to teach because he would be good at it (although she makes no reference to his obvious abilities in the world of finance, even though he had clearly done well in that industry for years). In telling her story, Lisa portrays her friend as being positively transformed by his financial misfortune, especially as he thinks about leaving his current profession for teaching. She suggests that in the clarity that can emerge from a crisis, a person can be spiritually transformed to consider pursuing works whose primary rewards are related to meaning, not money, and whose value is measured in how it directly serves others, especially those who are vulnerable. Lisa's story reflects a moral perspective on work, where the place of money in one's life is secondary to work that is oriented to service, and therefore religiously meaningful and morally exemplary. This perspective is commonly articulated at Saint Brigitta.

Perhaps it is not surprising, then, that lay leaders worked disproportionately in service-oriented helping professions. While those interviewed in the two parishes were similar in that most in each setting were lay leaders and had professional occupations, the clustering of the types of professions among interviewees and spouses differed, with a significant cluster of those at Saint Brigitta, 58 percent (14/24), working in the helping professions. Among men, four were in business or technical professions (including two organizational psychologists), three were attorneys, two were clinical psychologists, two did church work, one was a journalist, one a grocery store worker, and one a community organizer. Among women who worked for pay, nearly all were helping professionals: four were social workers, two were nurses, one was a psychologist, one did church work, one was a nursery school teacher, and one was in business (See table 5.1). Thus a substantial number of the most involved congregants at Saint Brigitta are helping professionals. They almost invariably talked about their careers more or less explicitly in terms of a sense of religious vocation, even when not in specifically religious occupations.

Moreover, professional culture generally and skills related to professions in particular predominate in parish culture at Saint Brigitta. Although professionals dominate the focal congregations at both Assumption and Saint Brigitta, the effects of professional culture are especially obvious where professional skills and conventions are practiced in volunteer service and even in worship. Stan Roberts, a longtime participant at the gym mass who is a semiskilled worker, described how preachers respond to participants during the dialogue homily in illustrating how professionalism manifests in its practice. He explained that his friend Sylvia often spoke during the dialogue but was frequently interrupted by the homilist; he observed, "The people who are allowed to speak uninterrupted have high-powered jobs and success orientations." And in fact, the different ways in which homilists treat dialogue participants at Saint Brigitta, and the general designation of leaders in the gym, do break down roughly along lines of social class. Those at the gym mass who speak regularly, at length, and uninterrupted tend to be professionals; often they have been trained to speak in an engaging or commanding style. But those who are less polished speakers and work in lower level or nonprofessional jobs tend to be interrupted by preachers, especially when they speak at length. Whether the less polished style of this second group is due to personal traits, work skills, generation, or other factors, these less accomplished participants possess neither the status nor the social power of their more articulate peers. Professional culture is unintentionally implicated in religious practice and in congregational perceptions of the nature of contribution.

But at the same time, Saint Brigitta actively tries to mobilize its laity, regardless of their class status, by means of a sense of vocation to the work of service, not only through one's profession but also through volunteerism. A large number of Saint Brigitta's members are actively involved in the parish, and the parish offers a multiplicity of organizations and activities for parishioner involvement; some groups focus on prayer and faith-sharing, some on religious ministries in the parish, some on work within the neighborhood and community, and some on larger political and social issues. To serve in one's work, whether in a profession or in volunteer activities, almost reaches the status of a moral imperative at Saint Brigitta—one that mobilizes parishioners to make active contributions to the church and society. The religious nature of this aspect of local culture is expressed by Brad Green, 67, as he talks about how he has counseled some of the resigned priests at Saint Brigitta. Brad was himself an ordained priest who resigned from the priesthood, married, and subsequently worked as an organizational psychologist. Although Brad here speaks specifically about how he has helped other resigned priests find work, his way of connecting people's experience of parish life and ministry with their professional work is common among Saint Brigitta's laity as well. Brad said,

> I suggest to them that their years in the priesthood, they're going to take that with them. And that no matter what they're doing, no matter what kind of job they get, that experience, and that business of what made you want to go into the priesthood in the first place, is going to be with you. And whether you tell somebody that you were a priest or not, you're going to act as a priest.

For men of Brad's generation who had a desire to pursue religious service, diocesan priesthood and religious life were the only available options. But for those Catholics who came of age during and after Vatican II, their options for religiously meaningful vocations were expanded by *Lumen Gentium*'s call to holiness for all and *Gaudium et Spes*'s articulation of the importance of the laity in the church's mission of service to the world.[29] Involved parishioners at Saint Brigitta enact these principles in professional work—especially if their work is service-oriented—as well as in volunteerism.

As a result, many parishioners have learned to think of both professional work and volunteerism as arenas to fulfill a religious vocation. Beth McGivern's discussion of her quest for work that expressed her religious commitments in the introduction to this chapter is one good example that illustrates this sensibility. Maggie McNeill provides another, when she explicitly describes her former work as a social worker at a Catholic residential institution for disabled children and adults as "at the intersection of faith and work." The intersection of faith and work for which Saint Brigitta's parishioners strive differs from Assumption's values in that it prioritizes particular professional works as religiously meaningful, although its outward evangelical thrust is similar to Assumption's. As those at Assumption do good works in the world, they are focused first on changing hearts and minds to the love of God, for their own and the world's salvation. But at Saint Brigitta, people ultimately strive for the salvation of the secular through concrete interventions in the world; they find religious meaning in trying to transform the structures and cultures of everyday life in small but significant ways.

In this effort, family in itself is not "the only salvation" as it is at Assumption; instead, it is a foundational institution where, supported by the church community, this work is nurtured. John Maloney-Jones articulates the desire that family life might be a seedbed for the support of the work of societal transformation, saying,

> Our desire is [for] a redefinition of the family in the first place, especially if we see the church, the faith community, as constitutive of the way we live our lives. In some ways I see the church as more important than the family, but the family is the most elemental building block in [the community]. What I'm really looking for is a faith and a body of people who are really going to be Christ in the world and transform the world. How people do that is most elementally lived out in how you have a family, how families live together.

John believes that family and work should be about the same objective: transforming the world. He understands that the setting in which most people will take up such a task will involve their families and thus will be fraught with the concrete details and constraints of balancing work outside the home, household work, and relationships within the family. In the current social and economic context, work-family balance is a challenge even for those who are fortunate enough to have a range of choices. John hopes that the church community will ideally support people to negotiate family life together in more cooperative ways than the modern nuclear family allows and so facilitate their work for social transformation.

In sum, John doesn't articulate the vocation of marriage and family life, per se; in his view, the family is primarily at the service of people's vocations in the wider world, rather than the source or fundamental location of their religious calling. While not all at Saint Brigitta would express a religious impulse to work for social change this fervently, most lay leaders would affirm the importance of working to alleviate social problems.

This understanding of the relation of the institutions of church and family is undergirded by, and has implications for, how the family is defined and imagined. In particular, while the nuclear family is important at Saint Brigitta and in some sense an ideal, a plurality of family forms is seen as more or less equally capable of the task of being Christ in the world, especially as the church helps families cooperate so that its members can be freed for mission-oriented work outside the home. With this goal, the defense of the modern nuclear family is less urgent, because the social problems that need addressing have solutions stemming from church, and one particular structure for families is not constitutive of this task. In other words, while both parishes are concerned with an evangelical world-saving mission, at Saint Brigitta families are understood to participate in this larger mission cooperatively as they are free to do so, whereas at Assumption modern nuclear families *are* the mission—that is, they accomplish salvation by the very work of family life.

Therefore, the vision of family and church at Saint Brigitta places the dominant perception of family-related public conflicts largely in opposition to those espoused at Assumption. The focus on a mission in which families participate, but which is centered in alleviating social injustices, emphasizes concerns over injustices suffered by socially marginalized groups, with women figuring prominently among then. This focus on social justice allows Catholics at Saint Brigitta to support pro-life positions as efforts to end injustice and recognize human dignity for the unborn. But, in concert with its public silence on abortion, Saint Brigitta also supports sentiments of concern about social injustices experienced by women with unwanted pregnancies, in the form of a lack of support and/or freedom; these concerns can cohere with both pro-life and pro-choice positions in ways that many at Assumption would reject.

The culture of work at Saint Brigitta thus supports a range of views on public cultural conflicts surrounding the family, and it does so precisely because these issues are largely identified and interpreted through a justice-oriented frame, rather than one concerned with the defense of the nuclear family, as at Assumption. Because these two different perspectives can each be perceived by the other as opposed to their moral view of the family in society—and this is despite the fact that they have much in common—the very constitution of these local cultures thereby contributes to the polarizing tendencies surrounding the family among Catholics.

Work in the World and the Work of the Family

The importance accorded work in the world at Saint Brigitta encourages both women and men to make contributory work central to their identities as professionals and as Catholics, creating coherence among several aspects of their public identities and providing a central frame for the meaning of human life and social relationships. This ethic has consequences for private life in provid-ing concrete religious and communal support for marital styles that honor both husbands' and wives' aspirations to social contribution through work. The work involved in keeping a home is ideally shared between family members in ways that often eschew older gendered perceptions of women's and men's roles in marriage—although couples also draw on, or acknowledge the influence of, these socially available gender role schemes. Habits that reflect the image of the church as a community ideally ground the realization of couples' contribu-tory work in marital practices by which couples adjust to one another in meet-ing their joint family obligations and free both spouses to pursue professional work and/or volunteer service. Thus the religious supports for women's pro-fessional work, together with congregational support for consensually negoti-ated marriages, implicitly reject traditional gender roles and therefore more or less explicitly oppose the retraditionalized gender roles valued in Assumption's milieu.

Moreover, the religious logic that emphasizes contributory work in the world, which, as we have seen, represents one side of polarized views of the family's role in contributing to the well-being of society, shares affinities with the practices of women as they negotiate vocational work in the world, which reinforce this polar perspective. However, this logic has both advantages and disadvantages for the congregation's women. It provides religious support for women's career identities and a basis for privileging women's autonomy in work-family balance negotia-tions. But this focus on contributory work in the world is not accompanied by an equally strong religious discourse surrounding family life, despite the fact that Saint Brigitta's women, like churchgoers generally, tend to be family oriented.[30] Both stay-at-home mothers and those who work for pay are highly articulate about the religious significance of their vocations in the world but less often explicitly ascribe religious meaning to their maternal identities—an additional difference between Saint Brigitta and Assumption that represents a source of cultural con-flict between their two milieus.

Stay-at-home mothers and work in the world

Stay-at-home mothers appealed to career identities in their self-presentations even long after they left the paid labor force and expressed these identities in volun-teer activities and future aspirations. Beth McGivern's story, told in the vignette that begins this chapter, is one good example of how at-home mothers at Saint Brigitta explain why they decide to become full-time mothers and homemakers and how they deal with the identity tensions resulting from their withdrawal from the labor force.

What is most apparent in Beth's story is her investment in work and its rela-tionship to her religious journey. Beth describes her search for meaningful work as emerging when she was in college, at the same time as she was connecting with peers who were asking religious and political questions, saying explicitly that the church was a part of her search, not through pious practice but through service experiences and reflection upon them. She tells a story in which her desire for meaningful work became increasingly connected with a religious ethic and practice, to such a degree that she pursued degrees in theology and social work concurrently. Although she struggled with the vocational issues that this choice evoked, she found in the practice of social work a religiously meaningful profession where she could participate in effecting small-scale social changes. She describes her professional work as a site of heavy personal investment, satisfaction, learning, and growth—and one expressive of her religious convictions and ideals.

However, when Beth and Peter decided to begin having children, she was faced with a range of unsatisfactory choices rooted, at least in part, in the structure of her job and the agency for which she worked. In ways similar to her high-achieving secular peers who have left professional work for full-time motherhood—and also similar to the experiences of some of Assumption's stay-at-home mothers—she believed that, once her child was born, the investment her job required would take too much time for her to also parent intensively, and there was no immediate job option that would allow her to adjust her job to her family life. Deciding against looking for a part-time option and doing "the juggle," she chose to stay at home full-time.

In telling this story, Beth reflects the experiences of many stay-at-home mothers who find their job options inadequately flexible or ill-suited for achieving a workable balance between work and family.[31] Similarly, like her secular peers, she brings her professional skills to her work within the home and retains her career identity. But she differs from them in *how* she frames the significance of her work in the home; consequentially, she explains her choice to stay at home in the same terms as she had made meaning of her career, describing it as another way to "make an impact"—this time with her child. In other words, she parallels the meaning of her work as a mother with the religious significance of her professional work, conveying the hope that, through the tasks of parenting, she might make a contribution that she can make sense of with her religious convictions. But at the same time, she expresses uncertainty about whether making an impact through childrearing will be enough for her. Although her life is satisfying in many respects, she still longs to find work that will allow her to contribute in a public setting.

As was true for Beth, tensions in maintaining a career identity while also spending significant time parenting children were felt broadly at Saint Brigitta, among both the mothers who worked outside the home and stay-at-home mothers. Maggie McNeill spoke in a particularly illuminating way about the effects of the choice to stay at home upon her sense of self. She followed a path that is similar to Beth's: like Beth, Maggie is a social worker, and she loved the work she did with disabled adults before leaving her job to stay at home full-time with her children. When Maggie was pregnant with her first child, Robbie, she planned to go back to work full-time after her maternity leave. But after Robbie was born, she changed her mind and returned to her job only to train her replacement because, she said, "It was killing me to think of going back and leaving [Robbie]. It became apparent that this is where I needed to be. What was important was being at home." Reflecting upon that choice, she explained,

> Having kids was definitely the most enormous identity change for every-one I know. Going from being a professional to being a mom [when I left Saint Mary's], I put my professional life on hold. It's the hardest thing about motherhood. We were the most ready people in the universe, but it was such a total blow to my identity—going from working to caring for children. I had trouble in the beginning.
>
> But it's a privilege to be able to be home with them. I worked very hard for seven years, and it sucks the life out of you, though I love it. And being at home is very hard, but I realize that it is all a gift. There are women who work so hard, who would give their right arm to be where I am. I should take this opportunity. Work will always be there.

Maggie is explicit that what is most difficult about the transition from working in the world to being a full-time mother is not what she actually does every day, but its significance for her sense of self, because moving from the professional world to the home involves a shift in her identity. Like Beth, her professional identity has religious meaning, in that she experienced her job as a caring professional at a Catholic institution as at the intersection of faith and work. Because of the religious context and her religious motivations for work, her narrative illuminates how religious supports at Saint Brigitta contribute to heightening the stakes she places in her professional identity. But the fact that Saint Brigitta emphasizes active public witness of faith in the world over the relation of faith to private life means that there are simply fewer religious resources for women to draw on in fashioning religious images of motherhood that might have mitigated Maggie's feelings of identity loss, once she stepped out of the paid labor force into stay-at-home motherhood.

However, Maggie finds the possibility of public contribution in stay-at-home motherhood in the experience and knowledge that she may be able to bring to caring institutions like Saint Mary's at a future time, when she resumes her career. She explains, "I was able to transition because of having a good relationship with Saint Mary's. It's all or nothing at Saint Mary's. I want to help them to see that there has to be middle ground. Maybe job sharing." Even though, as a not-for-profit religious institution, Saint Mary's is arguably less influenced by the capitalist work ethic than many other organizations, its religious mission nonetheless requires an intense vocational dedication among its staff. Maggie explained that Saint Mary's is run by a congregation of religious sisters who don't have spouses or children and that they expect of their married coworkers the same investment of time and dedication that the sisters can give. Maggie hopes to someday help the sisters at Saint Mary's to take into account the added claims married professionals have on their time and to encourage reshaping similar workplaces in a more family-friendly fashion.

One final consequence of the identity shift Maggie has undergone in withdrawing from the paid labor force is related to her marriage: in summing up her feelings about the transition to stay-at-home motherhood, she said, "To say for the first time, 'I don't work outside the home' is another level of identity. I have to figure out if that's what I really want. It doesn't feel very equal, but it's fine for now." Maggie's words imply that her transition to stay-at-home motherhood has introduced a felt sense of inequality, perhaps with her professional peers, but especially with her husband, who continues to work outside the home full-time. She doesn't specify how she experiences this sense of inequality and is willing to live with it as it is—but she also presents her decision to stay at home as revisable.

That mothers at Saint Brigitta who leave the paid labor force to stay at home feel a religious loss of meaning when they transition to childrearing and home-making is also evident in Ann Burke's account of why she left the paid labor force. For Beth and Maggie, leaving the labor force was a relatively free choice compared with the constraints that Ann faced before she became a stay-at-home mother. Ann had worked outside the home when her children were babies. But her youngest child was diagnosed with a learning disability and health problems at about the same time that her job was phased out. Her son's needs required much time and energy, and instead of the options Beth and Maggie had for continuing work—even if they were insufficiently flexible—she had no job at all. Ann chose to stay at home full-time rather than seek another nursing position. Ann's youngest is now seven, so she has been a stay-at-home mom a good deal longer than either Beth or Maggie. By staying at home, she said, she is able to create a placid home environment and be available for her children—a contribution to home life that she knows to be important to the quality of her family's life. She is available to take her youngest child to medical appointments and therapeutic sessions and to volunteer at her children's school. But Ann misses working outside the home.

> Now that my life is really involved with family, it's hard for me sometimes, remembering that what I'm doing is very ordinary, but that God is very present....
>
> What's been challenging for me is allowing Kevin to continue that...to allow that ministry to continue for him. It is very important for him,

important for my children to see that....We are committed to caring for
and serving other people, [but in staying at home, it is] just taking a different form. I liked it when I had a nursing practice that was helping people
and ministering.

Ann explicitly articulates how the religious sense of mission she shares with Kevin
is difficult for her to enact in her role as a mother and homemaker. For Ann, serving a larger group is an important characteristic of the ministry and mission that
enlivens her work and binds her to Kevin; playing a supportive role for Kevin's
ministry work, though important, does not yield the same meaning as her work
in the world. Her sense of her own vocational mission in "caring for and serving
other people" is implicitly directed to the wider world, rather than the home, and
even though she acknowledges that her work in the home is caring work, it is difficult for her to find it religiously meaningful, in the sense of feeling God's presence in it. By contrast with mothers at Assumption who experience the support
and acknowledgment of motherhood as a vocation in parish discourse, the work
of mothering is rarely talked about publicly at Saint Brigitta as a religious task.

These women experience parenting as a private endeavor, by contrast with
career experiences that engaged them in the work of service in the public sphere
among larger groups. Like their secular peers, they miss the larger world of adult
contacts involved in professional life—but they also feel the loss of its religious
meaning. Their sentiments reflect how religious meaning, professional aspirations, and the class cultures they inhabit intertwine in the processes that shape
their subjectivities. And even though Catholicism writ large offers other resources
for making religious sense of motherhood, such as those drawn on at Assumption,
women at Saint Brigitta almost never mentioned them. Instead, each struggles to
find religious meaning in their duties as mothers and homemakers, and they find
that the religious convictions they enacted in their careers translate imperfectly, if
at all, to their work in the home.

Why is it that these stay-at-home mothers struggle to find religious meanings
in motherhood, given the availability of images of motherhood in Catholicism's
storehouse of beliefs, practices, and traditions? One plausible answer is found in
the religious meanings of work that emphasize contribution in the wider world
rather than in the private sphere. But in addition, by contrast with Assumption,
although public talk about parenting at Saint Brigitta is not at all uncommon, there
is relatively little discussion in public settings specific to motherhood. Moreover,
although the Blessed Virgin Mary is a model at Saint Brigitta, she is appealed to
in a more reserved fashion, and in different ways, than at Assumption. This is, in
fact, a response to how Marian practices at parishes like Assumption are interwoven into narratives of family decline and public conflicts over issues like abortion;
Saint Brigitta chooses a different approach.

People at Saint Brigitta spoke explicitly about this. For instance, in speaking about Marian devotions, Father Theo worried that charismatic Catholics, who wanted the parish to explicitly address abortion, were "too attached" to Mary. He explained that he responded to charismatic parishioners, along with others who wanted him to address the abortion issue directly, by saying, "I just kind of avoid it, and say, no, we don't do that." This response directly opposes the practices of conservative milieus, intentionally situating Saint Brigitta at one pole against the other in this instance.

Not only does Saint Brigitta refuse to publicly engage the debate over abortion but also the meanings and practices surrounding Mary's role differ from those at Assumption. At Saint Brigitta, the symbolic role played by the Blessed Virgin Mary is one that tends to affirm women in a general way, rather than mothers specifically. Mary's motherhood *is* referenced in the parish's Elizabeth Ministry, which serves and assists pregnant women and new mothers—but this reference is directed toward Christian mission rather than motherhood per se. The ministry's name references the scriptural story in which Mary, when pregnant, went to visit her older cousin, Elizabeth, to assist her through her own pregnancy.[32] The image is of Mary, as a mother-to-be, spending time with and helping another mother. Although it is a maternal image, it is very different from the images of the Holy Family and Mary's motherhood of the church commonly referenced at Assumption. Moreover, Mary's portrait at Saint Brigitta is most often her image at the Visitation: proclaiming God's liberation of the lowly and oppressed in the Magnificat. Again, this is an image of a mother-to-be, but the emphasis here is on a woman who emphasizes her alliance with the poor and marginalized. This is, in fact, a symbolic role similar to that played by the congregation's women.

This thread, of identifying women and Marian devotion with roles or traditions that emphasize her care for her peers and her connection to the poor, rather than her daily tasks as the mother of a child, is consonant with, if not reflected in, Louis's ruminations on the Catholic devotions of his childhood:

One of the things I miss is praying the rosary as a family. Everyone got something different out of it, but at least we all engaged in it. Now, for me, I'd like to take the rosary, and instead of honoring Mary, I'd rather do the prayer of Saint Francis. I'd carry a rosary, but my meditation [would be], "Make me an instrument of your peace."

Louis appreciates older traditions of Catholic devotional life and sees them as potentially a part of his family's religious practice but suggests refashioning the rosary in ways that focus on a larger set of social relations than what is evoked for him by Mary's maternity. The roles of women at Saint Brigitta are reflected in how such imaginative practices surrounding Mary are shaped and reworked to address congregational concerns.

Even parish celebrations involving the commemoration of women historically and in the present tend to emphasize their public talents rather than the often hidden work of motherhood. For example, the parish celebrates the feast of Saint Mary Magdalene each year with a non-Eucharistic worship service at which women preside and preach; here the parish brings to the fore women's public ministerial gifts, not their roles within the family.

Thus, in a congregation that sacralizes works of public social contribution, religious meanings of work support mothers as they maintain career identities. Even when they leave the world of work and seek parallel religious meanings in childrearing, they struggle to make religious sense of motherhood. Religious meanings of motherhood are likewise mostly absent in discourses about public conflicts over the family. This is both a consequence of the emphasis on women's public social roles beyond the family and a reaction to the intertwining of traditional gender roles for women and family-related issues in more conservative Catholic milieus and in official church teachings and pronouncements.

Mothers working in the world: professions, vocation, and work-family balance

We have seen that, by contrast with Assumption's mothers, stay-at-home mothers at Saint Brigitta did not express worry or despair about their job chances when they decided it was time to return to their professions. In fact, they do not leave their career identities behind them, but merely put their work on hold. Similarly, mothers who did work outside the home reflected a sense of self rooted in career identities; for these mothers, however, their struggle was not grounded in the maintenance of these identities, but in how to sustain their work and find balance between work and home in the midst of multiple pressures. These women desired to significantly invest in both their work and their home lives, and they adjusted their schedules as necessary to achieve a life where they could both parent and practice their professions. Thus, these women's struggles primarily involved the practicalities of time management and career development rather than struggles surrounding identity. Their perspectives on public debates surrounding the family reflected an acute awareness of the strains, pressures, and disadvantages in the workplace they faced as women and the kinds of changes, both in social structures and in intimate relationships, that would make the workplace more family friendly.

As we saw in chapter 3, solutions to the problem of work-family balance at Saint Brigitta often involved women's active negotiation with their spouses. Some women's husbands intentionally chose jobs that afforded them a flexible co-parenting schedule; other men had more constrained work schedules that their wives accommodated. Still other women were single parents and managed work-family balance with the help of trusted friends. Regardless of their husbands' schedules or the presence of a partner at home, mothers sought balance between career and work by choosing flexible jobs that accommodated family responsibilities. Some women said that they chose particular career paths based in part on how they saw the capacity of its work practices to accommodate family life. Women's choice of professions among the interview group contains many that have flexible options for working hours, part-time employment, and entrepreneurship or contract work (see table 5.1). Most of the mothers interviewed who worked outside the home either worked for pay part-time or had trajectories where the amount and timing of their paid work varied over time.

Monica Maloney-Jones is a good example of a mother who has a co-parenting arrangement with her husband, John. His job affords him a fair amount of flexibility. Monica presently works part-time for pay as a psychotherapist and also does pro bono work with victims of violence. She negotiates her work-family balance with John through communication and adjustment of their schedules.[33] Monica left the paid labor force temporarily when her sons were babies before crafting her present work-family arrangement, which she believes has much improved the quality of her life. She explained,

> Now that the kids are older, I find myself with more energy. After two kids, I had a hard time staying home, and I remember saying to John, "I hate my life. Not existentially, not fundamentally—I just hate what I do every day. I am bored to tears." When they were younger, I was desperate to get out. I needed to preserve myself.

Monica did not explain why she initially chose to stay at home full-time when her sons were born, but focused instead on how difficult that period of her life was—so difficult that she portrays reentering the labor force as an act of self-preservation. At the same time, from early on she had determined that she did not want a career that left little time for family; Monica had begun college intending to be a medical doctor, but on learning about the demanding characteristics of doctors' schedules, she reconsidered this choice because she believed a career in medicine would leave her too little time for family. She changed her undergraduate major to psychology and decided to pursue a career as a therapist instead, since she perceived the options within that profession to afford her more flexibility and time for family life. Today she balances work and family in a way that integrates rather than separates these life arenas. In speaking about how and why Monica's work—and his own—is structured as it is, John speaks about their desires, practical motivations, and limitations.

I work [outside the home] more than she does....She wants to be around. I don't want to say it's more of a value [for her], but she sees the value in wanting to be around the boys more as their day-to-day things are taking care of. Not that I don't have that, but I don't really have the option of taking this job part-time or sharing or things like that, and this is not the best paying job in the world. She can make more money per hour as a therapist. Not that money is all she wants to have; she does great things with the job and the volunteer work....[Our schedules] constantly have to be attended to. To the degree I do have flexibility, having evening hours free me up in the days sometimes: working in the day, [home] while she's away, and going back at night, and things like that.

At least two aspects of John's statement bear mention. The first is that John and Monica have decided together to center their lives around the twin priorities of family and work, and they do this through frequent communication, which allows each of them to privilege both work and family in their daily routines. In fact, the routines of partnership influence their perspectives on family life generally, as well as their views of public family-related conflicts. Second, John makes clear that when it comes to work, it is the work and its mission that is their highest priority, not its material benefits, even though they cannot completely escape the constraints that are entailed by the necessity of making a living. Despite the fact that Monica's work is part-time, John presents both their jobs as being of equal priority. He explains that his work is full-time and Monica's is part-time partly for practical reasons but primarily because of Monica's desires for involvement with their children's everyday activities and for flexible work that she can easily balance with childrearing.

It is clear from the way Monica has structured her life that parenting intensively is an important priority for her and that she has been intentional about choosing a career path that will allow this while accomplishing meaningful work. However, she did not articulate the place of mothering in her life in vocational terms, even though she was especially articulate about the vocational aspects of her work outside the home. She explained her professional work this way.

I need to be connected to people, need to be swimming in a deeper stream of life than just my little vision of the world. I volunteer, I see some clients for [an organization] that treats victims of violence and political prisoners. I see people from different cultures. I need that, to stay how I want to be in the world.

And I have to have an intense one-on-one. I definitely feel that you can think about doing therapy in terms of structurally changing the world. In terms of a social justice bent. It bores me to run programs after a while. It doesn't reward me enough. I have to be with the person on their path.

Monica chose work that would allow her a flexible work-family balance but chose this particular profession, and her place in it, both for its personal satisfactions and because of her desire to help in the work of healing others—an aspiration that, even in college, was strongly motivated by religious faith. In particular, she is motivated by Catholic teachings on social justice and aims to work for social structural change, believing that it is possible to make such change by healing individuals. She has placed herself in a setting where she encounters people who have been victimized due to their social locations. In helping to heal others, she finds meaning, a sense of competence and contribution, and satisfaction in individual interactions with psychological depth and intimacy.

A second example of mothers' work-family balance at Saint Brigitta is Christine Todd-Aikens's arrangement, which is much more constrained than Monica's because of the inflexibility of her husband's job. Her husband, Brent, is a newspaper reporter, and because of his unpredictable schedule, the entire family is in the position of having to accommodate to its demands. Christine's vocational motivations are in many ways similar to Monica's, as is her professional work; she is a psychological social worker. Her work-family arrangement is likewise similar in her prioritizing both intensive parenting and career. But her children are teens, and she has been negotiating work and family much longer than Monica, so she gives us an example of a trajectory of work-family balance that extends over many years and allows us to see how women at Saint Brigitta negotiate career involvements with parenting over time.

Because of Brent's job, Christine requires job flexibility out of necessity rather than her own preferences. She describes the ways her work and parenting routines have changed over time.

> I worked outside the home when the kids were little. I went part-time for three months after [my son was born]. But I needed to be home with my child, [so] then I stopped. I had one or two clients that came my way; I rented an office and built a private practice. In the next seven or eight years I built up to three days [a week] while raising kids.
>
> When my daughter was small, if I was going to work away from home, I didn't want to be [away] evenings and weekends, but [I was and] it was good for Brent to have responsibility all day on Saturdays. The kids loved it. I felt like they were getting the fun days and I was getting the "sweat it out" days. And I never saw Brent. Sequential parenting is hard on a marriage. We did it while the kids were young and it covered child care, or most of it.

For the last eight years I've done half-time school social work and half-time private practice. Brent's job, his hours and demands, are really primary. Our family has to go on hold when he has to be at work. Mine and the children's lives are kind of interruptible, and that's the way it's always been.

Although Christine describes her position in the family as one that accommodates her husband's career as primary and as shouldering more of the work of the family than he does, they cooperate so significantly in co-parenting that they needed little paid child care for eight years. At the same time, she has been able to build her career entrepreneurially—and like Monica, she has taken the opportunity her flexibility affords to invest significantly as a volunteer in a community-organizing effort. At this point, she works close to full-time hours in two part-time positions, and she said that, now that her children are in their teens, she is ready to take on a full-time position when the right one comes along. Christine's work trajectory shows a style of flexibly managing a career over time that allows intensive mothering and accommodates the demands of her spouse's job.

Finally, some mothers working outside the home are single parents, and although their practical challenges differ since they do not have a partner, they illustrate how mothers at Saint Brigitta generally enlist the help of others in creating work-family balance—sharing or trading child care, depending on the generosity of friends, or employing help. Sandra Turner, who is divorced, illuminates these practices in an exemplary way. Sandra has spent most of her childrearing years as a single parent working full-time. A low-conflict divorce and an ex-husband nearby have allowed her to co-parent with him during the years when they have lived near one another. But at some points, her coworkers have also become surrogate family members. She explains how career success borne of hard work placed demands on her that required her to forge partnerships with caring friends and coworkers.

Every job I have had would start out in one position and then, because I did more than was asked, I'd be [promoted]. [When I was] at the police department [in the city I lived in before moving here], they pulled me out of research, and I became [a public official's] speechwriter and traveled with him.

My daughter was adopted by all the police officers. During this time...when I was [worried about her], they would make sure she was home, especially if she was late getting home, [or] I'd call somebody, because she got home and forgot to call me. So it was really a family. I still consider some of the people there her godfathers. As an adult she still connects with them.

Sandra, like others at Saint Brigitta, spoke of her work as religiously meaning-ful, as involved in the work of social change, and as religiously supported—but practically, as a single parent, she has also needed to work continuously and full-time for income. Thus Sandra has had to find support for the nitty-gritty details of parenting in community settings, which have included both religious settings like Saint Brigitta and work settings that have communal dimensions to them, as did the department in which she worked. For Sandra, childrearing has necessar-ily been a community endeavor, and her efforts to balance work and family have been enacted in the details and relationships of public work, as well as in more private settings. Of course, relationships among parents and others in which par-ents share childrearing tasks with other trusted adults are not unusual, but Saint Brigitta affirms these efforts religiously in its central self-image as a community, encouraging relationships of community intimate enough that they are described as fictive kin. In this way, Sandra's solution to problems of balancing work and family, and those of mothers like her, shares affinities with and at times trans-poses the metaphor of church as community into these solutions.

Therefore, by contrast with women at Assumption, mothers at Saint Brigitta who work in the world not only experience their work vocationally but also often choose career paths that allow them to balance family life with work such that they can invest intensively in both work and home. In some cases, these women's careers were chosen well before marriage—in anticipation, and with the explicit intention, of making a life that allowed them to combine professional work and family. Moreover—and again, by contrast with women at Our Lady of the Assumption—the location of many of these women in the helping professions often rested, at least in part, on their understanding of these professions as a place to work that would also have religious significance in their lives. In many cases, then, they brought this understanding of work with them to Saint Brigitta, finding that the parish's religious understanding of work was a good fit with, and support-ive of, a sensibility that they had learned elsewhere. This way of thinking about the religious meanings of work and women's roles provides an important contrast between Saint Brigitta and the milieu at Assumption, in that these two notions of women's vocations run counter to one another.

As we have seen, how the parish supports mothers working in the world—in its religious understandings of work, in the rituals that highlight women's contributions, and in its programs and everyday practices—tends to emphasize women's use of their gifts in public life. By contrast with Assumption, Saint Brigitta's parishioners do not necessarily directly link its culture of work to hot-button issues; in speaking about work-family balance, they did not mention their religious perspectives on cultural conflicts surrounding the family, but instead focused on broader religious issues of social justice. But in heavily supporting the contributions of women's work in the world, Saint Brigitta emphasizes concerns and values that shape parishioners' perspectives on family-related public conflicts, especially around issues of women's (and others') equality. Combined with ambivalence about or rejection of many of the church's teachings on sexuality, this culture of work supports a plurality of family forms, including same-sex couples. In its support of increasing women's options, it does not reject pro-life stances but has the capacity to support pro-choice positions, particularly because the public silence over abortion at Saint Brigitta leaves both options open.

Women may have few religious resources to apply to their work as mothers, but those who are combining work in the world with childrearing also, along with stay-at-home mothers, exercise leadership within the parish. As they go about the task of finding practical solutions to problems of work-family balance, they are also literally seen in the congregation as contributing to the church's mission— and thereby come to symbolize the efforts of a group that, though perceived structurally as second class, belies their status through their contributions. Despite the lack of a religious language for motherhood, Saint Brigitta appreciates the difficulty with which women balance mothering with other work, whether professional or volunteer, which allows them to symbolically parallel mothers with disadvantaged others who must surmount obstacles, thus giving expression to how groups with less power can overcome invisibility. These women, therefore, come to represent Saint Brigitta's protest against social injustices and structural inequality and its commitment to the dignity and equality of all persons. This symbolism of women's roles represents an alternative and competing vision of women and their contribution to Christian mission to that valued at Assumption, which, as we have seen, facilitates polarization over issues surrounding the family.

Conclusion

This analysis of how religion is implicated in women's efforts to balance work and family at Assumption and Saint Brigitta has shown how their choices and practices not only reflect the intertwining of religion and daily life but also how this intertwining supports and reproduces beliefs and attitudes at two poles of Catholics' engagement in public cultural conflicts over the family. It is in relation to each parish's culture of work that mothers' identities come most sharply into focus, helping us to identify the local cultures and practices that support women's senses of self. Despite the fact that women in each setting often confront similar situations and problems and often have similar desires, these parishes fashion different religious solutions to these problems, which are linked to cultural contests over different public issues.

The local cultures at Assumption and Saint Brigitta practice two different and competing visions of women's roles in family life. The differences in these visions are subtle but ultimately polarizing—an empirical reality that survey research and demographic studies of women and work cannot readily capture. At Assumption, concern with issues related to the decline of the nuclear family is reinforced and implicitly supported in women's efforts at work-family balance, especially in women's assessments of the world of work outside the home—whether those assessments are of this world's hostility to mothers, its inflexibility, or the overall structural and cultural degradation of society. Assumption's response to these assessments includes protest, together with a Catholic identity that defines itself squarely against family decline. By contrast, the concerns and critiques of society related to the efforts of Saint Brigitta's women to balance work and family are largely external to the family as an institution and centered instead in a set of beliefs and practices that seek to increase healing, opportunity, and participation for women and marginalized groups in society generally. As we saw with childrearing, this local culture surrounding women and work tends to focus family-related issues at the opposite pole, though its ethic of inclusivity and relative silence about the church's teachings on sexuality creates room for arguments that can either hold up the congregation's visions of the family, focus on specific social injustices, or attempt to reconcile the two.

Work-related discourses and practices in these different Catholic settings provide these different frames, along with different solutions to problems of work-family balance. As we have seen, the discourse and practice at Saint Brigitta sacralize work in a career as a religious contribution to the larger world, with men's and women's religious identities fundamentally grounded in this world of work, even in the arena of family life. This contrasts with the discourse and practice at Assumption, where, although work is understood to be an important vehicle for the sanctification of the self, identities are much less centered in work than in parental roles.

Why do women at Assumption and Saint Brigitta have such different ways of approaching questions of combining career and motherhood? In conjunction with these different approaches to the sacred in the world of work, women's career trajectories in each congregation are implicated in the choice to practice either liberal or conservative styles of Catholicism. We have seen that, earlier in their lives, women at Assumption tended to prepare for careers, such as law and journalism, that some found difficult to combine with mothering. Mothers at Saint Brigitta instead sought religiously meaningful careers, many in the helping professions, and generally anticipated future challenges of combining work and childrearing in their college years, sometimes switching out of careers like medicine that they perceived would restrict their ability to intensively parent. The sacralization of motherhood and family at Assumption and the sacralization of work, the ecclesial metaphor of community, and the consensus-based egalitarian ethic at Saint Brigitta, therefore, not only provide different religious meanings for work in the world but also constrain the solutions available and support different solutions to women's problematic choices around work and family. And among Assumption's and Saint Brigitta's mothers, we see that, although the religious supports for making sense of their maternal and professional identities differ in the two settings, women in both congregations inevitably find themselves attracted to, and even sometimes feel dogged by, the standards of the secular professional world.

The supports that different religious groups provide for particular styles of family life and work-family balance, together with the accumulation of choices families make, can result over time in a trajectory of lifestyle choices that limit a family's future options. For example, a dual-career marriage often raises a family's disposable income but can make the choice for one spouse to leave the workforce quite difficult, especially if they have come to depend on two incomes. Similarly, the choice to have a large family—especially in cultural contexts like that at Assumption—often limits women's availability to pursue a career. Thus, as families draw on the resources of religion to support and shape a balance between work and family, they often knowingly choose resources that support and clarify the meaning of their choices, but sometimes they face consequences of their beliefs, practices, and choices that are unforeseen.

Conclusion

RELIGION, MORAL POLARIZATION, AND THE
FRAGMENTATION OF TRADITION

MY GOAL IN writing this book has been to better understand how religion is implicated in cultural conflicts about the family among ordinary American Catholics. Given the increasing conflict and incivility in our public politics in the last few decades, understanding the processes involved in sustaining these polarizing tendencies among local groups has seemed to be a particularly urgent task.

Explaining this polarization among Americans is a complicated undertaking, and the analyses of this book are intended to contribute to a portion of an explanation that has been largely neglected in the so-called culture wars debate. We know that elite discourse and social movement activism in the public framings of these conflicts have channeled some of the ways in which Americans, and Catholics in particular, think about issues like abortion and same-sex marriage. And yet, analyses of public framing alone have been insufficient to explain their resonance locally or to explain why and how individuals in congregations come to the convictions they do, since their reasoning about these issues often moves beyond the contours of public discourse. Thus, an important presupposition of this study has been that to understand this resonance, we needed to look deeply at how people respond to the forces of family change by exploring the cares, concerns, and contexts of their everyday lives. I have attended to the effects of larger institutional and societal events and trends as they pertain to these local settings, but my primary focus has been to understand how religiousness in everyday life contributes to moral polarization. To this end, I have pursued a cultural analysis regarding the problems and pressures that people confront as they form families in a societal context of family change, as well as how their religious faith informs their efforts.

In so doing, I intentionally selected churches that would allow me to view ethnographically how the polar positions of these cultural conflicts are socially constructed. In studying the family among local religious groups—an arena where there is evidence of polarization in the American public generally—I have documented and analyzed social processes through which polarizing tendencies among Catholics are constituted and sustained culturally in local churches and seen how these processes impinge on the everyday lives of their members.

I chose these case studies carefully to come as close as possible to pertinent ideal types of Catholic churches, anticipating that they might yield insight into general patterns in the construction of polarization among Catholics and other religious groups.

In concluding this book, then, I discuss what we have learned about the relation of local cultures to polarization in cultural conflicts about the family. In doing this, I first consider the extent and limits of what we have learned by using a case study approach. Then, in the second and final section, I discuss how this study's main findings about religious identity support a more general explanation of moral polarization.

Case Studies as a Vehicle for Conceptualizing Culture and Identifying Social Processes

Although case studies focus on the concrete experiences of particular individuals and the institutional environments in which they are embedded, carefully chosen case studies ideally allow us to discern more general patterns in social life. In considering this analysis of family life at Our Lady of the Assumption and Saint Brigitta parishes, two specific contributions to our knowledge of polarization and the family become evident: that local religious cultures contribute to and support moral polarization and that local processes surrounding the practice of ecclesial metaphors and religious identity are implicated in polarizing tendencies among Catholics. First I consider what we have learned about the importance of local religious cultures through this study; then I consider its implications for understanding the role of ecclesial metaphors.

Conceptualizing Culture in the Study of Moral Polarization and Religion

The case study method utilized in this book shows the strengths of James Davison Hunter's approach to culture in his discussion of culture wars but moves beyond it, thereby enhancing our understanding of how culture, especially local culture, is implicated in moral polarization.[1] This study has afforded a detailed examination of social processes contributing to polarization operative in congregations, demonstrating that as conflicts about the family play out in local cultures, they contribute to polarizing tendencies in ways that reveal polarization to be more than a quantitative distribution of attitudes with two distinct peaks. Moreover, it has shown that polarization is neither based only on religious beliefs or understandings of God, nor determined solely by elite discourse. This study has moved beyond other conceptualizations of cultural conflicts about the family by showing *how* moral polarization is intertwined with *everyday concerns, life experiences,* and the *feelings* evoked by these concerns and experiences.

In theorizing cultural conflicts among Americans, Hunter described polarizing impulses toward orthodoxy and progressivism as culturally grounded in beliefs that lead to competing moral visions. According to Hunter, the orthodox vision is grounded in a transcendent God that evokes an unchanging authority, whereas the progressive vision is anchored in an immanent God accompanied by an authority grounded in personal experience and rationality in dialogue with religious traditions. However, I have shown that at local levels, these categories are empirically mixed, with personal experience playing a role in authority relations in both settings. Life experience is intertwined with autonomous authority at Saint Brigitta in ways similar to Hunter's progressive vision, but it also plays a role in the retraditionalized authority relations at Our Lady of the Assumption in confirming the truth of Catholic teachings for parishioners, especially those regarding human sexuality. And although competing orthodox and progressive visions are involved in polarizing tendencies in these local settings, additional aspects of belief and practice are also important in the construction of moral polarization, including patterns of social relations, religious conceptions of human nature, and beliefs about the church's mission. Particularly important to understanding polarizing tendencies among Catholics is the finding that the logics of church social relations can be transposed to and played out in family life, since in these affinities the actual routines and practices of families are related to particular moral stances on the family.

In addition, Hunter makes a strong distinction between private and public culture, arguing that culture wars are fought in the arena of public discourse because of the high payoffs involved in cultural dominance there. Although this may be true, Hunter's claim is too strong and his distinction between public and private too sharp. In focusing primarily on the public sphere, he neglects the importance of local cultures in how people construct and understand moral choices. As we have seen, elite public discourse is not wholly determinative of local cultures, polarization itself is not only an elite phenomenon, and empirically, private and public boundaries are often blurred or categories elided locally. As these case studies of Saint Brigitta and Assumption demonstrate, polarizing impulses reside in institutions not only at the macro level but also among smaller groups and at intermediate levels of analysis. These contexts are ones where individuals directly encounter mediating institutions such as parishes, and social processes that create and sustain polarization locally.

Finally, these local cultures have allowed us to see how emotions and patterns of sociation figure in polarization, shedding light on the sources of energy for polarizing conflicts. As we have seen, the cultural milieus represented at Assumption and Saint Brigitta not only define themselves in part in *disagreement* with one another but also feel *antagonism* toward some of the other's beliefs and outlooks. This antagonism, grounded in different understandings of their Catholic belonging, is a conflict between intimates—in Georg Simmel's phrase, those who share "common kinship"—and this intimate pattern of sociation tends to focus on small disagreements, with the intimacy of belonging to the same Catholic Church responsible for their intensity. Simmel's theory of conflict thus has drawn attention to and helped to explain how cultural conflict in religious settings derives its emotional energy.

The Utility and Limits of Case Studies in Understanding Social Processes: Ecclesial Metaphors

In addition to these findings about how local congregational cultures figure in moral polarization, the case study approach has also yielded specific findings about the social processes that foster it. In particular, this study has revealed how the practice of particular ecclesial metaphors can foster polarizing tendencies in congregations, especially through their practice in worship, which essentially summarizes these metaphors in practice.

We have seen that parishes express a central self-image in worship and that these images and the social relations of intimacy and authority that come along with them have affinities with, and can be applied to, other arenas of daily life. Moreover, when people worship, they enact dispositions expressing moral goods that figure concretely in the concerns of daily living. In these ways, parish worship provides support for the social forms and ongoing formation of family life. We saw this especially in how the relations and logics of worship at Assumption and Saint Brigitta are electively affined with those by which women and men structure their marriages, share parenting duties, and create work-family balance. These affinities suggest different ways of perceiving specific life problems and, often, alternative ways of solving them. They provide evidence that religious practices enact worldviews that make particular patterns of social relations and understandings of family life in each congregation not just plausible, but normative.[2]

The practices surrounding the expression of ecclesial metaphors therefore contribute to polarization locally because different metaphors tend to support different patterns of social relations and particular perceptions of family problems and goals. Expressed in worship, these metaphors thus support particular, practical family choices and routines. But they are also linked to symbolic struggles through the concerns from which they emerge, the emotions they generate, and the social relations they practice—as well as through the beliefs about the human person, work, vocation, and mission that underlie different understandings of the family. Because of this, polarizing tendencies often manifest themselves symbolically in cultural conflicts surrounding the family in ways that are linked to private life. For example, egalitarian negotiations as a practice of marital intimacy at Saint Brigitta, supported in the metaphor of the church as community, are logically and experientially linked to issues like homosexual sex through a moral outlook founded on values of individual dignity, equality, and autonomous authority. Similarly, at Assumption, women's practice of motherhood and its affirmation of marital and parenting roles in the nuclear family, supported in the metaphor of the church as family, undergird the logic and intensity of its pro-life stance on abortion.

To what extent can these case study findings from Assumption and Saint Brigitta inform our understanding of other local settings? Are similar affinities between worship and family life likely to be found in other Catholic parishes, other institutional and movement settings, and perhaps in congregations of other religious denominations? Even though many Catholic parishes exhibit more internal religious diversity than do Assumption and Saint Brigitta, extant studies suggest that similar patterns may be found in other Catholic contexts. Some of the fundamental characteristics and practices observed at Assumption and Saint Brigitta, such as their worship styles and their religious orientations, are readily recognizable in other Catholic parishes, as are their correlates in other religious congregations.[3]

Moreover, these affinities between church and family practices have been especially evident in Catholic movement organizations such as the Christian Family Movement and Women for Faith and Family. In addition, the relationship demonstrated here between ecclesial metaphors and congregational behavior is similar to those found in other studies, suggesting that they may support particular forms and styles of family life more generally.[4] It is also probable that similar patterns can occur with different ecclesial metaphors. Scholars have observed models of churches beyond the two models documented here, including, for example, metaphors of church as herald, as disciple, as house of worship, and as institution. Some of these models, in combination with other particular religious beliefs and practices, might similarly support perceptions and practices of family life close to the poles of current cultural contests, although others may not. These possibilities should be addressed through further comparative study.

At the same time, other congregations may well practice church metaphors that resist polarizing tendencies, perhaps especially among old ethnic churches, where ascription and belonging are still more salient than choice, or among Catholic churches in the Hispanic and African American communities, where public issues such as immigration and race relations are viewed as more important than, and at times inclusive of, those related to the family. Thus while it is likely that patterns similar to those found here also exist in other churches and that the relation between a congregation's central ecclesial metaphor and its dominant family practices constitutes a pattern that appears beyond these two cases, the logics involved in the relation of worship and family in other settings are probably more varied than the two models examined here.

The identification of affinities between logics of worship and family life may also help explain how churches support particular family styles for churchgoing congregants generally. We might expect that parish life would support and shape the outlooks of those with higher involvement more significantly than those who are less involved in their parishes. But even among the most committed families in these parishes, Sunday worship was most often the central setting where they encountered Catholicism and interacted with other Catholics, suggesting that worship is an important vehicle for family support across a wide spectrum of religious commitment. Precisely because local expressions of worship summarize and enact beliefs and social relations that are transposable to family life, worship has the capacity to support routines of marriage, childrearing, and work-family balance in ways similar to those we have encountered in this study, even for those whose involvement in parish life might be less intense or even minimal.

At the same time, the central congregational images and dominant discourses surrounding religion and family discussed in these chapters are just that: they are the dominant cultural materials available to people in these settings. We have seen that these resources vary in their actual utility for and influence on parishioners, depending on the fit between their life circumstances, the problems they perceive, and those framed and addressed by their local congregational culture. Parishioners use these resources in varied ways, but they can and do also draw on resources from Catholicism's tradition that may not be practiced in their local settings; examples include those at Saint Brigitta who practice traditional devotions and those at Assumption who study contemporary Catholic literary works (as did the women's book group described in chapter 5).

Moreover, people in both settings also sometimes drew on secular resources when these dominant images of church and family did not fit their life experience. Sometimes a poor fit between available resources and life experience resulted in individuals changing their style of Catholic practice, as we saw in some accounts of neotraditional reversion at Assumption. In other cases—such as a perceived need for religious meaning in the work of motherhood at Saint Brigitta or in the absence of a vocational language for combining a career with mothering at Assumption—people either remade the meaning of their circumstances according to available religious meanings or searched for other sources of meaning. In such instances, religious meaning sometimes receded from that sphere of living. In still other cases, such as in parishioners' accounts of past periods of disaffection from Catholicism, the gap between experience and religion may at times become so large that Catholicism recedes from most of life. This may well be the case, in fact, among a large portion of nonpracticing Catholics. This study thus contributes to a tradition of scholarship that demonstrates how religion's reach in contemporary societies, if not wholly an instrumental good, depends at least in part on the fit between people's life problems and experiences and the structures of meaning communicated in churches.

How Catholics' Identities, Choice, and Tradition Play Roles in Moral Polarization

We have seen that religious identity construction, the second of the processes discussed in this book, not only shapes local religious cultures and supports conceptions of the family but also is related to polarization in cultural conflicts about the family directly. Most people come to Assumption and Saint Brigitta with religious identities, but once they are part of parish life, they participate in the ongoing construction of Catholic identities in these settings. As we have seen, for some, membership at Assumption or Saint Brigitta causes change or development in the way they understand their Catholicism, and for others, it allows continuity. Regardless, these religious identities, continually constructed in parish interactions, support these Catholics' everyday lives and family practices. Especially in the tasks of creating bonds and boundaries, social groups define themselves against others and, in so doing, establish an opposition between groups that is a necessary condition for polarization.

The creation of identity boundaries between groups generally need not result in moral polarization; for instance, American Catholics have historically created boundaries with each other based primarily on ethnic heritage, which have at times produced conflicts between them but not necessarily ones that are polarizing around moral issues. But as others have chronicled, over the last half century a confluence of social changes, including the post–World War II restructuring of American religion, the social forces driving family change, and for Catholics, Vatican II, created a context in which salient religious boundaries have shifted from denominational ones to those of liberal-conservative opposition, in a time of dissensus over what constitutes the good citizen and the good society.

The multiple boundaries drawn against others over religious practice and family life—especially other Catholics—reflect these boundary shifts. As we have seen, parishioners at Assumption and Saint Brigitta draw boundaries over worship practices, experiences of religious socialization in the post–Vatican II church, their underlying ecclesiologies, the content of the church's mission to the world, assumptions about human nature, and the qualities of effective social relations. In so doing, they create a multiplicity of more or less binary oppositions that constitute a condition for polarization.

Why have these identity boundaries come to be constituted as they have, as binary oppositions that are evident in local settings? This study has shown that two larger trends, manifested locally, are implicated in religious identity construction and contribute to polarization in Catholic cultures: the prevalence of a broader culture of religious choice and the fragmentation of tradition in late modernity. In fact, we can now conclude from this study *how* both choice and tradition matter to the development of polarizing processes among Catholics.

Characteristics and Effects of Religious Choice

At both Assumption and Saint Brigitta, discourses of Catholic identity are infused with the notion of choice—and not just among those who are converts to Catholicism. I have shown that even those with ascribed religious identities practice achieved, or actively chosen, religious identities. In practice, cradle Catholics integrated their sense of identity as belonging with their achieved religious identities in one of a few ways: through return, through reversion, or through the assumption of an adult commitment to a particular religious ethic and the establishment of patterns of life conduct on the basis of that commitment. And although parishioners in this study exhibited patterns of choice that are in some respects specific to Catholicism, the prevalence of a discourse of choice in parishioners' narratives of belonging and discussions of family life reflects the predominance of a culture of choice on the American religious landscape generally.

Scholars have explained this culture of choice, and the individualism with which it is closely associated, as a growing trend since the Reformation that has its origins in Protestantism. For example, in Talcott Parsons's view, such trends are the result of the progression of the "Protestant principle," where increasing autonomous authority, along with the assumption of Christian values in the social fabric of Western societies and the privatization of religion, is a product of the historically progressive societal differentiation of religion.[5] Thus for Parsons and others, Protestantism has been highly influential in American society, effectively Christianizing its values.[6] We know, for example, that Protestantism has not only shaped the ways in which Western scholars think about religion but also helped to shape religion itself in the American context in the structural forms of denomination and congregation.

Some scholars have explained changes in American Catholicism over the last few decades, changes reflecting a culture of choice, as related to this Protestant principle, arguing that such changes are effectively a "protestantization" of Catholicism. For example, historian Michael Carroll explains that Catholic commentators have observed, "Since Vatican II, many American Catholic leaders and thinkers have increasingly embraced precisely that emphasis on religious individualism that used to be more uniquely associated with the Protestant tradition,"[7] and Jay Demerath and Rhys Williams show ethnographic evidence of protestantization of Catholicism at the parish level.[8] Such observations are not limited to scholars, nor are they necessarily confined to American religion. For example, some conservative Catholics decry the changes of Vatican II, saying they have led to a protestantization of Catholicism more broadly.[9]

But not everyone finds protestantization worrisome. For example, Michele Dillon argues that cafeteria Catholicism, which she understands as equated with its protestantization, is not diluting Catholicism, but rather shows Catholics as engaged with their tradition.[10]

If indeed, as I have argued, Catholics participate in a culture of choice that has consequences for religious practice, then through the construction of achieved identities created in and fostered by a culture of choice, polarizing tendencies have come to mirror those of Protestantism, at least in part because of Protestantism's emphasis on choice, an emphasis that has had effects on American culture generally. Moreover, the evidence of this study suggests that the Protestant influences shaping American religious and secular cultures may have been influential both indirectly and directly upon the polarizing processes documented in this study. If the emergence of a culture of choice in American culture has shaped Catholic identities such that polarizing outcomes are more likely in the establishment of religious boundaries with others, and the culture of choice is Protestantizing, then we can conclude that polarization among Catholics is also a continuing legacy of Protestantism. But at the same time, we have also seen specifically Catholic dimensions of the culture of choice at Assumption and Saint Brigitta. Let us consider three findings of this study that provide evidence that a religious culture of choice has had an effect on polarizing outcomes among Catholics locally, and consider to what extent they may arise from Protestant influence and/or contain elements that are distinctly Catholic.

First, despite the worries of scholars who have written about the culture of choice in American religion as secularizing, the religious identity narratives documented in this book show that choice is implicated in *religious reenchantment*. An argument can be made, correctly in my view, that a culture of religious choice is potentially both secularizing and reenchanting. But in this study, we have seen how and why choice in the American setting makes religious identities stronger, not weaker.[11] The very strength of these identities is found in the process of choice that legitimates them, which entails that religious identities are highly personal and individually meaningful. Such choices, and the personal commitment they necessitate, make it more likely that those espousing them will hold strong views and thereby create robust identity boundaries with others. In other words, people who choose religious practice as a validation of identity are likely to invest deeply in religious belief and practice and its moral outcomes, since commitment and the presentation of personal authenticity are interwoven. And in drawing moral boundaries against others that are undergirded by theological views—such as Christian anthropologies and understandings of vocation—both religious principles and personal identities are subsumed into morality, making the morality of family life something that people will contest in part by what, and whom, they define themselves against.

Second, at Assumption and Saint Brigitta, religion is a primary resource with which involved parishioners create *coherence of the self*, through which they make—and make sense of—serious life choices. None of my interlocutors in this study compartmentalized their religious identities but instead sought to extend them into various arenas of life as a way of making coherence of their personal identities overall. This impulse toward identity coherence through religion has the capacity to contribute to polarizing tendencies among Catholics because it entails nontrivial choices that can have serious consequences for families' life trajectories and because practicing self-coherence across different life arenas can dissolve or blur public-private boundaries.[12]

In fact, some of the ways in which individuals in this study negotiated marriage, parenting, and work-family balance were not confined to the private sphere, but reflected fluid boundaries between public and private life. We saw this, for example, at Assumption, where the reach of a dedifferentiated religious practice extended into public life in parents' schooling choices, in individuals' informal lobbying about abortion in professional contexts, and in their practice of prayer and devotion in the workplace; and at Saint Brigitta, in the public practice of religion in corporal works of mercy practiced in and beyond their neighborhoods and in religious social activism.

Perhaps more important, the commitment involved in parishioners' practice of identity coherence had serious consequences for people's lives. In these cases, their religious choices were neither inconsequential nor trivial: they significantly informed their patterns of life conduct in the formation and routines of their families and in other arenas that impinged on family life. At Assumption, we saw this, for example, in the choice to have large families out of religious convictions—and most vividly in couples' adherence to the church prohibition on artificial contraception, by which they effectively relinquished control over the size of their families, a control that the majority of Americans, and American Catholics, take for granted. Similarly, at Saint Brigitta, religion provides more than a sense-making rationale for the vocational choices and marital negotiations made by women and men there; it can also shape them through the adoption of a religious worldview with imperatives for action. The chapters of this book thus suggest a reconsideration of how we conceptualize the culture of choice in American religion today, in that they provide ample evidence that religious choices are not at all less significant merely because they are chosen; rather, these are quite serious choices. In fact, the seriousness of such religious choices heightens the stakes for those who make them, and thereby contributes to the strength of polarizing tendencies surrounding the family.

Third, the *configurations of choice* that we have observed at Assumption and Saint Brigitta also play a significant role in polarizing tendencies among Catholics— and in this sense, the characteristics of choice are not only protestantized but also follow patterns that are distinctively Catholic. We have seen that achieved identities, while diversified and highly personal, are not infinitely variable; rather, they occur in more or less predictable combinations. Moreover, although each of the churches studied contains internal variation in parishioners' moral beliefs and religious practices, each group also espouses a set of more or less internally shared *consistent* beliefs and practices. This suggests that, despite the ubiquity of the phrase 'cafeteria Catholics'—used to describe those who purportedly pick and choose among Catholicism's beliefs and practices, adhering to ones they like and rejecting those they don't—this appellation is largely a misnomer. At Assumption and Saint Brigitta, religious choice does not occur as in a cafeteria. Neither group just picks and chooses from Catholicism's beliefs and practices. Instead, those they emphasize and those they avoid or reject emerge from particular sets of *interwoven* beliefs and practices that have their own internal consistency. We see this in the patterned sets of opposed choices observed in these parishes, which are revealed in their responses to cultural conflicts about the family.

Moral Polarization and the Fragmentation of Tradition

We have seen that at Assumption and Saint Brigitta, the consequences of religious choice include the formation of more or less opposed Catholic milieus that not only choose to practice family life differently but also emphasize different religious beliefs and practices while each anchoring themselves in Catholicism's tradition. Both groups appeal to the Catholic tradition for the legitimacy of their beliefs and practices. Each group defines itself in terms of the elements of tradition that it emphasizes and against others who emphasize alternative parts of that tradition.

In fact, this study has demonstrated that polarizing tendencies among these Catholics, and those who are members of similar milieus, are largely constituted in the different appropriations of tradition that we find in parishes like Assumption and Saint Brigitta. But if this is indeed the case, how are we to best understand the role tradition plays in polarization? What ideas, descriptions, or definitions of tradition might help us to best explain how those at Assumption and Saint Brigitta (and Catholics more generally) differentially appropriate and define themselves and others vis-à-vis Catholic tradition? Because the evidence of this study has demonstrated the importance of religious tradition for explaining moral polarization surrounding the family, I conclude by discussing what we have learned about how both the content and our concept of Catholic tradition matter to understanding the moral polarization documented in the chapters of this book.

One approach to tradition that might help us understand its relation to the contemporary climate of moral polarization surrounding the family is found in philosopher Alisdair MacIntyre's discussion of tradition in *After Virtue*.[13] In explaining his view of tradition in modernity, MacIntyre notes that some have drawn a contrast between tradition and reason; we see this, for example, in Max Weber's ideal types of authority. But MacIntyre argues that this contrast, and the associated contrast between stability (tradition) and conflict (reason), is flawed because "all reasoning takes place within the context of some traditional mode of thought, transcending through criticism and invention the limitations of what had hitherto been reasoned in that tradition."[14] In other words, all cultures have historical content and therefore always involve dialogue with, and within, a tradition.[15] MacIntyre goes on to observe that it is characteristic of vital social traditions that those who espouse them are often involved in an argument about their purpose. He says, "Traditions, when vital, embody continuities of conflict."[16] Thus, according to MacIntyre, living traditions not only endure but endure through conflict—suggesting that conflict is a source of growth and change.

In some respects, this definition of tradition fits what we have observed in Catholics' cultural conflicts about the family. In fact, an argument could be made that this view of tradition underlies much contemporary public polarized discourse among Catholics, especially regarding what some have described as "neuralgic issues" among Catholics, such as issues of authority and church discipline. This is plausible because MacIntyre's way of conceptualizing tradition directs our attention to how conflicts over the family constitute a conflict over the goods of Catholicism—and not only in family-related issues but also as conflicts over ecclesiology, Christian anthropology, and theologies of work and mission. These are some of the very things we have observed to be important in the polarizing tendencies in the local cultures at Assumption and Saint Brigitta.

And if MacIntyre is correct, then we would expect that the identity-defining, polarizing conflicts represented in the contrasts between Assumption and Saint Brigitta to reflect the contemporary vitality of the Catholic tradition. But is this the case? Does the current environment of conflict, which includes not only antagonism but also incivility, disengagement, incomplete and sometimes politicized knowledge of tradition, and perhaps even stalemate, really reflect institutional vitality? In fact, are *all* conflicts over tradition ones that reflect vitality? Are all such conflicts institutionally productive? Such conflicts may promote change, but do they always produce growth?

There is reason for skepticism here. As Simmel observes, while the antagonism involved in conflict can be an integrative force to the extent to which it brings people into interaction with one another—that is, it can be a positive form of *sociation*—conflict that produces *indifference* or *disengagement* is negative because it produces *dissociation* between people.[17] Organizational studies that investigate environments with some of the characteristics we have witnessed at Assumption and Saint Brigitta, including indifference to other Catholics or disengagement from the church as a whole, suggest that such conflicts do not always result in institutional success or endurance.[18] Thus, to the extent that groups become disengaged from one another in conflicts over tradition, conflict has the potential to become enervating rather than vivifying.

This is where MacIntyre's view of tradition becomes less helpful: he does not explicitly address how the *characteristics* of conflict affect the vitality of a tradition, and for the most part, he does not consider how or to what extent the *processes* involved in conflict matter in a tradition's endurance, growth, and change. However, he does observe that traditions are strengthened by the exercise of virtue in choosing between the goods of a tradition. According to MacIntyre, the act of choosing can be better or worse. This moral view implies, in fact, that the conduct and process of conflict can and *does* matter to a tradition's strength—perhaps suggesting that we should indeed consider the conduct of conflicts in assessing their contribution to a tradition's vitality. But MacIntyre's definition of tradition is otherwise underdeveloped regarding the conditions under which conflict over a tradition reflects its vitality. Therefore, the question remains: Can this view of tradition correctly capture the relationship we have seen between tradition and polarizing tendencies among Catholics, or is there another concept of tradition that might allow us to better understand the origins and outcomes of the polarizing tendencies that we have observed in this study?

In answering this question, let us consider a second perspective on tradition by returning to Danièle Hervieu-Léger's work, which was introduced in the exploration of religious identity construction in part I of this book.[19] By contrast with MacIntyre, Hervieu-Léger believes that tradition is constituted differently in the modern world than in premodern societies. She argues that the pressures of modernity have effects on tradition, even when a tradition is supported by social structures and authority relations that support its worldview; in modernity, she observes, traditions are fragmented. And this fragmentation of tradition generally shapes the contemporary practice of religion.

Hervieu-Léger argues as follows. Religion has been displaced in modernity; people have become separated from the continuity of religious traditions through globalization, information, and science. The need for meaning, which religion provides, still exists, but believers also have a new need: a need to legitimate religious belief. In a world where tradition has not been displaced, this is not necessary, since the meaning that a tradition confers on life does not need confirmation. But its displacement prompts a need for the authority of religion *and* its legitimation.

At the same time, because traditional social institutions have largely collapsed in modernity, people's access to religion is primarily through fragmented traditions. According to Hervieu-Léger, traditions in modernity are no longer as strong as they once were because in the modern world, traditions are sustained primarily in voluntaristic affinity groups rather than by institutional belonging, and in the long run, the collective memory sustained in these voluntary groups—which are often pitted against one another[20]—becomes fragmentary with time.

Hervieu-Léger's observations about tradition in modernity have the capacity to illuminate how the local cultures at Assumption and Saint Brigitta stand in relation to the Catholic tradition and the larger Catholic Church. As we have seen, these two local cultures emphasize different aspects of the Catholic tradition, rather than both expressing a unified or comprehensive practice of Catholicism. We have seen this in the particular church doctrines each church emphasizes, in the styles of authority relations each practices, and in the dominant Catholic identities practiced in each setting. The different emphases practiced at each church tend to present only a partial view of Catholicism's tradition, even though the intent of the leadership in each church is not necessarily to ignore aspects of Catholicism that receive little attention.

Nevertheless, the pastors at each church captured this reality colloquially during interviews, when each independently volunteered that their church "was not everyone's cup of tea." Using the same phrase, each acknowledged their parishes as sites of local cultures with distinctive styles that are not universally appealing but are most attractive to particular kinds of Catholic identities. One might be tempted to think that this description supports a view of religion as mere lifestyle enclaves, but as we have seen, the distinctions in identity and practice to which each pastor referred in this comment are not trivial. Nor are they dependent on religious fusion with other social identities, such as ethnicity. Instead, the differences we have observed between Assumption and Saint Brigitta at times reach into the heart of Catholic belief and practice.

There is another side to this sort of local fragmentation: it sometimes also contains within it memories or aspects of the tradition not emphasized, but rather, remembered because they are rejected. We saw this in both cases: at Assumption, for example, in a retraditionalized approach to worship that integrates some of the aesthetic and ritual changes that have become common in the Vatican II church but eschews others, and at Saint Brigitta, in public silence about and parishioners' private rejection of church teachings on contraception.

Religious professionals, parish leaders, and committed and educated parishioners among each church's membership do often operate in the context of a larger view of Catholicism's tradition and participate in an argument about its contents, as MacIntyre suggests. However, we have seen that the actual discourses and practical conduct of parish life on a daily basis—and therefore, the primary resources available to parishioners in each setting—represent the tradition writ large, and a larger conversation over the Catholic tradition, only partially. In other words, even when pastors and leaders intend otherwise, the discourses and concrete activities of parish life institutionalize fragmentary Catholic traditions. The elements of tradition buttressing one side of contested issues are presented in these local cultures in a developed way, whereas the others are more often caricatured, rejected, cast as not authentically Catholic, or seen as not Catholic enough. Thus, these cultures could be thought of, not as *contained* in a traditional mode of thought, as MacIntyre might conceptualize them, but as *modes of thought in themselves.*

In fact, we observed different modes of thought at Assumption and Saint Brigitta in the ways in which identity boundaries were drawn in cultural conflicts surrounding the family. This was evident, for example, in these congregations' differing approaches to human nature, work, and mission, which underlie the family patterns in which they engage. Each congregation's local culture tended to emphasize either sin or grace, either work in the world or work in the home, and either internal or external ecclesial mission—and did so, at times, in ways that de-emphasized the other half of the pairing. But within Catholicism historically, these binary pairs, and others, have generally existed in a relationship with one another. Although one side of such pairs might be emphasized at particular historical times and in particular places—for example, in the importance of practices and beliefs about sin in Western churches prior to Vatican II—Catholic practice has emphasized a dialogic relationship between them, often in ways similar to MacIntyre's image of a vital tradition. But as we have seen, the repeated and patterned emphases on one side of binary pairs of Catholic beliefs, intertwined with the logics of family life, in large part comprise the architecture of contemporary moral polarization.[21]

We see a similar pattern in each parish's practice of central ecclesial metaphors. In each parish, one metaphor was dominant in such a way as to more or less preclude others. And yet, as Dulles documents, multiple models define Catholicism as it is represented in the documents of Vatican II: the church is imagined as institution, as mystical communion, as sacrament, as herald, as servant, and as disciple.[22] In contesting these ecclesial metaphors, groups are involved in integrative conflict. But in adopting one and refusing to engage others—and others who define themselves in terms of other models—conflict becomes dissociating, and the tradition less vital.

Both Assumption and Saint Brigitta earnestly seek to express an authentic Catholicism, but the unintended result of the processes we have observed in this study is the institutional fragmentation of tradition, passed on in parish settings that approximate the characteristics of the affinity groups Hervieu-Léger observes. This fragmentation, together with its oppositional character seen especially in public politics, supports polarization since the traditions on each side—and to which the appeal for confirmation is made—are incomplete because some aspects of the tradition have been delegitimized in these local cultures, are not practiced, or not known. This fragmentation, moreover, has been accentuated by the visceral nature of our public politics.

Note that these parishes were chosen for study not because they are typical, but because they are closer to ideal-typical examples—that is, local cultures that were purer in their religious orientations and therefore cultures in which we could more easily observe the processes involved in polarizing tendencies among Catholics. The results of this study suggest that we might expect similar divisions and a fragmentation of tradition in cases where the social processes documented in this book follow similar lines, even if their local cultures are more mixed. This is an empirical question that should be investigated in other studies.

Finally, the fragmentation of Catholic tradition we see occurring in settings like Assumption and Saint Brigitta suggests a rethinking of how we conceptualize and study moral polarization, especially as it concerns religion's contribution to polarizing impulses in American life. This study has demonstrated that polarizing tendencies in Catholic churches are not only about public political conflicts about the family, nor are they undergirded merely by local cultures' religious beliefs and worldviews. Rather, polarizing tendencies in Catholicism move *beyond* our public politics. They are constituted in the routines of everyday life, as well as by church practice, ecclesiology, social relations of authority, and Catholic tradition. Moreover, Catholicism has been not only restructured in the last several decades, in the sense of its internal religious worldviews and public politics aligning; instead, American Catholicism itself has become polarized *in its life as a church*. This empirical reality, therefore, has implications not only for the public politics of the family in American society but also for the Catholic Church itself.

These observations have both methodological and practical implications. Methodologically, they suggest that researchers study how religion is implicated in moral polarization in American society in ways that begin with—or, at least, take into account—the study of local religious cultures, rather than concentrating only on elites, large-scale institutions, or individual attitudes. And practically, it is clear that understanding the causes and processes of moral polarization is only a first step toward insight into its amelioration. Having identified some of the sources and carriers of polarizing tendencies, we can hypothesize how people might begin to engage and work together despite them, or recover a less fragmented Catholicism: one, perhaps, where local groups might more actively work to incorporate multiple ecclesial metaphors into their self-image and practice, or resist or expand affinity groups in parishes—something that Catholic parishes have done well historically. Future research should be directed to study parishes that resist polarization around family-related issues and/or creatively combine or tolerate polar views. In these ways, further studies of Catholicism can contribute not only to practical issues of pastoral practice but also to a better understanding of how religion is implicated in moral polarization generally.

Notes

INTRODUCTION

1 Quoted in Shear (2009). Full text of the commencement address is available in many locations, including www.nytimes.com/2009/05/17/us/politics/17text-obama.html?pagewanted=all.

2 Gilford (2009).

3 Gilford (2009). A Rasmussen poll conducted in the following week asked a related question. When asked about whether Notre Dame should obey guidelines issued by the U.S. bishops and refrain from awarding President Obama an honorary degree, 60 percent of U.S. Catholics responded affirmatively, while 25 percent said no (CNS Web 2009).

4 Reilly (2009). The petition was started online by the Cardinal Newman Society, which "promotes traditional Catholic teachings."

5 Clemmer (2009). Of this number, 258 were active bishops in May 2009, and 171 were retired bishops.

6 Gilbert (2009). The pronouncement, *Forming Consciences for Faithful Citizenship: A Call to Political Responsibility from the Catholic Bishops of the United States*, was approved by the USCCB in 2007. The document is available at http://usccb.org/issues-and-action/faithful-citizenship/upload/forming-consciences-for-faithful-citizenship.pdf.

7 Glendon (2009).

8 Staff Editorial (2009).

9 Shear (2009).

10 Regarding the deprivatization of religion in the West in the last three decades and the U.S. Catholic Bishops' public pronouncements as an instance of deprivatized religion, see Casanova (1994).

11 On changes in the constitution of the U.S. Catholic bishops during the papacy of John Paul II and changes in the priorities of the U.S. Conference of Catholic

Bishops, see, for instance, Curran (2008); McBrien (2004); Reese (1990, 1992, 1996).

12 Hunter (1991).

13 Hunter includes secular Americans in the progressive cultural group.

14 Wolfe (1999); DiMaggio et al. (1996); Campbell (2006).

15 Putnam and Campbell (2010); see also Galston (2012) and Abramowitz (2010).

16 Putnam and Campbell (2010).

17 Hunter (2006).

18 Campbell (2006); DiMaggio et al. (1996); Wolfe (2006:47).

19 Shields (2012).

20 Simmel (1971a:90).

21 Davidman (1991); Gallagher (2003); Wilcox (2004, 2009). Also, scholars of social movements have investigated some of the organizations and activists that provide public voices in debates about family-related issues, e.g., Katzenstein (1999), Munson (2008).

22 Luker (1985) and Manning (1999) are exceptions to this, as they do relate public conflict to everyday life. But other types of work focus, for example, on plausible frames rather than the conditions under which they are received favorably (cf. Benford and Snow 2000).

23 Chaves et al. (1999).

24 Wuthnow (1988).

25 See Alberigo (2006) and O'Malley (2008) for accounts of the history of Vatican II, Wilde (2007) for a sociological analysis of the council as an instance of religious change, and Abbott and Gallagher (1966) for compilations of the documents.

26 Cummings (2009); Dolan (1987/1992); Orsi (1985, 2005); Taves (1986).

27 Recent examples include D'Antonio et al. (2007); D'Antonio et al. (2001).

28 In so doing, I use the design and logic of the extended case method. See Burawoy (1991; 1998).

29 Hunter uses the terms *orthodox* and *progressive*, but because the term *orthodox* is quite contested among Catholics, I use the term *conservative* instead.

30 See, e.g., Warner (1993).

31 Cadge and Davidman (2006); Smith (1998); Starks (2009).

32 See Riesebrodt (1995/2000). See also Cadge and Davidman (2006).

33 These processes are empirically intertwined, but their analytic separation is useful in that it allows us to observe more clearly the ways in which each one helps to form groups relatively unified around family-related issues despite in-group variation.

34 Simmel (1971a:90).

35 Chaves et al. (1999).

36 Of course, there is a large literature on ethnicity and religion generally, including recently Chen (2008); Chong (1998); Kniss and Numrich (2007); and Nabhan-Warren (2005). Many (e.g., Wood 2002) include Catholic congregations, though

fewer sociological studies focus primarily on Catholics; in contrast, ethnicity among U.S. Catholics is well documented in historically oriented studies (e.g., Dolan 1987, chaps. 5, 11, and 13; Fichter 1954; Gleason 1964, 1970; Zahn 1962).

37 *Merriam Webster Online Dictionary* (2012). The changes of the council were many. They included liturgical reforms, such as changing the ritual of the mass and the language of the mass from Latin to the vernacular. But as Wilde (2007:1) notes, more important, "Vatican II changed the way the Church understood itself, as its identity went from being a hierarchical authority to a church conceived of as the people of God". See fn. 10 for citations of important scholarship on Vatican II and the documents promulgated by the Council.

38 The Magisterium is "the teaching authority of the Catholic Church. It resides in the Roman pontiff and the college of bishops as legitimate successors to St. Peter and the apostles of Jesus (*Lumen Gentium*, 18–25)." *New Catholic Encyclopedia* (2003:567).

39 For a history and characteristics of the post–Vatican II U.S. Catholic mainstream, see, e.g., Seidler and Meyer (1989) and Dillon (1999); for a discussion of Catholic liberal groups, see Weaver (1999). Regarding Catholic conservative movements, see Weaver and Appleby (1995); see Cuneo (1997) for a discussion of Catholic conservative dissent.

40 Founded in 1928 in Spain by Josemaria Escriva de Balaguer, Opus Dei is a world-wide organization of laity whose goal is to sanctify themselves and the secular world. Opus Dei includes celibate members or numeraries; married members or supernumeraries; cooperators, who participate in its programs and support its work; and priest chaplains. Members follow a rigorous daily program of prayer and self-discipline. Opus Dei has been criticized by liberal U.S. Catholics who object to its institutional politics, perceived secrecy, and religious practices. For a hagiography of its founder's life and work, see Berglar (1993); for a critical perspective of a former member, see del Tapia (1997).

41 See, e.g., Cuneo (1997).

42 For a discussion of liturgical and devotional practices among conservative Catholics, see Cuneo (1997).

43 See, for example, Cuneo (1997); Weaver and Appleby (1995).

44 See, for example, Carroll (2002); Davidman (1991).

45 Warner (1994), quoted in Baggett (2008:42–43).

46 Baggett (2008:42–43).

47 Wuthnow (1988); Hunter (1991).

CHAPTER 1

1 Our Lady of the Assumption Church is characterized in a church pamphlet as Roman Renaissance and is built in a Romanesque Revival style, which is charac-terized by "monochromatic brick or stone buildings, highlighted by semicircular

arches over window and door openings....The arches and capitals of columns are carved with geometrical medieval moldings. Facades are flanked by polygonal towers and covered with various roof shapes" Burden (2002:276).

2 The nave is "the principal or central part of a church; by extension, both middle and side aisles of a church, from the entrance to the crossing of the chancel; that part of the church intended for the general public" Burden (2002:219).

3 A baldacchino is a "permanent canopy, especially over an altar, throne, or tomb, usually supported on columns" Curl (1999:50).

4 "The gesture of bending the knee...an act of adoration of the Blessed Sacrament" (i.e., the Eucharist), *New Catholic Encyclopedia* (2003:648).

5 A cassock is a "close fitting ankle-length garment worn especially in Roman Catholic and Anglican churches by the clergy and by laypersons assisting in services." *Merriam-Webster Online Dictionary* (2012). A surplice is a "loose white outer ecclesiastical vestment usually of knee length with large open sleeves." *Merriam-Webster Online Dictionary* (2012).

6 A chasuble is "the principal and most conspicuous Mass vestment, covering all the rest....It consisted of a square or circular piece of cloth with the centre of which a hole was made; through this the head was passed. With the arms hanging town, this rude garment covered the whole figure." An alb is "a white linen vestment with close fitting sleeves, reaching nearly to the ground and secured round the waist by a girdle (cincture)." *New Catholic Encyclopedia* (2003).

7 Luke 18:9–14.

8 Recent studies demonstrate that worship generally, and Catholic worship in particular, varies not only by nation, ethnicity, and class, as has been the case historically (see especially Dolan [1987] and Appleby [1989]), but also according to religious orientation and aesthetic preferences (see, e.g., the parishes documented in Baggett [2008], Cuneo [1997]).

9 Mark Chaves (2004:5 and chap. 5) has shown that worship is the most widely shared of U.S. congregations' core activities, and worship is especially central to Catholic religious practice. American Catholics express an attachment to the rituals of Catholicism; not only is the celebration of the mass and the sacraments asserted as doctrine (see, e.g., *Sacrosanctum Concilium*) but also they are fundamental to the faith of ordinary Catholics, who respond in surveys that the sacraments are among the most important elements of Catholicism for them. See D'Antonio et al. (2007:23–26). Of Catholics surveyed, 81 percent responded that the real presence of Jesus in the Eucharist is essential to Catholicism, and 76 percent said the sacraments were essential—just behind helping the poor and Jesus' resurrection. These beliefs are especially important to high-commitment Catholics, 98 percent of whom named the sacraments as essential to their relationship with God; 82 percent of medium-commitment Catholics responded similarly (D'Antonio et al. 2007:63). This is the case for those Catholics who identify themselves as more traditional, as well as for progressives, like the

prochange Catholics studied by Michele Dillon (1999), whose attachment to the sacraments often cements attachment to the church as an institution and keeps dissenters from leaving.

10 Sewell (1992).
11 Geertz (1973a).
12 Geertz (1973b).
13 Brown (1991:14ff.).
14 Becker (1999); Dulles (1974).
15 Dulles (1974:25).
16 Dulles (1974:25).
17 Sewell (1992).
18 Sewell (1992:4).
19 Sewell (1992:18).
20 Bourdieu (1977:83), quoted in Sewell (1992:17).
21 Geertz (1973:90).
22 This definition of *habitus* differs from that of Pierre Bourdieu, the concept of habitus with which sociologists are most familiar. As Saba Mahmood (2005:136) makes clear, Bourdieu's definition of *habitus* explains "how the structural and class positions of individual subjects come to be embodied as dispositions— largely through unconscious processes." Bourdieu understands the schemes and values of *habitus* to be more fundamental than consciousness. But Aristotelian and Thomistic understandings emphasize that people also consciously choose to habituate themselves.
23 In her work on the Egyptian Islamic revival, Mahmood (2005) studies women's ritual practice to explore the possibility that religious observance in nonliberal traditions is not only determined by relations of domination. Mahmood shows that, even in a tradition that subordinates them to men, Muslim women can and do practice religious rituals in ways that allow them to gain creative control over their lives.
24 Mahmood distinguishes her use of the word *habitus* from Bourdieu's more contemporary use of the term to bring a somewhat greater degree of human agency to the discussion. Drawing on Aristotelian and Thomistic meanings of *habitus*, Mahmood contends that people must practice behaviors to become virtuous. Although rituals are culturally meaningful practices for Bourdieu, he does not directly connect the concept of virtue to his understanding of habitus, and he employs a more limited notion of agency in his emphasis on its learning rather than its intentional inculcation. No such meaning of virtue or agency exists in Bourdieu's notion, even while it is still based in practice. See Mahmood (2001b; 2005:134–139).
25 See also Ammerman (2007); McGuire (2008); Hall (1997).
26 Mahmood applies this perspective to understand why many, though not all, women who participate in the Egyptian Islamic revival wear the *hijab* (a veil). She

argues that such practices of modesty are desired by these women because they confer moral authority on them, guide their actions, and command the respect of men. In so doing, she contends, they exercise real agency in self-cultivation; their agency is not absolute, but neither is it merely constrained by the particularities of the institutions they inhabit. Rather, agency itself is *shaped* by the social contexts of culture and everyday life (Mahmood 2005). This argument is a response to critical feminist perspectives, which interpret practices such as these as the opposite of self cultivation, claiming instead that they are oppressive and a participation in a brand of false consciousness. For a theoretical elaboration of this argument, see Mahmood (2005:1–39, especially 5–25, and 195–199).

27 Otto ([1929] 1958).

28 See, for example, Neitz (1987); Becker (1999); Edgell (2006); Marler (1995); Stacey (1990).

29 Many of the church's objects of art reflect the sensibility of *l'art Saint Sulpice*—whose realistic images of the Catholic heavenly cohort were criticized beginning in the mid-20th century, because modern-leaning elites perceived them as encouraging a weak and feminized devotionalism. Borrowing from modernist trends in art, Catholic proponents of *l'art sacré* believed that simplicity in church environments and art best represents the sacred (see McDannell 1995). But I encountered many Catholics at both parishes who read such images not as feminized, but rather as traditional. For those at Assumption, in fact, these were not only objects of devotion and catechesis but also signs of a muscular, "true" church that has been neglected since Vatican II.

30 These devotions are also practiced less by members of post–Vatican II generations: D'Antonio et al. (2001:62) report that 40 percent of pre–Vatican II respondents recite the rosary, while only 11 percent of the post–Vatican II generation of respondents do. Similarly, 49 percent of the pre–Vatican II generation of respondents list devotion to Mary and the saints as important, compared with only 16 percent of the post–Vatican II generation of Catholics. Changes in Marian theology and devotional practice were among several important developments arising from Vatican II (Dolan 1987:431). On the Conciliar changes, see Wilde (2007).

31 The Angelus is "a short practice of devotion in honor of the Incarnation repeated three times each day, morning, noon, and evening, at the sound of the bell. It consists essentially in the triple repetition of the Hail Mary, to which in later times have been added three introductory versicles and a concluding versicle and prayer." *New Catholic Encyclopedia* (2003).

32 Konieczny (2009:429–430).

33 In describing the church as a mystical communion, Dulles (1974:51–52) draws on Ferdinand Tonnies's typology of *Gemeinshaft* and Charles Horton Cooley's concept of the primary group, together with the community's bond with the Holy Spirit.

34 Founded in 1946 and located in Fort Benning, Georgia, the School of the Americas, now named the Western Hemisphere Institute for Security Cooperation, is a U.S. Army international training ground for police and soldiers, especially those from Latin American countries. Human rights groups have long protested its continued operation because of the complicity of its graduates in political repression and torture. See, e.g., Gill (2004).

35 Christian base communities, modeled on Catholic Action cell groups, originated in Latin America, along with the birth of liberation theology. See Smith (1991).

36 Faith-sharing groups are not uncommon among Catholics. See Wedam and Warner (1994); Lee et al. (2000).

37 John 4:4–42.

38 These principles of social organization, which combine the affective dimensions of community with personal autonomy, are similar to Zablocki's (1971) observations of the late-20th-century communes he compares to the Bruderhof. Zablocki describes the motivations of commune members to include "reconstitution of the extended family, and the desire to be free" (Zablocki 1971:305) and goes on to discuss the fear and ambivalence with which they greet authorities. Significantly, affective ties, autonomy, and ambivalence toward institutionalized forms of authority are common in both settings. Both groups could be understood to have a similar type of response to Sennett's query about authority in late modernity—one that resolves tensions surrounding authority by emphasizing affectivity and autonomy.

39 Kanter (1972).

40 See McDannell (1995:163–197).

41 Joyce (1922).

42 Sennett (1980:27–36). I am grateful to Andreas Glaeser for directing me to Sennett's work on this topic.

43 See "Legitimate Domination" in Weber ([1922] 1978).

44 Sennett (1980:28).

45 Sennett (1980:28).

46 Edgell (2006).

47 A small but important point to note in relation to these examples is that, in both cases, parish priests not only exercise leadership and authority within their congregations but also tend to be highly regarded by parishioners. These parishes are not unusual in this respect, despite the sex abuse scandal among U.S. Catholic clergy that became public during my field research. While surveys of American Catholics demonstrate their shock and concern, their outrage at pedophile priests, and their disappointment with bishops' responses to the problem, 90 percent also somewhat or strongly agree that parish priests do a good job— about the same percentage as before the scandal broke (Gallup Poll of Catholics 2005)—and 80 percent of Catholics continue to participate in the church just as they did before the scandal (D'Antonio et al. 2007:75).

CHAPTER 2

1 Eliasoph and Lichterman (2003).
2 There is a large literature on this. For an introduction, see Dolan (1987) and Deck (1995).
3 On ascription and achievement in contemporary religion see Cadge and Davidman (2006).
4 D'Antonio et al. (2007); Hammond (1992); Hunter (1993); Lytch (2004); McNamara (1992); Roof (2001); Roof and Gesch (1995); Smith (1998); Smith and Denton (2005); Smith and Snell (2009); Wuthnow (2000).
5 Hoge et al. (2001:16).
6 Smith (1998:102–104); see also Ammerman (1987); Bellah et al. (1985); Ammerman and Roof (1995a).
7 Berger has since moved away from this view, but others ascribe to it. See, e.g., Hoge et al. (2001).
8 Smith and Snell (2009).
9 Smith (1998).
10 Ammerman (1987); Davidman (1991); Neitz (1987); Snow and Machalek (1982).
11 Smith (1998:104).
12 Hervieu-Léger (2000).
13 Mannheim (1952).
14 See chap. 4.
15 I had not heard this term before doing field research at Assumption. However, by the time of this writing, it had become a common enough term among some Catholics to have merited a reference in *Catholicism for Dummies* (Trigilio and Brighenti 2011).
16 In fact, survey researchers note that religious illiteracy has grown among Catholics in the last several decades; this happened during the post–Vatican II period with changes in theological emphases and methods of religious education; see Davidson et al. (1997:213–216); Smith and Snell (2009); Wilkes (1996:xix). Others point out that religious illiteracy was also a concern prior to Vatican II and that understanding religious literacy among Catholics generally is more complex. I thank Bryan Froehle for sharing his knowledge on this topic with me.
17 Kennedy (1995). See especially chaps. 1–3.
18 Kennedy (1995:10–16, especially 12–13).
19 See, e.g., Seidler and Meyer (1989).

CHAPTER 3

1 Paul VI, Pope (1968/2002).
2 John Paul II, Pope (1997).
3 Genesis 1:26–28.

4 Natural family planning (NFP) is defined by the USCCB as "an umbrella term for certain methods used to achieve and avoid pregnancies. These methods are based on observation of the naturally occurring signs and symptoms of the fertile and infertile phases of a woman's menstrual cycle. Couples using NFP to avoid pregnancy abstain from intercourse and genital contact during the fertile phase of the woman's cycle. No drugs, devices, or surgical procedures are used to avoid pregnancy" (www.usccb.org/issues-and-action/marriage-and-family/natural-family-planning/what-is-nfp/index.cfm). Catholic dioceses often offer training courses for couples interested in doing this, with a website sponsored by the USCCB with various resources: www.usccb.org/issues-and-action/marriage-and-family/natural-family-planning/find-an-nfp-class.cfm. Today conservative Catholics have varied attitudes and experiences with NFP (for one example of these discussions, see: http://forums.catholic.com/forumdisplay.php?s=949e02c11410b6f319e386ac80076093&f=12).

5 Chris and Assumption young adults are here discussing the *Catechism of the Catholic Church* (2000).

6 Ephesians 5:22ff.

7 Although some recent studies of religion and marriage have investigated religious conservatives, fewer studies examine marriage outside conservative settings, examine internal denominational variations in marriage, or utilize qualitative comparison to explore the effects of local contexts on marriage practice. Comparative analyses, such as Brad Wilcox's (2004) study of marital work among Protestants, tend to focus at larger levels of analysis. And while existing comparative studies have revealed general religious differences in marital behavior, we know much less about how congregational processes facilitate these differences.

8 Edin and Kefalas (2007); Furstenberg (2007); Hackstaff (1999); Hernandez (2007); Stacey (1990).

9 The literature on cohabitation is extensive; see, e.g., Seltzer (2000, 2004); Smock (2000). For earlier discussions, particularly on the relationship between cohabitation and marital stability, see, e.g., Bennett et al. (1988); Schoen (1992). The varied approaches to same-sex marriage in American and European cultures are discussed in Cherlin (2009:116–130). See also Krause (2000); Olson et al. (2006).

10 See, for example, Beck and Beck-Gernsheim (1995); Cherlin (2004, 2009); Giddens (1991, 1992, 1999); Hackstaff (1999); Wilcox (2004).

11 Cherlin (2009).

12 See Stacey (1990:9) and Bellah et al. (1985).

13 Bellah et al. (1985), chap. 4, "Love and Marriage," esp. 97–107.

14 Swidler (2001).

15 Amato (2004); Cherlin (2009); Whitehead and Popenoe (2001:6).

16 Some of this recent history involves Catholics' current marital practices and trends. For instance, although fertility among Catholics was markedly higher

than that of Protestants in the 1950s and 1960s, by 1975 family size among Catholics had become roughly similar to that of Protestants (see Christiano 2000; Mosher et al. 1992). And although family behavior of U.S. Catholics is today similar to that of mainline Protestants generally, Catholics still marry later—an artifact, some suggest, of the Catholic proscription against divorce (see Lehrer 2004:718).

17 Tentler (2004). The Cana Conference and the Christian Family Movement were programs for married people that date from the 1940s. Tentler explains that "Cana was the more conventionally educational of the two, primarily oriented to the support of a distinctively Catholic family life by means of retreat-like group programs and the sponsoring of local clubs, where five to six couples, meeting regularly, discussed their particular problems and needs with regard to Christian living" (Tentler 2004:194). Pre-Cana programs are marriage preparation programs originating out of the Cana Conference. As Tentler describes, "the Christian Family Movement...thought in somewhat broader terms [than the Cana Conference]: the problems of individual families could not be fully addressed without simultaneously addressing societal patterns of injustice...they were as apt to discuss the wrongs of racial segregation as topics like "the Mass and the family" (Tentler 2004:194).

18 Taves (1986).

19 Cummings (2009).

20 Orsi (1985, 1998, 2005).

21 Swidler (2001).

22 Their efforts include supports through catechesis during worship, at Young Adult Group meetings, at a parish pre-Cana program, during monthly Evenings of Reflection, and in Opus Dei Cooperators' Circles.

23 Evidence for the capacity of religion to shape particular ways of family living also has been found in other studies. See, e.g., Warner (1988:124–127).

24 Gallagher and Smith (1999); Gallagher (2003).

25 Manning (1999).

26 Luker (1985).

27 Shields (2012).

28 Shields's indicator of gender egalitarianism is a forced-choice question, with respondents who say that "women should have an equal role with men in running business, industry, and government," rather than "women's place is in the home," which is an indicator of gender traditionalism (2012:44).

29 Moreover, Julia's gender traditionalism, like most of the women at Assumption, is much more nuanced than what can be captured by survey indicators about whether women belong in the public sphere or in the home.

30 Christiano (2000).

31 Greeley (1991:189). See also Christiano (2000:51).

32 Lehrer and Chiswick (1993:386). See Christiano (2000).

33 Bernardin (1983); see Bernardin and Fuechtmann (1988) for other talks and for a symposium on this theme.

34 Wedam (1997).

35 Newport (2009).

36 Davidson (2005). See also D'Antonio, Davidson, Hoge, and Gautier 2007.

37 Davidson (2005). This suggests Catholics of younger generations may be on average more inclined to be attracted to churches that do not evince strong polar positions on abortion—although, again, churchgoing Catholics generally are more likely to take pro-life positions on the issue.

38 Davidson (2005).

CHAPTER 4

1   E.g., see Edgell (2006).

2   Lenski (1961).

3   See Alwin (1984, 1986, 1990).

4   Starks and Robinson (2007).

5   Bartkowski and Ellison (1995); Ellison (1996); Ellison and Sherkat (1993a, 1993b); Ellison et al. (1996).

6   Bartkowski (1995); Bartkowski and Ellison (1995); Bartkowski and Wilcox (2000); Wilcox (1998).

7   Mintz (2007:301).

8   Kline (1998:96).

9   Aries (1998:41–47).

10 On class, Jean Anyon has shown how schools located in neighborhoods with different bases and combinations of social class imagine children's capabilities differently, teach them differently, and shape them for different roles in capitalist production (Anyon 2006. See also Bernstein 1977; MacLeod 2001; Turner 2001). Annette Lareau (2002, 2003) has further shown how U.S. class contexts carry different notions of what children need and that these different ideas about childhood produce different parenting strategies: working-class parents work to accomplish natural growth in their children, whereas middle-class parents promote a concerted cultivation of their talents and skills. Regarding gender, a large literature shows that a traditionally gendered social organization is produced even in elementary schools (Thorne 1993) and in other institutional settings for children, such as Little League baseball (Fine 1987). Parents, too, socialize children into gender stereotypes, sometimes unconsciously, by treating boys and girls differently: giving them different toys, furnishing their rooms differently, or giving them different types of household chores (Coltrane 2006). Moreover, parenting strategies that seek less differentiable gendered patterns have the capacity to produce children of both sexes with more gender-neutral attributes and attitudes (Risman and Myers 2006).

11   Synott (2006:25–42). On images of childhood, adult's responses, and children's culture, see Aries (1962); Pollock (1983); Zelizer (1985); Jenkins (1998); and Lareau (2003).

12   Synott (2006:26–28).

13   Simmel (1971a:90–95).

14   One example is parents' concerns about the inculcation of violence through video games. During a Sunday brunch conversation, a group of mothers became uncomfortable when my then ten-year-old son described the "Stress Relief" computer game he played—one that involved a lot of breaking of things and shooting things. As he described the satisfaction of the "rat-a-tat-tat" as the player shoots insects on the screen, the mothers remained silent, but a couple of them visibly cringed. This took place during a discussion of violence in video games, in which mothers expressed concerns that video games have potential to teach children habits of violence; their reactions suggest that they would have sought to protect their own children from this game, even though it lacked the blood, gore, and weaponry of many video games.

15   The majority of parents interviewed at Assumption send their children to private or public schools; a few, like June, homeschool their children. Although home-schooling parents' concerns about schools tend to be particular, they generally reflect the moral and intellectual concerns of the parents at Assumption more broadly. However, they are often exceptionally articulate about these broader concerns, perhaps because, as Mitch Stevens (2003) observes, they are used to explaining and defending their decision to homeschool their children.

16   Lareau (2002, 2003).

17   Synott (2006:26–27).

18   Lareau (2002, 2003).

19   Lareau (2002, 2003).

20   This experience was common among Christine's mother's generation of Catholics; see Tentler (2004:204–244).

21   Dillon and Wink (2007); Greeley (1989); Stolzenberg et al. (1994).

22   Smith with Snell (2009:112).

23   Smith with Snell (2009:254).

24   Smith with Snell (2009:97).

25   Smith with Snell (2009:279–299).

26   Blair-Loy (2003); Gerson and Jacobs (2007); Hochschild (2001); Hochschild with Machung (2007); Jacobs and Gerson (2004); Presser (2003, 2007); Warren and Tyagi (2003).

27   Some of these solutions surround work-family balance are discussed at length in chapter 5. For example, some fathers chose less consuming professional work once they became parents so that they could be at home in the evenings, or they chose flexible work that allowed them daytime presence with children. Mothers often either left careers to stay at home full-time with children,

chose jobs that accommodated or included children, or managed their careers flexibly.

28 Bartkowski and Wilcox (2000); Wilcox (1998, 2004).

CHAPTER 5

1 Lewis (1943).

2 Stacey (1990:251–270).

3 Recent scholarship documenting the relation of religion to work-family balance has mostly focused on families in conservative religious groups, in which questions of women's rising labor force participation are particularly acute because of these groups' tendency to emphasize homemaking and childrearing as mothers' primary vocation (Bartkowski 2001; Davidman 1991; Gallagher 2003; Wilcox 2004; see also Edgell 2006; Stacey 1990).

4 For example, in Lynn Davidman's (1991) study, by contrast with a Lubavitch center that emphasizes women's marriage roles in the home and arranging marriages, an Orthodox synagogue in New York City that focuses on drawing upper-middle-class young adult Jews and converts to Orthodoxy allows women's work outside the home. This is a responsive strategy, since the synagogue attracts numbers of single women who, because they did not find marriage partners earlier in their lives, have focused on careers.

A similar range of approaches can be found among Christian evangelicals. Sally Gallagher and Christian Smith have shown that evangelical Christians' doctrine of submission is often combined with a practical egalitarianism that makes varied patterns of work-family balance possible for couples (Gallagher and Smith 1999). Moreover, Gallagher (2003) shows that, as evangelical women have increased their labor force participation, evangelical leaders' responses to issues of work-family balance have moved from a rather exclusive portrayal of women's vocational role in the home to emphasizing women's duties as wife and mother while allowing room for their work outside the home, because of either necessity or personal inclination.

5 For example, among studies of conservative religions, Gallagher and Smith (1999) and Stacey (1990) address how women combine work and mothering.

6 Gerson and Jacobs (2004).

7 Gerson and Jacobs (2004). See also Hochschild (2001).

8 Gerson and Jacobs (2004).

9 Bianchi et al. (2000).

10 Bianchi et al. (2000:206, 212–215).

11 Pew Research Center (2007). This represents a substantial decrease; 32 percent of women considered full-time work ideal in 1997. Instead, women today largely prefer part-time work: 60 percent said that part-time work was ideal for them (compared with 48 percent in 1997), and 51 percent report that part-time work was best for their children.

12 Edgell (2006:58–65).
13 Edgell (2006:64).
14 Edgell (2006:63).
15 Luke 16:1–13.
16 Information Office of Opus Dei (2000:2).
17 In addition, in saying that the church calls everyone to be saints, he makes a reference to Vatican II's call to holiness in its *Dogmatic Constitution on the Church, Lumen Gentium* (1964/1966, chap. 5), a document and a call that was frequently quoted from the Assumption pulpit.
18 Tocqueville (1835).
19 See chapter 4.
20 In 1997, 77 percent of women worked for pay, with 48.7 percent working full-time, 28.3 percent working part-time, and 23.1 percent not working for pay. See Waite and Nielsen (2001). By 2010, according to a U.S. Department of Labor Fact Sheet, among women who worked for pay, 73 percent of employed women worked full-time, and 27 percent worked part-time; this among 58.6 percent of women who were working or looking for work.
21 Stone (2007).
22 Stone (2007).
23 See Julia's story in chapter 3.
24 Stone (2007).
25 See, e.g., Pamela's story in Stacey (1990), chaps. 3–7.
26 This aspect of Assumption's ethos appears to be very similar to evangelical Protestant ethos that supports and encourages fathers' familistic involvements (Wilcox 2004; Bartkowski 2004).
27 Stone (2007).
28 Historical examples are documented, for example, by Bass (1979) and Clark (1987). A contemporary example is documented by Chong's (2008) study of Korean women and evangelical Christianity.
29 Pope Paul VI (1964, 1965). *Lumen Gentium* is known as the *Dogmatic Constitution on the Church* (1964); *Gaudium et Spes* is also known as *The Pastoral Constitution on the Church in the Modern World* (1965).
30 Edgell (2006).
31 Stone (2007).
32 Luke 1:39–56.
33 See chapter 3 vignette.

CONCLUSION

1 Hunter (1991).
2 For a compatible theoretical view of this relationship, see the essay "Ethos, World View, and the Analysis of Sacred Symbols" in Geertz (1973c).

3   Among Catholic parishes in particular, see, e.g., Baggett (2008); Neitz (1987).

4   Becker (1999); Dulles (1974); Geertz (1973b); Orsi (1985).

5   Parsons (1967). For a brief discussion of this point, see Roof and Gesch (1995) in Ammerman and Roof (1995a:63).

6   Parsons claims that this differentiation has likewise led to secularization. In fact, Jay Demerath (1995:461–463) follows this basic line of argument in explaining that values such as individualism, freedom, and pluralism have unintentionally undercut liberal Protestantism's organizational vitality by de-emphasizing obedience and loyalty and making its virtues relative.

7   Carroll (2007:166). Similarly but even more broadly, Melissa Wilde has shown Protestant pressures upon Catholicism to be a factor in the political processes that produced the documents of the Second Vatican Council (Wilde [2007]).

8   Demerath et al. (1998).

9   See, for example, Cuneo (1997).

10 Dillon (1999:253).

11 This view concurs with Dillon's (1999) point about contemporary Catholics' engagement with the Catholic tradition.

12 That people use religion as a way of establishing identity coherence in multiple arenas of life has also been observed by others; see, e.g., Ammerman (1987).

13 MacIntyre (2007:204–226, esp. 221–226).

14 MacIntyre (2007:222).

15 This argument shares a sensibility with Max Weber's argument about history, culture, and explanation in his famous essay "Objectivity in Social Science" (Weber in Heydebrand [2006:248–259]).

16 Weber in Heydebrand (2006:248–259).

17 Simmel (1971a:70–71).

18 E.g., Dark (2007); Cameron et al. (1987).

19 Hervieu-Léger (2000).

20 Hervieu-Léger (2000:156).

21 The exception to these patterned emphases on one side of beliefs related as binaries is found the Christian anthropologies that underlie childrearing, where both congregations, in different ways, express the goodness of children, together with the recognition of their weaknesses. Importantly, despite their differences, Assumption and Saint Brigitta are more similar in their approaches to children than in other arenas of family life.

22 Dulles (1974).

Bibliography

Abbott, Walter M. SJ and Joseph Gallagher, eds. 1966. *The Documents of Vatican II.* New York: Guild Press.

Abramowitz, Alan. 2010. *The Disappearing Center: Engaged Citizens, Polarization, and American Democracy.* New Haven, CT: Yale University Press.

Aguilar, Nona. 2002. *The New No-Pill No-Risk Birth Control.* New York: Scribner.

Alberigo, Guiseppe. 2006. *A Brief History of Vatican II.* New York: Orbis Books.

Alwin, Duane F. 1984. "Trends in Parental Socialization Values: Detroit, 1958–1963." *American Journal of Sociology* 90:359–82.

———. 1986. "Religion and Parental Child-Rearing Orientations: Evidence of a Catholic-Protestant Convergence." *American Journal of Sociology* 92:412–40.

———. 1990. "Cohort Replacement and Changes in Parental Socialization Values." *Journal of Marriage and Family* 52:347–60.

Amato, Paul. R. 2004. "Tension between Institutional and Individual Views of Marriage." *Journal of Marriage and Family* 66:959–65.

Ammerman, Nancy Tatom. 1987. *Bible Believers: Fundamentalists in the Modern World.* Piscataway, NJ: Rutgers University Press.

———. 2007. *Everyday Religion: Observing Modern Religious Lives.* New York: Oxford University Press.

Ammerman, Nancy Tatom and Wade Clark Roof. 1995a. *Work, Family, and Religion in Contemporary Society.* New York: Routledge.

———. 1995b. "Introduction: Old Patterns, New Trends, Fragile Experiments." Pp. 1–22 in *Work, Family, and Religion in Contemporary Society.* New York: Routledge.

Anyon, Jean. 2006. "Social Class and the Hidden Curriculum of Work." Pp. 369–394 in *Childhood Socialization.* 2nd ed., edited by Gerald Handel. New Brunswick, NJ: Aldine Transaction.

Appleby, R. Scott. 1989. "The Era of the Ombudsman: 1930–1954." Pp. 7–23 in *Transforming Parish Ministry: The Changing Roles of Catholic Clergy, Laity, and*

Women Religious, edited by Jay Dolan, R. Scott Appleby, Patricia Byrne, and Debra Campbell. New York: Crossroad.

Aries, Philip. 1962. *Centuries of Childhood: A Social History of Family Life*. New York: Alfred A. Knopf.

———. 1998. "From Immodesty to Innocence." Pp. 41–57 in *The Children's Culture Reader*, edited by Harry Jenkins.New York: New York University Press.

Baggett, Jerome P. 2008. *Sense of the Faithful: How American Catholics Live Their Faith*. New York: Oxford University Press.

Bartkowski, John P. 1995. "Divergent Models of Childrearing in Popular Models: Conservative Protestants vs. the Mainstream Experts." *Sociology of Religion* 56:1, 21–34.

———. 2001. *Remaking the Godly Marriage: Gender Negotiation in Evangelical Families*. Piscataway, NJ: Rutgers University Press.

———. 2004. *The Promise Keepers: Servants, Soldiers, and Godly Men*. Piscataway, NJ: Rutgers University Press.

Bartkowski, John P. and Christopher G. Ellison. 1995. "Divergent Models of Childrearing in Popular Manuals: Conservative Protestants vs. the Mainstream Experts." *Sociology of Religion* 56:21–34.

Bartkowski, John P. and W. Bradford Wilcox. 2000. "Conservative Protestant Child Discipline: The Case of Parental Yelling." *Social Forces* 79:265–90.

Bass, Dorothy C. 1979. "'Their Prodigious Influence': Women, Religion and Reform in Antebellum America." Pp. 279–300 in *Women of Spirit: Female Leadership in the Jewish and Christian Traditions*, edited by Rosemary Radford Ruether and Eleanor McLaughlin. New York: Simon and Schuster.

Beck, Ulrich and Elisabeth Beck-Gernsheim. 1995. *The Normal Chaos of Love*. Malden, MA: Wiley-Blackwell.

Becker, Penny Edgell. 1998. "Congregational Models and Conflict: A Study of How Institutions Shape Organizational Process." Pp. 231–55 in *Sacred Companies: Organizational Aspects of Religion and Religious Aspects of Organizations*, edited by Nicholas Jay Demerath, Peter Dobkin Hall, Terry Schmitt, and Rhys H. Williams. New York: Oxford University Press.

———. 1999. *Congregations in Conflict: Cultural Models of Local Religious Life*. New York: Cambridge University Press.

Becker, Penny Edgell and Nancy L. Eiesland. 1997. *Contemporary American Religion: An Ethnographic Reader*. Lanham, MD: Rowman Altamira.

Bell, Catherine. 1992. *Ritual Theory, Ritual Practice*. New York: Oxford University Press.

Bellah, Robert N., Richard Madsen, William M. Sullivan, Ann Swidler, and Steven M. Tipton. 1985. *Habits of the Heart: Individualism and Commitment in American Life*. Berkeley: University of California Press.

Benford, Robert D., and David A. Snow. 2000. "Framing Processes and Social Movements: An Overview and Assessment." *Annual Review of Sociology* 26: 611-639.

Bennett, Neil G., Ann Klimas Blanc, and David E. Bloom. 1988. "Commitment and the Modern Union: Assessing the Link between Premarital Cohabitation and Subsequent Marital Stability." *American Sociological Review* 53:127–38.

Berger, Peter L. 1967. *The Sacred Canopy: Elements of a Sociological Theory of Religion.* New York: Anchor Books.

Berglar, Peter. 1993. *Opus Dei: Life and Work of Its Founder.* Princeton, NJ: Scepter.

Bernardin, Joseph Louis. 1983. "A Consistent Ethic of Life: An American-Catholic Dialogue." www.priestsforlife.org/magisterium/bernardingannon.html.

Bernardin, Joseph Louis and Thomas G. Fuechtmann. 1988. *Consistent Ethic of Life.* Lanham, MD: Rowman & Littlefield.

Bernstein, Basil. 1977. *Class, Codes and Control, vol. 3, Towards a Theory of Educational Transmission.* 2nd ed. London, England: Routledge and Kegan Paul.

Bianchi, Suzanne M., Melissa A. Milkie, Liana C. Sayer, and John P. Robinson. 2000. "Is Anyone Doing the Housework? Trends in the Gender Division of Household Labor." *Social Forces* 79:1, 191–228.

Blair, Sampson Lee and Michael P. Johnson. 1992. "Wives' Perceptions of the Fairness of the Division of Household Labor: The Intersection of Housework and Ideology." *Journal of Marriage and Family* 54: 570–81.

Blair-Loy, Mary. 2003. *Competing Devotions: Career and Family among Women Executives.* Cambridge, MA: Harvard University Press.

Bourdieu, Pierre. 1977. *Outline of a Theory of Practice.* New York: Cambridge University Press.

———. 1979. *Distinction: A Social Critique of the Judgment of Taste.* Cambridge, MA: Harvard University Press.

———. 1980. *The Logic of Practice.* Stanford, CA: Stanford University Press.

Brines, Julie. 1994. "Economic Dependency, Gender, and the Division of Labor at Home." *American Journal of Sociology* 100:652–88.

Brown, Karen McCarthy. 1991. *Mama Lola: A Vodou Priestess in Brooklyn.* Berkeley: University of California Press.

Browning, Don S. 1991. "Family Ethics and the Ethics of Ministerial Leadership." Pp. 198–214 in *Clergy Ethics in a Changing Society: Mapping the Terrain*, edited by James P. Wind, Russell Burck, Paul F. Camenisch, and Dennis P. McCann. Louisville, KY: Westminster/John Knox Press.

———. 1995. "Religion and Family Ethics: A New Strategy for the Church." Pp. 157–176 in *Work, Family, and Religion in Contemporary Society*, edited by Nancy Tatom Ammerman and Wade Clark Roof. New York: Routledge.

Brusco, Elizabeth Ellen. 1995. *The Reformation of Machismo: Evangelical Conversion and Gender in Colombia.* Austin: University of Texas Press.

Burawoy, Michael. 1991. *Ethnography Unbound: Power and Resistance in the Modern Metropolis.* Berkeley: University of California Press.

———. 1998. "The Extended Case Method." *Sociological Theory* 16(1):4–33.

Burden, Ernest. 2002. *Illustrated Dictionary of Architecture.* New York: McGraw Hill.

Burdick, John. 1996. *Looking for God in Brazil: The Progressive Catholic Church in Urban Brazil's Religious Arena*. Berkeley: University of California Press.

Burns, Gene. 2005. *The Moral Veto: Framing Contraception, Abortion, and Cultural Pluralism in the United States*. New York: Cambridge University Press.

Butler, Judith. 1990/1999. *Gender Trouble: Feminism and the Subversion of Identity*. New York: Routledge.

Cadge, Wendy and Lynn Davidman. 2006. "Ascription, Choice, and the Construction of Religious Identities in the Contemporary United States." *Journal for the Scientific Study of Religion* 45(1):23–38.

Cameron, Kim S., Myung U. Kim, and David A. Whetten. 1987. "Organizational Effects of Decline and Turbulence." *Administrative Science Quarterly* 32(2):222–40.

Campbell, David. 2006. "A House Divided? What Social Science Has to Say about the Culture War." *William & Mary Bill of Rights Journal* 15:1–17.

Carroll, Colleen. 2002. *The New Faithful: Why Young Adults Are Embracing Christian Orthodoxy*. Chicago, IL: Loyola Press.

Carroll, Michael. 2007. *American Catholics in the Protestant Imagination: Rethinking the Academic Study of Religion*. Baltimore, MD: Johns Hopkins University Press.

Casanova, Jose. 1994. *Public Religions in the Modern World*. Chicago, IL: University of Chicago Press.

Catechism of the Catholic Church. 2000. Huntington, IN: Our Sunday Visitor.

Chaves, Mark. 1997. *Ordaining Women: Culture and Conflict in Religious Organizations*. Cambridge, MA: Harvard University Press.

———. 2004. *Congregations in America*. Cambridge, MA: Harvard University Press.

Chaves, Mark, Mary Ellen Konieczny, Kraig Beyerlein, and Emily Barman. 1999. "The National Congregations Study: Background, Methods, and Selected Results." *Journal for the Scientific Study of Religion* 38:458–76.

Chen, Carolyn. 2008. *Getting Saved in America: Taiwanese Immigration and Religious Experience*. Princeton, NJ: Princeton University Press.

Cherlin, Andrew J. 2004. "The Deinstitutionalization of American Marriage." *Journal of Marriage and Family* 66:848–61.

———. 2009. *The Marriage-Go-Round: The State of Marriage and the Family in America Today*. New York: Random House.

Chong, Kelly H. 1998. "What It Means to Be Christian: The Role of Religion in the Construction of Ethnic Identity and Boundary among Second-Generation Korean Americans." *Sociology of Religion* 59:259–86.

———. 2008. *Deliverance and Submission: Evangelical Women and the Negotiation of Patriarchy in South Korea*. Cambridge, MA: Harvard University Asia Center.

Christiano, K. 2000. "Religion and the Family in Modern American Culture." Pp. 43–78 in *Family, Religion, and Social Change in Diverse Societies*, edited by Sharon K. Houseknecht and Jerry G. Pankhurst. New York: Oxford University Press.

Clark, Elizabeth A. 1987. "Women and Religion in America, 1870–1920." Pp. 373–425 in *Church and State in America: A Bibliographic Guide: The Civil War to the Present Day*, edited by John F. Wilson. Westport, CT: Greenwood Press.

Clemmer, Don. 2009. "New Numbers among the Bishops." United States Conference of Catholic Bishops Media Blog. November 4, 2009. http://usccb-media.blogspot.com/2009/11/new-numbers-among-bishops.html.

CNSweb. 2009. "Catholics Overwhelmingly Oppose Notre Dame Honor to Obama, Poll Finds." *Cardinal Newman Society*. www.cardinalnewmansociety.org/PressReleases/tabid/54/itemid/545/amid/452/catholics-overwhelmingly-oppose-notre-dame-honor-to-obama-poll-finds.aspx.

Collins, Patricia Hill. 1990/2000. *Black Feminist Thought: Knowledge, Consciousness, and the Politics of Empowerment*. New York: Routledge.

Coltrane, Scott. 1989. "Household Labor and the Routine Production of Gender." *Social Problems* 36:473–90.

———. 2006. "Engendering Children." Pp. 279–310 in *Childhood Socialiation*. 2nd ed, edited by Gerald Handel. New Brunswick, NJ: Aldine Transaction.

Coontz, Stephanie. 2005. *Marriage, a History: From Obedience to Intimacy or How Love Conquered Marriage*. New York: Viking.

Cummings, Kathleen Sprows. 2009. *New Women of the Old Faith: Gender and American Catholicism in the Progressive Era*. Chapel Hill: University of North Carolina Press.

Cuneo, Michael W. 1997. *The Smoke of Satan: Conservative and Traditionalist Dissent in Contemporary American Catholicism*. Baltimore, MD: Johns Hopkins University Press.

Curl, James Stevens. 1999. *A Dictionary of Architecture*. New York: Oxford University Press.

Curran, Charles. 2008. *Catholic Moral Theology in the United States: A History*. Washington, DC: Georgetown University Press.

D'Antonio, William and Anthony Pogorelc. 2007. *Voices of the Faithful: Loyal Catholics Striving for Change*. New York: Crossroad.

D'Antonio, William V., James D. Davidson, Dean R. Hoge, and Katherine Meyer. 2001. *American Catholics: Gender, Generation, and Commitment*. Lanham, MD: Rowman Altamira.

D'Antonio, William V., James D. Davidson, Dean R. Hoge, and Mary L. Gautier. 2007. *American Catholics Today: New Realities of Their Faith and Their Church*. Lanham, MD: Rowman & Littlefield.

D'Antonio, William V., James D. Davidson, Dean R. Hoge, and Ruth A. Wallace. 1996. *Laity, American and Catholic: Transforming the Church*. Kansas City, MO: Sheed & Ward.

Dark, Taylor. 2007. "Organization Theory and Stages of Decline." *International Journal of Organization and Behavior* 10(2):213–44.

Davidman, Lynn. 1991. *Tradition in a Rootless World: Women Turn to Orthodox Judaism*. Berkeley: University of California Press.

Davidson, James D. 2005. "What Catholics Believe about Abortion and the Death Penalty." *National Catholic Reporter*, September 30, 2005.

Davidson, James D., William J. Whalen, Patricia Wittberg, Andrea S. Williams, and Richard A. Lamanna. 1997. *The Search for Common Ground: What Unites and Divides Catholic Americans*. Huntington, IN: Our Sunday Visitor Publishing.

Day, Dorothy. 1952. *The Long Loneliness: The Autobiography of Dorothy Day*. New York: Harper Collins.

Deck, Allan Figueora. 1995. "'A Pox on Both Your Houses': A View of Catholic Conservative-Liberal Polarities from the Hispanic Margins." Pp. 88–106 in *Being Right: Conservative Catholics in America*, edited by Mary Jo Weaver and R. Scott Appleby. Bloomington: Indiana University Press.

Del Tapia, Maria Carmen. 1997. *Beyond the Threshold: A Life in Opus Dei*. New York: Continuum.

Demerath, Nicholas J. 1995. "Cultural Victory and Organizational Defeat in the Paradoxical Decline of Liberal Protestantism." *Journal for the Scientific Study of Religion* 34(4):458–69.

Demerath, Nicholas Jay, Peter Dobkin Hall, Terry Schmitt, and Rhys H. Williams. 1998. *Sacred Companies: Organizational Aspects of Religion and Religious Aspects of Organizations*. New York: Oxford University Press.

Dillon, Michele. 1999. *Catholic Identity: Balancing Reason, Faith, and Power*. New York: Cambridge University Press.

Dillon, Michele and Paul Wink. 2007. *In the Course of a Lifetime: Tracing Religious Belief, Practice, and Change*. Berkeley: University of California Press.

DiMaggio, Paul, John Evans, and Bethany Bryson. 1996. "Have Americans' Social Attitudes Become More Polarized?" *American Journal of Sociology* 102:690–755.

Dolan, Jay P. 1987/1992. *The American Catholic Experience: A History from Colonial Times to the Present*. Notre Dame, IN: University of Notre Dame Press.

Dolan, Jay P., R. Scott Appleby, Patricia Byrne, and Debra Campbell. 1989. *Transforming Parish Ministry: The Changing Roles of Catholic Clergy, Laity, and Women Religious*. New York: Crossroad.

Dulles, Avery. 1974. *Models of the Church*. Garden City, NY: Doubleday.

———. 1991. *Models of the Church*. 2nd ed. New York: Random House.

Edgell, Penny. 2006. *Religion and Family in a Changing Society*. Princeton, NJ: Princeton University Press.

Edin, Kathryn and Maria Kefalas. 2007. *Promises I Can Keep: Why Poor Women Put Motherhood before Marriage*. Berkeley: University of California Press.

Eliasoph, Nina and Paul Lichterman. 2003. "Culture in Interaction." *American Journal of Sociology* 108:735–94.

Ellison, Christopher G. 1996. "Conservative Protestantism and the Corporal Punishment of Children: Clarifying the Issues." *Journal for the Scientific Study of Religion* 35:1–16.

Ellison, Christopher G., John P. Bartkowski, and Michelle L. Segal. 1996. "Conservative Protestantism and the Parental Use of Corporal Punishment." *Social Forces* 74:1003–28.

Ellison, Christopher G. and Darren E. Sherkat. 1993a. "Conservative Protestantism and Support for Corporal Punishment." *American Sociological Review* 58:131–44.

———. 1993b. "Obedience and Autonomy: Religion and Parental Values Reconsidered." *Journal for the Scientific Study of Religion* 32:313–29.

Fenn, Richard K. 2001. *The Blackwell Companion to Sociology of Religion.* Hoboken, NJ: Wiley-Blackwell.

Feree, Myra Marx. 1990. "Beyond Separate Spheres: Feminism and Family Research." *Journal of Marriage and Family* 52:866–84.

Fichter, Joseph Henry. 1954. *Social Relations in the Urban Parish.* Chicago, IL: University of Chicago Press.

———. 1978. *Dynamics of a City Church.* Manchester, NH: Ayer.

Fine, Gary Alan. 1987. *With the Boys: Little League Baseball and Preadolescent Culture.* Chicago, IL: University of Chicago Press.

Furstenberg, Frank F., Jr. 2007. "Can Marriage Be Saved?" Pp. 182–187 in *Family in Transition.* 14th ed, edited by Arlene S. Skolnick and Jerome H. Skolnick. Boston, MA: Allyn & Bacon.

Gallagher, Sally K. 2003. *Evangelical Identity and Gendered Family Life.* Piscataway, NJ: Rutgers University Press.

Gallagher, Sally K. and Christian Smith. 1999. "Symbolic Traditionalism and Pragmatic Egalitarianism: Contemporary Evangelicals, Families, and Gender." *Gender and Society* 13:211–33.

Gallup, George and Jim Castelli. 1987. *The American Catholic People: Their Beliefs, Practices, and Values.* New York: Doubleday.

Gallup Poll of Catholics. 2005. "CLRGYJOB," variable 33. www.thearda.com/ Archive/Files/Analysis/GALLUP05/GALLUP05_Var33_1.asp.

Galston, William. 2012. "Why Republicans Aren't the Only Ones to Blame for Polarization." *New Republic*, May 18, 2012.

Geertz, Clifford. 1973. *The Interpretation of Cultures.* New York: Basic Books.

———. 1973a. "Deep Play: Notes on the Balinese Cockfight." Pp. 412–454 in *The Interpretation of Cultures.* New York: Basic Books.

———. 1973b. "Religion as a Cultural System." Pp. 87–125 in *The Interpretation of Cultures.* New York: Basic Books.

———. 1973c. "Ethos, World View, and the Analysis of Sacred Symbols." Pp. 126–141 in *The Interpretation of Cultures.* New York: Basic Books.

Gerson, Kathleen. 1986. *Hard Choices: How Women Decide about Work, Career, and Motherhood.* Berkeley: University of California Press.

Gerson, Kathleen and Jerry A. Jacobs. 2004. "The Work-Home Crunch," *Contexts* 3:29–37.

———. 2007. "The Work-Home Crunch." Pp. 350–359 in *Family in Transition*. 14th ed., edited by Arlene S. Skolnick and Jerome H. Skolnick. Boston, MA: Allyn & Bacon.

Giddens, Anthony. 1991. *Modernity and Self-Identity: Self and Society in the Late Modern Age*. Stanford, CA: Stanford University Press.

———. 1992. *The Transformation of Intimacy: Sexuality, Love and Eroticism in Modern Societies*. Stanford, CA: Stanford University Press.

———. 1999. *Runaway World: How Globalization Is Reshaping Our Lives*. New York: Routledge.

Giele, Janet Z. 1996. "Decline of the Family: Conservative, Liberal, and Feminist Views." Pp. 89–115 in *Promises to Keep: Decline and Renewal of Marriage in America*, edited by David Popenoe, Jean Bethke Elshtain, and David Blankenhorn. Lanham, MD: Rowman & Littlefield.

Gilbert, Kathleen. 2009. "83: Bishops Opposing Obama Honor Continue to Surface Following ND Commencement." LifeSiteNews.com. May 19, 2009. www.lifesite-news.com/news/archive/ldn/2009/may/09051910.

Gilford, Dan. 2009. "Poll: Minority of Catholics Oppose Notre Dame's Obama Invite." US News-Politics: Online. April 30, 2009. www.usnews.com/news/blogs/god-and-country/2009/04/30/poll-minority-of-catholics-oppose-notre-dames-obama-invite.

Gill, Lesley. 2004. *The School of the Americas: Military Training and Political Violence in the Americas*. Durham, NC: Duke University Press.

Glaser, Barney G. and Anselm L. Strauss. 1967. *The Discovery of Grounded Theory: Strategies for Qualitative Research*. New Brunswick, NJ: Transaction.

Gleason, Philip. 1964. "Immigration and American Catholic Intellectual Life." *Review of Politics* 26:147–73.

———. 1968. *The Conservative Reformers: German-American Catholics and the Social Order*. Notre Dame, IN: University of Notre Dame Press.

———. 1970. *Catholicism in America*. New York: Harper & Row.

Glendon, Mary Ann. 2009. "Declining Notre Dame: A Letter from Mary Ann Glendon," *First Things*, April 27, 2009. www.firstthings.com/blogs/first-thoughts/2009/04/27/declining-notre-dame-a-letter-from-mary-ann-glendon/.

Goffman, Erving. 1959. *The Presentation of Self in Everyday Life*. New York: Penguin.

———. 1966. *Behavior in Public Places: Notes on the Social Organization of Gatherings*. New York: Simon and Schuster.

Greeley, Andrew M. 1989. *Religious Change in America*. Cambridge, MA: Harvard University Press.

———. 1991. *Faithful Attraction: Discovering Intimacy, Love, and Fidelity in American Marriage*. New York: Tor Books.

Greenstein, Theodore M. 2004. "Economic Dependence, Gender, and the Division of Labor in the Home: A Replication and Extension." *Journal of Marriage and Family* 62:2, 322–35.

Griffith, R. Marie. 1997. *God's Daughters: Evangelical Women and the Power of Submission*. Berkeley: University of California Press.

Grusky, David B. 2001. *Social Stratification: Class, Race, and Gender in Sociological Perspective*. Boulder, CO: Westview Press.

Hackstaff, Karla B. 1999. *Marriage in a Culture of Divorce*. Philadelphia, PA: Temple University Press.

———. 2007. "Divorce Culture: A Quest for Relational Equality in Marriage." Pp. 188–199 in *Family in Transition*. 14th ed., edited by Arlene S. Skolnick and Jerome H. Skolnick. Boston, MA: Allyn & Bacon.

Hall, David D. 1997. *Lived Religion in America: Toward a History of Practice*. Princeton, NJ: Princeton University Press.

Hammond, Phillip E. 1992. *Religion and Personal Autonomy: The Third Disestablishment in America*. Columbia: University of South Carolina Press.

Handel, Gerald. 2006. *Childhood Socialiation*. 2nd ed. New Brunswick, NJ: Aldine Transaction.

Hartmann, Heidi I. 1979. "The Unhappy Marriage of Marxism and Feminism: Towards a More Progressive Union." *Capital & Class* 3:1–33.

———. 1981. "The Family as the Locus of Gender, Class, and Political Struggle: The Example of Housework." *Signs* 6:366–94.

Hays, Sharon. 1998. *The Cultural Contradictions of Motherhood*. New Haven, CT: Yale University Press.

Hernandez, Donald J. 2007. "Changes in the Demographics of Families over the Course of American History." Pp. 40–58 in *Family in Transition*. 14th ed., edited by Arlene S. Skolnick and Jerome H. Skolnick. Boston, MA: Allyn & Bacon.

Hertz, Rosanna and Nancy L. Marshall, eds. 2001. *Working Families: The Transformation of the American Home*. Berkeley: University of California Press.

Hervieu-Léger, Danièle. 2000. *Religion as a Chain of Memory*. Piscataway, NJ: Rutgers University Press.

Heydebrand, Wolf. 2006. *Max Weber: Sociological Writings*. New York: Continuum.

Hochschild, Arlie Russell. 1989. *The Second Shift*. New York: Penguin Books.

———. 2001. *The Time Bind: When Work Becomes Home and Home Becomes Work*. New York: Holt.

Hochschild, Arlie Russell with Anne Machung. 2007. "The Second Shift: Working Parents and the Revolution at Home." Pp. 343–49 in *Family in Transition*. 14th ed., edited by Arlene S. Skolnick and Jerome H. Skolnick. Boston, MA: Allyn & Bacon.

Hoffmann, J. P. and A. S. Miller. 1998. "Denominational Influences on Socially Divisive Issues: Polarization or Continuity?" *Journal for the Scientific Study of Religion* 37:528–46.

Hoge, Dean R., William Dinges, Mary Johnson, and Juan Gonzales. 2001. *Young Adult Catholics: Religion in the Culture of Choice*. Notre Dame, IN: University of Notre Dame Press.

Houseknecht, Sharon K. and Jerry G. Pankhurst. 2000. *Family, Religion, and Social Change in Diverse Societies*. New York: Oxford University Press.

Hunter, James Davison. 1991. *Culture Wars: The Struggle to Define America*. New York: Basic Books.

———. 1993. *Evangelicalism: The Coming Generation*. Chicagoi IL: University of Chicago Press.

———. 2006. "The Enduring Culture War." Pp. 10–40 in *Is There a Culture War? A Dialogue on American Values and Public Life*, edited by James Davison Hunter and Alan Wolfe. Washington, DC: Pew Research Center.

Hunter, James Davison and Alan Wolfe. 2006. *Is There a Culture War? A Dialogue on American Values and Public Life*. Washington, DC: Pew Research Center.

Hurley, Dan. 2005. "Divorce Rate: It's Not as High as You Think." *New York Times*, April 19, 2005.

Information Office of Opus Dei. 2000. *Cooperators of Opus Dei*. (Brochure)

Jacobs, Jerry A. and Kathleen Gerson. 2004. *The Time Divide: Work, Family, and Gender Inequality*. Cambridge, MA: Harvard University Press.

Jenkins, Henry. 1998. *The Children's Culture Reader*. New York: New York University Press.

———. 1998a. "Introduction: Childhood Innocence and Other Modern Myths." Pp. 1–37 in *The Children's Culture Reader*. New York: New York University Press.

Jenkins, K. E. 2005. *Awesome Families: The Promise of Healing Relationships in the International Churches of Christ*. Piscataway, NJ: Rutgers University Press.

John Paul II, Pope. 1997. *The Theology of the Body: Human Love in the Divine Plan*. Boston, MA: Pauline Books & Media.

Joyce, James. 1922. *Ulysses*. New York: Penguin Classics.

———. 1999. *Finnegans Wake*. New York: Penguin.

Kanter, Rosabeth Moss. 1972. *Commitment and Community: Communes and Utopias in Sociological Perspective*. Cambridge, MA: Harvard University Press.

Katzenstein, Mary Fainsod. 1999. *Faithful and Fearless: Moving Feminist Protest inside the Church and Military*. Princeton, NJ: Princeton University Press.

Kaufman, Debra R. 1991. *Rachel's Daughters: Newly Orthodox Jewish Women*. Piscataway, NJ: Rutgers University Press.

Kennedy, Eugene C. 1995. *Tomorrow's Catholics Yesterday's Church: The Two Cultures of American Catholicism*. Liguori, MO: Liguori Publications.

Kippley, John F. and Sheila Kippley. 1996/2009. *Natural Family Planning: The Complete Approach*. Cincinnati, OH: Couple to Couple League International.

Kline, Steven. 1998. "The Making of Children's Culture." Pp. 95–109 in *The Children's Culture Reader*, edited by Harry Jenkins. New York: New York University Press.

Kniss, Fred Lamar, and Paul David Numrich. 2007. *Sacred Assemblies and Civic Engagement: How Religion Matters for America's Newest Immigrants*. Piscataway, NJ: Rutgers University Press.

Konieczny, Mary Ellen. 2009. "Sacred Places, Domestic Spaces: Material Culture, Church, and Home at Our Lady of the Assumption and St. Brigitta." *Journal for the Scientific Study of Religion* 48:419–42.

Krause, Harry D. 2000. "Marriage for the New Millennium: Heterosexual, Same Sex—or Not at All?" *Deutsches und Europisches Familienrecht* 2:208–21.

Lareau, Annette. 2002. "Invisible Inequality: Social Class and Childrearing in Black Families and White Families." *American Sociological Review* 67:747–76.

———. 2003. *Unequal Childhoods: Class, Race, and Family Life.* Berkeley: University of California Press.

Lee, Bernard J., William V. D'Antonio, and Virgilio P. Elizondo. 2000. *The Catholic Experience of Small Christian Communities.* Mahwah, NJ: Paulist Press.

Lehman, Edward C. 1993. *Gender and Work: The Case of the Clergy.* Albany: State University of New York Press.

Lehrer, Evelyn L. 2004. "Religion as a Determinant of Economic and Demographic Behavior in the United States." *Population and Development Review* 30:707–26.

Lehrer, Evelyn L. and Carmel U. Chiswick. 1993. "Religion as a Determinant of Marital Stability." *Demography* 30:385–404.

Lenski, G. 1961. *The Religious Factor: A Sociological Study of Religion's Impact on Politics, Economics, and Family Life.* New York: Doubleday.

Lewis, Clive Staples. 1943. *Out of the Silent Planet.* New York: Scribner.

Luckmann, Thomas. 1967. *The Invisible Religion: The Problem of Religion in Modern Society.* New York: Macmillan.

Luker, Kristin. 1985. *Abortion and the Politics of Motherhood.* Berkeley: University of California Press.

Lumen Gentium (Dogmatic Constitution on the Church). 1964/1966. Pp. 14–101 in *The Documents of Vatican II*, edited by Walter M. Abbott, SJ. New York: Guild Press.

Lytch, Carol E. 2004. *Choosing Church: What Makes a Difference for Teens.* Louisville, KY: Westminster/John Knox Press.

MacIntyre, Alasdair. [1981] 2007. *After Virtue: A Study in Moral Theory.* 3rd ed. Notre Dame, IN: University of Notre Dame Press.

MacKinnon, Catharine A. 1987. *Feminism Unmodified: Discourses on Life and Law.* Cambridge, MA: Harvard University Press.

MacLeod, Jay. 2001. "Ain't No Makin' It: Leveled Aspirations in a Low-Income Neighborhood." Pp. 421-34 in *Social Stratification: Class, Race, and Gender in Sociological Perspective*, edited by David B. Grusky. Boulder, CO: Westview Press.

Mahmood, Saba. 2001a. "Rehearsed Spontaneity and the Conventionality of Ritual: Disciplines of *Salat*." *American Ethnologist* 28:827–53.

———. 2001b. "Feminist Theory, Embodiment, and the Docile Agent: Some Reflections on the Egyptian Islamic Revival." *Cultural Anthropology* 16:202–36.

———. 2005. *Politics of Piety: The Islamic Revival and the Feminist Subject.* Princeton, NJ: Princeton University Press.

Mannheim, Karl. 1952. *Essays on the Sociology of Knowledge.* London: Routledge.

Manning, Christel. 1999. *God Gave Us the Right: Conservative Catholic, Evangelical Protestant, and Orthodox Jewish Women Grapple with Feminism.* Piscataway, NJ: Rutgers University Press.

Marler, Penny L. 1995. "Lost in the Fifties: The Changing Family and the Nostalgic Church." Pp. 23–60 in *Work, Family, and Religion in Contemporary Society,* edited by Nancy Tatom Ammerman and Wade Clark Roof. New York: Routledge.

Martin, Bernice. 2001. "The Pentecostal Gender Paradox: A Cautionary Tale for the Sociology of Religion." Pp. 52–66 in *The Blackwell Companion to Sociology of Religion,* edited by Richard K. Fenn. Hoboken, NJ: Wiley-Blackwell.

Massa, Mark S. 2010. *The American Catholic Revolution: How the '60s Changed the Church Forever.* New York: Oxford University Press.

McBrien, Richard. 2004. "Challenges Facing the Next Pope," *Church* 20(4): 5–8.

McDannell, Colleen. 1995. *Material Christianity: Religion and Popular Culture in America.* New Haven, CT: Yale University Press.

McGuire, Meredith B. 2008. *Lived Religion: Faith and Practice in Everyday Life.* New York: Oxford University Press.

McNamara, Patrick H. 1992. *Conscience First, Tradition Second: A Study of Young American Catholics.* Albany: State University of New York Press.

Merton, Thomas. 1948. *The Seven Storey Mountain.* Orlando, FL: Harcourt.

Merriam-Webster Online Dictionary. 2012. www.merriamwebster.com/dictionary.

Mintz, Steven. 2007. "Beyond Sentimentality: American Childhood as a Social Construct and Cultural Construct." Pp. 291–303 in *Family in Transition.* 14th ed., edited by Arlene S. Skolnick and Jerome H. Skolnick. Boston, MA: Allyn & Bacon.

Mooney, Margarita. 2009. *Faith Makes Us Live: Surviving and Thriving in the Haitian Diaspora.* Berkeley: University of California Press.

Morgan, David. 1998. *Visual Piety.* Berkeley: University of California Press.

Munson, Ziad. 2008. *The Making of Pro-Life Activists.* Chicago and London: University of Chicago Press.

Mosher, William D., Linda B. Williams, and David P. Johnson. 1992. "Religion and Fertility in the United States: New Patterns." *Demography* 29:199–214.

Nabhan-Warren, Kristy. 2005. *The Virgin of El Barrio: Marian Apparitions, Catholic Evangelizing, and Mexican American Activism.* New York: New York University Press.

Neitz, Mary Jo. 1987. *Charisma and Community: A Study of Religious Commitment within the Charismatic Renewal.* New Brunswick, NJ: Transaction.

———. 1995. "Constructing Women's Rituals: Roman Catholic Women and 'Limina.'" Pp. 283–304 in *Work, Family, and Religion in Contemporary Society,* edited by Nancy Tatom Ammerman and Wade Clark Roof. New York: Routledge.

Nesbitt, Paula D. 1997. *Feminization of the Clergy in America: Occupational and Organizational Perspectives.* New York: Oxford University Press.

New Catholic Encyclopedia.2003. Detroit, MI: Thomson/Gale. www.newadvent.org.

Newport, Frank. 2009. "Catholics Similar to Mainstream on Abortion, Stem Cells." Gallup, March 30, 2009. www.gallup.com/poll/117154/catholics-similar-mainstream-abortion-stem-cells.aspx.

Olson, Laura R., Wendy Cadge, and James T. Harrison. 2006. "Religion and Public Opinion about Same-Sex Marriage." *Social Science Quarterly* 87:340–60.

O'Malley, John W. 2008. *What Happened at Vatican II*. Cambridge, MA: Harvard University Press.

Orsi, Robert A. 1985. *The Madonna of 115th Street: Faith and Community in Italian Harlem, 1880–1950*. New Haven, CT: Yale University Press.

———. 1998. *Thank You, St. Jude: Women`s Devotion to the Patron Saint of Hopeless Causes*. New Haven, CT: Yale University Press.

———. 2005. *Between Heaven and Earth: The Religious Worlds People Make and the Scholars Who Study Them*. Princeton, NJ: Princeton University Press.

Otto, Rudolf. 1929/1958. *The Idea of the Holy: An Inquiry into the Non-Rational Factor in the Idea of the Divine and Its Relation to the Rational*. New York: Oxford University Press.

Parsons, Talcott. 1967. *Sociological Theory and Modern Society*. New York: Free Press.

Paul VI, Pope. 1964. *Lumen Gentium*. www.vatican.va/archive/hist_councils/ ii_vatican_council/documents/vat-ii_const_19641121_lumen-gentium_en.html.

———. 1965. *Gaudium et Spes*. www.vatican.va/archive/hist_councils/ ii_vatican_council/documents/vat-ii_cons_19651207_gaudium-et-spes_en.html.

———. 1968/2002. *Humanae Vitae*. San Francisco, CA: Ignatius Press.

Perl, Paul, and Jamie S. McClintock. 2001. "The Catholic 'Consistent Life Ethic' and Attitudes toward Capital Punishment and Welfare Reform." *Sociology of Religion* 62:275.

Pew Research Center. 2007. "Fewer Mothers Prefer Full-Time Work." http://pewresearch.org/pubs/536/working-women.

Pollock, Linda A. 1983. *Forgotten Children: Parent-Child Relations from 1500 to 1900*. New York: Cambridge University Press.

Popenoe, David, Jean Bethke Elshtain, and David Blankenhorn. 1996. *Promises to Keep: Decline and Renewal of Marriage in America*. Lanham, MD: Rowman & Littlefield.

Presser, Harriet B. 2003. *Working in a 24/7 Economy: Challenges for American Families*. New York: Russell Sage Foundation.

———. 2007. "The Economy That Never Sleeps." Pp. 377–383 in *Family in Transition*. 14th ed., edited by Arlene S. Skolnick and Jerome H. Skolnick. Boston, MA: Allyn & Bacon.

Putnam, Robert D. and David E Campbell. 2010. *American Grace: How Religion Divides and Unites Us*. New York: Simon & Schuster.

Reese, Thomas. 1990. "Inside the Laghi Legacy," *America*, June 23, 1990.

———. 1992. *A Flock of Shepherds: The National Conference of Catholic Bishops.* Kansas City, MO: Sheed & Ward.

———. 1996. *Inside the Vatican: The Politics and Organization of the Catholic Church.* Cambridge, MA.: Harvard University Press.

Reilly, Patrick J. 2009. "The Cardinal Newman Society's Stance on Notre Dame." Los Angeles Times Online. May 16, 2009. http://articles.latimes.com/2009/may/16/opinion/oe-reilly16.

Riesebrodt, Martin. 1993. *Pious Passion: The Emergence of Modern Fundamentalism in the United States and Iran.* Berkeley: University of California Press.

———. 1995/2000. "Class Cultures and Cultural Milieus: On the Conceptualizaton and Interpretation of Group Formation," published as "Fundamentalismus als Kulturmilieu," chap. 3 in *Die Ruchkehr der Religionen*. Munchen: Beck.

Riesebrodt, Martin, and Kelly H. Chong. 1999. "Fundamentalisms and Patriarchal Gender Politics." *Journal of Women's History* 10:55–77.

Risman, Barbara J. and Kristin Myers. 2006. "As the Twig Is Bent: Children Reared in Feminist Households." Pp. 65–88 in *Childhood Socialization*. 2nd ed., edited by Gerald Handel. New Brunswick, NJ: Aldine Transaction.

Roof, Wade Clark. 2001. *Spiritual Marketplace: Baby Boomers and the Remaking of American Religion.* Princeton, NJ: Princeton University Press.

Roof, Wade Clark and Lyn Gesch. 1995. "Boomers and the Culture of Choice: Changing Patterns of Work, Family, and Religion." Pp. 61–80 in *Work, Family, and Religion in Contemporary Society*, edited by Nancy Tatom Ammerman and Wade Clark Roof. New York: Routledge.

Rubin, Lillian B. 1976. *Worlds of Pain: Life in the Working-Class Family.* New York: Basic Books.

Ruether, Rosemary Radford and Eleanor McLaughlin, eds. 1979. *Women of Spirit: Female Leadership in the Jewish and Christian Traditions.* New York: Simon and Schuster.

Sacrosanctum Concilium (Constitution on the Sacred Liturgy). 1963/1966. Pp. 137–78 in *The Documents of Vatican II*, edited by Walter M. Abbott, SJ. New York: Guild Press.

Schoen, Robert. 1992. "First Unions and the Stability of First Marriages." *Journal of Marriage and Family* 54:281–84.

Scott, Joan Wallach. 1988/1999. *Gender and the Politics of History.* New York: Columbia University Press.

Seidler, John, and Katherine Meyer. 1989. *Conflict and Change in the Catholic Church.* Piscataway, NJ: Rutgers University Press.

Seltzer, Judith A. 2000. "Families Formed outside of Marriage." *Journal of Marriage and Family* 62:1247–68.

———. 2004. "Cohabitation in the United States and Britain: Demography, Kinship, and the Future." *Journal of Marriage and Family* 66:921–28.

Sennett, Richard. 1980. *Authority.* New York: W. W. Norton.

Sewell, William H. Jr. 1992. "A Theory of Structure: Duality, Agency, and Transformation." *American Journal of Sociology* 98:1–29.

Shear, Michael D. 2009. "Obama Addresses Abortion Protests in Commencement Speech at Notre Dame," *Washington Post*, May 18, 2009. www.washingtonpost.com/wp-dyn/content/article/2009/05/17/AR2009051701622_2.html?sid=ST2009051701939.

Shields, Jon. 2012. "The Politics of Motherhood Revisited." *Contemporary Sociology* 41(1):43–48.

Simmel, Georg. 1971a. "Conflict." Pp. 70–95 in *On Individuality and Social Forms*, edited by Donald N. Levine. Chicago: University of Chicago Press.

———. 1971b. "Group Expansion and the Development of Individuality." Pp. 251–93 in *On Individuality and Social Forms*, edited by Donald N. Levine. Chicago: University of Chicago Press.

Skolnick, Arlene S. and Jerome H. Skolnick. 2007. *Family in Transition*. 14th ed. Boston: Allyn & Bacon.

Smith, Christian. 1991. *The Emergence of Liberation Theology*. Chicago: University of Chicago Press.

Smith, Christian. 1998. *American Evangelicalism: Embattled and Thriving*. Chicago: University of Chicago Press.

Smith, Christian with Melinda Lundquist Denton. 2005. *Soul Searching: The Religious and Spiritual Lives of American Teenagers*. New York: Oxford University Press.

Smith, Christian with Patricia Snell. 2009. *Souls in Transition: The Religious and Spiritual Lives of Emerging Adults*. New York: Oxford University Press.

Smith, Herbert F. 1996. *Natural Family Planning—Why It Succeeds*. Boston: Pauline Books & Media.

Smock, Pamela J. 2000. "Cohabitation in the United States: An Appraisal of Research Themes, Findings, and Implications." *Annual Review of Sociology* 26:1–20.

Snow, David A. and Richard Machalek. 1982. "On the Presumed Fragility of Unconventional Beliefs." *Journal for the Scientific Study of Religion* 21:15–26.

South, Scott and Glenna Spitze. 1994. "Housework in Marital and Nonmarital Households." *American Sociological Review* 59:327–47.

Stacey, Judith. 1990. *Brave New Families: Stories of Domestic Upheaval in Late-Twentieth-Century America*. Berkeley: University of California Press.

Staff Editorial. 2009. "Constructive Debate Welcome." The Observer Online. March 27, 2009. www.ndsmcobserver.com/2.2756/constructive-debate-welcome-1.255492#.TsQg8OV2N8E.

Starks, Brian. 2009. "Self-Identified Traditional, Moderate, and Liberal Catholics: Movement-Based Identities or Something Else?" *Qualitative Sociology* 32:1–32.

Starks, Brian and Robert V. Robinson. 2007. "Moral Cosmology, Religion, and Adult Values for Children." *Journal for the Scientific Study of Religion* 46(1):17–35.

Stevens, Mitchell. 2003. *Kingdom of Children: Culture and Controversy in the Homeschooling Movement*. Princeton, NJ: Princeton University Press.

Stocks, Janet. 1997. "To Stay or to Leave? Organizational Legitimacy in the Struggle for Change among Evangelical Feminists." Pp. 99–120 in *Contemporary American Religion: An Ethnographic Reader*, edited by Penny Edgell Becker and Nancy L. Eiesland. Lanham, MD: Rowman Altamira.

Stolzenberg, Ross M., Mary Blair-Loy, Linda J. Waite, and University of Chicago Population Research Center. 1994. *Religious Participation over the Early Life Course: Age and Family Life Cycle Effects on Church Membership*. Chicago, IL: Population Research Center, NORC, and the University of Chicago.

Stone, Pamela. 2007. *Opting Out? Why Women Really Quit Careers and Head Home*. Berkeley: University of California Press.

Swidler, Ann. 2001. *Talk of Love: How Culture Matters*. Chicago, IL: University of Chicago Press.

Synott, Anthony. 2006. "Little Angels, Little Devils: A Sociology of Children." Pp. 25–42 in *Childhood Socialiation*. 2nd ed., edited by Gerald Handel. New Brunswick, NJ: Aldine Transaction.

Taves, Ann. 1986. *The Household of Faith: Roman Catholic Devotions in Mid-Nineteenth-Century America*. Notre Dame, IN: University of Notre Dame Press.

Tentler, Leslie Woodcock. 2004. *Catholics and Contraception: An American History*. Ithaca, NY: Cornell University Press.

Teresa of Avila. 1565/1957. *The Life of Saint Teresa of Ávila by Herself*. New York: Penguin Classics.

Teresa of Calcutta, Mother. 2007. *Mother Teresa: Come Be My Light: The Private Writings of the "Saint of Calcutta,"* edited by Brian Kolodiejchuk. New York: Random House.

Thorne, Barrie. 1993. *Gender Play: Girls and Boys in School*. Piscataway, NJ: Rutgers University Press.

Tocqueville, Alexis de. 1835. *Democracy in America*. London, England: Saunders & Otley.

Trigilio, John and Kenneth Brighenti. 2011. *Catholicism for Dummies*. Hoboken, NJ: John Wiley and Sons.

Turner, Ralph H. 2001. "Sponsored and Contest Mobility and the School System." Pp. 319–24 in *Social Stratification: Class, Race, and Gender in Sociological Perspective*, edited by David B. Grusky. Boulder, CO: Westview Press.

Turner, Victor. 1974. *Dramas, Fields, and Metaphors: Symbolic Action in Human Society*. Ithaca, NY: Cornell University Press.

United States Conference of Catholic Bishops. 2011. "Natural Family Planning." Obtained January 18, 2011, from www.usccb.org/prolife/issues/nfp/index.shtml.

Vanauken, Sheldon. 1977. *A Severe Mercy*. San Francisco, CA: Harper & Row.

Waite, Linda J. and Mark Nielsen. 2001. "The Rise of the Dual-Earner Family, 1963-1997." Pp. 23-41 in *Working Families: The Transformation of the American Home*, edited by Rosanna Hertz and Nancy L. Marshall. Berkeley: University of California Press.

Wallace, Ruth A. 1992. *They Call Her Pastor: A New Role for Catholic Women.* New York: State University of New York Press.

Warner, R. Stephen. 1988. *New Wine in Old Wineskins: Evangelicals and Liberals in a Small-Town Church.* Berkeley: University of California Press.

———. 1993. "Work in Progress toward a New Paradigm for the Sociological Study of Religion in the United States." *American Journal of Sociology* 98: 1044–93.

———. 1994. "The Place of the Congregation in the Contemporary American Religious Configuration." Pp. 54-99 in Volume 2, *American Congregations: Portraits of Twelve Religious Congregations,* edited by James P. Wind and James W. Lewis. Chicago, IL: University of Chicago Press.

Warren, Elizabeth and Amelia Warren Tyagi. 2003. *The Two-Income Trap: Why Middle-class Mothers and Fathers Are Going Broke.* New York: Basic Books.

Weaver, Mary Jo. 1999. *What's Left?: Liberal American Catholics.* Bloomington: Indiana University Press.

Weaver, Mary Jo, and R. Scott Appleby. 1995. *Being Right: Conservative Catholics in America.* Bloomington: Indiana University Press.

Weber, Max. 1922/1978. *Economy and Society,* edited by Guenther Roth and Claus Wittich. Berkeley: University of California Press.

Wedam, Elfriede. 1997. "Splitting Interests or Common Causes: Styles of Moral Reasoning in Opposing Abortion." Pp. 147–168 in *Contemporary American Religion: An Ethnographic Reader,* edited by Penny Edgell Becjer and Nancy L. Eiesland. Lanham, MD: Rowman Altamira.

Wedam, Elfriede and R. Stephen Warner. 1994. "Sacred Space on Tuesday: A Study of the Institutionalization of Charisma." Pp. 143–178 in *"I Come Away Stronger": How Small Groups Are Shaping American Religion,* edited by Robert Wuthnow. Grand Rapids, MI: Eerdmans.

Wessinger, Catherine. 1996. *Religious Institutions and Women's Leadership: New Roles inside the Mainstream.* Columbia: University of South Carolina Press.

Whitehead, Barbara D. and David Popenoe. 2001. "Who Wants to Marry a Soul Mate?" Pp. 6–16 in *The State of Our Unions 2001: The Social Health of Marriage in America, edited by Barbara D. Whitehead and David Popenoe.* New Brunswick, NJ: National Marriage Project.

Whitnah, Meredith C. 2010. "The Discourse of American Evangelical Gender Ideology and Intimate Partner Violence." M.A. Thesis, University of Notre Dame.

Wilcox, W. Bradford. 1998. "Conservative Protestant Childrearing: Authoritarian or Authoritative?" *American Sociological Review* 63:796–809.

———. 2004. *Soft Patriarchs, New Men: How Christianity Shapes Fathers and Husbands.* Chicago, IL: University of Chicago Press.

———. 2009. "The Evolution of Divorce." *National Affairs* 1:81–94.

Wilde, Melissa J. 2007. *Vatican II: A Sociological Analysis of Religious Change.* Princeton, NJ: Princeton University Press.

Wilkes, Paul. 1996. *The Good Enough Catholic: A Guide for the Perplexed*. New York: Ballantine Books.

Williams, Rhys H. 1996. "Religion as Political Resource: Culture or Ideology?" *Journal for the Scientific Study of Religion* 35:368–78.

——. 1997. *Cultural Wars in American Politics: Critical Reviews of a Popular Myth*. Hawthorne, NY: Aldine de Gruyter.

Wilson, John F., ed. 1987. *Church and State in America: A Bibliographic Guide: The Civil War to the Present Day*. Westport, CT: Greenwood Press.

Wind, James P. and James Welborn Lewis. 1994. *American Congregations: Portraits of Twelve Religious Communities*. Chicago, IL: University of Chicago Press.

Winter, Miriam Therese, Adair T. Lummis, and Allison Stokes. 1994. *Defecting in Place: Women Claiming Responsibility for Their Own Spiritual Lives*. New York: Crossroad.

Wolfe, Alan. 1999. *One Nation, After All*. New York: Penguin Books.

——. 2006. "The Culture War That Never Came." Pp. 41–73 in *Is There a Culture War? A Dialogue on American Values and Public Life*, edited by James Davison Hunter and Alan Wolfe. Washington, DC: Brookings Institution and Pew Research Center.

Wood, Richard L. 2002. *Faith in Action: Religion, Race, and Democratic Organizing in America*. Chicago, IL: University of Chicago Press.

Woodhead, Linda. 2001. "Feminism and the Sociology of Religion: From Gender-Blindness to Gendered Difference." Pp. 67–84 in *The Blackwell Companion to the Sociology of Religion*, edited by Richard K. Fenn. Hoboken, NJ: Wiley-Blackwell.

Wuthnow, Robert. 1988. *The Restructuring of American Religion: Society and Faith since World War II*. Princeton, NJ: Princeton University Press.

——. 1994. *"I Come Away Stronger": How Small Groups Are Shaping American Religion*. Grand Rapids, MI: Eerdmans.

——. 2000. *After Heaven: Spirituality in America since the 1950s*. Berkeley: University of California Press.

Zablocki, Benjamin. 1971. *The Joyful Community*. New York: Penguin.

Zahn, Gordon Charles. 1962. *German Catholics and Hitler's Wars: A Study in Social Control*. New York: Dutton.

Zelizer, Viviana A. Rotman. 1985. *Pricing the Priceless Child: The Changing Social Value of Children*. Princeton, NJ: Princeton University Press.

Zikmund, Barbara Brown, Adair T. Lummis, and Patricia M. Y. Chang. 1998. *Clergy Women: An Uphill Calling*. Louisville, KY: Westminster/John Knox Press.

Index

Tables are represented by an italic *t* following the page number.

CPSIA information can be obtained at www.ICGtesting.com
Printed in the USA
BVOW01s0744180314

347964BV00001B/1/P